The
Family
in
Global
Perspective

D0124540

to
ZOË

ELAINE LEEDER

Sonoma State University

The Family in Global Perspective

A Gendered Journey

SAGE Publications
International Educational and Professional Publisher
Thousand Oaks ▪ London ▪ New Delhi

For information:

Sage Publications, Inc.
2455 Teller Road
Thousand Oaks, California 91320
E-mail: order@sagepub.com

Sage Publications Ltd.
6 Bonhill Street
London EC2A 4PU
United Kingdom

Sage Publications India Pvt. Ltd.
B-42, Panchsheel Enclave
Post Box 4109
New Delhi 110 017 India

Printed in the United States of America

Library of Congress Cataloging-in-Publication Data

Leeder, Elaine J.
The family in global perspective : a gendered journey / Elaine Leeder.
     p. cm.
Includes bibliographical references and index.
ISBN 0-7619-2837-5 (Paper)
    1. Family. 2. Family—Cross-cultural studies. 3. Sex role. I. Title.
HQ519.L44 2004
306.85—dc222

                                                          2003017828

03   04   05   06   07   10   9   8   7   6   5   4   3   2   1

Acquiring Editor:	Jim Brace-Thompson
Editorial Assistant:	Karen Ehrmann
Production Editor:	Sanford Robinson
Typesetter:	C&M Digitals (P) Ltd.
Copy Editor:	Pam Suwinsky
Indexer:	Sheila Bodell
Cover Designer:	Michelle Lee

Contents

Photographs

Acknowledgments

A work of this length takes many years to complete and countless people to assist in its research and writing. There are a number of people who worked with me as research assistants, editors, and supporters during the seven years it took me to write this book, from conception to publication. My research assistants from Ithaca College were Jessie Falk, Pat Yevchak, Mollie Pasqualone, Tamara Ochoa, Craig Murphy, and Sara Curtis. My assistant from Sonoma State University was Megan Lewis, and Tonya Ward helped me on Semester at Sea. Thanks to Madeleine Rose and Chris Salvano at Sonoma State University for their literature review additions. I appreciate all the time and energy it took all who helped me find the sources that inform this work. Also at Sonoma State, Erica Wilcher, Jane Wright, and Connie Lewsadder have been my thoughtful and kind supports while putting the final finishing touches on this manuscript.

There were also editors all along the way, especially Diane McPherson and Barbara Adams, two superior writing professionals who helped me choose my words carefully and taught me how to be a much better writer. Other colleagues at Ithaca College helped me significantly with the content. I appreciate the wisdom of Jim Rothenberg, Jonathan Laskowitz, Julian Euell, Margo Ramlal-Nankoe, Judith Barker, and Hector Velez, who all helped me think through some of the tangled parts of the theories and race chapters, and talked me through some of my concerns. Thanks to Larry Shinagawa for his thorough read and recommendations.

My two photographers, Mary Thieme and Patti Carman, traveled with me on Semester at Sea and shared their glorious pictures generously. I am thrilled that their work has brought to life the images that we shared as we traveled together.

A number of dear friends and family have helped me through the painful stages of writing this book. I so appreciate Peggy Williams, Mary Corsaro, Craig Longley, Bob Armstrong, Yvonne Fogarty, Debbie Crown, Ellyn Kaschak, Sandy Pollack, Ann Wexler, David Schwartz, Cleo Gorman, Ron Ackerman, and my daughter Abigail Leeder for all their support. Thanks to Esinet Mapondera, my friend of many years, and her family in Zimbabwe and the United States, who helped me see the importance of a cross-cultural understanding of families. I want to especially thank Zoë Sodja, who helped finalize this book and send it off into the world.

To Jim Brace-Thompson, Karen Ehrmann, and Sanford Robinson of Sage Publications, my deepest appreciation for seeing the merit in this work. To Pam Suwinsky, I thank you for the exceptionally well-done final editing. To any whom I might have forgotten, my apologies and my thanks.

I appreciate all the help that I received from those named, but I take full responsibility for the content and for any errors found within.

Elaine Leeder
Sebastopol, California

Preface

In the summer of 2000 I attended a seminar at the United States Holocaust Memorial Museum. It was a two-week workshop for college professors, to assist them in teaching courses on the Holocaust. While I was there I began to do research on my own family, both on my father's and my mother's sides. In the course of the research and the seminar, I learned in vast detail what happened to the Jews of Eastern Europe as well as to my own family. For the past 26 years I have been teaching sociology to college students, knowing that I was a Holocaust refugee's daughter and that the Holocaust had impacted me in some way. I knew that I was the family "memorial candle" who would carry on the family history and who felt an imperative to do something about the atrocities done to others in the world.

This book is the product of those years of preparing myself and educating others about difference. Because of people's intolerance of difference and racism against Jews, Gypsies, and Poles, to name a few, as well as hostilities against those in the former Soviet Union, the Holocaust occurred. Not understanding others and not accepting difference leads to suffering on a daily basis in countries all over the world. It also happens within our own country. It is for this reason that I try to educate readers about difference, about people who might be unlike ourselves, who live in countries the world over.

I lead you through a series of chapters that lay out the basics of family life, looking at how families are similar and how they differ from each other. In Chapter 1, I begin with a series of vignettes from my own travels, then talk about the need for a theory to explain what we see. In Chapter 2, I develop a few commonalities in function exhibited by families as well as the diversity that can be observed in structure and family purposes or goals. I discuss several of the theories that have been used to explain family life and the structure of society in Chapter 3.

As we proceed through the book, in Chapters 4 and 5 we work to develop a perspective on the history of family life in the developed parts of the world, and then compare it to places in Africa, Asia, and Latin America. We see how capitalism and power differentials have affected the course of family history and family life today for different groups of people. Families, of course, are where intimate relationships take place. In Chapter 6 we explore gender relations in the family, and then in Chapter 7 look at how race, ethnicity, and class manifest themselves in family life.

In Chapter 8 we look at love, marriage, and the dissolution of relationships, and in Chapter 9 at intergenerational relationships and how they operate in a vast array of countries. In Chapter 10 we focus on some of the difficulties families face, such as domestic violence, war, and economic hardships, and in Chapter 11, the final chapter of the book, we explore the effects of globalization and the future of the family.

When I began writing this book, I had hoped to choose four or five countries or cultures and make them the central areas that we learn from. Unfortunately there is not enough information on specific countries in developing parts of the world to cover *all* the issues that I hoped to address. Thus I have created a mosaic of cultures for us to study. In this way I hope to keep the reader interested and challenged. I have tried to organize the chapters in such a way as to make it clear what we are to learn from each one. I have also included material on the United States as a basis of comparison, since this book is primarily intended for a Western audience. I expect that this book might be used in conjunction with a primary text, so the information on the United States is not my specific focus.

I should say at the outset that I am a feminist. I have been one for most of my adult life, and that perspective informs all that I do and teach. This in no way means that this book is man-hating. It is, nonetheless, honest about structural inequities as they impact men and women, as well as people in different class and racial status groups. Where possible I provide statistical evidence to document my assertions, as well as anecdotal data from the years of study and visits I have made to many parts of the globe.

At this time of increasing globalization, mass commercialism, and industrialization, it becomes more imperative than ever to understand others. Economies are changing, global capital is moving from country to country, boundaries are permeated in ways that have never been seen before. The Internet, transnational corporations, and a new global culture are upon us, and we need to understand them and how they impact one of the most private and yet public institutions, the family. I present this book to you in the hope that you will begin to enjoy the variability and diversity of family forms worldwide and that you will become interested in knowing them and perhaps visiting a few of these places some day.

CHAPTER 1

Focusing on the Family

The mother was about 20 years old. We were sitting on a crowded airplane traveling from Newark to Santa Domingo, in the Dominican Republic. The baby was an infant, no more than three months old. As the child began to cry, the young mother began to sing to her baby. She did not just sing. She danced, clicked her mouth, and held the baby's hand as she began to do the salsa, the merengue, and the numerous dances of her culture. She could have been a mother anywhere in the world, but at the same time, hers was a unique way of teaching and soothing her child. In this simple act of love and nurturance from a mother to her crying infant, I knew that I was encountering the family, its socialization, and a unique culture.

It is not an easy task to undertake a comprehensive study of the family, particularly from a global perspective. The family, as we will see in this book, is both surprisingly complex and simple. We assume that we know what *family* is, since we all come from families and have had personal experience with them. Learning about the family, though, is not like studying science or mathematics. It is a close-up process, one that deals with familiar territory and yet requires the development of a critical eye. We must step back and try to understand the very phenomenon from which we come. We must realize that even though we know families, we don't really know them, especially what families are like outside our own cultural spheres.

Much has been written about the family, particularly the Western and the American family, by sociologists, psychologists, anthropologists, and psychotherapists. Texts abound, and critiques have been written and rewritten about this social form. Historians, feminists, theorists, and other scholars have all looked deeply at family structure, family functioning, family in the economic sphere, family dynamics, family composition, family demise, and other areas of analysis. It has been said that the family is dying; that the family as it once existed ideally is being destroyed by forces beyond its control.

The family has been around since the beginning of humankind and clearly will exist in some form forever. However, what it looks like, what it does, and how it operates depends on variables that are complex. The structural arrangements of society affect the family and influence the entity the family becomes. The family does not operate in a vacuum. In order to work with and understand it, one needs to see the family in the context of these structural arrangements and social order. If you are to become a practitioner working with families, or merely a citizen of the world, an appreciation of this complexity is part of your education.

Some of us assume that the family is the most loving institution of society. But it is more than that. It exists within an environment; it is not merely the product of change. In a dynamic process, the family acts and reacts to the social, political, environmental, and economic forces (structural arrangements) around it. Understanding this dynamic interaction, the reciprocal relationship between families and the larger society—that will be the challenge to our learning. The family in the world is in process: Resilient, the family copes with the forces acting on it and adapts in an ongoing manner that makes it a highly elastic and changeable form. The family is reacting to the changes in economy, in the transnational nature of global capitalism. What the World Trade Organization and the International Monetary Fund do has a direct impact on family life. Consumerism is a driving force that impacts how families work, live, and die. We live in a period of rapid globalization and need to understand its impact on family life.

The Journey

In 1992 and again in 1999 I was lucky enough to travel around the world on a university ship, teaching American college students about the family and about the geography of the countries we visited. Traveling to the Bahamas, Cuba, Venezuela, Brazil, South Africa, Kenya, India, Malaysia, Vietnam, China, Taiwan, and Japan, I was able to study firsthand the topics I was teaching. My students, some 900 in total, studied families as we traveled. We would return to the ship after each port of call and share what we had learned. In addition, in the summer of 1997, I co-led a group of 19 students to the Dominican Republic, where we took an in-depth look at the family in that Latin Caribbean country. As a consultant and educator, I have visited Zimbabwe, the Philippines, Jamaica, and a total of 28 other countries. In quite a few of those countries, I have maintained contact with a number of professionals, including scholars and social workers, some of whom have contributed their knowledge of the families in their countries to this book.

In many of the countries I conducted focus groups in which family professionals and lay citizens told me about their family lives. Often informal, these groups were always informational. I asked people what their daily lives were like and how their family relationships and family structures appeared to them. I compared what I was told to what my research assistants and I found in the literature about those countries. The process, begun informally in 1967 and continuing more formally through the 1990s, has taught me much about the family as it exists in the early twenty-first century. It is that learning, from personal observation, student thinking and writing, literature review, discussion and thinking with other professionals, and deep reflection, that I share with you.

For many years I practiced psychotherapy in the United States in a family and individual practice. My focus was domestic violence, and I saw the tragedy and resilience of people who dealt with enormous distress and trauma. Once I felt I had an understanding of violence in families in American society, I began to study it cross-culturally. I have been trying to develop a global perspective on how and why people who are so intimate can hurt each other so badly. I have visited shelters and programs in other countries to see how the problem is being combated outside the United States. Some of that learning is discussed later in this book, to detail how social problems can lead to social change.

For the past 25 years I have taught sociology and social work to college students at Ithaca College and Sonoma State University. I have encouraged them to develop a critical awareness of the world around them. In studying the family, social change, or social work, I have always emphasized a need for what is called a *critical consciousness: developing an understanding and awareness that all social relationships are based on inequality and that each of us comes from a position within a social structure that colors our view of the world.* It is awareness that there is a hierarchical social stratification system. Critical consciousness is the opposite of *false consciousness,* which is *the belief that all people have equal opportunity. To be falsely conscious means that we are not aware of a social stratification system and where each of us falls in that system.* It is important to understand that each of us views life and the social world from a unique perspective, based on our life experience, race, class, gender, sexuality, and ethnic background. This makes it harder to walk in another's shoes or to understand completely what another human being experiences.

Being critically conscious means attempting to understand such inequalities and to position oneself and others within the surrounding social, economic, and political system. I cannot ignore that my standpoint is that of a white, middle-aged college professor, one who lives in a developed country and who has a position of privilege and power in the world. Standpoint theory, a feminist theory, argues that everyone's experiential reality is structured, shaped, limited, and organized by the social location in which one exists (Lorber, 1998, 115–127). My labor and thinking will differ from a man's because of my experience in the world. A complete worldview would include multiple subjects and equal representation of all viewpoints. My viewpoint in this book is just one, and by its very nature is biased and incomplete. I can try to present as thorough an explanation as possible, but the nature of knowledge is that it can never be complete.

In this book you are invited on this journey of attempted understanding. I have been traveling the world for 30 years, with my major focus on the family. I share with you what I have seen, what I have studied, and what I have found, and weave into it writings and findings of other global family studies researchers and writers. Perhaps some of you might go on similar journeys yourselves, but if not, this is one you can take in the comfort of your own room. We will learn that the family, although quite dissimilar in various places, shares certain characteristics worldwide. In its diversity and its multiple forms, the family is very much alive and well.

Vignettes

As we make our way on this journey I share with you images from my own travels that have stayed with me. Some of these images are typical of their societies; others are key to understanding those places. I start with some recent ones and work backward, so that you can see some of the changes that reflect the global and universal character of the family. The story at the beginning of this chapter, for example, describes a first interaction with the Dominican culture. One's own reflections, however, should not be universal generalizations. Generalizations never do justice to the complexities of an issue.

The scientific method demands that one first observe and then later incorporate observation into a larger picture, which through analysis can lead to greater learning. It involves developing a logical system of processing information through direct and organized observation. One might first see, then develop a theory about what one sees, and finally compare that observation to what others have observed. With a theory, one can develop a hypothesis and set out to test whether or not that theory holds true, based on evidence. From such a process one attempts to be objective, realizing that everything we see is not always true. It is the beginning of that process that we engage in now.

One hot holiday at Boca Chica, Dominican Republic, I was sitting with a group of students and a colleague under the palm trees, avoiding the hot Caribbean sun. The beach was filled with thousands of Dominicans who were listening to music, playing in the water with their children, flirting, vending, sunning, eating, and, most of all, visiting with their families. At a large table next to us was a family of four generations, with a great-grandmother in the seat of honor. With her were her daughters and their husbands and children, great-grandchildren, and even one infant child of the great-grandchild. A daughter had once lived in the United States but came home because she missed her family, and was now able to help her family out financially. The family was enormously proud of their large numbers and their beauty. There was lots of touching and laughter. When we asked to take their picture, the family proudly posed, clearly reflecting the importance that each person played in this large, multigenerational extended family. The great-grandmother told us that this was one of her happiest moments, to be surrounded by all her family on this festive day at the beach. Right there I learned about the importance of elders in the Dominican culture. I saw the appreciation for the large extended family, and I saw the immigration process in operation. In one interaction I had a sociological picture of family life in the Dominican society.

◆ ◆ ◆ ◆

A few days later a group of us visited a Haitian camp for sugar cane cutters in the Dominican Republic, in the rural region of Bayauguana. There were two sets of accommodations: one for the Dominican workers, the other for

Haitians. We were led there by a missionary nun, Sister Lettie, who worked with the Haitians. They had fled their neighboring homeland to escape difficult political conditions and the abject (or absolute) poverty that puts people's lives at risk and fails to provide even the minimum level of nutrition and health care to sustain life. The workers lived in huts that reminded me of the stalls we use for cows in upstate New York. There were five or six family members to a room, with rags on the floor for sleeping and tattered clothing and minimal food for the children. Scores of children followed us around, begging for food or candy. We approached one of the huts where a family of six Haitians stood out front. There in the father's arms was a beautiful infant, naked, smiling, and bouncing. All around us was poverty. Bitter, brutal, and ugly. Yet there was a family, its members coexisting in conditions some of us could not even comprehend. The father proudly showed me his baby, smiling and waving at us, as we trooped through the compound, overwhelmed by the squalor yet inspired by the vibrancy of life. Here I learned that families can exist under all conditions and thrive even under the greatest poverty brought on as the consequences of a one-crop-based economy.

Another day we were traveling by publico, *a privately owned bus that drives around and picks up as many passengers as possible on its way to a predetermined destination. Twenty-one of us were crammed in with local residents, old and young alike. Music blasted, babies were passed, lunch was eaten—it felt like a free-for-all. Out the window I noticed something I have only begun to see in other parts of the world: a woman in her twenties driving a motorcycle. Although it was not surprising to see a female driver, behind her was a woman who appeared to be her mother, riding astride the cycle, with a young girl of four or five riding between them. The sight of three generations of women on the motorcycle, with a female driving, was most amusing. Observing them, I began to think about gender roles and the changing role of women in this society. (Gender roles are the attitudes and expectations that a culture links to each sex.) Here I was seeing the redefinition of what was considered appropriate for a woman to do in this part of the world. In fact, I have only begun to see it anywhere else before, except for a few norm breakers in the United States.*

◆ ◆ ◆ ◆

In March 1992 I visited Kialisha, a squatter camp for the homeless outside of Cape Town, South Africa. Thousands of people had moved there from their rural homelands seeking employment in booming Cape Town. At that time, they were unable to live in the city because of apartheid, *the systematic separation of the races through a series of policies employed by the white minority against the African majority from 1948 until 1992. People in these camps built homes out of any materials they could find: boxes, tin, paper, plastic sheets. There were no electricity, plumbing, or sewage systems. Every couple of miles there was a single spigot of water from which to hand-carry buckets to*

Photo 1.1   South African mother and child in Kialisha squatter camp, one of the most densely populated and squalid of the camps set up to accommodate migration to the city of Cape Town. Photographer: Patti Carman

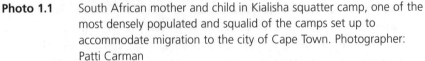

the hovels. I saw a baby eating a raw chicken leg, and I also encountered a child dressed in a black garbage bag. In the middle of this onslaught to my senses I encountered a woman dancing to Afro-pop music and flirting with the man she was with. She looked me straight in the eye and said, "Don't pity us, there is life in these places and we are happy." From that simple interaction I learned much about survival and about not judging other people's lives.

◆ ◆ ◆ ◆

On a later stop in 1992, I was walking though an untouchable (dalit) *village in rural, southern India, where I observed the caste system in operation. A caste is a form of social stratification that is based on the group into which one is born— not one that you can readily move in or out of. According to the Indian caste system, untouchables are the lowest members of society. Although the Indian government abolished the caste system in 1949, untouchables are still treated poorly and discriminated against in their society. In this village there was a funeral going on, with chanting, wailing, and singing. As a group of students and I walked the streets, with the smell of jasmine on one side and cow manure on the other, we encountered a young mother with a string of six children trailing behind her. She brought us over to the small plot of land that she and her children were tending as a garden and proudly pointed out the newly sprouting plants. After showing us into her simple, clean hut, she looked at me and asked, "What is it that you will do to help me?" I had nothing to say. She already had quite a lot, with her family, her home, and her garden. But I also knew that I would share her story.*

◆ ◆ ◆ ◆

Three years earlier, in the summer of 1989, I had been invited to Zimbabwe, Africa, to visit an old friend and colleague. She was on the board of a women's bank that lent money to women starting their own small businesses in rural regions of the country. One day I was invited to accompany her to a presentation about financial support at a small women's farming cooperative. When the van pulled into the yard, a group of 100 African women greeted us, clapping and singing their welcome to us, the dignitaries. After the ceremonies, I sat with the women at an open fire, as they stirred a large pot of sadza, *a cornmeal porridge. They were gleeful at having a woman from the United States sit with them, stir the pot, and sing their songs rather than sitting with the government officials, as would be expected. Here I was, another woman, one who cooked at home for my own child, learning to prepare the local food. I was with women much like myself in age, but different in lifestyle, cooking dinner and chatting. I saw so clearly how similar we all are when it comes to caring for families and being a member of a community.*

Another day in Zimbabwe I was out walking with a Nigerian friend. We happened upon a stand, a circle of grass-roofed huts in the rural countryside. There was a man tending his maize (corn) crop, and we began chatting. Having attended a missionary school, he spoke English. He invited us into his home. One of the huts, which he shared with his wife, was for cooking and sleeping, another was for the children, another for his mother-in-law, who lived with them. A fourth was for storing the maize, and a fifth housed the

Photo 1.2   Women at the cooking pot, Zimbabwe. These women are making *sadza*, the traditional food of the Shona people. Photographer: Elaine Leeder

animals. The main home was dirt-floored and incredibly well tended and cleanly swept. An altar was built into one wall, where ancestors were revered. Beside it were gleaming and well-kept pots and pans. The house was immaculate, even out in the bush, surrounded by dust and fields of crops. We sat on the ground sharing tea and chatting, as easily as old friends might.

◆ ◆ ◆ ◆

Returning from my trip to Africa in 1989, I walked into a delicatessen in New York City. There on the shelves, I found egg rolls, a Chinese delicacy; Pad Thai noodles, an East Asian staple; bagels from Jewish ancestry; spaghetti—which originated in China but was adopted by Italians and is sold everywhere in the world; mango juice from the Caribbean; and Russian breads. I had just traveled all over the world, and I came almost all the way home to find a cross-section of the globe in a small local deli. But already I knew that it was a small world.

Abstracting from What We See: Getting a Theory

As beginning students in family studies, sociology, or social work, we must understand that observation is just the beginning of learning. We must then make sense of what we see. Embedded in the previous vignettes were a number of important concepts, all of which have a large body of information and research concealed behind the terms. After observation comes the need to understand that these social factors are produced by social forces that are often beyond the control of those who are affected by them.

One of the concepts embedded in these examples is the transnational and global nature of the family. A global perspective promotes an understanding that all people are connected, no matter how far-flung they are. Those connections are based on a global system of relationships, from one country to another and among groups of people within those countries. In every group there is a hierarchy, a pecking order with rules of domination and subordination between people. The rules specify who has access to resources and who controls, manages, and oppresses other people. The transnational or global nature of the world means that there are distinctions among people based on their race, their class, their ethnicity, their gender, their sexual orientation, and the places from which they come.

To consider this is to begin to think theoretically. Often people are afraid to think theoretically, believing that theories are abstract, hard to follow, and irrelevant to their own lives. Yet each person has a theory, a way of seeing the world and explaining it. Often we are not conscious of what our theory is and how it is relevant to our daily functioning. To have a theory is to have a way of explaining the world—an understanding that the world is not just a random series of events and experiences.

Having a theoretical understanding of what one sees helps one think about what to do: how to relate and then perhaps effect change. Theories help us to develop ways of studying and then altering our own lives and the lives of those around us. Theory grounds us; it gives us a lens through which to make sense of the many pieces of information we process every day. Theories, then, drive a research question, which can be framed in terms of the theoretical perspective one takes. It also helps us consider alternative actions that can be taken in dealing with a social problem. For these reasons, theories are introduced early in this book and are woven throughout the text.

This book is based on the belief that all people are trying to make a living, feed their families, and raise their children. Although this might sound simple, it is not. We are all connected through a global economy, and we all use resources that are produced in other parts of the world. The world is connected through a global system; what occurs in one part impacts the rest. Thus, although the families I described might look different from one another, they are all influenced by the global hierarchy and the market system under which they operate. Different theories exist to try to explain that connection. For example, one currently influential sociologist, Immanuel Wallerstein (1974, 1989, 1992), has argued that the developed parts of the world need the less developed parts of the world to remain poor and impoverished. In other words, the rich countries need the poor countries' resources and cheap labor, and we need those countries to stay dependent on us. Let me give you some examples.

Places like the Dominican Republic, Haiti, the Philippines, and Zimbabwe have become one-crop economies or sites of trade zones, which produce materials that the developed parts of the world need. This process creates classes of landless rural laborers or dependent factory workers. The only work available for locals in these countries is working for the multinational corporations; they are unable to engage in the subsistence farming they once did. Their foods are imported because their land is used for crops that can't sustain them. That is why the Haitian family I described to you living in the Dominican Republic was in such abject poverty. This is the essence of Wallerstein's theory and explains why people in these countries are rarely seen tending small garden plots, even if they live in beautiful, tropical, and lush climates. This practice of encouraging the growing of single crops and deciding what shall be grown and produced is made by multinational corporations. It is part of the international exchange of commodities. We buy a country's resources and sell them back as finished products at higher prices.

That is why there are Coca-Colas and McDonald's in every part of the world. It also explains why the first thing I saw as I entered into the main port in Venezuela was a Marlboro man advertisement dominating the skyline. This was particularly provocative given the recent decline in smoking among U.S. citizens. The billboard reminds us that the tobacco industry is in search of new markets; it is an example of the global nature of the world and its connections.

These examples also explain why groups such as those protesting the World Trade Organization and the World Bank were demonstrating in Seattle in 1999. The activists understand the global implications of policies made by a handful of entrepreneurs seeking profit as their ultimate goal.

Global Social Change

To understand what is happening to the family, recognize that societies do not remain stable and static. In your lifetime you have already seen extensive technological change—the development of VCRs, cellular phones, sophisticated computer systems, and high-imaging television. Things have certainly changed. Also, your own family has probably seen changes as a result of employment, shifts in education, physical moves, or aging.

Social change occurs at many levels of society, in social institutions, technology, culture, communities, as well as in roles and relationships among people. Forces within a society and outside it influence how change will occur. Generally, social change is not orderly, although sometimes it is planned. However, it does happen everywhere. For simplicity's sake we will define *social change* as *a transformation of a society, both planned and unplanned, evolutionary or revolutionary, that alters the patterns of people's interaction.*

The theme of social change pervades this book. Families, as the primary unit of every society, are altered as a result of social change. Usually such change is not easy; it may result in distress. If a mother has to go to work because her income is needed, if a father has to move to another city to find employment, or if a daughter has to leave home and emigrate to better her life, all these families must adapt and change. The globalization process is changing family life on a day-to-day basis, altering previously accepted patterns of interaction.

Social change occurs at three levels: in a society's norms and values, in its laws and institutions, and in its popular culture. Change can take a long time to occur,

Photo 1.3   Global social change: Older Chinese women eating ice cream with Pepsi signs behind them. Western products find their way into the global economy. Photographer: Patti Carman

and it must permeate a society and culture in order to bring about any long-term effect. It does not seem important which level of change comes first; however, for change to occur it must be synthesized at all levels.

Social change is a dynamic process. It can occur through conflict and tension between groups of people, as in wars and revolutions. The consequences of that can be devastating to families, as we have learned from recent atrocities in Rwanda, Burundi, and Bosnia. Change can occur because of demographic shifts, such as movements of people to other locations. Throughout this book we pay attention to how social change affects the family and examine the family's adaptability in dealing with those forces.

Social change reverberates throughout the world, a shift in one place altering life in another. When jobs leave the northeastern part of the United States and move to Asia, those transformations have an impact on the families in both places. Capitalism, the economic system under which most of the world lives, needs all the labor power it can find. Corporations move in order to find cheaper labor to minimize their costs and to make more profit, which is the point of capitalism. Families provide the labor and also train their children to enter the workplace. These families are affected when those jobs move to other parts of the world. Social change is like dropping a stone into water: The circles move outward from the center, and one never knows how great the effect of that initial impulse will be.

Culture

Entire cultures change as a result of social change. By *culture*, I mean *the language, beliefs, values, behavior, and material objects that a people share*. Cultures vary a great deal, but all have symbols, language, values, and norms. Sometimes we think of culture only as art, music, or literature. But as a term used by social scientists, *culture* refers to everything that people do, their means of communication, as well as what is handed down from generation to generation. It is everything that people learn, and it is socially constructed. So culture includes all ideas and beliefs, possessions, music, language, art, customs, and concepts about what is important. It is usually families who carry the culture and teach it to their children.

Language is considered a human universal through which people teach their culture. There is certainly scientific evidence that animals communicate through language, too, but for the purposes of explaining the family we will limit ourselves to humans. Each culture has a language that conveys to its members what is important to them. Edward Sapir and Benjamin Whorf developed a *theory of linguistic determinism and linguistic relativity* (Sapir, 1958; Whorf, 1966). The first (determinism) says that the way we interpret the world is influenced by our language. We see the world because our language habits predispose certain choices of interpretation. The relativity component of the theory says that if language determines thought, then speakers of different languages will have different life experiences.

We can see the importance of language in conveying culture and the impact of social change on culture in the Shona people of Zimbabwe, for example. The poetry and various Shona sayings reveal that women and men once enjoyed complementary roles (Chitauro, 1995, 10). In pre-colonial Shona history (prior to the 1890s), women worked in the households, while men raised the animals, and both worked in the fields. Women's and men's positions may not have been entirely equitable, but there was some balance. Then, slowly, with the addition of European (British) culture, men began to be called "breadwinners " and women "housewives." Western ideals promoted the idea that "proper" women were domestic. It seems that "these notions of domesticity were manipulated to maintain colonial class relations" (10), which sent men to the cities and maintained women in the rural areas. As a result, the British did not have to provide housing for displaced families, and gradually women's work became marginalized and considered irrelevant (9).

Society

A society differs from a culture. A *society* is *a group of people organized within a specific territory to carry out the basic functions of daily life*. Often we use the words *culture* and *society* interchangeably, but they do mean different things. One might be living within American society, but partake in many different cultures. Culture is a social heritage, while a society is composed of institutions and organizations, established to implement social needs. Societies are organized in some cooperative manner to provide food, shelter, and other basics necessary to sustain life. Society is about social relationships and interactions between people to form social institutions that are stable and continue over time, such as religion, law, and education. It is passed down through the generations. When social change occurs, it can and does occur on both societal and cultural levels. Often the institutions and the roles that people play within a society change, as do the traditions, language, symbols, and everything else we define as cultural.

World Systems Theory

In order to make sense of what all this means and to help develop a critical perspective on the structural arrangements of the family, we need to understand how society and social systems operate on a macro, or big picture, level. Wallerstein's *world systems theory* (1974) helps by dividing the world using language that defines *the core states, semiperipheral areas,* and *peripheral areas.* The core states include the United States, England, France, Russia, Germany, and Japan, as well as Italy, in most groupings. These countries are technologically advanced and dominate the world economy through banking and financial dealings. The semiperiphery includes places like Spain and Portugal as well as Brazil, Mexico, Venezuela, and the oil-producing Middle Eastern countries. All of these countries are somewhat independent in industry and finance, but are still dependent on the financial fluctuations of the core states. All need the technology that the core has developed.

The periphery consists of places in Africa, Asia, and Latin America, where the basic resources and labor are provided to keep the countries of the core and semiperiphery functioning. With this kind of economic dependency, there is little occasion for military or political domination, since most of the power already resides in the core and semiperiphery countries.

With this theory in mind, it becomes painfully obvious that the world is intimately connected. The woman growing her garden in India may be doing so for multinational reasons. She may not be able to feed her family from her income alone, because there is no employment for her in the global economy. The Haitian sugar cane cutter's family labors because sugar is needed for coffee, which is also imported from the periphery. Once we understand the global nature of all societies and the transnational networks that exist economically, we can also realize the importance of developing a global perspective. We see that in fact, we *are* family, and that we are connected to the African man and his family in the stand.

Some economists say that the development of the core countries leads to the dependency of the periphery, actually hindering their economic development. It leads them to do things that are not always self-beneficial. For example, this interpretation might explain why certain parts of the world become single-crop economies: The core needs certain crops, and the periphery countries produce them because they need the core's payments to sustain themselves. Rather than developing self-sufficient, self-sustaining economies, they become dependent on what the core needs. This reality is important to the family as it tries to carry on its important functions and as people try to make a living and feed their children. It matters when a man has to leave the land to find work to send money home to his wife, who remains in a rural region, raising the children.

Dependency Theory

Wallerstein's world systems notion of the core and periphery is part of a larger body of work called *dependency theories*. These theories are relevant to the family because the family is the basic social unit of any society. When the larger public sphere changes, the family is forced to react to its environment. Dependency theory is one of the more accepted ideas of the construction of the world economy. It is somewhat pessimistic in that it says that inequities are getting worse and poverty is growing, not diminishing. As social scientist Thomas O'Toole (1996) says, "In most of the world's poorest nations economic growth has been shaky, the trickling down sparse and the dependency of the North deepening." O'Toole is using the term *North* as we have used the term *core*.

According to Wallerstein, the core has become rich through the exploitation of the periphery parts of the world, first through slavery, then through colonization, pillage, and assumption of control over others' destinies. The periphery is in the Southern Hemisphere of the world, the core in the Northern. Even today, some theorists argue, people in the South are politically manipulated, economically controlled, and culturally imposed upon by the wealthy elites of the North. Using this theory, one could explain why American popular songs from the '50s through the '90s are continually popular in the Philippines and why English is spoken nearly universally. It explains why most of the population wears American-designed jeans that are sewn in Latin American countries and exported to Asia.

Dependency theorists argue that peripheral countries will never have economic equality with core countries as long as this system is in place. Seeking equity, they argue that perhaps not all countries should become industrialized and part of the global marketplace. In fact, they say, there needs to be freedom from the global economy, with countries of the South banding together, helping each other by feeding themselves internally and regionally, and freeing themselves from the North. They argue that industries should produce not for export, but for themselves. In fact, until the periphery begins to produce for itself and becomes self-sufficient, becoming an equal partner, no change can occur.

Some social scientists argue that in fact, even in many developed countries some places resemble the periphery and are colonies, much like those in other parts of the world. *Internal colonial theorists*, people from the periphery and people outside the dominant groups in the West, believe there are reasons why we have ghettos and poverty areas, even in rich countries. They say that we have *internal colonies*, racial groupings that create the same inequity we see in developing parts of the world (Barker, 1991).

In such a system, the dominant groups need the cheap labor and resources that others can provide in order to serve the economic order of capitalism as well as national and multinational interests. White Europeans in core countries are still at the center, especially in the countries that they populate heavily. And the internal colonies—like barrios, ghettos, Chinatowns, and reservations—still provide labor to serve the economy, whether it be in other parts of the world or in our own American cities. This creates racial and class differences between groups of people and maintains a structural hierarchy of inequality.

There are 187 countries in the world. Most people in the world are not rich; in 1995, there were nearly 6 billion people in the world, and nearly three-fourths of them lived in poverty-stricken countries. According to O'Toole, nearly 800 million people faced starvation by the year 2001. So as we approach the family in the world, we must see that global poverty is an important factor in explaining how the family looks and operates.

Modernization Theory

For a long time social scientists believed that poorer parts of the globe were likely to emulate the West in the development of industrialization, urbanization, and the evolution of democratic governments. The term *modernization* usually means technological changes, a move away from subsistence agriculture toward specialization of crops, a growth of urban centers and the development of production in factories, and a market-based (competitive) economy. The West began a move in this direction with the rise of the Industrial Revolution, and by World War II had actually become wealthy. Modernization theory is based on the idea that with free markets and the rise of capitalism, all countries of the world would be free to compete with each other and eventually have equal access to becoming affluent and modernizing.

Modernization theory has been heavily critiqued by social scientists who note that poor countries have not come into parity with the richer ones even after technological development, and that they might never do so. In fact, modernization theory has fallen out of favor, even though it is still part of the thinking in popular culture. Social scientists understand now that the nature of the world system makes it impossible for the rest of the world to catch up with the West. It is important for students in the social sciences to unlearn this theory, because it makes little sense given the global nature of the world economy. For anyone who has traveled abroad, it is easy to see that there are many differentials that make "catching up" quite unlikely.

Post-Colonial Theory

There is a growing body of knowledge coming from writers whose work is based in the periphery and semiperipheral countries of the world. Their scholarship is called *post-colonial theory;* it is relevant to the discussion here because these scholars are helping us to understand the experience of those who were once on the fringe—the marginalized, the powerless in the world order. This theory, only about ten years old, involves "discussion about migration, slavery, suppression, resistance, representation, difference, race, gender, place and responses to the influential master discourses of imperial Europe such as history, philosophy, linguistics" (Ashcroft, Griffiths, & Tiffin, 1995, 2).

The work of these scholars begins with the historical fact of colonization. It seeks to understand what the process was: how were people colonized and what impact did it have on the material lives of the colonized? It also sees that the colonization did not end when the colonizers left the countries. In fact, colonization goes on today through a "continuing process of imperial suppressions and exchanges through a diverse range of countries" (3). The writers refer to colonization as "imperialism."

Different societies experienced settler/invasion scenarios, but different reactions occurred within the countries. Sometimes they were oppositional to the settler, other times they may have appeared to be complicit. The scholars talk about resistance to the settler and seek to understand that there is no easy answer about the complex process of these relations (Said, 1978, 87–91). There is also an argument that the very nature of colonization has created a "hybridism" by which one can never *really* know what came before the colonized experience (Ashcroft, Griffiths, & Tiffin, 4). But there is an effort to try to understand, not supplant, the indigenous peoples and languages of post-colonial societies.

One writer from this school of thought is Jamaica Kincaid (1988), a novelist who writes about her experience in Antigua from the view of a local woman watching with disgust as the tourists arrive. Her anger is also evident when she describes the colonizers who came before. Her books are useful for readers who want to understand the view from the colonized (also called *subalterns* in the language of post-colonial studies). For example, she says, "I met the world through England, and if the world wanted to meet me it would have to do so through England. . . . " (94).

Edward Said (1978), another important post-colonial thinker, has written of "The Orient" as a social construction, a place that might have been based in some reality, but was also a product of the West interacting with that area of the world, to create a whole entity to be studied, analyzed, idealized, and stereotyped. Both of these authors are well worth reading on your own.

Post-colonial theory is a good way to understand some of the current developments in peripheral countries. For example, the Islamic revolutions in Iran and Afghanistan can be explained by this theory. In those countries, fundamentalist religious organizations have taken over the governments and imposed traditionalist order upon the society. Families have been forced to take on an anti-materialist, anti-Western attitude. They are told to practice the traditional Muslim religion, take on traditional gender behaviors in family life, give up Western music and lifestyles, and adopt traditional practices in dress, values, and ways of being. The country and people within it are strongly anti-imperialist and stand in opposition to the materialist values of the core countries. In fact, their opposition to the West takes on a strongly nationalistic flavor. These behaviors are not unexplainable; they are a post-colonial reaction. Post-colonial theory also helps us to situate and understand the poverty and continued economic and political problems in many of the countries that were colonized.

Shifting the Lens

Most maps of the world that we see in the West have the United States at their center; this is a visual representation of Eurocentrism, seeing the world from the perspective that everything is in relation to ourselves. A map prepared by someone in Asia would have a different vantage point and a whole other way of telling the story.

Although this book is called a global, transnational, or cross-cultural family text, I should note that it is *Eurocentric*. The term means that the knowledge and information herein are centered on Western society, and that we will compare other countries in the world to what we know in the United States.

We need to understand that when we study the family in its cross-cultural complexity, there is a dynamic interaction between the *macrosocietal forces* and the *microsocietal forces*. Macro forces are those like economics and politics, which are concerned with the large-scale patterns that describe society as a whole. Micro forces are the small-scale patterns of social interactions, such as relationships, intergroup interactions, and family dynamics. In any study of the family, the interaction between the macro and the micro explains how family members' lives are shaped. This approach includes ideas about race, class, gender, and ethnicity.

The family differs depending on where you come from. If you are poor in a developing part of the world, where there are sharp divisions between the poor and the rich, your life experience will be very different from that of a wealthy person in the very same country. A woman's life will differ from those of men in the same family; the experiences of a minority ethnic group differ from those of the people in the majority. There is conflict in the world, between nations, between groups of people within nations, within families, in the economic sphere. The family is not always "a haven in a heartless world" (Lasch, 1977). Even though the family might be positive in some of its consequences, it can be negative for some individuals within the same families.

Ethnocentrism and Cultural Relativity

Because of our individual biases, most of us engage in ethnocentrism and need to try to understand cultural relativity. *Ethnocentrism* is the judgment of another culture according to the standards of one's own culture. It also assumes that one's own culture is superior. In the vignettes presented earlier in the chapter, when I saw the child eating a raw chicken leg in South Africa, or an Indian family squatting in the field to relieve themselves rather than using a bathroom, my stomach turned.

All of these phenomena have to be viewed with *cultural relativity*, or *the practice of evaluating any culture by its own standards*. There are reasons that groups of people do what they do, often reasons that make perfectly good sense to them. Cultural relativity means walking in the shoes of other people, understanding their reasons for doing things, and trying not to project your value system onto them. Many of us tend toward ethnocentrism until we confront our own biases. As we embark on this journey, I hope that you will attempt to suspend judgment, to try to understand how and why things are done as they are, and to engage in cultural relativity as much as possible.

On that trip to the stand in Zimbabwe, after spending the day with the family I offered the farmer some money for the food and for the photos I had taken. Later, I was rebuked by my Nigerian friend, who told me that I had been an "ugly American." I could not understand why, until he told me that in the Shona tribe, of which the family was a part, the proper thing to do would have been to give a gift to the mother-in-law for her hospitality and cooking. To give money to the father directly was disrespectful. In the United States, to tip directly is common, but I was being ethnocentric in assuming that was how it was done in Zimbabwe. The distinctions between ethnocentrism and cultural relativity are subtle, and understanding them requires knowledge about another useful related concept, jingoism.

Jingoism is *a chauvinistic patriotism that is somewhat bellicose in nature.* It is a form of intolerance somewhat like ethnocentrism, but in a more extreme form. A jingoist believes that the culture from whence he or she comes is the best, and is willing to go to war for that belief. She or he goes beyond believing to the point of action and intolerance. A jingoist tends to be patriotic and a bit of a flag waver, sometimes with little understanding of that which he is espousing. In dealing with a global perspective, it is useful to understand that many of us have developed jingoistic attitudes and that a critical consciousness is necessary to confront those internalized values. A case in point might be the 1996 Olympic Games held in Atlanta, Georgia.

At those games the United States did quite well, garnering many medals. Other countries did equally well. However, if one watched only U.S. television, including CNN, one would think that only the United States had been so successful. The media featured mainly U.S. athletes, and showed only events in which the United States triumphed. This is an example of jingoism, which led to embarrassment on the part of those who have a more global perspective.

Objectivity and complete cultural relativity is, of course, a difficult feat to accomplish. One is born into a certain culture and develops a viewpoint and worldview in accordance with that perspective. All of us filter what we see through the personal values and biases that we have developed. However, we can try to maintain some objectivity by understanding and owning our personal biases rather than claiming complete neutrality. Max Weber, a German sociologist, argued that researchers must try to be value-free and to discover "truth" as it is, rather than as it should be. But others have argued (Lorber, 1998, 112) that all research is political and is related to issues of power. Clearly, my perspective takes this view as well. I doubt that any of us can be completely neutral as we approach looking at the family in the world: what we can do is articulate our biases and be conscious of our own value-based viewpoints.

With those biased viewpoints can come value judgments that lead us to believe that we have nothing to learn from places or people unlike ourselves, particularly people who might be materially less well-off. By studying the family, we learn that every interaction, every piece of reading about families in the world, adds to a knowledge and information base.

Terminology

There has long been debate about what to call those countries that have gained independence from colonial domination since World War II and what to call those countries that are the major industrial powers, as well as what to call the former communist countries. For a long time the phrase "First World" has been used to designate the nations that were the first to industrialize and modernize and have since become technological and economic world leaders. We, as U.S. citizens, are part of the first world; our lives are quite comfortable. We are wealthy, by world standards. For example, Americans spend more on cosmetics, $8 billion annually, and Europeans on ice cream, $11 billion, than it is estimated it would cost to provide basic education ($6 billion) or water and sanitation ($9 billion) to more than 2 billion people worldwide who go without schools and toilets (Crossette, 1998a, 1). These rich countries are all *capitalist countries;* they have also been called "the West." They would be called the "core" in Wallerstein's theory.

Countries of the "Second World" are countries that are not central to the world economy but have industrialized and done well for themselves economically. They are places like Brazil, Mexico, Venezuela, Malaysia, those that had modernized in certain economic arenas but were still dependent and not economically in leadership positions. These would be the "semiperiphery" according to Wallerstein's theory. The phrase "Third World" designates those countries that were not aligned with any other country and whose resources and labor were expendable and not completely necessary to those in the First World. These are agricultural and land-based countries that were once colonies of the West, and are chiefly located in Latin American, Africa, and Southeast and South Asia. They are the poorer countries of the world, the "periphery" in Wallerstein's language. The term "Third World" has fallen out of favor.

Some writers have more recently begun referring to the world in terms of development (Mies, 1986, 39). Thus the First and Second World are called the "Developed (or even 'Overdeveloped') Nations," while "Developing Nations" are those countries developing more technology and industry, as well as the related social institutions of health, education, and democratic politics. Their argument is that the developed parts of the world have not stopped "developing," and the limitless expansion of accumulating wealth has become like a cancer that is progressively destructive to those who are exploited in this process as well as to those who benefit from it.

It has also been suggested that we should be using the words *North* and *South* to make distinctions. The North would be those countries in the Northern Hemisphere that were expansionist historically, which industrialized early and developed colonies in the South because they needed the resources. The South would be the poorer countries south of the Tropic of Cancer, which are less developed. For the purposes of this book I use the terms *developed, core,* or *West* for the countries that have been known as "First World." I call those that were formerly known as "Third World" either *developing* or *periphery,* and refer to those that have made recent progress in industrializing as the *semiperiphery.*

Packing Your Suitcase

A traveler needs to pack a suitcase, one equipped with the items necessary for getting by and handling whatever comes one's way while traveling. On this journey you are asked to bring a cultural relativity, an understanding that you need to suspend judgment and observe what you are seeing. You are asked to try to stand outside of what you are observing and think theoretically. As we continue on the journey, you will be provided with a number of different theories with which to view families. In this chapter you were lent the world system theory lens; later you will learn about and be asked to look through others. You will be asked to think about the nature of global social change and the reverberations of this change on families. You will need an appreciation that what happens to a family is not merely cultural, that there are structural conditions that impact families, and that the social structure determines the forms that the family takes. Finally, you will be asked to see that the family takes many different forms, that it is variable, elastic, and does not fit any common image.

Some Final Thoughts

One cannot universalize the family. There is no monolithic family, either in the United States or in the world. Just as in the United States families are quite complex, they are complex around the globe. There are single-parent families, dual-career families, gay and lesbian families, two-parent families, nuclear families, large extended families, merged and blended families, and people with no families, just to name a few. Thus the "global family" is impossible to describe. Through snapshots, anecdotes, and data gathered by those who have studied the family in various parts of the world, readers of this book will perceive a glimmer of the complexity that exists.

We are about to engage in a journey out of the center. As a traveler, one moves away from the core into the margins, realizing full well that most of the readers of this book live within the core and that we need to hear the voices of those who are shouting or living quietly on the margins. To them, it is not the margins; it is their lives. They are part of this journey. We will shift our paradigm (or way of seeing) to include their multitude of experiences.

The United States is a much more multicultural place than it was in the past. The fact that it is so diverse and un-unifiable is to be rejoiced at. The fact that we have many affinities, that all of us come from multiple backgrounds, from different races, classes, ethnic backgrounds, value systems and history, means that we need to begin to see the rest of the world in that way, too.

Because the world is changing so rapidly, we must revise the way we think about it and learn about it. In order to become compassionate, we must include in this change recognition, sensitivity, and appreciation for differences. The people in the families we study are much like you and me. They are born, raised with family, strive to live, and die. They may be different in the way they look, but they do not differ in their humanity. The children we meet are like children everywhere; their desires are like yours and mine. When we approach these families with love, with open hearts and minds, we encounter and learn much. To open to them is to grow. It is for this reason that I invite you on this journey with me, into the family in its plurality, its transcendence.

Summary

In this chapter we looked at the family by beginning a journey into the world, where we worked to develop a global and transnational perspective. We found that (1) families face common challenges; (2) they respond in different ways, due in part to different cultures; (3) their situations or resources differ due to their location in the class structures of their society and their society's location in the world order; and (4) cultural diffusion and global capitalism are changing families around the world.

By looking at a few vignettes, we began to develop a theoretical understanding of the relationship between societies and inequality in the world and how that impacts families and real people. We defined terms crucial to the understanding of family in the world, like *social change, culture, language, symbols, society, norms*, and *values*.

We defined important terms like *core, periphery,* and *semiperiphery, apartheid, caste, abject* or *absolute poverty, macrosocietal* and *microsocietal forces*. We utilized world systems theory and dependency theory to look at how the world is structured; then we compared those theories to modernization theory. Internal colonial theory can be used to explain some kinds of poverty in the core. We began to understand the difference between ethnocentrism and cultural relativity. We then considered jingoism and how Eurocentrism might impact the way we see people in the world. Finally, we began to develop a post-colonial analysis of how to approach the family, and we began the journey into the cross-cultural multiplicity and variability in the family.

CHAPTER 2

Defining Families in Global Terms

n Chapter 1 we looked at the multiple forms that the family can take and defined terms that are useful in getting a handle on "the family." *Family* is a simple word, yet it means so much. In working with families, we learn that individual families do not always look the way we have been taught to think of them. As students of the family, your understanding of families will have to be revised to include those that might be beyond your own experience. In this chapter we examine the diversity of structures and commonality of functions that exist in families.

The family may be defined one way in terms of biology and another way in a social context. In fact, *family* has many meanings. Biologically, the term *family* usually refers to the mating of partners who satisfy physiological needs and produce children; this mating then leads to the rearing of the offspring. Mating is usually impersonal, random, and temporary, and is purely about raising children to self-sufficiency. However, it is not the biological interpretation of family with which we are concerned here.

Instead, the family with which we are concerned is the social unit. Sociologically, the family is a far more complex form than the simple biological one.

Historically, sociologists and anthropologists have defined *family* as a social grouping in which there is common residence, economic cooperation, and reproduction, and which includes adults of both sexes—at least two of whom maintain a socially approved relationship—and one or more children, the biological or adopted offspring of the sexually cohabiting pair (Murdock, 1949, 2–3). But as we know, the family today encompasses far more than that definition. First, not all families live together, nor are they always economically interdependent. Families may not receive social approval and may not include children, nor are the partners always of both sexes. The definition of the family has evolved to include partners who are not always married. They may be living in common law, or merely consider themselves partners in life.

Photo 2.1   Author with Mapondera family "kin" in Harare, Zimbabwe.
Photographer: Elaine Leeder

Even though some readers of this book might come from traditional families with a dad, mom, and kids, we all know families that do not fit that profile. So too, around the globe, that image of the family is in the minority, and in fact is an ideal form that is not the norm in most parts of the world.

When I was in Zimbabwe in 1989, I stayed with my friend Esinet's family. Often I would come into the living room and be introduced to someone who was called her niece, or her cousin or her aunt or uncle. I was amazed at how many relatives she had. The house, a small British colonial house, was often filled with dozens of people, whose connections to the family I never got right. I got used to a houseful of people at all times and stopped asking how they were related. I knew who Esinet's children were, but I never understood the rest of the relatives' relationship to the nuclear family.

Later, after I returned to United States, Esinet's "niece" Sarah came to visit. She came to call me "aunt," and she listed me as her next of kin and relative living in the United States. I had been adopted into the "family" even though I had no blood relation. That summer, when Sarah came to my home, an eight-room Cape Cod in which I lived alone, the house was quiet and orderly, the way I liked it. Sarah looked at me and said, "This is unnatural." To her, my single woman's isolated life was completely foreign and contrary to Sarah's definition of family and what a home or household should be. Her reaction surprised me, and yet I knew that compared to the family as she knew it, my way of living *was* unnatural.

Contemporary family has taken on many faces. In the United States, it no longer matches the idealized image of father, mother, and two children living contentedly in the suburbs in a home with a white picket fence. In fact, the family has *never* fit that model, as we will see when we look at the history of the family in the United

States. Nor has the family ever fit that model in other parts of the globe. For example, for many years my daughter lived in Oregon and I lived in New York. Now we live an hour apart. I am a single mother and I have a grown child, yet she and I are still a family. Esinet's family in Zimbabwe has five children and a huge extended family. Members come and go from her home daily, all considered cousins, sisters, aunts, and uncles. That is her family. In India, my colleague Anita lives with her husband and son in an apartment. Near her live her father, mother, sisters, and their husbands and children. These are her family. My friend Sheila lives in Cape Town, South Africa, with her female partner and two daughters that they adopted. They too are a family.

The family is not limited by blood relations, legal or formal marriage, adoption of children, or even procreation. We cannot say that all families have children, nor that they all socialize them. Families are not all nuclear, nor extended. Not all families have married partners, nor do family members always live together. It is actually easier to say what a family *is not* than to say what a family *is*.

The definition of the family varies from culture to culture. In India, even as late as 1993,

> the institution of marriage and the event of child bearing are considered so essential for family life that couples staying together without marriage, single parent families and childless families are not accepted as complete or normal families. (TISS, 1993, as quoted in Gulati, 1995)

Indian society can be said to be totally preoccupied with marriage and the birth of children within marriage; Indians believe in the universality of marriage between men and women, able-bodied or disabled (Gulati, 1995, 134–135). Marriage must be arranged early and within the same caste group, particularly in rural areas. Women who are obtaining a college education or pursuing professional studies are allowed to marry a bit later. Very clearly, the family in India is quite dissimilar to the family in the United States.

For example, in the United States there is currently a debate over whether or not same-sex couples living together should be considered "married" and a family for purposes of health insurance benefit coverage. Conservative and liberal forces are doing battle, working to define and redefine what is considered family. Recently the state of Vermont legalized same-sex unions, but conservative forces have mobilized to challenge this law.

In other parts of the globe that same battle is going on, with different issues at stake and debated. In Zimbabwe, the president of the country, Robert Mugabe, believes that gays and lesbians should not be given credence; he banned gays and lesbians and their books from an international book fair in the capital, Harare, in 1996. In support of the president, the board of censors issued an official banning order, but later the high court of that country overturned the order on the grounds that the board of censors could not ban materials it did not screen.

In Zimbabwe, the family, particularly among the Shona, which is the dominant ethnic cluster, is traditionally a large extended family system. Male-headed households are the ideal, and the ultimate decision making resides with the male, who controls all forms of property. In Shona culture a bride price is paid to the family of the bride by the respective groom's family as a form of purchase of her labor and as payment to the family for having raised her. In fact, her children are claimed by the husband's family (Riphenburg, 1997). The bride's paternal aunt negotiates the payment; she has very strong control over the niece's marriage. However, since the process is a long one and the traditional society is changing, this kind of family is becoming less common. There are now common-law families, which tend to be dis-approved of (Meekers, 1994). How the family is defined among the Shona will impact how social workers and practitioners interact with families should there be any problems. From this example, we can see that it would be as hard to generalize about what is a family in Zimbabwe as it is in the United States. To define the term *family* one must use wide and all-inclusive language that does not limit the possi-bilities and is not myopic or narrow.

What Is a Family?

Perhaps in the broadest sense of the word, a *family is a group of people who have intimate social relationships and have a history together.* Families are of the same or different genders, of the same or different generations, and interact with strong ties of solidarity. Relationships of power and authority are developed, as are resources for meeting the basic human needs of the members. Rights and responsibilities are determined based on the cultural norms, age, sex, and position within the system, and the patterns are established based on the social context within which the family operates. Sometimes people choose to call themselves family and pretend that they are kin, a phenomenon we call "fictive kin," or kin defined by a fiction. They too are family.

Just as it is difficult to define the family, so too it is a challenge to define the *nuclear family.* Most cultures in the world have some form of nuclear families, which is also called a "conjugal group" or "marriage group" in the earlier literature. The *nuclear family is an adult (or two adults) living in an intimate relationship with their own or adopted children.* The nuclear family seems to be universal, even in places where other family forms play a significant role. Although universal, the nuclear family is sometimes more autonomous than the extended family.

In the United States, for example, more emphasis is placed on the nuclear family. Although people might belong to an extended family, they may live far away from them. We would call these nuclear families *conjugal families,* which means that *the relationship between the adult persons who are living together intimately is primary. The emphasis here is on the "marital bond" or intimacy between mates.* In other words, the large extended family is of less importance than it is, say, in Latin American or African societies. Conjugal families in the United States are somewhat transitory and fragile, affected by divorce, death of a partner, or separation (Hutter, 1998).

The nuclear family takes on many forms worldwide. The definition of a nuclear family once included the phrase "socially approved sexual relationship" (Murdock, 1949), but even that idea is now debatable, since many people live in nuclear families that might not be socially approved.

Photo 2.2   Nuclear family in contemporary China. Photographer: Patti Carman

Some families, like unmarried couples with children, gay and lesbian couples, and unwed mothers with children, might not be socially accepted by some people, but they can still be considered nuclear families. For example, in Latin America the traditional family with mother, father, and children was once the dominant form of nuclear family. Now single parenthood is on the rise, with nearly 20 percent of all Latin American families being single-parented by women (Sales & Tuirán, 1997, 145).

In the nuclear family there is more emphasis placed on individualism, romantic love, freedom to choose one's partner, separate residence from the extended family, and strong intimate relationships. This separateness also means that the family is less able to turn to extended family members for help and support in times of need.

There is enormous debate among historians and social scientists about whether or not the nuclear family is a historical form that has evolved in all societies as a result of modernization. Current research seems to indicate that it is not a historical progression that large, extended families become nuclear as societies modernize. With modernization, independence of nuclear families from their extended families does not always develop, and not all nuclear families become self-sufficient and autonomous. Work by historian Peter Laslett (Laslett & Wall, 1972) found that household size has not varied much for hundreds of years and that extended families were not the norm in the United States even in colonial times. Families in core countries tend toward the nuclear, but there is some indication that families in the periphery have different compositions and different patterns of adaptation (Wallerstein & Smith, 1991). This means that, although a family might look like a nuclear family, it may well be an adaptation of the extended family.

The *extended family* is comprised of *persons of common lineage with combined nuclear families and the primary connection coming through the parent-child relationship.* This results in family units of three or more generations. Here the emphasis is on blood ties between generations or between siblings. Interestingly, extended family lives on forever, in that it continues to exist even if family members die or there is a divorce. On a recent trip to the Dominican Republic, my students were surprised to see that many families lived in small apartments or homes and looked like the nuclear families with which we were familiar at home. However, upon further investigation they discovered that the small groups were closely connected to their larger extended families; they just did not live together.

In an extended family, all members may not reside with the head of the family or with the elders. Nonetheless there is intimate, ongoing economic and psychological interaction. Sometimes, because of immigration, the family might be separated by thousands of miles. Still, money is sent home to the family, regular phone calls maintain the emotional bonds, and visits take place back and forth frequently. One of my students, while in the Dominican Republic, met her grandmother and aunts for the first time. She was instantly welcomed into the fold, cooked for, given gifts, and within a week of meeting them was integrally involved in the daily life of her large extended family. She was a United States' citizen, an all-American college student, and yet she was part of an extended family that had expectations and connections that were blood related and deeply entrenched. For her the extended family was as important as her nuclear family at home.

There are also downsides to extended families. It is sometimes the case that poor relatives are exploited by the more prosperous kin for the labor they can provide. Sometimes the needs of the extended family hold individuals back from getting ahead financially, and there are economic and emotional obligations when one has an extended family. From the outside, extended families may look appealing, but they can have their negative consequences.

Another term that we need to define is *household.* A household is *a group of people who are responsible for their basic and continuing reproduction needs,* like food, clothing, and shelter, and who put together different kinds of income to meet those needs (Wallerstein & Smith, 1991, 228). *Households are places where people live together and share assets. Household implies common residence, economic cooperation, and socialization of children.* In any society, a family may or may not form a household. Households can be made up of individuals from more than one family. In fact, the word *family* comes from the Roman term *familia,* which refers to what we think of as a household, including slaves, servants, boarders, and others.

Families and households are related, but not all families live in the same households, and not all households are families. In the United States (Thorne, 1982, 16), there are class-based differences in the ability of households to realize the ideal of being autonomous and self-supporting. In other words, one might be part of a family in the world but not be able to live within that family because of economic conditions, which force flexibility and varied ways of obtaining money. So, for example, in South Africa, men who migrate to the gold mines or to the cities far from home sometimes create households in which they pool resources so that they can send money home to their families.

In Malaysia, young women leaving home to work in the free trade zone industries sometimes form households of non-related women who share expenses and

Photo 2.3   Extended family in contemporary India. Photographer: Patti Carman

accommodations. Economic necessity leads to forming a different social unit than living within the family. In the Caribbean, nuclear family units may be scattered in several different households, with the husband-father living with his mother, one or more children living with maternal relatives, and the mother working as a live-in maid. In Bangladesh, a household may be groups of people living together, but the family is the people who share the same bowl of food (Feldman, 1992, 8–10).

Kinship is the term that is used to explain *the role relationships used by people who consider themselves related.* These are also fictive kin, people who call themselves family but are not blood related. Terms we know are *father, mother, brother, sister, aunt, uncle, cousins, grandfather, grandmother.* But in other parts of the world, other types of relationships might be emphasized. For example, among the Shona, the father's sister, or the *tete*, is extremely important in relationships with the children. In that culture there is the word *amai*, which means both mother and mother's sisters, and the word *tete* is used for both a husband's sisters and father's sisters. The word *murume* is used for man, husband, and even husband's siblings and cousins (Chitauro, 1995). The nature of the relationships is reflected by the words chosen and the roles that the people play in a family member's life. One's aunt might be more important than one's biological mother in playing the role of teacher or matchmaker, as among the Shona.

Authority

Besides thinking of the family in terms of composition or roles, one might also think of it in terms of who has *power: the authority, the ability to make someone in the family do something they would not ordinarily do, and often the ability to control resources.* Most societies in the world have been *patriarchies,* which means that the authority is held by the male, usually the father or the eldest male. Historically, patriarchy has been the dominant form of authority, and although changing, it still remains the most common authority arrangement in the world today. Older men are given the right to make decisions that affect the overall operation of the family, and the children and even the wife are expected to submit and be obedient to that authority. Patriarchy usually refers to social relationships in which males dominate females, and power and prestige are accorded to the males. This is an example of one of the structural conditions that makes for inequity within the family.

Patriarchy impacts work, gender relations, sexuality, marriage, politics, economy, and, in fact, all human interactions. Suffice it to say now that the consequences of patriarchy have been the subject of endless debate, particularly in the past 25 years, with the development of feminist scholarship and critique of society. This book has a feminist orientation; it argues that the nature of patriarchy informs and influences every sphere of life, and that one needs to employ the "lens of gender" to understand just how deep and significant that influence is. Gender relationships is another "lens" through which we can view human familial interactions.

Examples abound of patriarchal societies. Most definitions of family assume a male head of household who is the breadwinner, a housebound wife, and related children. The case of women in the Middle East, particularly contemporary Iran, is a good one to illustrate the definition of patriarchy. In 1979, after the overthrow of the modernist Pahlavi regime, the Islamic fundamentalist cleric Khomeini was installed as supreme religious and nationalist leader. A year and a half after the revolution, Iranian women faced a number of restrictions on and violations of their rights. These included:

> 1) compulsory hijab (proper Islamic dress for women that covers the whole body except the face and hands) for Muslim as well as non-Muslim women in public—failure to adopt the hijab became punishable by public flogging and/or imprisonment; 2) the segregation of women in public institutions, schools and universities as well as buses; 3) lowering of the marriage age for girls to thirteen; 4) the reinstitution of easy divorce and polygamy for men; 5) pressure on young educated urban women and men to accept the Shiite Islamic tradition of Mut'ah or temporary marriage; 6) limited custody rights for mothers and a reversal of the Family Protection Law which gave mothers guardianship over their children after the father's death; 7) a reinstitution of male guardianship in all major decisions of life, such as permission for employment or travel; 8) significant restrictions on women's employment; 9) the closing of day care centers to discourage women's employment; and 10) a broad definition of adultery that included the prohibition of sex between unmarried but consenting adults. (Avary, 1996, 43)

Although there have been some modifications and compromises in the law in the intervening years, much remains the same today in this patriarchal society. Let us not assume, however, that because the United States does not have such restrictive laws, we do not live in a patriarchy. In the United States, too, power resides in the hands of the males. Although we are evolving toward a more egalitarian society, in which power is equally distributed, there are countless ways in which inequality between the genders is still part of our power relationships. Domestic violence, including wife battering, and child sexual abuse are just two examples.

Perhaps the most egalitarian country in the world is Sweden (Popenoe, 1988, 179). There the highest proportion of workers in the labor force is mothers with young children under age seven, and the Swedes have the lowest proportion of full-time housewives. They also have the highest rate of voluntary singlehood, nonmarital cohabitation, and other indicators of family change and nontraditional family roles. The dominant cultural motif seems to be informality, permissiveness, and egalitarianism (167). This society is considered by some to be one to emulate, and an example of where the family is heading in an advanced capitalist world.

Matriarchies exist when the authority is held by the eldest female in the family. There are a number of matriarchies in Vietnam at this time. For example, among the Cham, who live in the central part of the country (Vietnam News Agency, 1996), men play a major role in the family, but the heads of the families are often the aged women. Cham custom dictates that the daughters take the family name of the mother. After marriage the groom comes to live in his wife's house, and the right of inheritance is reserved for the daughters only. In particular, the youngest daughter is given a greater part of the inheritance because she is expected to care for the aging parents (34).

Contrary to popular conception in the United States, African American families are not matriarchal. In fact, black marriages are often more equal than are white marriages (John, Shelton, & Luschen, 1995). Recently, black women have been entering the labor market in greater numbers, and related to that rising economic position, the incidence of wife battering in black families is diminishing. African American males do not seem to be threatened by women working; this results in more egalitarian relationships than within white families in the United States (Hines & Boyd-Franklin, 1996, 69). In earlier studies the same finding was discovered. In the 1970s, Dietrich (1977) determined that even though the popular conception of lower-class black families seemed to be the stereotype of female-dominated homes, the reality was that men, although perceived as less active in decision making, were equal in decisions about handling the children and spending money (285).

In looking for international examples of matriarchal forms, one discovers that there are very few matriarchies in the world and that "even in societies organized about women, in societies that follow matrilineal descent, inheritance and residence, power tends to be held by males in the female lineage. Power usually is held by the women's brothers—from the viewpoint of ego, by the maternal uncle" (Leslie & Korman, 1985, 47).

Recently, Peggy Sanday (2002) studied matriarchies in Indonesia and found that if one changes the definition of matriarchies, there are cultures that reflect female power. Among the Minangkabau ethnic group in West Sumatra, male aggression is contained by the social structure that shuns those who violate the norms of nonviolence. There, women may not be in power politically, as we might expect of a matriarchy. However, they are crucially important in determining the cultural symbols and practices associated with the maternal as the origin and center of life (Sanday, 2002, 237).

Family sociologists, anthropologists, and feminist matriarchalists like to speak about the existence of matriarchies in prehistory, but the reality is that there were very few. Marija Gimbutas (1999) studied prehistoric goddesses in Old Europe (7,000–3,000 B.C.E.) and found that there were matrilineal societies where women were economically viable, because they could inherit goods. This did lead to greater female autonomy and greater respect for the woman, because these societies honored both mortal females and female deities. As a result, in Gimbutas's opinion, these societies were more egalitarian and honored both men and women (xix). However, they were not matriarchies. In fact, one researcher (Eller, 2000) argues that "theoretically, prehistory could have been matriarchal, but it probably wasn't, and nothing offered up in support of the matriarchal thesis is especially persuasive" (6).

Types of Marriages

So far we have been looking at types of families and defining them. Although not all people marry to be in families, as we have seen, some people do, and *relationships in which there are formal ceremonies and established norms about mating can be called marriages.* Regardless of the structure of a marriage or the type of wedding ceremony that takes place, marriages are socially constructed and are what members of a society choose to recognize as a marriage.

In essence there are two kinds of marriages: monogamy and polygamy. *Monogamy* is the most widely practiced form of marriage, in which there is one sexual partner. The two people in the marriage have an exclusive sexual partnership. In the United States, we currently tend to follow a pattern of *serial monogamy,* which is having one partner at a time. Partners may change over time because of divorce, death, or relationship endings. *Polygamy* is the situation of having a plurality of partners. There are two kinds of polygamy: polygyny and polyandry. *Polygyny* occurs when a man has more than one wife, and *polyandry* is when a woman has more than one husband. Polyandry, I should note, is extremely rare in the world.

In the United States, some people are appalled by the idea of multiple wives, which is the most common form of polygamy. In fact, we historically have had polygamous marriages in Utah, among the Mormons. Although polygamy was outlawed in 1890, the Church of Jesus Christ of Latter-Day Saints officially sanctioned it for 50 years, and only changed the policy because of governmental pressure when Utah became a state. Even into the 2000s there have been "unofficial" examples of the continuation of polygynous patterns among the Mormons.

There have been efforts to make polygyny a legally recognized lifestyle in the United States, and as many as 50,000 people in the Rocky Mountain States live in such relationships. Many people have no problem with this type of relationship, arguing that it is a fundamentalist religious practice and that it helps women in raising children. This is relevant to social workers and family practitioners, since, although illegal, the practice seems to be popular in Arizona, Utah, and Colorado.

The legal authorities find it problematic. There have been recent incidents of physical abuse of teenagers who have refused to enter into such marriages, which have caused renewed interest in polygamist practices. Another problem is that polygamous marriages are not legally recognized, and the "wives" have no marital rights. These families tend to rely on public assistance. Thus, this marital structure does not fit into the contemporary economic system.

Polygyny is still a fairly common practice in the world today. There are many reasons why it exists; sometimes for economic reasons, so that co-wives can aid each other in the work; sometimes it reflects material wealth and status in a society, because only men who can afford it can have more than one wife. It actually makes families wealthier, because there are more hands working toward the upkeep of the family. Sometimes there are not formal "marriages" that take place. Instead a man may have a mistress or even a concubine who is his sexual partner, but they are not officially married. Children may be born into such unions. Polyandry exists when men are too poor to be monogamous, and polygyny exists when men are well-off enough to have many wives (Ishwaran, 1992, 49).

In Africa the percentage of men who have more than one wife approximates 25 percent (Ramsay, 1999). There polygyny is practiced to take care of the surplus of women, and is also accepted when a woman is barren; this allows her husband to take another wife to give him children, since having many children is very important in African society. It also exists so that a man with a large plot of land can have assistance to work the soil and to feed the family. Sometimes the wives live near each other, but today it is possible that a man will keep co-wives who do not know of each other's existence.

Polygyny usually exists in societies in which patriarchy and the male power differential predominate. It is often a manifestation of the authority and power given to men and can be justified by females in support of that power structure. Sometimes the consequences of polygyny are problems for the children of the co-wives, such as favoritism of the first wife's children.

Lineage

Family lines of descent are also used to describe family structure. When the inheritance, names, rights, and duties are traced through either the mother's or the father's side, or both sides, various terms are given to explain the nature of that relationship.

In the United States, for example, we are generally *bilineal* or *bilateral,* meaning that *we trace our parentage through both mother's and father's sides.* This is what is considered normal to us. But what is normal in one society might be considered unusual in another.

Another way to trace the line is through the father, which is called *patrilineal*; this is the most common form in Western societies. The inheritance and the most important family ties are through the males from father to son to grandson and so on. In such a situation, the woman generally marries into her husband's family, and the children become members of her husband's family, not hers. Among the Fulani of Nigeria, even the name for family is the same term for a man and his wife, a household, or for all the male and female descendants of one living man. The Fulani, an ethnically diverse but related people, are patrilineal, and the woman belongs to her husband's household. The cattle on which they depend also belong to him, and he decides where they go. His is the sole lineage that is traced, and he obtains his cattle from his father and passes them on to his sons. The woman may bring some cattle to the family upon marriage, but those are given to her sons when they begin their own families (Otite, 1991, 25–30).

Matrilineal descent occurs when *the lineage and inheritance comes through the mother's line.* Even in societies where the line is through the mother, there is still much importance and respect accorded to her brothers, who have roles and responsibilities to the woman's children. In fact, her husband has responsibilities to his sister's children, although not to his own children. Farber (1964) says that in some matrilineal societies the man still retains supervisory obligations over his lineage, while the woman has no such responsibilities.

Living Arrangements

When a couple resides with the male's side of the family after marriage, it is called *patrilocal.* When they reside with the woman's side, it is called *matrilocal;* if they form their own independent household, it is called *neolocal,* which means "new place" in Greek.

Patrilocality is a common way for families to take up residence. Matrilocal couples move with the woman's family. Historical examples of matrilocality include Old Europe from 7,000 to 3,000 B.C.E. and the Native Americans a hundred years or more ago. Some scholars also suspect that the ancient Hebrews were once matrilocal. Historically, Mexican families were matrilocal, but within contemporary society there is more neolocality, with families living near their large extended families. Many of the matrilocal cultures have evolved away from that form as people move closer to cities for employment.

Some Final Terms

The term *bride price* or *dowry* is a fairly common one. Has your grandmother put aside any silverware or linen for the women in your family? Have you heard the word *trousseau?* What about *hope chest?* These are words that have come out of the concept of dowry or bride price. Sometimes the terms mean different things, and other times they mean the same thing. They are usually *a form of payment (money or goods) at the time of marriage, given from one family to the other.* In some societies, like the Shona described earlier, the payment is to the father of the woman for the raising of his daughter, and as reimbursement for the loss of her services and income to his family.

In Zimbabwe, bride price or *lobola,* as it is called, led to problems for awhile in the 1980s. As a result of women moving to the cities, the aunt *(tete)* was less involved in the girl's upbringing, and arranged marriages seemed to dwindle. Young women seeking employment moved away from the traditional family in the rural regions. Because birth control is only available with a husband's permission, because abortion is hard to come by and adoption is frowned upon out of respect and reverence to one's ancestors, young women were having children. There was a rise in the incidence of infanticide (the killing of infant children) among these young women, who would have been considered "tainted goods" if they had come home with a child born out of wedlock (Leeder, 1994). When the government realized the problem, social workers were sent in to find solutions. Homes for unwed mothers were established, and a system was worked out so that the putative father of the baby paid the woman's father "damages" in the form of a lesser financial amount than the dowry. Then the girl was free to return to the family of origin.

In other societies, such as in India, dowry is payment by the woman's family to the groom's side, to make her more attractive and marriageable to a prospective suitor. Murdock (1949) found that dowry payments happened more frequently in patrilocal societies when the women left their family homes.

Bride prices or dowries are part of the system of patriarchy, in which women are seen as commodities or possessions, like other parts of the household. Since marriage in many parts of the world is considered an economic arrangement rather than a romantic or emotion-based relationship, bride price or dowry makes sense. However, it is also true that these economic issues have led to social problems. Women, as property, have been greatly harmed by this system. Dowries are no longer legal in India, but some people still exploit the custom for economic gain instead of honoring a tradition of sincere marriage.

Romantic love is yet another of the terms used to contrast the family globally. In the United States we believe that we are free to choose our partner. We also believe that it is important to partner with the person with whom we fall in love. However, although love is a universal phenomenon, its meaning differs cross-culturally, and it is not always an important factor in determining with whom one partners.

Romantic love is based on valuing its immediate expression, with its uncontrollable passion, in contrast with the control of its expression by the individual's society (Murstein, 1974, 383). Romantic love comes from an era in which there was a rebellion from the constraints of traditional society, and to this day we hold on to those ideals. In the United States we value wining, dining, romantic music, "falling in love," and "living happily ever after." Our image is based on myths that evolve from this romantic ideal in which love occurs at first sight and "love conquers all." Other images, like a "white wedding" (Ingraham, 1999), shape our expectations. These myths have also come out of the traditions of Christian belief that love was forever, under God's recognition, based on a marriage contract with formal vows. Thus "[divorce] is an inevitable correlate of love matches, when love vanishes the partner must be replaced by a new lover" (Murstein, 1974, 560).

As we will see when we look at the institutions of courtship, marriage, and partnering, there are other ways of finding a mate. *Arranged marriages* are the norm in many parts of the world. For example, 95 percent of all Indian marriages are arranged (Bumiller, 1990, 24), because there marriages are economic agreements between families of the same caste system. When a couple marry, it is the joining of

Photo 2.4   Contemporary family in India, with all daughters, for whom arranged marriages and dowry will be likely. Photographer: Mary Thieme

two families and communities, not just two individuals. According to the Hindu religion, a person's fate is predestined by *karma*, which is the sum of all previous actions of that person's former existences. Thus karma dictates that the union of two people was meant to happen and that individuals should not interfere with what was meant to be. "It is the biggest gamble of one's life, why leave it to destiny?" (Murstein, 1974, 33).

Arranged marriages help maintain the social order or social stratification system of a given society; they also strengthen parental power over children as well as keeping family traditions and value systems intact. They create a bond between the kinship group, consolidate and extend family property, and even keep young people safe from the uncertainty of finding mates. Even if it is hard for some of us to imagine preferring an arranged marriage, many people in the world would have it no other way. Details concerning arranged marriages are changing in some areas (India and Zimbabwe are two such examples), but this form of bonding is acceptable in many parts of the world.

Love is not always about one's own desire. Love is often about community. As a society, we in the United States believe in LOVE and seek and crave it, long for it. In other parts of the world, love may be important, but so is doing what is right for the family, for the community. Love may be about growing together over time, about the development of a relationship that is initially determined by status and community. It is the family, the community, and not the individual nuclear relationship based on love that binds people together.

Commonality in Functions of the Family

Families across the world have much in common. Sometimes they look different based on dress, food, or rituals, but underneath they have a number of similarities. In fact, the family is diverse in its structure but common in its basic functions.

Procreation

One of the unifying themes among all families is the fact that they are the source of *procreation*. It is within families that *children are born and reared.* This seems to be a universal truth about families and one of the few "universal functions" on which anthropologists and sociologists can agree (Murdock, 1949). As we know, not all families raise their children, but it is within families that children are born. Societies must have a means of perpetuating themselves, and procreation is that means.

However, procreation is more than birthing. There are dissimilarities when it comes to how those births occur, where they happen, the life chances of those babies and mothers, and the resources available to them. All mothers birth babies, but even the circumstances of those births will depend on the social order and the structural conditions under which they exist. Birthing huts in rural Africa certainly differ from birthing rooms in hospitals in the United States. Whether or not a mother or baby survive any complications around the pregnancy and birth will depend on economic conditions and the material conditions of the society, where that family fits in the social stratification system, and where they are in the world.

For example, in most industrialized countries, except in Eastern Europe, at least 99 out of 100 girls born will survive their first five years. Hong Kong, Israel, Singapore, Greece, and Costa Rica also fall into this category (Population Crisis Committee, 1988, 2). In contrast, fewer than 80 out of 100 girls born in Afghanistan, Bangladesh, Mali, North Yemen, and Pakistan will survive to age five. In one-third of 99 countries studied, fewer than 90 out of 100 girls survive to age five.

In the world's poorest countries, mothers are up to 200 times more likely to die as a result of complications of pregnancy or childbirth as women in the richest countries. Since women in these poorer countries are also pregnant more often, maternal mortality often represents a major cause of death among women of child-bearing age. Worldwide, more than half a million women die every year because of inadequate reproductive health care. For every one woman who dies, an additional 10 to 15 suffer serious complications in childbirth, such as hemorrhage or infection. In more than one-fourth of the 99 countries studied, 1 in 10 women will die between ages 15 and 45 (3). Structural conditions even impact the most basic of family truths, procreation.

Socialization

Another condition unifying families is that they are primary agents of *socialization.* Socialization is *the process of learning who people are supposed to be in their society and social group.* Socialization depends very much on where one fits in terms of race, class, gender, ethnicity, and culture, but it is a social learning that takes place throughout a lifetime, not just in childhood. Most of this book is about the socialization process and how different cultures define what is normal and acceptable behavior within the family. Sometimes socialization is intentional, and often it is not; it is emulation of the people around us.

In the social sciences there is the understanding that the self is constructed by the social forces surrounding the individual. There are some characteristics that people are born with, but the environment helps to mold that raw material into the people they become. This is the old nature-versus-nurture debate. Families help to do that construction of the self through the roles that individuals are taught to play within the family. It is hard to determine what an individual is born with and what she is taught, but we do know that nurturing matters a great deal, far more than nature in shaping human behavior.

Socialization is carried out by primary agents of socialization, like the family, schools, peers, community, and the media. It also never stops, with adults being socialized into new roles later in life and different agents of socialization playing key roles within one's employment, social network, and changing family compositions. Television, for example, is one of the primary agents of socialization in the United States. The average American home has TV on for an average of 7 hours a day (Arendell, 1997). In fact, the more hours a child watches TV, the more he or she tends to hold traditional views, behave aggressively, and want more advertised products (10). Children who watch greater amounts of TV also have poorer quality social relationships and perform more poorly in school than children who watch less television.

One can also be resocialized by learning new behaviors like giving up drugs, alcohol, or other addictions. Groups become primary tools of resocialization, and it seems that socialization goes on throughout one's life, up until death, as one learns how to approach and handle challenges.

Socialization is very dependent on the structural conditions inside and outside of the family. Through gender socialization one learns the cultural norms for being masculine and feminine in a society. How one is socialized will differ depending on if one is a boy or a girl. Gender relationships within the family are an internal structural condition. For example, a girl raised among the Sambia in Papua, New Guinea, resides with her family until she is married, but boys are removed to a men's clubhouse at seven to ten years old and receive their first initiation into warriorhood. The boy is trained in developing strength, which is a primary male characteristic, and even in contemporary society among the Sambia there is an unbending definition of manhood. Women are seen as dangerous and polluting inferiors and men are seen as tough, strident, and highly masculine (Herdt, 1982, 50–57). This socialization process of difference begins at birth and continues through a lifetime of training. This is a structural condition of inequality and perpetuates a hierarchy of power within families that is also part of the socialization process.

Socialization teaches the norms and values of a society, the status and roles that we each take on in that society, how the institutions function, and our roles within them. Without socialization we would all simply be human animals, lacking the important societal skills needed to survive. We are social animals, and socialization teaches us how to be so (Nock, 1987).

Division of Labor

Another theme that seems to underlie most families is that they teach and perpetuate a *division of labor*. This means that families teach what kind of work will be done by family members. Division of labor refers to *the specialized economic activity that people do* (Durkheim, 1893). This term usually refers to gendered behaviors, what men and women do in the society, so it is also about the socialization process.

What one does for work in a society is determined by that society. Although the traditional family has come to mean women raising children and men going out and earning a living, that has changed dramatically in Western societies as the need for dual-career families has arisen. And it is not always true that mothers nurture and fathers work.

For example—in yet another culture—in Papua, New Guinea, the people of Sudest Island (locally called Vanatinai) arrange their work lives in ways very unlike anything we in the West might imagine. Men and women work as virtual equals (Lepowsky, 1994), and boys and girls care for younger siblings and younger children. Men are expected to share in child care as fathers and both sexes participate in the planting of the yams, one of the island's main crops. Now that the society is no longer warlike, there is far more equality, but even in this seemingly egalitarian society the average man spends more time hunting wild boar in the rain forest with his spear than does the average woman. His hunting seems to be more highly valued than her cleaning the hamlet and the house.

This culture is quite unique because it has had minimal contact with the West, and although both sexes do not live in perfect harmony, they do come close. For example, there is sexual equality in decision making, in which everyone participates in community forums. There is no chief, and because the island is small (2,300 people), they can meet face to face and not have to delegate responsibility to a few leaders. This is one of the few societies that is truly matrilineal, in which the kinship is traced through the mother's clan and women inherit and own land and other property. Women here are seen as *taubwaragha*, which means "ancient" and "the way of the ancestors" (Wilford, 1996).

In fact, women and men have equal access to the culture's form of authority, which is the idea of the giver. Through hard work, ritual generosity, and gaining supernatural powers one attains the job of being a "big man" who accumulates many goods and then gives them away at ritual feasts. Women and men have equal access to acquiring ceremonial valuables, and both sexes can lead their own trips to other islands to trade with others. This is the distribution of labor that is passed on to the children, and the culture allocates this responsibility fairly equally.

Regulation of Sexual Behavior

All families regulate and legitimate sexual behaviors. In Western societies the ideal is that the bond between two partners creates sexual exclusivity and solidifies the commitment they make to each other and then to the family. Part of the control of sexuality includes controlling premarital sexuality in preparation for marriage and contribution to the family and the community. Remember that marriage is often part of an economic arrangement.

Premarital sex seems to be the type of sexual behavior that is controlled by families and part of the sexual regulatory role of families. Murdock found that 70 percent of the societies he studied permitted premarital sex. Today in the United States, by the time American women are aged 20, 4 out of 10 of them will become pregnant. The U.S. rates of sexual activity among teens is declining, with 48 percent of all high school students sexually active. That is down from 54 percent in 1990. But interestingly, American teen pregnancy rates lead the developed world, with rates the highest in the industrialized world (Health Central News, 1999).

Some cultures approve of sex before marriage and encourage it. Others, having once prohibited it, are now trying to find ways to accommodate it as a result of changing social mores. Many definitions of what are acceptable sexual behaviors are evolving as a result of rapid importation of sexual ideas from the core countries. In a study done comparing 24 mostly Western countries (Widmer, Treas, & Newcomb, 1998), 61 percent of the countries agreed that premarital sex is not wrong at all. However, 58 percent condemned young teenagers having sex, with the majority limiting premarital sex to adults. And the majority of countries believed that extramarital sex was wrong, with only 4 percent reporting that it was not wrong at all for married people to have sex with someone besides their husband or wife (352).

A good example of the regulation of sexual behavior done by families is in rural Haiti (Allman, 1980, 35). Traditional norms seem to predominate for young women and men. A girl is expected to observe a strict code of behavior aimed at protecting her reputation, ensuring that she obtains a decent marriage or a common-law union. Even though people do not often formally marry in Haiti, there is the expectation that people will not have sex until age 20–21, and young people are still considered children at that age. Sexual experience is expected to remain within some union, particularly for young women, and there is very little pregnancy before the age of 20. Once a woman is settled into a union she tends to stay there, and women seem to have fewer sexual partners than has been found in other Caribbean countries (36).

Interestingly, the regulation of sexual behavior seems most often to focus on control of the female's activity. Feminists would argue that this is the nature of the patriarchy, which dictates the dominant social construction of sexual relations. When one looks at the proscriptions against premarital sexuality, the locus of responsibility tends to be on keeping the young women chaste and pure. Men are encouraged to experiment, while women are taught to guard their virginity.

Care and Economic Provision for Family Members

Another thematic link that seems to hold cross-culturally is that families are responsible for the care and economic provision of their members. What defines care might differ from culture to culture and family to family, but it appears that this job is entrusted to those who are closest to each other. There is some argument, though, that the family once provided far more than is now the case, with more responsibilities now being entrusted to the government and other social institutions.

The state or government plays a very important role in dealing with families' responsibility for each other. The laws, policies, ideologies, and entitlements provided by the government mediate between the family and the demands of the economy. It is the government that often determines who is family, who is obligated to care for the others, and sometimes provides monies and programs to aid family members. There is often a sharing of caretaking roles with institutions like schools, the workplace, welfare agencies, and social service facilities; however, in many parts of the world the family still provides for that kind of basic survival.

Structural conditions play a big role in how well a family will be able to provide basic necessities for family members. Depending on class and economic condition in the world, children will be provided for differently, with those of the upper classes and in core countries coming to expect far more materially than will those of poorer classes and in peripheral countries.

In a fascinating book produced by the Sierra Club in 1994 for the United Nations International Year of the Family, Peter Menzel and a team photographed selected families from around the world seated outside their homes surrounded by *all* their material possessions. Through the most graphic and pictorial representation, the viewer could see the inequities worldwide in what people were able to provide for their families.

One photo, of a family in Mali, one of the poorest countries in the world, in the west of Africa, showed the Natomo family sitting on the roof of their dirt house surrounded by three mortars and pestles, mosquito netting, a broken pot, two watering cans, one of which was broken, a few washing tubs, cultivating instruments, a battery-powered radio/cassette tape player, and five ceramic pots. There were few other possessions, and the eleven family members had a per capita income (U.S.) of $251 (Menzel, 1994, 15–16). The total fertility rate for women in that country is 7.1 children, and the life expectancy for women is 50. For men it is 47 (17).

In contrast, the Pfitzner family of Cologne, Germany, was surrounded by hundreds of items, including bookshelves, a dining room set, a TV, sofas, paintings, desks, beds, a car and a motorcycle, a dishwasher, a stove, and numerous other objects with which those in the developed part of the world are familiar. The per capita income in Germany is $19,204 (U.S.) with the fertility rate being 1.5 children per woman. The life expectancy for women is 79 and for men is 73 (180–184).

The contrast between the two families was noteworthy, and the fact that Germany is Europe's largest and most powerful country and Mali is one of Africa's poorest was obviously reflected in each family's ability or inability to provide for themselves.

In contrast with both of these countries, the family in the United States, the Skeen family of Texas, seemed to "have it all." There were stereos, beds, desks, three cars, two TVs, two sewing machines, a washer, a microwave, a clothes dryer with food processor, mixer, coffee maker, and pots on top, a stove, a computer and a piano and bench, to name just a few of their items. When that book was published in 1994, the per capita income was $22,356, and the life expectancy was 79 years old for women and 72 for men. The literacy rate was 95 percent for women and 96 percent for men, and fertility was 2.1 children per woman. By 2000 the median family income for a family of four in the United States was $56,061 (United States Bureau of Census, 2000a).

Through the visual representation of the family in its own surroundings, the viewer could see how much space each family had, the reflected health of the members, the material possessions that they owned, and some of their human emotions, like pride, exhaustion, and curiosity, as they provided for each other.

Affectional and Emotional Needs

Besides materially caring and providing for family members, families share the common theme of *attempting* to provide for them affectionally. Some have called the family a refuge from which members escape modern society and are loved and protected emotionally within a warm environment (Lasch, 1977); families are often thought to be a place for fun and self-growth. These might well be myths, perpetuated to make it appear that all families can be generalized about and that all people experience such affection. Let us remember also that many of these ideas about the family are based on observations from developed parts of the world and do not take into account what families do elsewhere.

What we can say is that families do evoke emotions and that affectional needs are provided for within a family, even if not always from parents who care for the children. Siblings, grandparents, and other kin, including community members, can also become caretakers and emotional supports. Affection means being emotionally close to one's kin, whoever they may be. Families in various parts of the world can determine who will be close to whom emotionally and provide for the bonds of intimacy and closeness.

In the United States there is usually the expectation that partners will provide for each other emotionally and that parents will nurture and attend to the emotional needs of their children. These expectations are not always met, as we can see from the fact that the divorce rate is 4.6 divorces per 1,000 population (Centers for Disease Control, 1995), and from the increasing incidence of wife battering and child abuse.

Often someone emerges within a family to whom another family member may turn. For example, children who have experienced severe forms of poverty, parental psychopathology, breakup of the family, or serious caregiving deficits can become *resilient* children when they form deep emotional bonds with someone who emerges to throw them a lifeline and provide support after the trauma (Werner, 1995, 81). Grandparents, older siblings, members of the extended family have become emotional helpers for these children. These people become substitute caregivers or surrogate parents, and in turn the children themselves take care of younger siblings and help members of their family who are ill or incapacitated (83).

In other parts of the globe, families can be structured to provide for affectional needs, which is a basic human desire. For example, in Muslim countries, where men and women are kept in separate quarters and women spend their lives in *purdah* (seclusion) and living behind the veil, a particularly strong emotional bond is formed between women, be they co-wives, mothers-in-law, or sisters-in-law. Because men and women do not eat together and husbands and wives do not speak to each other in public, women create an active "underlife culture and support system" (O'Kelly & Carney, 1986, 245). Tedious hours doing household maintenance and meal preparation is spent in the presence of other females, and this company actually adds an element of pleasure to otherwise boring tasks. This is not to say, by the way, that such a life is idyllic. However, it provides us with an excellent example of affectional needs being met by family members.

In African families, as another example of the meeting of affectional needs, often the eldest sisters are the source of nurturance and emotional support. A good case in point are the Igbo of Nigeria. Since children are the most valuable asset of the Igbo family, a strong family bond is formed between many family members and the child. The child is socialized within the family, but not by parents alone. Grandparents, aunts, and uncles play important roles. Sisters rear younger children, and often the eldest sisters play the roles that in the West we would think of as "parental." Other family members function as the child's first significant others, and they provide physical and emotional care, teach young members the parents' culture, and influence how cultural and social realities around them are interpreted (Offoha, 1996, 67). As a result of this kind of socialization, the children learn their future economic roles early on.

Girls in Igboland often perform domestic tasks like cooking, finding firewood, carrying water, and other tasks they will be responsible for once married. Boys go farther from home, learning skilled work and training for the traditional role of breadwinners. Children learn these roles early, watching their siblings and elders in their assigned tasks. Caretaking is a community and family affair (68). Emotional and affectional needs are met by a wide variety of family members, who surround the children from the moment they are born.

But all is not joyous in Igboland, since family relations are also a source of conflict; this conflict generally comes from the in-laws, and wives are maltreated, primarily by their husband's sisters and brothers. Some in-laws feel deprived of access to their son or brother, especially among the lower class or less educated. The in-laws tend to blame any mistake on the new wife, and the man is often caught between his wife and his family, trying to play "the good son" (70).

Status-Giving Qualities of Families

Another theme that emerges when looking at families in the world is the observation that families provide status to their members. *Status* consists of the positions that are recognized by a society and usually refers to a pecking order or hierarchy of accepted relationships based on one's position in the status-giving system. Status is conferred on individuals by their families when they are born; they may be able to change their status positions later, depending on whether or not the structural arrangements of society allow for such change.

Ascribed status is the status one is born with; it is involuntary and is given and may continue throughout life. It is a socially defined position. *Achieved status* is that which one can impact and change based on one's individual abilities or on the availability of means for mobility. Examples of ascribed status are the *harijans* (untouchables) in India, one's gender, or one's ethnic group, race, or class background. Being born poor in a developing part of the world, or being born in an industrialized Western society to a family of wealth are ascribed status. Examples of achieved status are becoming a bank president, being a winner of the lottery, becoming a model or a corporate executive.

In some societies people have less mobility and less opportunity to achieve status than others. Those with ascribed status also have less mobility than those with achieved status. Whether one can move in and out of a status is called *social mobility*. Usually open societies (in which there are less rigid boundaries for movement) make *upward mobility* more likely, and closed societies with rigid definitions of status keep people from moving. *Downward mobility* can occur when one loses status, perhaps because of loss of money or the death of the status-giving family member.

Families confer status. This means that where a family is in the social stratification system will determine where the family members who are born into it will be. *Class, race, ethnicity, sexuality,* and *gender* are status-giving positions in society and are part of the structural arrangements of a society that determine a person's ascribed status. Structural arrangements define the opportunity structures that are available to members of a society and determine whether someone is able to change their status position or is in a closed system with little opportunity for movement.

The family is the place in society where race, class, gender, and ethnicity come together. It is the locus of intersection of all these forces. The simple family, one in which people love, nurture, and raise children, is a complex institution in which most of the structural arrangements show up. In the interactions of men and women, we see gendered social arrangements. In the interactions between generations, one can discern differences based on race, class, and ethnic variability. All of these structural issues have simple families interacting with the larger society, reflecting structural inequities in the larger society, and replicating the social system within family interactions. This nexus of race, class, gender, and ethnicity is present without much consciousness on the part of the family members about its impact on them.

Consider an example of the status-giving power of families in contemporary Japan. Since World War II, the West has held the belief that Japan is homogeneous and that there is in that country an absence of class or status inequality (Lie, 1996, 35). Rapid and compressed industrial growth, with booming industries and an expanding economy, gave the impression that postwar Japan was a classless society. However, when we look at class, gender, and ethnicity more recently, there seems to be evidence that Japan has persistent class inequality and lack of social mobility. There still exists the idea of coming from a "good family," and there are many day workers and homeless people (37). Rural areas differ very much from the urban splendor of Tokyo, and there are many disintegrating farming communities (38).

Japan has long been considered a place where people can change their status by hard work, through what appears to be a superior educational system. But now there is evidence that gender discrimination, lack of opportunities for deviant students, and enforcement of conformity might hinder mobility. Lie found that there was a distinct hierarchy based on being well-off that affected what happened to children, and that parents who encouraged their children's education resulted in "children of the well-off having built-in advantages over their less privileged counterparts" (40).

Photo 2.5   Multiracial mother and daughter in Brazil. Photographer: Patti Carman

There is also much evidence that in Japan there is ethnic discrimination as well. It is true that Japan is multiethnic, with Koreans, Chinese, Okinawans, Ainus, Southeast Asians, and indigenous peoples, of which there are more than 3 million (43). However, Japan is portrayed by its government as *monoethnic* (one ethnicity), and there is evidence that minority groups are silenced in an effort to convey equanimity in that society. It appears that in Japan children who are born into families in which they are ethnic minorities, of lower classes or born as females, experience structural forms of discrimination. Lie argues that "the very fact that Japan can be characterized as economically unequal, gendered and ethnically diverse brings into question most theories of Japanese uniqueness" (46). Thus even though Japan looks equal to those outside and even to those within, the family one is born into determines one's status and position in that society.

Race is also a most important category for determining one's status in all societies. By taking a structural approach and understanding that people of minority positions are blocked from access to societal resources, one can argue that being born in any society will lead to different life chances and upward mobility. Material conditions (access to resources, power, ability to control one's own work life, control over others, ability to decide one's own fate, ability to make free decisions) are most important in determining how well a family survives and thrives.

Race is a social construction, very much determined by the people doing the defining. For example, in South Africa, until the abolition of apartheid, there were racial distinctions among whites, blacks, and colored (a distinction not noted in the United States). In fact, people still use those categories for social interactions. In contrast, in Brazil and other Latin American countries, people use the phrase "Money lightens," which means that the more money one has, the more likely one will be defined as white, even with dark skin. In the Dominican Republic there are no official racial distinctions; all people, dark-skinned of African heritage, or lighter-skinned with Spanish heritage, are called "Dominicans."

In the United States, race tends to be seen in terms of skin color, even though other characteristics are also important identifiers. What it means to be "white" has changed over time. Various ethnic groupings like Italians, Jews, and Irish became "white" only after many members of these groups became upwardly mobile and obtained social and economic power. Asians now appear to be becoming "white." We can see this by the male–female intimacy displayed in motion pictures; for example, white–Asian love relationships. The question is what will happen to Latinos, especially Mexican Americans, as they move up socioeconomically. And the question remains whether or not African Americans will ever make it (Heller, 2000).

Certainly power and access to it is part of a racial definition: who has the power and who doesn't influences what are defined as racial categories. Even to call someone a "minority" or a "person of color" connotes some specific way of seeing people who are not of the dominant culture (Asante, 1996, 62), and such people are lumped together and compared to those in structurally dominant positions.

Families Are Embedded in Communities

Communities are groups of people who interact while carrying out necessary social functions; they are usually in close proximity to one another and provide support—economic, social, or spiritual. A family is never far from what is happening around it.

In social science literature, one often sees the argument that as a society modernizes there is a loss of community, a sense of growing alienation, a decline in small, traditional communities, and a growing acceptance of rootless and impersonal relationships. One could cite the crime rates in inner cities as examples of the decline of society that results from such a lack of community.

However, one might also argue that communities are in fact alive and well in the world, much as the family is. It is the nature of the community that is changing. Communities might not be based solely on geographical units, but on mutual interests or on geographical units smaller than entire villages or agrarian settings. In the United States there has been a resurgence of block associations in the inner cities, suburban programs for neighborhood watches. The crime rate seems to be diminishing as people, disturbed by what appears to be lack of community, are attempting to build networks to provide connection and support for each other.

Programs like Alcoholics Anonymous, teen parenting groups, support groups for battered women, and other private sector programs are all thriving in the United States. There is community; it is just not the form that might once have existed in traditional agrarian societies, nor does it take the form that traditional sociologists have sought in defining community. Communities may still be distinct geographic units in some parts of the world, but in other places they have become like-minded people who have something in common. Communities remain crucial to family life; they just do not fit traditional definitions of community.

Data indicates that families are very much networked with their communities (Canian, Goodman, & Smith, 1978–79; Saitoti, 1995; Sidel, 1974). Visits to any part of the world indicate that neighbors know each other and each other's business. Cafés in semiperipheral countries remain important centers for social and political life, where matters of personal import are discussed with people with whom a community member has something in common. Communities in peripheral countries are centers for social and economic life, and do not replicate the alleged alienation of Western city living.

For women in developing parts of the world, community is often provided at the watering hole or around the communal cooking pot. Levinson (1989) found that in the 18 societies out of 90 studied that did not have wife battering, there was less incidence of abuse when women formed closely knit networks for mutual support and there was regular intervention by neighbors and kin. This is not restricted to rural areas, either; often in cities, women working in marketplaces selling their wares are just as networked with women around them. In other words, less violence occurs when there is a sense of community.

In a classic study by Elizabeth Bott (1968), in which families were interviewed in London, the results indicated that urban families have an "individuated" set of relationships (217). By this I mean that everyone in a family has a network of people to which they relate, but in a city those networks do not overlap with each other, as they would in a rural community. Families in the city are more private and free to regulate their own affairs, while rural families are contained in organized groups that control many aspects of their daily activities.

Perhaps one interesting contemporary example of the embeddedness of families within communities is the Maasai of Kenya and Tanzania. The Maasai are a tall, handsome, and very proud people who live herding cattle, sheep, and goats in and around the Great Rift Valley. An important ritual that moves children to adulthood is the circumcision procedure that takes place within the community. Girls are segregated with other about-to-be circumcised young women, and the boys are likewise segregated. The young men about to be initiated into masculinity through this procedure are isolated with others. Prior to circumcision boys and girls interact freely; after the ceremony they separate, and soon the young women are married.

Just prior to the ceremony, young men are summoned by other newly circumcised warriors to a procedure of insulting and humiliating the soon-to-be circumcised men so that they will bear up and not cry at the pain of what will be done. Songs are sung to them praising warriorhood and encouraging them to achieve it at all costs (Saitoti, 1986). Participation in this ceremony deepens their bond with the community.

In the United States and other parts of the world, women have networks of communities in which they participate that enhance their lives and the lives of others within their communities. Women's community participation is a way to better their own lives, their family lives, and their community lives (Abrahams, 1996, 768). For example, women often care for other people's children. In fact, in African American families there is the "othermother," who meshes smoothly with the wider black community. These women create black female spheres of influence, authority, and power (Collins, 1990, 147).

Summary

The theme of this chapter is that, globally, families are diverse in structure but similar in function. We added to the suitcase students were asked to prepare in Chapter 1, packed with definitions for some of the ideas needed to explore the family cross-culturally. Terms like *extended* and *nuclear families* began to illustrate the complexity of family forms. Further concepts such as household and kinship, authority patterns like patriarchy, matriarchy, and egalitarian were discussed, so that the student can learn the language of family relationships. We explored living patterns, lineage patterns, bride price and dowry, and the differences between romantic love and arranged marriages. Within this chapter we began to understand the structural conditions under which families operate and explored the themes that seem to unite families cross-culturally.

Families have in common the procreative role; the socialization responsibility, including teaching gendered behaviors; and the economic responsibility of dividing labor among family members. Families are also charged with regulating sexual behavior, with the care of and economic provision for its members, with meeting affectional and emotional needs, and with providing the status position of their members. Status is very much related to race, class, ethnicity, and gender. Finally, students were shown that families are related to communities and embedded in environments that exceed their own boundaries.

CHAPTER 3

Theories on the Family

Often when someone opens a book and sees a title that includes the word *theory*, the reader experiences a negative reaction and a sense that the material will be dry, boring, and irrelevant. But theories help to explain what we are seeing and help us make sense of the world. Have you ever seen the bumper sticker that reads, "Subvert the Dominant Paradigm"? What that bumper sticker is saying is that there is an overarching theory and model that pervades our society's thinking (the "dominant paradigm"), and that it is time to do away with the ways that we have been explaining things and develop a new theory.

A theory is an idea, a supposition, a belief system, a reason for something, an explanation for what we believe to be true. Theories answer questions about what is going on, give us a perspective from which to operate, and may even provide a model from which to explain that which we see. Theories explain and predict. From a theory emanates a hypothesis, which is used later for testing and then generalizing about the findings.

In this chapter you will read about a few of the major theories that have been developed to explain the family. There are countless theories about the family; fields like psychology, sociology, anthropology, and home economics have all developed theories to explain family construction, functioning, evolution, and destruction.

Here we focus on the social theories of the family. While we are looking at the family cross-culturally, it can be difficult to get into the dynamics *within* families. Cross-cultural comparisons lend themselves more easily to looking at how societies construct their families, how the families appear from the outside, what their kinship patterns are, and what the family structure's relationship is to the social construction of that society. It is far more difficult to ascertain how people within cultures treat each other interpersonally and then to compare them, although some theorists, particularly in cross-cultural psychology, have attempted to do so.

Without a theoretical understanding of the family, you just get a lot of facts, vague stories that don't hold together. With a theory, you can see that "every way of seeing is a way of not seeing" (Laskowitz, 1998) and that you need to pack in that suitcase of yours a critical consciousness that frames and challenges what you observe.

I focus in this chapter on two main schools of thought: structural functionalism and social conflict theory. There are contemporary developments that are offshoots of those main theories; each of those perspectives has a very long and complicated history, and it is impossible to summarize and do justice to them. Instead, what works best for our purposes is to provide an outline of those perspectives and apply them to the family. We also discuss a few of the main theorists' ideas as their thinking has impacted the development of family theory.

The Major Frameworks

To explain a field that is compact, deep, and very historically grounded, it is easiest to step outside and ask: How does this theorist view the world? What is his or her way of seeing? What are some of the basic tenets of her theory? All *macro theories* try to explain how societies function or operate, how change occurs, how to create change, what is the image of an ideal society. They try to explain the whole society and the experiences of people within that society's systems. The family is one of the institutions in a society that theorists look at and attempt to explain.

In addition, *micro theories* look at individual interactions in society and attempt to explain the self, what is happening within the individual. These theories look at the dynamic social activities that take place between persons. Symbolic interactionism is one such theory. However, in this book we are concerned only with macro theories, because they are more relevant to our discussion of global forces as they impact the family.

For the purpose of simplicity, the first two sets of theories—structural functionalism and social conflict—are best described in terms of a consensus-versus-conflict (Rothenberg, 1997) view of the world. The consensus or *structural functionalist* view sees society as harmonious and ordered. It describes social phenomena as an organism, like a biological entity. These theorists believe that humankind is basically good, and people can achieve whatever they set out to do because the society is integrated and whole and, for the most part, at peace. *Social conflict* theorists take another tack. They view the world in terms of struggle between groups of people in a hierarchical system. They say that the world is about scarce resources and power—who has it and who does not.

It is these two major paradigms that have informed the study of the family, with other explanations emerging more recently. In Chapter 1 we discussed modernization theory and dependency theory. Modernization is considered a consensus or functionalist theory; dependency theory is considered part of a conflict perspective. Post-colonialism, the other theory we touched upon, is also described as an outgrowth of conflict theory.

As you read about these theories, try to situate your own view of the world into them. Which theories make the most sense to you? Which ones resonate and seem to explain what you see? Each of us has a theory; but we are not always conscious of how it is that we think.

Structural Functionalists

Structural functionalist theories argue that society and the family are harmonious entities and that harmony is the natural state of people. Their belief is that stability dominates, and that all societies and families seek equilibrium. Even if a system is out of balance, the natural order of things is to find that state of peace and get back to order. These theorists look at a society and the families within it as an integrated whole that all fits together and works, almost like an engine that hums along well. It might need a tune-up now and then, but in general you try to keep it functioning well. If that system is not working, if it has a disruption or breakdown, the system has not yet accommodated and adjusted its own maintenance.

The early functionalists were anthropologists and sociologists (Malinowski, 1922; Durkheim, 1897) whose work focused on how each part of the structure worked together to keep society going. This theory talks about social institutions, such as family, and the roles and positions that people play in those institutions.

When looking at power relationships, structural functionalists say that everyone has power; it is within all of us, and there is an open system in which everyone can move. Open mobility comes through hard work. A structural functionalist argument holds that we all share common values and that even people who are in power positions, like those who are rich or educated, are there because of an open system that allows them equal access. They believe that authorities are there for the common good and have been inspired to carry out a public trust. There is also a belief that these authorities help to keep the system functioning and that they are needed to maintain the public good.

If there are problems, like racism or sexism or other forms of inequality, structural functionalists say these are necessary and "functional." They serve a purpose (Davis & Moore, 1945). For example, if there are poor people or people cast in minority status, they are in the system for the purpose of doing certain types of work, or they are there to keep the society going. Maybe they provide incentives to the system to progress or improve overall standards. Thus inequality is inevitable, but functional. If a component seems to be dysfunctional, old institutions may change and new ones may be created or emerge to fix the system. These theorists believe that associations can promote change within the system and that a pluralistic debate and political activity can improve the system. Social institutions might also stay dysfunctional, which means there is a negative consequence to someone (Merton, 1949/1968).

Change, following this view, comes from people working together and collaborating to bring about change. Through rational, collaborative problem solving, all problems can be worked out, and the building of trust between groups of people will bring about that change. In fact, if change is supported by authorities, it is more likely to have lasting impact and replace the dysfunction within the system. This theory is a rational one, based on the idea that with logical thought and dialogue, change can happen.

If people are problematic, if they break norms or values and act deviantly or in some maladjusted way, it is because of some problem in those people, not in the system. Perhaps the malcontents or troublemakers are unsocialized or mentally ill, or troubled because they are deviating from the universal values that most people share in that society.

One might ask, How does all this relate to the family? Structural functionalism was a very important theory in the development of family studies, particularly from the 1950s until the 1970s. Talcott Parsons, one of the most influential sociologists of the time, wrote about the American nuclear family and its isolation. His theories have been tested in the United States and applied to other parts of the world. He looked at what happens to families when industrialization and urbanization occur and how the roles that people play in families are impacted by these conditions. His theories were later incorporated, elaborated on, and extended by William Goode, whose modernization theory has influenced interpretations of the family around the globe.

Structural functionalism is quite important to our understanding of how families in other parts of the world have been explained and the lens through which families have been viewed. However, it is a way of seeing that is now being challenged by other theorists and might not hold true in a transnational twenty-first-century world.

Talcott Parsons and the Nuclear Family

Parsons's most important contribution to the study of the family was his development of *expressive versus instrumental roles* (Parsons & Bales, 1955, 1966). Parsons argued that because of the industrialization and modernization of American society, families have become primarily nuclear, and that the normal household consists of husband, wife, and children who are independent of their extended families. Parsons argued that the family is indispensable for social stability and that the family internalizes a social control function that keeps a society running. In order for a society to function properly, there must be a sexual division of labor in which men and women play different roles.

The roles that men and women play have become highly "differentiated"; women are primarily charged with taking care of the home, emotional life, and the "affective roles" that families need to function efficiently and well under a technological and industrialized economic system. Men, on the other hand, are given "instrumental roles" in this well-functioning system, which means that they become the breadwinners and go outside of the home to earn money and to provide the material goods necessary for a decent living. The well-functioning family system is always trying to maintain its equilibrium, balancing these roles, and the family is a microcosm of the larger, functioning society.

Another contribution of Parsons's theory is the idea that the educational, religious, political, economic functions that families once served are now being taken over by other institutions of society through differentiation of those responsibilities. These roles have been given up by the family as a result of the need for mobility and independence from their extended families. In essence, modern societies need families to be unencumbered by familial obligations and responsibilities. The primary duty of families is to socialize children and to earn money; this leaves the need for a social welfare system, an educational system, mental health programs, and health facilities. As a society becomes complex, the families become more nuclear and isolated, and social institutions take over family functions.

Many of Parsons's ideas on families were taken seriously as the model for what all families would become within industrialized societies. Eventually, what were unique observations about family life in America were exported and applied to families elsewhere, so this view and language held sway for a long time in application to family life around the world.

William Goode and Modernization Theory

Historically speaking, the dominant way that social thinkers have looked at the family since the mid-twentieth century is that the family has been part of the process of industrialization that occurred first in the West, then in other parts of the globe. The idea is that this industrial process (starting with the Industrial Revolution) has changed the family from large, extended, and rurally based to city-centered, more egalitarian, and far less stable (thus the high divorce rates in the West).

This view, called *modernization theory,* has been developed by a number of consensus theorists. One of the primary thinkers was William J. Goode, who wrote *World Revolution and Family Patterns* (1963). His work built on the work of Parsons and included ideas of Charles Darwin (1859) on the evolution of the species and the survival of the fittest. Goode's argument is that as societies modernize (the assumption being that all of them will), families move away from large, extended families and become nuclear. He chooses to use the term *conjugal* (we used this term interchangeably with *nuclear* in Chapter 2), which means that the husband, wife, and children, although not cut off from their extended families, do not live with them (Goode, 1982, 176).

Such conjugal families become more independent of their larger families, and people become freer to choose their own mates. Dowry and bride price usage disappears, the families become more egalitarian in terms of parents' authority over children and husbands' authority over wives, and what was once traditional family concern for all gives way to a focus on individual welfare.

Family forms in traditional, agrarian, and nonindustrialized countries were seen as quite diverse, with polyandry, polygyny, and matrilineal descent as just a few examples. However, Goode argued that as societies became more modern, those multiple forms would give way to the conjugal family type, which was somehow better suited to an industrial economy. Goode's work, superb in its vastness and comprehensive analysis, was widely cited, and many studies followed to corroborate or refute it.

Ideology

I would argue that the ideas about structural functionalism have moved from theory into ideology. Theory is a way to explain and predict, a logical explanation that can be subjected to an empirical test, while an *ideology* can be defined as *a dominant idea of our time* (Laskowitz, 1998). Ideology is the thought, notions, opinions, and system of meaning that people attach to phenomena. In other words, it is a worldview or cultural belief system that develops over time. As ideologies become codified and incorporated into how phenomena are viewed, they become the ways conditions are described and explained. Modernization and structural functionalist theories, other theorists have noted, codify a worldview of inequality and structural arrangements that keep some groups of people powerless.

In other words, as societies, economies, and technologies change, the ideologies that develop within them justify the unequal power relationships and judge the people with less power as inferior. In the traditional sense, ideologies legitimize an existing social condition with justifications derived from the status quo and repress the possibility of historical alternatives. Then they deny any historical limitation on these social conditions (Offe, 1977, 12–14, as quoted in Osmond, 1987, 111). Ideologies present the social structure as inevitable, as unchangeable and as universal human nature; they legitimate and reinforce the given system, regardless of that system's deficiencies (Osmond, 111).

Karl Marx, the conflict theorists, and later theorists influenced by the conflict perspective say that there is a cultural *hegemony*. This means that there is a reigning way of thinking that is based not just on ownership but also on the ideas the powerful use to dominate and support those power relationships. In other words, it is every way that we think, all the relationships among people, the media, the government, and all other social institutions and social interactions that support the dominant and unequal relationships that exist in a society. Our minds are trained and shaped by the dominant way of seeing that then supports the way it is (see Gramsci, 1932; Laclau & Mouffe, 1985), based on the cultural leadership that links thought to action. Thus this cultural leadership, exercised by the ruling class, does not have to be violent or even externally coercive; instead it permeates the culture, espoused by the intellectuals as well as other leaders. It is also assented to by the masses who go along with it all (Ritzer, 2000, 283).

An example of how Goode's ideas have been used in ideological colonization is work done by John C. Caldwell (1982). He posits a theory of fertility transition that shows how the theory that Goode describes—that of marriage centered on the couple rather than the broader kin group—was imported to Africa by missionaries and aided in placing Africa in an inferior position and vulnerable to further colonization. The way that this was done was by limiting fertility and imposing Western models of population control.

The Conflict Perspective*

The founders of the conflict perspective on society and the family were Karl Marx and his collaborator Frederick Engels (1884/1972). Since their work began to gain prominence, their ideas have been taken much further than the authors originally wrote and intended. The basic principles of the conflict perspective are that the

---

*Author's Note: With thanks to Jim Rothenberg for the development of this explanation.

nature of society is inherently a battle, and that struggle is a natural part of life. In fact, a state of flux dominates, and stability, as described by the functionalists, is quite unusual. In all spheres of life, economic, political, and cultural, there is invariably a struggle for power and dominance and control both within groups and between groups of people. Based on this thinking, everyone is associated with a special interest group defined in comparison to another group: rich versus poor, black versus white, men versus women, old versus young, gay versus straight, and so on.

With this perspective comes the idea that society is a struggle for domination and that everyone's experience, depending on the group from which one comes, is different and cannot be understood by others not in that group.

Power is about control of resources, ownership of the means of production, and the ability to control others, which comes from those who have historically been dominant. This usually means that those who are rich, white, male, and self-interested have power. These elites, as they are called, hold power, which comes sometimes from inherited wealth but also from their position in the status hierarchy, which is influenced by being white or male or older or better educated. Because they are in these positions of power, accountability for their behavior is limited; they are rarely called into question for what they do in their own self-interest.

When it comes to relations between classes and cultures, a conflict perspective would hold that different groups have different values and that there is a hierarchy of cultures that defines who will be excluded and who will be assimilated into the dominant pecking order. Thus there is major stratification and segregation in most societies (and in most families), and it is quite unusual not to find such systems. They exist in every human interaction, the conflict theorists argue.

Leaders and authorities in such a system are there to advance the special interests of the elites, even if they are not aware of it. These leaders are in their positions not necessarily because they are competent, but because they are attached in some way to those in power or because they do not threaten the dominant order in any fundamental way. Since authority works in mysterious ways, incompetence is hidden, and it is rare that there is a challenge to those who are truly in power.

Norms, values, and beliefs are imposed as a result of the powerful group's views, and generally reflect maintenance of the status quo, keeping that power and not allowing the boat to be rocked. When, through some form of communication, the differing needs of groups of people come to public awareness, this leads to conflict; then comes negotiation, which might lead to a working agreement between conflicting groups of people. What this means is that those in power give a little when they are threatened and see that they have to give up something in order to maintain their positions.

Real change, in this view, comes from dissent and agitation by those of the excluded groups who fight for their own needs. Often the people at the top do not want to change and do not support these changes, at least at the beginning. In order to suppress conflict, those in power will make changes as a means of social control and to cool down troublemakers, rather than to give up any real power and share the decision making. In other words, through conflict and making trouble, those in lower-status positions gain only a semblance of power.

Thus, it becomes necessary for lower-status power groups to advocate for their own needs and make coalitions with other low-status groups to get anywhere. It is only through the generation of challenge and threat that "the powers that be" will give anything. It is through collective advocacy and bargaining, and *not* through problem solving, that anything ever really gets done.

Karl Marx and Frederick Engels

Karl Marx and Frederick Engels (1848/1948), among the original conflict theorists, did work on class conflict and the family. Marx believed that capitalist society and its gross inequalities was a necessary step toward building a socialist society.

He believed that all inequality was rooted in the relationship that people had to the means of production under capitalism. He used concepts like the *bourgeoisie,* who owned the factories or other businesses that supported the factories, and the *proletariat,* who sold their labor to the owners in order to make a living. Under capitalism there would always be class conflict between those who own and those who work. There would always be *alienation* of the workers, because the profit motive would keep conditions abominable.

Marx also believed that eventually the workers, because of the exploitative conditions under which they worked, would rise up in rebellion and take over the "means of production" like the factories to create a socialist revolution. Marx believed, as did other social thinkers at the time, that revolution was inevitable because of the contradictions inherent in capitalism.

Another key term that helps us understand Marx, particularly, is the concept of the *dialectic* or *dialectical materialism.* The dialectic is a concept that Marx borrowed from the German philosopher G. W. F. Hegel, and says that change is not linear, not causal and direct. You can never know what "causes" anything; all you can know is that there are conflicts and contradictions between structures of society and actors within society. People interact with society and society interacts with people to create change.

Dialectical materialism focuses on the change that happens in the material world, not just in consciousness or in our heads. The material world is real commodities, real objects, real items like our jobs, items we need to survive. Change happens when the contradictions occur in that real world, and the contradictions between those who "have" material wealth and those who "have not" become so extreme and contradictory that those who have not rise up and take what they need.

Marx and Engels on the Family

Marx and Engels did the first economic analysis of the family. They looked at changes in the nuclear family that came as a result of the rise of capitalism, and said that this system separated the spheres of work and the home, taking workers away from home and into the factories (Hutter, 1998, 31–32). Men became wage earners, dependent on their bourgeois bosses, and women became dependent on their husbands and fathers. Poor women, if they had no husbands, and children without fathers were the most marginal laborers and worked in the most exploitative conditions.

This new economic system, capitalism, hurt women particularly, argued Engels, because it confined women to the home, doing housework and taking care of the children, putting women in a subservient position. In pre-industrial society, women were out in the "public" sphere and had freedom and empowered social status. Under capitalism they were relegated to a private role that supported the male in serving capitalist economic needs. This led to the "world historic defeat of the female sex" (Engels as quoted in Lengermann & Niebrugge-Brantley, 2000, 436). He wrote that the word *family* derives from the Latin word for servant, and that the family is overwhelmingly a system of dominant and subordinate roles. In fact, he argued that families did not exist, historically, until capitalism; formerly people were organized in "kin networks" of large-scale associations among people sharing blood ties (Lengermann & Niebrugge-Brantley, 2000, 436). Engels believed that when women participated in socially productive work, when domestic duties were only a minor part of their jobs, there would be liberation of women.

The key to Marx's and Engels' importance to the study of the family is that they believed that removing the family from the public world, from economic community activity, and putting it into the private sector caused the family to become a basis for social inequality, particularly class inequality. The sexual differentiation of labor and the differing roles that male and females play become very important historically in understanding how the family has become privatized. Marx and Engels thought that it is not only the economic situations in which families operate that are important, but also how families interact with those structural conditions and impact and change society and themselves.

Marx's and Engels' descriptions of the family have been important to the development of thinking on the family, and have led to neo-Marxist, Marxist feminist, and socialist feminist analysis of the family (Eisenstein, 1979). Marx's thinking has been thoroughly critiqued, and it has been taken much further than he originally intended. Marx, writing in the mid-nineteenth century, expected that revolution would happen in the not-too-distant future. Capitalism, he argued, had the seeds of its own destruction within it, and workers of the world would unite to overthrow capitalism and substitute worker-run economies. As we know from contemporary developments, this revolution never occurred in capitalist countries. (Marx never expected that revolution would take place in peasant, agrarian economies like Russia, China, or Cuba.)

Marx did not foresee that capitalism would evolve as far as it has, nor that it would learn to accommodate some of the contradictions inherent within it. For example, he did not foresee that labor unions would win rights and benefits for their workers that would make work under capitalism possible. He did not foresee that women would be accommodated into the workforce in such large numbers. He did not foresee that the government would provide benefits to unemployed workers, or that protections would be provided for workers when they were unable to work.

There are many points made by Marx, however, that other social conflict theorists still adhere to and that are part of contemporary theory development. In fact, much of the feminist critique, and the theories of those who analyze world economic systems and transnational capitalism, use many of Marx's arguments applied to contemporary issues. Many conflict theorists (see Domhoff, 1998, and Giddens, 1982) point out that some of his predictions are still relevant. For example, workers still do not receive an equitable distribution of profits. Wealth is highly concentrated in the hands of the few, and this seems to be getting worse. The 20 percent of people in high-income countries account for 86 percent of private consumption; the poorest 10 percent of the world's people consume only 1.4 percent (Crossette, 1998a).

Post-Marxist thinkers also argue that women, although synthesized into the workforce, do most if not all of the housework (Hochschild, 1989) and are still at the lower end of the pay scale. They also point out that "capital travels," and now workers in periphery countries are the ones who are exploited, just as the workers during the Industrial Revolution were exploited. Only the site of the exploitation has changed. Post-Marxist thinkers have evidence to show that Marx's ideas are still important and play a role in international relations and the capitalist hegemony that now dominates the world. The argument is that global capitalism proves that Marx was right.

We now turn to some of the other conflict theorists whose ideas were influenced and informed by Marxian analysis, and try to explain the family using a contemporary application of this perspective.

Eli Zaretsky: Capitalism, the Family, and Personal Life

Eli Zaretsky (1976) followed up on the "public" versus "private" split described in Engels' work. He argued that the split between the family and the economy is a false dichotomy and that they are linked (Osmond, 1987, 116) and are an integrated system. This apparent split, begun when the Industrial Revolution took place, made it seem like there were two worlds. It also idealized the family as a place to hide from a hostile world.

In fact, Zaretsky argues, family life and work life are really one. Children are taught how to participate in the economic system, and the separation of women's and men's work leads to the trivialization of that which women do and the idealization of male occupations. By focusing discussions about the family on its internal dynamics, rather than seeing that the family is influenced by structures outside of itself, we lose sight of the fact that the family found in society is socially determined and its form arises out of specific social conditions (Zaretsky, 1976). In the history of the family in other parts of the world, this analysis is relevant to understanding the evolution of family life and the devaluation of community, personal relationships, and extended kinship networks. They did not serve the economic order well, and thus have been devalued and trivialized, as has been women's work.

Radical Critical Theories

Contemporary evolutions of conflict theories continue the line of reasoning by Marx, but go much further in describing contemporary family life. This school of thought, now called *radical critical theories* (Osmond, 1987, 103–124), argues that "family studies," in which sociologists look at the internal life of families and the dynamics between people, do not really understand the macrosocietal forces that impact the family and by so doing reinforce the subordinate role of women (119). They argue that race, class, ethnicity, religion, and gender composition, to name just a few forces, must be explored to understand the full complexity of the family. They use the term "dialectic," and say that families reflect that dialectic.

The dialectic, as applied to families, means that there are power imbalances in all relationships: husband over wife, parents over children. Thus in contemporary family life, there is domestic violence, divorce, and other family crises because inherent in all social structures are internal contradictions that lead to these crises. This theoretical orientation says troubles develop because of outside social conditions, not because of internal troubles caused by faulty family dynamics. For example, there is wife battering because of gender inequality in the larger society, which is reflected in personal family situations, not just because of one "sick" man who beats his wife. As part of this example, radical critical theorists would say that family violence is caused by the ideology of patriarchy, which is reproduced in the family, leads to power imbalances between men and women, and ends with a man hitting his wife.

This line of thinking is a segue into the analysis of the family done by *feminist theorists,* who have made significant contributions to theories on the family during the past 25 years.

Feminist Theories on the Family

Feminist theories aim at synthesizing a micro- and macroanalysis of the family. Feminists argue that "the personal is political," and thus when looking at family life, what goes on privately is very political and is influenced by social forces that enforce power relationships. Therefore they aim the lens of the family onto both family interactions and dynamics and the structural conditions of society.

Contemporary feminist theorists are sociologists, political scientists, historians, anthropologists, lawyers, psychologists, economists, biologists, and just about any other discipline that might be interested in conditions for women. Feminist theory is an interdisciplinary field. It is a field of thought that holds that women have been left out of theory building, that most of the major theories are derived from a male experience and then generalized to the conditions of women, and that this is a biased and narrow focus. Theory, until just 25 years ago, has been made by "dead white men," is what the argument says, and the time has come to include women in theory development; conditions for women must be included in the structural analysis of society (Barker, 1991).

Feminist theory is, foremost, women-centered (Flax, 1996, 19). Feminists argue that men and women have different experiences in the world, and women's experiences must be explained by women. According to feminist theory, the oppression that women experience in the world is rooted in the patriarchal social system, one that is historical, psychological, and economically based. They argue that it is not a historical accident that men oppress women; there is a payoff to men for this system.

Feminist theorists argue that *gender is socially constructed.* In other words, it is not biology but society and culture that determine what men and women are all about. The social construction of gender is reflected in the different opportunity structures available to males and females and the differences in power and control that reflect those gender inequities. An example of social construction of gender would be the prohibiting of women behind the veil (particularly women in Muslim countries) from working in public employment, while in the West and developed parts of the world the assumption is that women should and must work because of the need for income to support families.

Feminist theorists have a number of sub-schools of thought. There are liberal feminists, who believe that women's inequality comes from women's being relegated to the private sector, to homemaking and childcare. The idea is that society is basically "just and fair," and if one can "add women and mix," equality will occur; women merely need to be added to the public sphere (the workplace and politics) and everything will work out. The inequities are holdouts from an earlier economic system, and with legislation and proper education these practices will be eradicated. Liberal feminists believe that "sexism" is about prejudices and discriminatory practices, and that these can be eliminated if laws are changed, if families engage in sharing responsibilities more fairly, and if "sexism" is confronted whenever it is manifested (Lengermann & Niebrugge-Brantley, 2000, 450–454). The idea is that inequities based on gender can be rectified.

Marxist feminists take Marx's and Engels' ideas and help us bring them to contemporary relevance. Since the fall of the former Soviet Union, Marxist feminism is not as active, but it is useful to understand Marxist feminist arguments because they help us to understand current explanations of family life using Marxist terms; it is also an important theory in current academic thinking (454). These feminists say that gender inequality is due to the class inequities under contemporary capitalism. "From this theoretical vantage point, the quality of each individual's life experiences is a reflection first of his or her class position and only second of his or her gender" (456).

Women of different classes have different experiences depending on their positions in the class system, and have little in common with women of other classes. Women also make less money than do men, because under capitalism it pays to keep wages low, so that capitalists will make more profit. It also helps to keep women as surplus labor, a pool of workers who threaten unions and can be tapped as alternative workers (457). Women serve capitalism by consuming goods and services for their households, therefore providing new markets under which capitalism can sell its commodities and continue to make money. Women also do unpaid child care and housework, which further supports the capitalist economic system. Woman becomes "the slave of the slave" (MacKinnon, 1982, 8, as quoted in Lengermann & Niebrugge-Brantley, 2000, 457). In other words, the family becomes the nexus of the capitalist economic system, according to this way of thinking. One cannot look at the family without seeing the reflection in gender relations of the economic system under which that family lives and all gender relations reflect that system.

Radical feminists are the most militant of feminist theorists, and believe that women everywhere are *oppressed* by the system of patriarchy. It is gender oppression, not class oppression, that is the source of women's difficulties in society. Here the word is *oppression* and not *inequality:* There is actually victimization and exploitation of women. The radical feminist position is that women have an absolute positive value in society as women (461) and have been undervalued and denied their just due in a completely unjust social system. Radical feminists would also argue that the nexus of the problem lies within the family, but this time the focus is more on violence than it is on class relations and relationship to the means of production.

The radical feminist argument is that violence is the source of the control that men have over women, and that the entire patriarchy is constructed in such a way as to maintain that control. The power resources of an entire society are constructed to maintain that power: economic, ideological, legal, and emotional. Radical feminists point to sadism in pornography, Chinese foot-binding, forced suicides of Hindu wives, female circumcision, persecution of lesbians, witch burning, and female infanticide as the literal manifestation of patriarchy (462). They would say that the family is the place where this power dynamic is most clearly played out, and it is within the family that gender conflict occurs.

Socialist feminism seems to combine the theories of Marxist feminism and radical feminism in the idea of "capitalist patriarchy" (Eisenstein, 1979). *Capitalist patriarchy* is an entire system that subjugates all women, no matter who they are. The socialist feminists look at the commonalties and variations in women's experience of subordination. They combine an understanding of class inequities with an understanding of other gender inequities to talk about race, ethnicity, age, sexual preference, and location within the global hierarchy of nations. They also say that there is a "multifaceted system of domination" that includes the micro level of interpersonal relationships and sexuality and the macro level of economics and politics. In other words, domination goes beyond gender to race, class, ethnicity, and sexual orientation and is not just about men in power over women, but about certain men in power over certain groups of people in a form of domination (Lengermann & Niebrugge-Brantley, 2000, 466).

Third wave feminism is a recent addition to feminist theory. Women from peripheral countries, as well as women from marginalized groups in the core countries, have argued that feminist theory is white, middle class, and written by women centered at the core. You could say it has been written by live white women, instead of dead white men. First wave feminism arose during the era of women's suffrage, and it was about helping privileged white women get the vote. The second wave of feminism took place from the 1960s until today, and includes the feminist theories that we looked at earlier (socialist feminism, liberal feminism, radical feminism, Marxist feminism). Third wave feminism is written by women who are on the edges, the margins. It is written by women who are part of a global feminist movement and who are different from those at the "center." It is part of the post-colonial theoretical development.

The premise of this brand of feminist theory is that imagining women as a generic category of people misses the differences among people (468). Instead, there is a diversity of women's experiences, and there are "vectors of subordination and privilege—gender, race, class, age, ethnicity, global location, and affectional

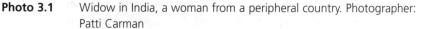

Photo 3.1   Widow in India, a woman from a peripheral country. Photographer: Patti Carman

preference—both interact structurally and intersect dynamically in people's lives to create oppression and inequality" (468).

The point is that "not all suffering is equal, that there is a calculus of pain" (Arguelles, 1993, as quoted in Lengermann & Niebrugge-Brantley, 2000, 470) in which people's locations in the structure lead to individual pain, and which intersects with the macro-level forces that put them there. So the challenge to feminist thinkers is to position themselves and differing groups of people, to say what women's experiences are, but then to situate women in terms of where they are depending on race, class, age, global location, or other "vectors of oppression and privilege."

In other words, a woman's experience in the United States is different from a woman's experience in a peripheral country, and each experience must be described and explained and seen as not equal suffering, because of the access (or lack thereof) that different women have to power. So the life of a woman in a family in the United States, even if poor, is quite different from that of a woman living in wealth in Brazil or in poverty in India. Third wave feminism says that there are no universal truths about women in the world, except that they are oppressed.

World Systems Theory

Although it is not a feminist theory, it is appropriate to elaborate here on the theory presented in Chapter 1. World systems theory, like third wave feminism, combines some thinking from Marxist feminism, is viewed from a conflict perspective, and moves our thinking into a geographical explanation that is relevant to our discussion of the family globally. One could say that this theory, quite popular among global sociologists, is a unique combination and critique of all the theories described so far. It seems to be part of the post-colonial thinking that has developed during the past decade.

Wallerstein says that there are two historical eras. The first is one in which there was a *world empire* system, of which Rome is an example (Wallerstein as cited in Ritzer, 2000, 307–313); in that era most of the world was organized through political and military domination. Now we are in a period of a *capitalist world economy,* in which economic domination is the basis for organization. Wallerstein (1992) studied historical eras and argued that modern capitalism grew out of geographical expansion through exploration and colonization.

The system went through a series of stages, ending with where we are today. In the geographic expansion phase, countries like Portugal and other European nations took the lead, and, in their own interests, found places for overseas expansion. An example would be the slave trade, which gave those countries a labor force to serve the building of the capitalist economy. Colonial expansion also gave them raw materials like gold, sugar, and other items necessary to expand development (310).

Once the world underwent geographical expansion, the next stage was the division of labor. This, Wallerstein argued, based on his Marxist analysis, was a conflictual stage (310). It was not done equally; different parts of the capitalist world system came to specialize in specific functions. For example, Africa produced slaves, Western and Southern Europe had peasant tenant farmers, and Western Europe became the center of wage workers, ruling classes, and supervisors for the rest of the economic system. The core countries also had free labor, in which workers could choose to sell their employment to the owners, while the periphery had forced labor like slavery or involuntary servitude. The semiperiphery had sharecroppers, who were the center of their economic structure.

Wallerstein argued that the key to capitalism lies in a core dominated by a free labor market for skilled workers and a coercive labor market for less skilled workers in peripheral areas. In fact, this is the essence of capitalism. Another key idea is that some regions of the world started with small advantages, and those advantages moved them to positions of domination. Those at the periphery stagnated and became single-focus societies (310).

The final stage of development of this world system was the political sector being established to protect and advance the interests of the core countries (310). Those at the periphery developed weak political systems, and in the process the core took over, through such means as creating modern armies and bureaucratic systems. Even though recent history might find a shift of who is in power at the core (for example, England and France each seeking domination, and the emergence of the

United States), the basic system has been in place since the 1730s, and little has happened to shift the balance of power (312).

As for the conditions in the global economy today, Wallerstein has said that the United States was a "hegemonic power in the world system from 1945 to 1990" (312) but that it is now in a state of decline. Western Europe and Japan are catching up, and there is a widening gap between rich and poor in the United States and the rest of the world, which means that "the heyday of U.S. prosperity is over. The scaffolding is being dismantled" (Wallerstein, 1992, 16, as quoted in Ritzer, 1996, 313). In addition, Wallerstein predicts a major redistribution of the wealth because the well-to-do core and the impoverished periphery have some major restructuring to do (313). Wallerstein is not sure in just what way this restructuring will take place.

The Family and World Systems Theory

World systems theorists are attempting to analyze the world economic system and make global connections and historical analyses that have heretofore been uncharted. It is a big job, and one that is difficult to do. Some of the theorists in the field are now just starting to apply the ideas to the specifics of family life. Historians have done work on the family in the United States and in Europe, but to make the global connections is a challenge.

One such theorist, Maria Mies (1999), has argued that the concept of the family is one that has developed as the world system has developed (103) and that the concept of the nuclear family was necessary to continue expansionism and the global capitalist system.

Mies seems to combine radical feminist theory with world systems theory, to say that the process of turning the family into the institution we know it to be today was a violent and destructive one (74–111). She says that the process by which this was done was predatory and that "progress" is really the destruction of people, old ideas of the family, and separation and subordination of human beings. Men were separated from women, one's own people were separated from others, who became "heathen" or "foreigners." This she attributes to the capitalist patriarchy.

So as capitalism expanded, land was appropriated, natural resources and people in Africa, Asia, and Central and South America were exploited, and the social relationships among people were challenged because the global economic system needed them as workers (103–104). Mies argues that the concept of the monogamous nuclear family was an idea exported from the core because the economic system needed husband as head of household and breadwinner, and wife as housewife and caretaker. In fact, what this really accomplished was to disrupt historical kinship patterns that were the basis for family organization prior to the imposition of this economic system.

Mies believes that the family as we think of it today was not destroyed by capitalism; in fact, it was *created* by capitalism. The economy needed housewives and breadwinners, and could be seen as part of an internal colonial process that re-created conditions like those of the core countries. She calls this process "housewifization," in which children were "bred" for participation in the capitalist

Photo 3.2   Women as cheap labor selling wares, Bali. Photographer: Mary
Thieme

economy and women were taught to become consumers for that economy
(see discussion of work of Tilly and Scott in Chapter 4 for further discussion).
She also argues that when the economy needed these women they were available
as cheap labor, to mbe expelled back into unemployment when the market could
not accommodate them (106).

Mies also argues that this process continues to this day, with the multinational
corporations using workers in the periphery for the work that has been exported
from the core and semiperiphery. Thus the work is in free trade zones and other
large-scale manufacturing industries, agricultural production, and small-scale
manufacturing like making handicrafts, food processing, or creating art objects for
tourists or for export (112–144).

But the definition of family is changing once again to suit the needs of the global economy. Now there is a need for cheap labor, so women, leaving their families or as heads of households, are the source of that labor, in competition with men, even men in their own families. Women are becoming producers, because in peripheral countries it is necessary to have two wage earners (if the couple lives together) or certainly one wage earner (if the woman is a single parent).

The Challenge to Understand Families Theoretically

In a post-colonial, multicultural age, perhaps there can be no theories that totally explain the family. In fact, there never have been. Any grand theory would be "essentialist," meaning that it would reduce people to fixed, basic, and unchanging conceptions; this is impossible to do. Instead, all we can hope to do is to listen to the stories of people in their lives, and to try to understand their racial, ethnic, class, gender, and sexual orientation perspectives.

The purpose of this chapter has been to situate the global family in the theoretical debates about whether the family is a pawn in a global system or an active participant in creating itself. I do not think that the question can easily be answered. Your answer depends on your viewpoint. Your theoretical perspective will color the way you see the family. Is it harmonious? Is it conflictual? Is it a stable entity in an ordered world? Is it battered and bruised from an assault by global capitalism? This is for you to decide, depending on your own theoretical perspective.

Unpacking Your Suitcase

In the first chapter I asked you to pack your suitcase, to suspend your ethnocentrism, put on your critically conscious sunglasses, and become culturally aware. Now I am suggesting that you unpack a different suitcase, one that you might have been carrying around as baggage. The old baggage in that suitcase says that modern is good, that progress is more technology, that the world should look like the industrialized West, that the family can be explained by theories developed by thinkers in the West and exported and applied elsewhere. Now we can see that the nuclear family in the West, while not always structurally sound and up to meeting all challenges, has come about because of economic variables; the inequities that have evolved are best explained with the use of conflict theory. Furthermore, suggestions for possible equitable and productive change might best come from a conflict theory–based analysis. Both sets of theories have something to recommend them, and both fail to explain other observations, specifically global ones; thus we need to hear the post-colonial voices. In other words, when you pack new bags, be sure to include some of the old luggage and mix it liberally with the new.

The suitcase we carry is one that others have carried before us and that we have picked up and carried on. As we take this global journey into the family, we see that those old explanations might not work anymore, that perhaps the stories have not yet been told, that there are many theories yet to be developed, by people out there who have yet to write them.

Summary

In this chapter we learned about some of the major theories utilized to explain and understand the family. First, *theory* was defined. Then, we moved to some of the "big ideas" of our times, especially the macro theories that have been employed to make sense of family life and society. Structural functionalism was compared to conflict theory. Structural functionalism was described as a view of society as ordered, harmonious, and seeking balance. Social conflict theory was described as one that viewed society as hierarchical, with struggle and power battles between the "haves" and the "have nots."

In describing structural functionalism, the work of Talcott Parsons was detailed, with emphasis on his ideas on the nuclear family and the differentiated roles played by males and females: instrumental versus expressive. We then saw how his theory was further developed by William Goode, who described the family using modernization theory and the belief that all societies would eventually emulate the West in modernization.

In exploring social conflict theory, we began with the thinking of Marx, particularly his ideas on capitalism and the structure of society based on economic relationships. We defined *bourgeoisie, proletariat, alienation, dialectic,* and *dialectical materialism* and worked on understanding the nature of power and the concept of hegemony. We then moved onto the work of Eli Zaretsky and the radical critical theorists who have built on a Marxist analysis, challenging the dominant thinking on the family. Then we tried to define the differences among the types of feminist theories and how each would explain the family life, particularly as they relate to conditions of women. We began to see that feminists argue that gender is a social construction.

Finally, we described world systems theory as an outgrowth of the economic explanations of family life, looking at Wallerstein's view of history in terms of the core, semiperiphery, and periphery. Then we applied this theory to family life as developed by Mies.

CHAPTER 4

The History of the Family in the United States

Needless to say, even to consider writing the history of the family in the United States is nearly an impossible undertaking. The cultural and intellectual dilemma of trying to generalize about the United States and to put the family in historical perspective worldwide is a daunting task. It is barely possible to describe the history of the family in even one country: one has to account for gender, racial, ethnic, sexuality, and class differences. Often, the history of a place has been written by those who can write and who thus are of the dominant group in that society. Then there is the complexity of explaining what has occurred by continent and by country, a task almost beyond comprehension.

Nonetheless, scholars in various parts of the world have made efforts to explain some of the dominant themes that have prevailed in Western and non-Western societies. Certainly much is missing from the picture; we are only beginning to get a glimpse of what life was like for people of the past. Most history has been written about kings, queens, wars, and politics. It has only been since the 1960s that a new form of history, called *social history,* has gained prominence and has begun to tell the story of common people living ordinary lives. This new social history offers an alternative take on what history can be. By describing the lives of communities, immigrants, women, marginalized peoples, gays, and workers, the focus has shifted away from those who are in power in the public sphere to those who have little power but have attempted to influence the course of their own lives and their communities.

Prior to Industrialization

Prior to the arrival of white settlers there were Native peoples living in America. Early Spanish explorers first gave them one name, "Indios," which lumped all peoples into one category rather than seeing them individually. However, prior to European entry there were more than 2,000 cultures and societies practicing a multiplicity of customs and lifestyles (Sutton & Broken Nose, 1996, 31). They held an enormous variety of values and beliefs and spoke numerous languages. Prior to contact with Europeans, the tribes of North America had a self-awareness of their own identities and raised and educated their children in relative isolation from each other. Each group taught their children about their cultural heritages, spiritual and religious practices, and economic survival skills (Tafoya & Del Vecchio, 1996, 48).

The seasons determined the activities of the group, with storytelling during the cold weather, religious rituals to ensure harvests and hunts, and a sense of cultural continuity that was ensured by the accumulation of the stories told over the seasons (48). Hands-on instruction and stories told by families passed on the cultural heritages of tribes from generation to generation.

Families, as the central institution of cultures of Native peoples, were crucial to the survival of the tribes. A Native American elder who was more than 100 years old in 1940 told his very moving remembrances of family life to an oral historian (Aginsky, 1940). This Pomo Indian from California remembered the changing family situation in this way:

> What is a man? A man is nothing. Without his family he is of less importance than a bug. . . . A man must be with his family to amount to anything with us. If he had nobody else to help him, the first trouble he got into he would be killed by his enemies because there would be no relatives to help him fight the poison of the other group. No woman would marry him because her family would not let her marry a man with no family. He would be poorer than a newborn child; he would be poorer than a worm, and the family would not consider him worth anything. . . . The family is important. In the white ways of doing things the family is not so important. The police and soldiers take care of protecting you, the courts give you justice, the post office carries messages for you, the school teaches you. Everything is taken care of, even your children, if you die; but with us the family must do all of that. (53)

After the arrival of the white settlers, the situation changed, with Native peoples slowly taking on some of the characteristics of the whites who followed.

After America was colonized, agriculture was the dominant economic system, and with it came a family structure suited to that undertaking. The typical white family farmed, kept animals, grew crops, made its own clothes, and attempted self-sufficiency. There were also craftsmen, merchants, and servants, as well as slaves, who assisted the family in meeting its needs. During this time, especially in the colonial era, families were primary caregivers and performed many of the functions that we now turn over to institutions like hospitals, schools, and social welfare agencies. People lived closely together, in small homes with little privacy, each person involved in the family's activities.

That system changed with the advent of industrialization, moving the family away from this family-based economy to a family-wage economy. Rising agricultural productivity—due to the use of new crops (like potatoes), multi-cropping, and better fertilizer practices—gave rise to a larger population that was able to work in the factories. Then the factories' growth prompted the expansionist trade and led to the enclosure and casting out of farmers so that cash crops could be grown more efficiently on large farm tracts. Once capitalism began to emerge in full force, power differentials and inequality began to manifest more clearly, affecting the course of family history for different groups.

Industrialization, Modernization, and Western Domination

When trying to explain the history of the family, we must begin by looking at world history for the period from 1800 to the present, because of two major developments: the growth of industrialization and Western domination of the world. The Industrial Revolution was one of the major forces for change in the nineteenth century (Duiker & Spielvogel, 1994, 764) and led to the beginning of what we now call the modern era. As the core countries industrialized, they achieved domination of much of the rest of the world by the end of the nineteenth century. Thus everything we study and say about families is based on those historical facts. By the end of the 1800s, Europeans had expanded into the Americas and Australia, and most of Africa and Asia was divided up into European colonies and spheres of influence. Even today, in many parts of the world people speak primarily English, French, or Spanish, in addition to their indigenous languages.

Industrialization began in Great Britain by the late 1780s and expanded through continental Europe and the United States. It then reached into the rest of Europe and other parts of the West. Prior to this time most of the world had been agrarian, with very few cities and most workers employed as farmers. After this period, economies began to focus on production in factories, and on the use of machinery and technology in development. Industrialization and modernization spread from Britain to the rest of the West from 1800 to the 1870s.

As Europeans began to migrate to other parts of the world, there was an era of imperialism in which Europeans carved up the world and expanded their technological developments. Beginning in the 1880s, European states scrambled for overseas territory, especially because of the dramatic increase in the European population. Parts of the world that had been ignored in terms of technological development, such as Africa and Asia, were now included in industrialization and were vied for as markets, as suppliers of resources, and as places of production by the European powers. Although there was resistance to this form of imperialism, Western industrial technology had the upper hand, and for the most part the indigenous peoples in Latin America, Asia, and Africa suffered defeats at the hands of the Europeans. In other cases Europeans were welcomed because of the technology they brought with them.

"Accustomed to rule by small elites, many native peoples then simply accepted their new governors, making western colonial rule relatively easy" (Duiker & Spielvogel, 1994, 766). Although there was often resistance to commercial penetration by the Europeans, ultimately expansion of Western business and technologies was complete.

The Industrial Revolution changed the social life of Europe and then the rest of the world, including the United States. Populations increased as death rates diminished; more food was available because of the use of machinery; cities and towns grew and became places for manufacturing and industry. With the emergence of the steam engine, businesses could be located in cities and goods could be transported. In fact, during the era from 1871 to 1914, many Europeans believed that they were living in the age of progress and that most human problems could be solved with the scientific developments of the time (817).

This new urban and industrial world created what has been called a "mass society," in which large numbers of people were able to participate in public life. The mass press, improvement in the standard of living, the extension of voting rights, and the beginnings of compulsory education all had their origins in this era. Nonetheless there were also flaws in this development. For example, urban centers contributed to health and safety problems; squalid living conditions caused epidemic diseases; and overcrowding of the workers in slums led to moral and political problems (825).

Class Relations

This era was the beginning of industrial capitalism and gave rise to a new set of class relations. There developed an industrial upper middle class who were the owners of the factories and the professionals involved in commerce, industry, and banking, as well as lawyers, teachers, government officials, and doctors. There were also merchants and craftsmen who were at the lower end of that socioeconomic group. The earliest workers in the factories in the West were children, women, and young people who had left the farms. Later immigrants and the poor became factory workers. These workers were at first employed in textiles, railroads, iron, and coal. However, by the late 1880s and until World War I, the second industrial revolution led to the production of steel, chemicals, electricity, and petroleum.

By 1900, economic developments and transportation growth, including marine transport and railroads, fostered the true beginnings of a world economy (Duiker & Spielvogel, 1994, 819). Europeans were receiving goods from all over the world: coffee from Brazil, sugar from Java, iron from North Africa. The world had become a small one, with Western investment taking place on every continent and foreign countries providing markets for the surplus manufactured goods of Europe. In this global economy there was a growing disparity between the wealthy and the workers. Often the owners were Western industrialists who enlisted the wealthy of the countries in question to invest with them or to manage the industries that the companies established. The workers were most often poor locals and new immigrants who were glad for employment. However, the conditions under which they worked were often assembly lines with poor ventilation, unsafe conditions, and work speed-ups to ensure profitability.

At the top of European and American society stood a wealthy elite, a mere 5 percent of the population who controlled 30–40 percent of the wealth (825–826).

These elite were the new industrialists as well as the old aristocracy. Through common interests and bonds like school and country clubs, they assumed leadership roles in government and the military. The middle class became even further divided into the upper middle class, who were the doctors, lawyers, and civil servants and some of the moderately wealthy business owners. The middle-middle class became those employed as business managers, and new professionals like engineers, architects, accountants, and other solid and comfortable citizens. The lower middle class became the small shopkeepers, traders, manufacturers, and well-off peasants who provided goods and services for those in the classes above them. Finally there developed the lower classes, the salesmen, bank tellers, department store salespeople, secretaries, and finally the factory workers (825–826).

The working classes (lower middle class) were actually 80 percent of the population in Europe and the United States. The elite of the working class were the artisans who made things like cabinets and jewelry. In the middle of the working class there were machine-tool specialists, shipbuilders, and metal workers. Semiskilled laborers such as carpenters, bricklayers, and factory workers were just below them in the social stratification system. Finally there were the unskilled laborers, the day laborers who worked irregularly for low wages. They also included women who would work as domestic servants to the wealthier classes.

These categories are still relevant and helpful in understanding today's world. More often than not, U.S. citizens have no class consciousness or awareness of differences in what life is like within each class and what cross-class relations are all about. In fact, we have a myth of classlessness in our society.

Lifestyles of the Classes

In the late nineteenth century, life for the upper classes was lavish and aristocratic. The wealthy were able to buy splendid estates in the country and magnificent town houses with the money they were earning as their businesses thrived. These wealthy men invested in railway shares, public utilities, government bonds, and production factories. When they and their children married, they married into other wealthy families, which ensured even greater wealth. This was the time when such families as the DuPonts, the Carnegies, and the Rockefellers amassed their great wealth.

The middle class attempted to emulate the values and lifestyles of the rich. They emphasized the need for progress and the value of science. They believed in hard work, thrift, churchgoing, and good Christian morality, and held firm to the principle of doing things the right way. In fact, they developed social programs for themselves and for those beneath them in socioeconomic status, in order to teach the workers and new immigrants how to become good and solid citizens. As a result of the growth of industry and the resultant modernization and urbanization of the Western world, the nineteenth and early twentieth centuries led to great changes in the social fabric and family relationships. However, life for the poor remained harsh. Workers labored long hours and lived in squalid conditions. Life expectancy, health, and educational attainment were far less than those of the upper classes.

Changes in the Family

The Industrial Revolution significantly altered family life, first in the West, although elements eventually spread to the rest of the world. Prior to the rise of industrial capitalism, as previously noted, all of the domestic economic functions were taken care of on the farm. Families raised their children while growing the crops and tending to their small plots of land. There was a prevalence of subsistence farming, growing enough to feed the family and maybe to sell to neighbors or in a market-place. The center of the farm was the household, which was both shop and home (Tilly & Scott, 1987, 12). In what is called the *domestic mode of production,* all of the labor of the household was done by the men, women, and children. Their work fed the family, and the household was the center around which resources, labor, and consumption were balanced. This form of family life was called the *family-based economy.*

Family-Based Economy

Although historians have studied this form of family life in Britain and France, the form was also prevalent in most other parts of the world prior to industrializa-tion. In fact, this form is still in existence in many rural economies to this day.

These rural-based economies provided for a family life that was difficult; it was a subsistence living. Sometimes families would produce clothing or cloth that they sold to supplement their earnings, but for the most part they subsisted on what they could produce themselves. The family worked together to produce that which it needed to survive. Families were large because of a high mortality rate, and because families needed children to contribute to the families' survival. People married late, which led to the birth of fewer children, and each household provided for itself based on what the family could produce on their own land (227). Eventually land was bought up by wealthier landowners, who farmed their tracts with the use of day laborers who became agricultural wage earners.

Sometimes families who lost their land turned to cottage industries like cotton weaving and worked for wages for the wealthier entrepreneur. The family remained household-based, in that family members controlled their own pace and organiza-tion and continued to work together at home with other family members.

In the cities, during the family-based era, people still worked toward the eco-nomic interests of their families. Decisions were made in the interest of the group and not the individual; the whole family was an enterprise in which each person's work was defined by his or her family position (21). Among the poor, men, women, and children all worked; among those with wealth, everyone was expected to con-tribute to the best of their ability and for the prosperity of the family. Often it was the father, however, who determined what was in the best interest of the family.

Young women either worked in the home or for other families as servants. Single women were the servants of their families, and if they were employed out of the home they lived with other families or with other women like themselves (31). Once they married, women brought dowries and even a marketable skill. There was a division of labor based on age and sex, and as children got older, the levels of expectations increased as to their participation in chores and earning. And "the normative family division of labor tended to give men jobs away from the home or jobs which required long and uninterrupted commitments of time or extensive travel, while women's work was performed more often at home and permitted flexible time arrangements" (44).

In the United States this time period was that of our colonial era, in which the family was the center of each member's life. Often the family served as church, hospital, school, house of correction, orphanage, poor house, old people's home, and welfare institution (Demos, 1970, 183–184). In fact, during this time families took in non-kin members of the household, like boarders who helped pay the rent. The family was integrally related to the community, and people were invited into the home as they needed assistance.

The argument among historians of this era is that as industrialization developed, all of these family caretaking functions were taken over by other social institutions, and that as a result the family became more isolated and detached from the community. During the family-based era, all the social functions were maintained by this one institution; eventually, with modernization, the family became responsible only for the psychological well-being of its members. There is some debate about this point, but for some time this was the narrative and point presented by people who studied the family. They argued that the family became a private retreat once historical forces pushed the family into the industrializing world, and that a public/private split took place as the economy industrialized and as people increasingly moved to cities for employment, leaving their communities and families behind.

Family-Wage Economy

Tilly and Scott (1987) argue that as industrialization moved labor and resources away from agriculture, fishing, and forestry and into manufacturing, commercial, and service activities, the family gradually adapted its form to that of the *family-wage economy* (63). What had once been the form followed only by people without land became the norm. This rise of European industrial capitalism substituted work done in factories, away from home, for the work done in the home and on the farm. Now goods and services that were once produced by families for themselves were produced elsewhere, and the family lost its once-important functions to other social institutions.

Starting in the 1870s, the role of the family became one of providing emotional support for its members. Where social welfare and support of family members were once the job of the family, the state now took over those responsibilities. "The family became a specialized unit, its tasks limited primarily to procreation, consumption and child rearing" (Parsons & Bales, 1955, 1966).

The family became an emotional refuge from the modernizing world and a place where family members could retreat. However, even if the family no longer served as the locus of production, it still served important functions economically, in that it regulated the work and occupational choices of its members as part of the collective effort to provide for the family's economic well-being (Hareven, 1976,

199). As Hareven has put it, the family was an agent of change as well as a custodian of tradition (2000, xxi). Mothers worked when the household needed their wages, and in the course of their lifetimes women alternated between productive and reproductive work (1976, 228). Daughters were wage earners, as were sons and husbands, particularly in the working classes of the early twentieth century. The family helped determine what kind of work each family member would do in the outside world. The power differentials were changing within family life.

Members of the family, once involved on a daily basis with their families and larger communities in rural areas, became involved in the urban areas to which they were moving. The mass society (institutions that served the needs and provided services to large numbers of people) saw the rise of trade unions and political parties. Community centers, schools, benevolent associations, and literary organizations developed to meet the needs that had once been met within the family. While education had once been done at home or in small rural schools with a few families present, mass education now developed during the late nineteenth and early twentieth centuries. Education that had only been available for the rich became available to all and became compulsory. Industrialization demanded skilled labor, and as jobs became more diverse, trained and educated workers were needed.

Mass education served other important functions as well. It led to a rise in literacy and helped to educate the public to become part of the electoral process. Education instilled patriotism. The local region and family had once been the place where religion and nationalism were taught, but now that the family was losing those functions, schools became the vehicles for indoctrination of national values (Duiker & Spielvogel, 1994, 831).

Schools also taught the basics like reading, writing, and arithmetic, while turning the curriculum toward patriotic views of national history, literature, and geography. Education of boys and girls varied, and sexes were separated. Girls were taught domestic skills and how to become good wives and mothers, while boys were taught workplace skills as well as math and science. All the schools inculcated the middle-class values of hard work, thrift, sobriety, cleanliness, and respect for the family (831).

As the end of the family-wage economy evolved, social and leisure functions were shifted from the family to other institutions as well. Where once the social life of families was based on the seasons and located within the family home, now the mass society developed recreational and leisure activities to meet people's needs to play. Factories demanded new rhythms of daily life, to accommodate machines, clocks, and a faster pace of life. Now leisure was seen as what one did after work, and family life began to be organized around the concept of weekends, the work week, workday hours, and even summers (832).

During this era families began to spend their time doing leisure activities together, like going to amusement parks, enjoying movies, engaging in athletic games, and listening to music (833). The idea of the family vacation emerged at this time, when people who no longer spent all their time with their families in family-based labor began to have time off from work at the factory.

Families of workers often took in boarders to assist them financially and also to provide housing for the rural-to-urban migrants. However, families had always had strangers living with them. In the family-based economy, apprentices, servants, orphans, extended family members, and non-kin strangers lived with families. As the family became wage-based, others came into the home as paying boarders. It was not until the 1920s, with more houses available and the growing privatization of the family, that this practice ceased (Hareven, 1976, 195). In fact, whenever families ran into financial pressures this practice of taking in others reappeared.

Family-Consumer Economy

Toward the end of the nineteenth century and certainly by the mid-twentieth century, a third economic period developed that was an outgrowth of the family-wage economy. The *family-consumer economy* (Tilly & Scott, 1987, 176) was different from its predecessor in that men's wages were increasing. This, coupled with the availability of cheaper consumer goods, made it less necessary for women and children to work.

As a result, the father became the primary breadwinner, especially in middle- and upper-class families, and the family increasingly emphasized consumption rather than wage earning. The division of labor among men, women, and children became even further differentiated because of the increasing complexity of the urban environment and of money and family affairs. Husbands and unmarried children were the wage earners, and wives were given the tasks of child care and household management (176). The power differentials in family life began to shift, with men becoming more central to the economic function of the family.

Child labor laws had been passed by the late 1880s in the United States, and children were no longer allowed employment. With the rise of compulsory education, school-aged children did not contribute to the family's income, although poorer children often worked after school or truanted so as to mind the other children while mothers worked. Girls were allowed to work until they married, and more often than not, if they were poorer, they were allowed to be servants, factory workers, and shop girls.

Within the family-consumer economy, there were differences between races, classes, ethnicities, and region. But what they all had in common was that, rather than working together or contributing to the family upkeep, the family now centered on purchasing and consuming the wide array of products and goods that became available as capitalism expanded its markets and developed more commodities.

We must also remember that although these forms were typical of family life, there were plenty of people who did not follow the norm. The family ideals of breadwinning husbands, homemaker wives, families as caring havens from commerce were all popularized social constructions. They were also ways to control immigrants and the working class and to serve as ideals to which these peoples were supposed to aspire.

The Cult of True Womanhood and the Upper Classes

Perhaps one of the more interesting developments arising from these changes in family life was the separation of men's and women's spheres of influence, especially in England and the United States. When families lived and worked together in the family-based economy, although there was a distinction between men's and women's work, roles and responsibilities were more fluid and flexible. The power was shared somewhat more equally. However, with the removal of the economics of family life from the home, and with workers going out of the home for employment, a separation developed between what were considered the public and private sectors. This "doctrine of two spheres" led to the *belief* that married women should stay home, creating a home and haven for their husbands and children. Married men were expected to earn the money to support the family by entering the marketplace and selling their labor as workers or as lucrative businessmen. We must remember that this was a belief, an ideology. It does not mean that all families did this, just that it was an ideal to be modeled and emulated.

Women had always been in an inferior position within the family and as citizens, not having the vote, and being defined by their household tasks. However, the Industrial Revolution codified women's inferiority and defined women's roles according to traditional gender expectations, particularly in England and the United States. Marriage was the only honorable and available career open to most women, and women were always expected to marry. If they worked outside the home, it was before they married or to supplement a husband's wages, or to support families when their husbands were unemployed or died.

An ideology developed that women were morally superior to men and that their role was to watch over and act as guardians and angels of the household. This ideology was called *the cult of true womanhood;* it developed out of the upper classes, but was soon taken up as the model for all females, especially in England and the United States.

Barbara Welter (1973) surveyed U.S. women's magazines, religious tracts, and sermons from the era, as well as cookbooks, diaries, and personal papers written from 1820 to 1860. She noted that a "woman was a true woman, wherever she was found" (313).

A true woman would have "piety, purity, submissiveness and domesticity. Put them all together and they spelled mother, daughter, sister, wife-woman" (313). Religion and piety were supposed to be the core of women's virtue and inherently a part of all women, but not of men. In fact, a woman's intellect was sometimes thought to be determined by her hymen, not by her brain, and a woman was expected to fight off man's assaults upon her to prove her superiority and ultimate power over him (314).

Women were to be modest, innocent, humble, pliable, silent in handling adversity, and totally accepting of their lot in life. They were to comfort the sick, engage in morally uplifting activities, do needlework, tend flowers, know their way around the kitchen, and above all else, devote themselves first to their husbands and then to their children (322–325). They were to infuse their children with a sense of patriotism and good Christian morals. If they dared ask for more, they were considered troublemakers. Those who lobbied for the vote for women or for more involvement in the public sector were seen as sexually questionable (326).

But as Welter notes, eventually the seeds of destruction of that ideology developed (327). Because there were so many social problems, women began to feel compelled to do something about them, moving out of the private sphere and into the public, thus giving up the role of angel.

It is necessary to note that this ideology was very much a class-based ideology. The cult of true womanhood was developed by upper- and middle-class thinkers to make a distinction between the wealthy and working classes. Poor women had to work in order to support their families, and to be a "lady" was a status symbol. This ideology idealized the private family for all classes of women and helped to preserve class distinctions. Poor women did not have this luxury; they had to work, while richer women were able to afford hired help.

Women, in fact, have always worked. They were employed throughout their lives, both in the home and in factories. First they were employed in the textile mills of The United States and Western Europe, engaging in spinning, weaving, and sewing. Later, as industries expanded they were employed in shoe production and the less heavy industries. Young women were expected to work outside of the home until they married, and to return to the workforce later, when their children were raised. Married women also worked in the home, taking in piecework and employing themselves in cottage industries so they could still be at home.

The Cult of True Manhood

The parallel view about men, especially in the United States, was that he would be devoted to hard work and material success. Such men were to be "pure" in their sexuality, which meant controlled but yet insistent, as well as assertive. He was to be very much the patriarch, a benevolent ruler. These were the characteristics of the true male, who would love rewards in this world and would struggle to obtain them. Yet he was also to sublimate his lust into the procreation of children. He was authoritarian and independent; above all else he was to protect his wife and family (Gordon, 1980, 145–157).

This division into true men and true women was necessary as capitalism grew and developed. Men were needed as workers or businessmen, women were needed as mothers and wives, to fuel the economic development that was occurring at the time. The social construction of roles linked biology and destiny. What one was born would determine what one did and what one became: the economically dependent woman controlled the domestic sphere; the aggressive, benevolent patriarch went into the world to earn. The power differentials in family life were set by ideology and social construction, mostly externally defined.

The Cult of Normal Sex

If men and women did not adhere to these definitions, they were considered godless, and people who dared to fall outside of these narrow definitions were negatively labeled. Since chastity and purity were held in highest esteem, if one were at all deviant, unwilling or unable to conform, or if a woman spoke out against these constrictions of the Victorian era, they were called "semi women and mental hermaphrodites" (Katz, 1983, 140). Women were also called "unsexed or sexual perverts" if they loved other women, cross-dressed, or did not follow the norm. There was a great deal of debate about women's roles, and there were "new women" who were educated and economically independent from men. These women challenged existing gender relations and the distribution of power (Smith-Rosenberg, 1989, 264) and were defined as "unnatural": a symptom of a diseased society, because they challenged the bourgeois social order.

If relationships were nonsexual, then individuals were allowed to love people of the same sex. In fact, according to Smith-Rosenberg, this was very much allowed in the United States until well into the end of the 1800s. These nonsexual relationships were actually revered, and were considered the highest form of love because they did not include the nasty form of lust. Lust was separated from love, and if a man were to express his lust it could only be with prostitutes or even with other men: it had nothing to do with love and procreation, which were centered in family life.

People who engage in same-sex love and sexuality have been around in most societies since the beginning of recorded history. It had long been legitimate for two males to have sexual relations with each other. But there were two restrictions: that adult men who have sexual relations with males also marry women and produce families, and that the adult male in the sexual act always take the active or penetrator's role. History is replete with examples, from many societies, of same-sex love. It has existed throughout history, sometimes accepted and sometimes not. But as modern Western societies began to develop, unacceptance became the norm.

From 1880 on, doctors began to develop the *idea of normal love*, and it became a medical concept. No longer were lust and love separated, with lust being ghettoized (Katz, 1983, 143). It now meant that normal love included the sexual, the erotic. One should feel this kind of passion for one's wife or husband. Women's normal love should be for a male and a man's should be for a female; love for the same sex was inappropriate and viewed as abnormal. Thus came the idea of the "pervert": someone who did not procreate, did not make babies, who did not follow the commandment to go forth and multiply. The procreative norm was seen as innate, biologically determined, and the purpose of male and female bodies (142).

"Normal," by the late 1800s, became defined as that which most people did. It was how the majority engaged in sex and what was "ordinary." We must remember that the term *normal* is that which is defined as acceptable by a society. It is not good, bad, or inherently anything until a society makes a judgment about it. In the case of same-sex love and genital sexuality, because only a small percentage of society engaged in it, it became "deviant" and a "perversion." At this time, fewer than 3 percent of men and 2 percent of women identify themselves as homosexual or bisexual (Laumann, Gagnon, Michaels, & Michaels, 1994).

This new definition of what was acceptable sexually was a result of the change from a rural-based, family economy to a wage-based urban economy. There was a new emphasis on industrialization, which relied upon commodification and on numbers, on using statistical evidence to determine the standard; it was linked to the spread of the capitalist ethic, "the more the better" (Katz, 1983, 143).

It also served an important economic purpose: to set heterosexual, procreative sexuality as the standard. It paved the way for people to serve the growing capitalist economic system, which needed male laborers and businesspeople, and female mothers and wives to raise the children and provide nurturance to men out in the workplace. With the growing dichotomization of the public and private sectors, sexuality became an important area for social control and for the pathologizing of those who did not adhere to the norm. It became one new way to define power differentials between certain groups of people in society, those who were "normal" sexually and those who were not.

Types of Family Structure

There is a debate among historians and sociologists about the form that families have taken as a result of urbanization and modernization. The reigning argument had been that the large extended family of the agrarian world gave way to the nuclear family when industrialization moved people to the cities. Parsons argued that the family had become nuclear to fit the need for isolation and the rise of capitalism. However, historians like Tamara Hareven (1976) have found that the modern family in fact might well be a modified extended one.

The modified extended family structure is one that is quite common in contemporary parts of the globe. The term *modified extended family* was coined by sociologist Eugene Litwak in 1960 to refer to American families in Buffalo, New York, in the nineteenth century, which did not require geographic closeness or job patronage or strict authority relations. They had egalitarian relationships and provided aid to the nuclear family related to standard of living, like housing, illness, and leisure pursuits, rather than to occupational appointments or promotions (Litwak, 1960, 385). Certainly his definition of *egalitarian* might be problematic. Why then, we might ask, was it necessary for suffragists to bother with the first wave of the feminist movement?

Modified extended families aided in the rural–urban migration, and they were equally important in the migration of European immigrants to the United States. Even with rural–urban migration, there was still a reliance placed on kin, who were reconstructed through *chain migration:* people influenced each other in choosing where they moved and what jobs they entered. Relatives helped each other migrate, provided housing and resources, and eased the transition to a new place. Friends and family brought others from their home areas to the centers in which they now resided. These types of families helped people adapt to the industrial system. Modified extended families continue to play a significant role in contemporary family forms, as newer immigrants leave their homelands to settle abroad.

Workers migrated in kin groups and carried with them traditional patterns of kin assistance. They adapted these patterns to the industrial system and developed new functions for kin that were considerably different from those customarily performed in rural society (Hareven, 1976, 197).

Families could be modern at work and go back to their traditional family habits at home. Hareven found that modernization is, in fact, a very complex process and not a direct progression. She found that even in the same time period, different ethnic groups and socioeconomic groupings adapted differently (205). Using the modified extended family typology can be helpful in understanding how different groups of people maintain family relationships. I would argue that in contemporary society it is one of the dominant family structures in most parts of the developing world.

Ethnicity and Class Distinctions in Industrialization

The story I have told you about the history of the family is very much the story of the white middle and upper classes of Western society. There is another story to tell about life for immigrants and racial and ethnic minorities in the West. When the history of the family was first written, it was based on documents and materials gathered from records like Census Bureau data and household size. Historians analyzed birth, death, marriage data, and even the physical layout of people's homes. This was called the *family reconstitution technique.* Using the newest forms of historical analysis, the social history I described, we are now able to say more about what life was like for those who did not leave this kind of data. People like you and me, common folk living ordinary lives.

The period of time from 1880 to 1924 brought massive numbers of immigrants to the United States from Southern and Eastern Europe. This was the second wave of immigration, the first being smaller numbers of Scandinavians, English, Irish, Scots, French, and Germans who arrived between 1820 and 1880. The second wave came from Austria-Hungary, Greece, Italy, Poland, Rumania, Russia, Serbia, China, Japan, Mexico, French Canada, and the West Indies (Hutter, 1988, 107). More than a million of these immigrants came as a result of population explosions in their own countries and political and economic dislocations. The labor markets in their own countries were overcrowded, while skilled labor was in demand in the United States. The immigrants were employed in the burgeoning industries.

The conditions to which they came were less than ideal. Poverty and horrible living conditions were the norm. Housing in the major cities of the United States was dirty, overcrowded, smelly, and with poor air quality and inadequate heating. Families lived in immigrant ghettos based on networks of friends and families who had come to the cities earlier (chain migration, such as had occurred in the rural–urban migration of workers in previous eras). Usually young men and women who were single or young married couples came first, establishing a base, saving money, and eventually sending for other family members as they could afford to.

These new immigrants were poor and were considered *working class.* They clearly maintained their ethnic identity while trying to assimilate into American society. Different ethnic groups had different work patterns. Italians, for example, tended to go into the building trades, Jews engaged in the needle trades and manufacturing, Scandinavians and Germans often went into farming. They retained their traditional ways of life and used their traditional family patterns to survive.

Immigrant women were treated somewhat better than they had been in the old country. Irish domestic workers, for example, enjoyed greater freedom than they had at home. Very few married women worked in factories, while young daughters were encouraged to work outside of the home. If married women did work, they did so to supplement the family income. This was much like white working-class women, who were not seen as primary income earners for the family.

Ethnic working-class families were very adaptable and resilient, as families have been historically. They responded to the stresses of immigration and employment in the industrial sector by adjusting and changing as need be, while still trying to maintain their ethnic identities.

Again the family form seemed to be modified extended families. Modified extended families still lived near each other as they emigrated from the old country. Families played an important role economically and provided emotional assistance and support. Even if the extended family did not live in the same house, members were involved in the daily life of the family, watching the children, sharing holidays and festivities, and socializing children and newcomers into the ways of the new world. We have no concrete data to indicate exactly how many families lived in close proximity to each other. But as Litwak mentions, at least in Buffalo, the modified extended family was the norm.

During this time there was much negative commentary by the upper and middle classes about new immigrants. Prejudice and discrimination was not uncommon, and social agencies were developed to try to bring the newcomers into the American mainstream and have them "Americanize" as quickly as possible. They were taught English, proper manners, and hygiene as well as middle-class values of child rearing and gender roles. The dominant ideology of the time was that America was a "melting pot" and that within a few generations all ethnic and class distinctions would be eliminated. Old-world ways were viewed negatively and were also seen as pathological. Assimilation was the goal, seen as inevitable, both by the immigrants and by the dominant white culture. The cult of true womanhood and manhood were the models to emulate. In fact, the profession of social work developed during this era to bring enlightenment and American values to the new immigrants.

Racial Considerations

The situation for racial minorities has been quite a bit different than for Caucasian immigrants. For black families as well as Asians and Latinos, negative stereotypes have made integration into the dominant white culture quite a bit more complicated. Because of the differences in skin color, historical forces that brought them to the West under differing conditions than did white immigrants, and the nature of prejudice and discrimination, negative images of these groups have dominated Western thinking and actions toward them.

To understand those who are considered racial or ethnic minorities in the United States, we must see that those who are called "people of color" were brought in order to serve the need for cheap labor. The very fact that they are called people of color lumps all of them together, in a way that defines them as different from the mainstream and says that they are all the same, even though they come from enormously different places and backgrounds. Many of these peoples, such as Asians,

African Americans, and Latinos, have a very different history than do the Caucasian immigrants who first entered the United States.

The term *race* is very much a social construction. What is one race in one society might have a very different definition in another, or at a different point in history. Race in and of itself does not exist; it is merely what is defined by the dominant society as its own racial groupings. The definition of race changes over time. Groups that were once considered minority can move into the majority over generations. The Irish, when they first came to the United States, were at the lowest rung on society, socializing and intermarrying with blacks. In fact, they were themselves considered black. Within a few generations they had become "white" and had moved up on the socioeconomic scale (Ignatiev, 1995).

The term *colonized minorities* is also used to describe the people who came here following differing patterns than the Caucasian immigrants. The non-European immigrants were helpful in serving the needs of growing industrialization in the major Eastern cities in the United States. They received low wages, but there was still more and different work that needed doing, and colonized minorities were brought or recruited to go to the West, Southwest, and South. For example, Chinese men were an important part of the workforce in completing the railroads, doing laundry and domestic work in California, and working in agriculture. Chicanos (Mexicans) were miners, railroad workers, and agricultural migrants in the far West. Blacks were important sources of labor in the South.

While these racial minority groups were important sources of labor, they were not able to move up socioeconomically because of the way they had entered the United States, where they came from, and the prejudices against them. They came from areas that had been colonized by the West, and they maintained their colonized status upon arrival to the United States. In fact, it was argued that once they arrived here they continued to live in little colonies, internal colonies, in which they were maintained in unequal status from the Anglo mainstream. This colonized status influenced their family structures as well. While wealthy families, those of European ancestry, could follow the division of the public/private sphere, with women staying home and men going out to work, poverty and the need for economic survival made it more likely that all immigrant family members worked when they arrived in the West. The power differentials established by advancing capitalism were reflected in family life and the history of minority families in the United States. The rise of industrialism, consumerism, and class exploitation played a significant role in the way that the history of the family played out for the colonized minorities.

African Americans

It is useful to remember that, historically, Africans entered the core countries in a manner unlike that of other immigrants. They came from many different countries in Africa over four centuries, and because of slavery they arrived in chains, against their will, and without connections to their extended families back home. *Point-of-entry theory* (Feagin & Feagin, 1993) argues that the way one enters a new society will determine the nature of one's future interactions with that society. Africans did not come of their own volition, and they were forced into conditions that were brutal and dehumanizing. During the expansionist eras, while the West was exploring Asia, Africa, and Latin America and finding labor and resources to enhance the West's economic position, slaves were one commodity that was exported. They were not seen as people, but rather as cattle who could work on plantations. This image of blacks as less than human fit the popular conception that was based on Charles Darwin's doctrine of the "survival of the fittest." This pseudoscientific theory maintained that certain individuals, groups of peoples, and societies adapted to changing circumstances in order to survive and prosper in the world. If they did not do so, then they were considered on their way to extinction and less than human beings.

Blacks were pathologized as having unstable families and chaotic, disorganized relationships. "Negroes," as they were called, were described as having disrupted and disintegrated home lives as a result of the dissolution of families under slavery. The actual truth of the matter, historians are now arguing, is that African Americans have been extremely resilient in surviving the harsh conditions under which they have been living for 300 years. They came from enormously diverse backgrounds, based on geography, age, religion, skin color, cultural beliefs, and traditions.

In fact, African American families have not broken down. They have adapted and survived, although in a form that does not emulate the white dominant culture. African Americans had to abandon their native languages, names, occupations, religions, partners, foods, and customs. For a time men and women were not allowed to marry under slavery, and frequent partners were the rule, because individuals were often sold away from their families. Black men were often seen as breeders for increasing the labor supply, and black women were raped and sexually exploited by their masters. But "despite these extreme hardships, slaves sought to form new family units to compensate for losses due to death and slavery. Even after emancipation, many former slaves remained on plantations, hoping that family members might return" (Hines & Boyd-Franklin, 1996, 66).

In Africa, and then in the United States, strong kinship bonds were most important. In African philosophy there is the belief that "we are, therefore I am" (Nobles, 1985). The individual owes his or her existence to the tribe. So uncles, aunts, grandparents, boyfriends, older siblings, deacons, and even neighbors become part of the family network (68). Carol Stack (1974) looked at African American kin in the United States and found that young black children are born into personal networks that include "essential kin," those people who actively accept responsibility toward them and some relatives who do not actively create reciprocal obligations. This folk system of "kin" is people whom the family has determined are relatives, even if they are not related by blood (46).

African American families tend to be caught between conflicting demands: there are economic pressures, as well as physical demands, social, psychological, and spiritual needs of the kin (Billingsley, 1992). In order to meet these needs, the African American family has evolved into many forms, including nuclear families made up of married couples with and without children, extended families, and the augmented family, which is primary family members plus nonrelatives (32). In order to cope with its stresses, many family members work together to assist others. In fact, the single-mother, female-headed household is the minority of family form for blacks (35). Billingsley described a single mother raising her own and others' children as the "modified nuclear" family.

If one adopts a balanced perspective on the African American family, one can see that there are strengths as well as weaknesses within family life. For example, religion has always played a significant role in black American families. The church has served as a refuge, source of community, and a source of strength. There are also weaknesses, the residuals of slavery and of having been exploited, marginalized, and victimized for generations. For example, kin will help each other out in times of need, but they can also make it difficult for low-income blacks to rise out of poverty. A person who raises his or her level of living cannot really do so until everyone in the network is able to raise his or her level too. Nor is the extended family able to eliminate the hardships that beset single-parent black families (Cherlin, 1981, 111).

African American women have been important sources of strength within the family and have worked outside of the home since their arrival in the West. They never fell into the "cult of true womanhood," both because of their class status in the West and the fact that they were mainly employed serving members of the upper classes, in child rearing and housekeeping. Class exploitation played a significant role in how family life played out for blacks in the industrialized West.

Many of the features the West has attributed to the pathology of African American families, in fact, may not be pathologies at all. Instead they are forms of adaptation to Western society as well as uniquely African cultural traditions and kinship systems. Perhaps it is not the dysfunctional behaviors of the "underclass" that need attending to, but those of the "plunderclass" who are greedy (Tolnay, 1999, 178).

In a fascinating book by Stewart Tolnay (1999), in which he studied African Americans at the "bottom rung" of the southern agricultural ladder, the author found that early southern farming practices required early marriage and large numbers of children in black families. As mechanization took place, fewer workers were needed and blacks were left without a niche in the rural economy (171). When they moved to the cities in search of employment, they were forced to live under racial segregation, which eventually led to an "oppositional culture," one in which blacks refused to get married and raise children within marriage (172). He also noted that as work disappeared from inner cities, blacks (the men especially) were displaced in the labor force, and eventually family life was impacted, with marriage declining. Now, without jobs, marriage became less likely, although having children and raising families was still an adaptive response to the structural conditions of the American economic system (174–175).

Currently there seems to be a crisis in African American gender relations and in marriage and families. The legacy of slavery has impacted gender relations among blacks. In recent decades the external economic environment for black women has improved, but it has stagnated for black men. While this has been going on, the internal gender environment (male and female relationships among blacks) has deteriorated for women, partly because of the conservatism of black men's gender attitudes. The current low marriage rate for blacks reflects differing values between men and women, with black men being more permissive sexually and black women believing in fidelity. These facts leave black children growing up fatherless, many impoverished single mothers stressed, women living adulthood as singles, and men under forty going through life either single or in short-lived relationships.

Black women, studied by Elaine Bell Kaplan (1997), often become single mothers because of structural conditions such as economic subordination, which contributes to their performance (4). She argues that because young black mothers have faulty information about sexual matters, and because they attempt to live according to the family-values models of the larger society, they act on distorted views, thus creating even more problems for themselves, which they take into their adult lives. For example, young black women, according to Kaplan, may desire to have children in order to make a family for themselves.

Clearly the consequences of structural conditions have their impact today on relations in the black family.

Latinos

It is useful to note that there is debate today as to what to call someone who has immigrated from Latin America. The term *Hispanic* is seen as a politically conservative term that is gender neutral, and thus unlike any Spanish word a Latin American might call him- or herself. The terms *Latino/Latina* are more progressive; they are Spanish, rather than English like *Hispanic*. For Latinos, the label "Hispanic" takes away their national origin and symbolizes a loss of identity (Garcia-Preto, 1996a, 141).

There are many Latino groups who immigrated to the United States, including Mexicans, Puerto Ricans, Dominicans, Brazilians, Cubans, Central Americans, and South Americans. To lump them all together does a great disservice to all of the groups, whose ways of entry have differed depending on forces within their own countries, as well as in the West. They have different values, patterns, and characteristics of family life.

Latinos have been in the United States since the 1500s, when the Spanish settled in what is now New Mexico. They later moved into areas in what is now Texas, Arizona, California, Colorado, Nevada, Utah, and Wyoming. The major waves of Latin immigrants came after World War II; their entry usually followed economic depression or political revolution in their own countries. Usually they are poor, or intellectuals escaping persecution, or the very wealthy who come with money (144).

The first Latin group to officially become part of the United States in significant numbers was Mexicans living in what became New Mexico after the Mexican American War. In 1848 they were granted U.S. citizenship when the government appropriated their lands as part of the United States. Once their lands were taken, Mexicans were relegated to cheap labor in agriculture. As Caucasians (called *Anglos* by Latinos) moved further west, they brought prejudices with them, and Mexicans became further impoverished, losing lands and then status. Today most Mexican Americans still live in the Southwest, bolstered in their numbers by additional more recent immigration from Mexico.

Photo 4.1   Contemporary Cuban family. Photographer: Patti Carman

Other Latino groups arrived later. Puerto Ricans began arriving in the 1940s and 1950s and are primarily based in the Northeast, with some representation in Texas, Florida, and Illinois. Since Puerto Rico is a protectorate of the United States, its citizens are granted citizenship and there is a back-and-forth migration from the mainland.

Cubans began arriving in great numbers after the Cuban revolution in 1959 and are primarily based in Florida, New York, and New Jersey, but they have been migrating to the United States since the nineteenth century. They come from two distinct classes: the rich, who came early, fleeing Fidel Castro; and the poorer, darker-skinned Cubans who arrived in the 1980s and 1990s when Castro opened the doors to hospitals, prisons, and mental hospitals, to expel dissidents and troublemakers from his regime. Many of these immigrants traveled by raft, at great risk. Because of the ideologic conflict between the United States and Cuba, there is still a blockade under which immigration is not allowed.

Dominicans are a growing group of Latin immigrants who have entered the United States recently. Primarily made up of people of mixed Spanish, Indian, and African heritage, they came to escape poverty and economic troubles. The history of the Dominican Republic is one related to the history of colonization, the expansion of Western markets, and the source of labor for capitalism. Today, because the number of Dominicans allowed to enter the United States is limited, some flee to Puerto Rico so they can pass as Puerto Ricans. Dominicans are known as industrious and somewhat aggressive, opening businesses particularly in the northeastern parts of this country. They maintain strong allegiances to their families back home and maintain modified extended families upon immigrating to the United States. Like other Latin immigrants, they engage in chain migration, bringing family members to join them in the States as soon as they can afford to do so.

There are a vast number of other Latinos whose history of entry into the United States is more recent. Central Americans from Nicaragua, Guatemala, and El Salvador have all come because of political upheaval in their own countries. These countries were conquered by the Spanish in the 1500s, with a massive extermination of the native populations through war, disease, and enslavement. During the colonial period the white elite ruled, and with the class configuration, mixed bloods *(mestizos)* were of higher social status than pure Indians. In the nineteenth century the British established Central American countries as exporters of coffee and bananas, and a system of wealthy landowners worked hand in hand with military and civilian dictatorships to rule and thus increase the class differences. In the twentieth century, through a series of revolutions there have been efforts to overthrow this oppressive sociopolitical system (Hernandez, 1996, 214).

Recently, war, poverty, and racial and ethnic conflict between whites and native peoples in Central America have made immigrants' entry into the United States far more traumatic. Many of these immigrants have histories of being tortured, traumatized, and brutalized. Their entry is sometimes illegal, as they come seeking political sanctuary from the ravages of conditions in their own homes.

Family life for Latinos is not easily summarized. They share a common language (although Brazilians speak Portuguese) and they do share a common religion. The Roman Catholic faith is crucially important in the history and dynamics of Latinos. There is an emphasis on spiritual values and a willingness to sacrifice material comforts for spirituality (151). Family life is one of the most important values. The emphasis is on the group and *not* on the individual, and families share a deep sense of family commitment, obligation, and responsibility. The family takes care of all family members, and there is the expectation that if there are problems others will help. Once again kinship is most important. Godparents, adopted children, and non-blood relations are as important as those related by blood, and all kin are expected to encourage, correct, and care for others in the family (151). Even strangers are expected to assume responsibility for others' children. Authority is always respected, and it sometimes makes for fear in speaking up for one's rights. Music, foods, dancing, and a sense of community are extremely important cultural components in the life of Latinos.

Latino families are patriarchal, and men and women have separate spheres of influence. There is often a stereotype about the *machismo* of Latin men, which has become associated with sexism. However, culturally this refers to self-respect and a responsibility for protecting and providing for the family. This attitude can become negative when it leads to possessiveness, but it also has positive values of protecting and honoring one's family. For women, who are seen as morally and spiritually superior to men, the concept is known as *marianismo*. A woman should be respected, and if she is not she is known as a whore. Women are also expected to strong, to be flexible, and to have perseverance and the ability to survive, almost to be superwomen (183).

Latin families today represent a kind of transnational family, with branches of family members living in more than one society. This kind of modified extended family, with kin living near and far, is one manifestation of the new kind of family that is impacted by the global context in which they live. Familism helps Latino families gain entry into their communities when they move from their homelands. Among Chicanas, for example, familism and patriarchy are closely connected. There are very traditional divisions of labor that bind women to the role of mother and household caretaker, while still pushing her into the labor market because of economic necessity. Women often take the lead in defining the goals for the family, while the husband determines who can work and who should go to school (Segura, 1986).

Latino families are often the victims of discrimination and class exploitation as they enter American society, reflecting the inequitable structural conditions that impact their families' lives.

Asians

Another group strongly affected by the global context and discrimination are Asians. To summarize the history of Asian immigrants to the United States is, again, a nearly impossible task. Certainly the experiences of Chinese, Japanese, Korean, Filipinos, Vietnamese, and Cambodians in settling in the United States have all differed. Among Asian American groups there are more than 32 different primary languages. Religious beliefs vary greatly, with Chinese following Buddhism and Christianity; Japanese following Shintoism, Buddhism, and Christianity; Filipinos being Catholic; Koreans primarily Protestant; and Southeast Asians, like Vietnamese, being Buddhist and Catholic. It is best to separate their stories following a chronology of immigration.

Chinese

The first Asian immigrants were Chinese men who came as early as 1785, although the large numbers began arriving in 1848 with the discovery of gold in California. They worked in the West in railroads, laundry, and agriculture. They left China seeking the "gold mountain" (Lee, 1996, 250). After the U.S. government passed the Chinese Exclusion Act in 1882, no further Chinese laborers were allowed into the country, and those who were here were not allowed to bring in family members. The men lived family-less, without connection to their homes and heritage. America's capitalist economy wanted Asian men as workers, but not their families, because it was more profitable. If families were not with the workers, the companies did not have to pay for housing, clothing, education (Espiritu, 1997). The unattached male could be a more flexible source of labor (17).

When the law was changed in 1930, Chinese merchants once again brought to America their families and women whom they could marry. By this time Chinese citizens were able to buy businesses and develop into small producers who owned family-run establishments (Lee, 1996, 251). They were very much like the wage-economy type we saw in Western families, in that everyone contributed to the family upkeep, and income was pooled.

From 1943 to 1965, when the quota law was finally repealed, the main Chinese immigrants were women coming to be reunited with their husbands, or young women who had been matched up with the Chinese men who were here earlier. Until the 1970s, Chinese immigrants were entire families who settled in metropolitan areas in Chinatowns and worked as service workers and laborers (251). They worked long hours in garment sweatshops and restaurants, and spent little time with their families, in an effort to ensure economic survival. Asians in the United States have had to struggle to maintain family and community life in a non-supportive environment (Espiritu, 1997, 21). Early on they formed bachelor communities, when they could not import their families, and maintained wives and families in Asia.

The most recent Chinese immigrants are those who come to the United States for education from Hong Kong, Taiwan, and China. Some were worried about the transfer of Hong Kong from British to Chinese rule, and others maintain two homes, one in Hong Kong and another in the United States. These Chinese are of a different socioeconomic status than the first waves of Chinese immigrants. They come educated and with money, ready to enter the middle classes of U.S. society.

In addition, there are migrants struggling their way to the United States, sometimes using illegitimate means in a desperate attempt to improve their lives. Recently there has been a rise of illegal immigration of Chinese seeking jobs in the West. Some resort to extraordinary means, like hiding in boxcars or cargo vans to make their way to the United States.

Traditional Chinese families put an emphasis on Confucian religion, which focuses on harmonious relationships and interdependence. The extended family often lived within the same complex; the family was patriarchal, with males, especially fathers and eldest sons, in the positions of power. Marriages were arranged with husbands dealing in the outside world and providing for the families and wives caring for the homes, following a similar path to the cult of true womanhood in the West. Mothers were self-sacrificing and were told to be "thrice obeying": expected to obey their fathers and eldest brothers in youth, their husbands when they married, and their sons, upon the deaths of their husbands. Historically, this was the way the traditional Chinese family operated (Lee, 1996, 252).

Contemporary Chinese families have changed their functioning, with a shift to more nuclear families, more involvement of women in decision making, less reliance on children to care for the elderly, and earning power shared by all family members (254). Chinese families in the United States tend to maintain a chain migration and a modified extended family structure.

Japanese

Japanese immigration to the United States came as a result of changes in Japan starting in 1868, when the old, feudal system was overthrown by a coup. Japan began to modernize, in reaction to Western modernization and in fear that the West would try to colonize Japan. The country quickly introduced industrialization, and farmers were forced to pay higher taxes to finance the overhaul of the economy. Many peasants came to the United States in order to send home money to pay the farm taxes (Matsui, 1996, 269). The traditions of the *issei* (first-generation immigrants) closely followed those practiced at home. The *nisei* were the second generation in the United States; they were the children born here. *Sansei* are the third generation, born from 1945 to 1965; *yonsei* and *gosei* are the fourth and fifth generations, respectively, born in the United States.

In the first immigration era, when Japanese were allowed to leave their country after two centuries of not being allowed to travel outside of Japan, the premodern family had a sense of filial piety, which was a respect for age, seniority, and a deep preference for male children. There were clear-cut patterns of deference for elders and others in authority. Families valued cohesion and harmony over individual achievement, and there were specific roles taken between generations of family members (269).

The first wave of immigrants went to Hawaii as contract workers on the plantations, but soon after arriving they were lured to the mainland by the promise of higher wages. Single men would often choose brides from home, selecting from photographs for arranged marriages. In 1905, there was an anti-Japanese movement in the United States, mainly because organized labor found Japanese workers a threat to their own employment. This anti-Japanese sentiment grew, and in California legislation was passed that prohibited Japanese from buying land; eventually the U.S. government passed the Immigration Act of 1924 that halted any further Japanese immigration.

In 1942, Franklin Roosevelt signed Executive Order 9066, which authorized the military to exclude anyone from a community without a trial should the government deem it necessary to do so. Between April and September 1942, more than 120,000 Japanese American citizens were rounded up and placed in "relocation camps" because the military believed them to be a threat to national security. The United States was in the midst of World War II at the time, and there was fear that these citizens were somehow more loyal to the emperor of Japan than to the U.S. government. This wartime evacuation lasted until 1945. The United States did not have similar types of camps for German Americans or Italian Americans, although it was at war with both those countries as well. Some were interned in the Japanese camps.

Japanese families traditionally have shown great respect for the older generations, with women being considered the transmitters of traditions (273). Hierarchy is important in Japanese families, with ranking based on gender and age. The fathers and sons hold the most power, and the earlier immigrant generations are more likely to follow the traditional patriarchal and hierarchical family structure. Families are restrained in their communication patterns, so that one is hesitant to ask questions or speak out in groups, following the tradition of respecting elders and those of higher rank. Mothers and children form very strong bonds, with children sleeping with their parents until they are quite old. The group is most important, so that one is expected to be conforming, moral, and responsible. People fear ostracism from the family and the group; it is crucial to belong at all costs.

Newer Asian Immigrants: Koreans, Filipinos, Vietnamese, Cambodians

In 1965, the Amendment to the Immigration and Naturalization Service Act of 1955 opened doors for Asian immigrants and led to an influx of groups that previously had been restricted. Again, chain migration and the modified extended family played an important role in the migration of Asians. The change in laws brought Koreans who came with their nuclear families, bringing other family members as soon as they could afford to. The Koreans were better educated and upwardly mobile, willing to move wherever jobs, schools, or opportunities were available (Kim, 1996, 283). Because they are recent immigrants, they still maintain contact with Korea through newspapers, radio, and phone, and they return home regularly.

They, too, follow the hierarchy described for other Asian groups, with strict segregation of the sexes and clear role expectations. Generational boundaries are firm, with a respect for elders and those of higher rank (284). Marriage is the joining of two families, not individuals, and couples are expected to be faithful, to have mutual respect, and to make joint decisions. The major source of family problems seems to be in-law relations, particularly between daughters-in-law and mothers-in-law because of the possessiveness of mothers over their sons.

Filipino families came from a tropical archipelago of more than 7,000 islands in the middle of the Asian trade routes (Santa Rita, 1996, 324). Their country has quite a varied history, having been colonized and settled by the Spanish, Chinese, Indonesians, Indians, and Malaysians, to name just a few. The Philippines was also an American colony from 1898 to 1946. Spanish Christian missionaries taught the Filipinos to fear retribution and to submit to authority, while the United States shaped the economy to meet its need for cheap labor and raw materials. Immigrants came to the U.S. mainland starting as farm workers in the 1920s. During World War II, Filipino soldiers served with the Allies and were allowed to enter the country as a result of their service. The United States established a military and naval base there, which only recently closed. More recently, Filipino working-class immigrants have been arriving as domestics, with the higher class entering as professionals.

Family life in the Philippines is very much the center of a person's world. This primacy of family leads to a loss of individuality in service to others. Gender roles are strict, and there is an "optimistic fatalism" (325) about one's future. This is the belief that things will probably go badly, but there is hope that it will not. Shame is to be avoided at all costs, and one is expected to return favors and be gracious. It is most important to belong and respect family and authority. Because Catholicism plays such an important role in Filipino society, the church is often the arbiter and mediator in times of stress. Allegiance and loyalty are primary among family members.

Vietnamese immigrants have come to the United States only within the past 20 years, in the aftermath of war in their country. Vietnam has gone through tremendous changes since the beginning of the twentieth century, first with French colonial rule, then Japanese occupation in World War II, and then the war between North and South Vietnam over freedom and reunification. The United States also intervened in that country's civil war.

Traditional Vietnam was heavily influenced by China in commerce, religion, and culture. Because China is a larger northern neighbor, Confucianism was exported early, and reverence for authority and hierarchy pervades this culture as well. The "self" is minimized for the good of the family and the society. The goal is harmony at all times. Ancestor worship plays an important part in the family, and elders are revered and respected. There are traditional rules of etiquette for family relations, and family members are expected to stay in their roles.

Because of the political upheavals in Vietnam the traditional family has been disrupted. Families were pitted against each other, depending on their political allegiances. In 1954 the Geneva Agreement divided Vietnam. Some families living in the north of Vietnam fled communist rule, and whole families were broken up when this political decision was made. War broke out between the two halves, and there was a massive exodus, with many refugees coming to the United States to escape the turmoil. Those who were loyal to the United States, which was intervening to aid South Vietnam, fled Saigon when the U.S. forces left the country.

This disruption led to massive changes in family structure. Where once families were large and extended, with generations living in the same household or in close proximity, now they were in small nuclear family groupings or living as individuals, without any family. The loss of the large extended family "meant a loss of a natural and familiar supportive system and an associated identity that one could only attain while living among a network of related people" (300).

Needless to say, there are many cultural differences between Vietnamese and Americans. When new Vietnamese come to the United States, conflicts arise based on these differing values. Often the children are forced to Americanize, while still maintaining Vietnamese values, like parental authority and respect for elders, which is supposed to last for a lifetime (Bankston & Zhou, 1998). Children are supposed to provide a lifetime of social security for their parents, which leads to culture clashes as the children become more assimilated (167).

Cambodian immigrants have an even more traumatic immigration history. Cambodia is a Southeast Asian country surrounded by Thailand, Laos, and Vietnam. The people are known as Khmer and are primarily Buddhist. Cambodia was primarily an agricultural country and a French colony, with very little interaction with the West until 1970, when it had the unfortunate position of being close to Vietnam during that country's war. In 1970 Cambodia was bombed by the U.S. military because supplies used in that war were being transported along the Ho Chi Minh Trail, which ran through eastern Cambodia. Thousands were homeless, and the bombings and disruption led to an overthrow of the government, which had been run by Prince Sihanouk. In 1975 the government of Cambodia came under the control of the Khmer Rouge, an authoritarian rule led by Pol Pot. His attempt to rid Cambodia of all Western influences resulted in a genocide.

Under Pol Pot and the Khmer Rouge, an estimated 2 million people were killed. In what has been called the "killing fields," whole families were slaughtered, tortured, disemboweled, and maimed. Children were separated from their families and placed in camps, forced to inform on their own parents. The horror that occurred has led to a form of hysterical blindness among many mothers and women, who were forced to watch the brutalities acted on their families. In 1978, the Vietnamese Army invaded Cambodia, and millions of refugees fled the country seeking safety, as they ran to Thailand across mine fields. This caused further maiming and death. Finally, when those who survived reached safety, they lingered in refugee camps.

Eventually, in 1980, the United States opened its doors to these refugees. Many of them have arrived with trauma deep in their psyches. The experience has had severe consequences in terms of their family lives, and many of them arrived poor and in need of extensive assistance. But Cambodians are a very proud people, seeking harmony and maintaining politeness. Family life, although disrupted, is still most important, for the maintenance of culture and for their very survival.

Summary

In this chapter we looked at the historical developments of the Western family, particularly in England and the United States. Using the ideas of the family-based, family-wage, and family-consumer economy, we began to understand that the family has evolved in relation to the development of industry, the move to the cities, and the growing modernization taking place under capitalism. By looking at the ideology of the cult of true womanhood, true manhood, and the construction of "normal" sexuality, we traced the rise of the modern era and began to look at whether the family was nuclear, extended, or a modified extended family.

Seeing that the family seems to have developed a modified extended family form, we looked at immigrant families and the point-of-entry theory. We saw the importance of chain migration and the modified extended family in the immigrant experience, and we explored family life among African Americans, Latinos, and Asians who were employed as laborers in the United States. Finally we looked at some of the newer immigrant groups to the United States, the process by which they came to this country, and the impact on their family life.

Throughout this discussion we found that capitalism and the power differentials generated from it have affected the course of family history for different groups of people. We saw that the history of the family influences how the family operates in today's society and that structural conditions from the past inform structural conditions in contemporary society.

CHAPTER 5

History of the Family in the Semiperiphery and Periphery

F or peoples in parts of the world other than the West—particularly those parts colonized by the West—the story of the family is quite different than the one told in previous chapters. Although industrialization, urbanization, and modernization occurred in these periphery and semiperiphery countries, it came later and as an exported force. Great Britain, France, Germany, Spain, Portugal, and the United States needed expanded markets, as well as resources and labor to fuel their development processes. For these they turned to Latin America, Asia, and parts of Africa. Thus, perhaps the best way to understand the lives of immigrants in the United States and to frame the history of the family in parts of the world other than the core is to understand the nature of colonialism and the rise of Western imperialism as they have impacted the internal histories of the countries with which we deal next. Each country and culture has its own unique history. But with colonization, an international movement toward industrialization, urbanization, and modernization has had significant impact on each place. A dynamic process of acculturation occurred, creating a whole new entity of family life.

In this chapter, we focus on family life in Latin America, Africa, and Asia, because we in the West know so little about families in those parts of the world. Also, there is enough material available about individual countries on these continents to give readers an overview of family practices there.

Colonialism

As industrialization was growing in the West during the nineteenth and early twentieth centuries, European nations began to view Latin American, Asian, and African societies as a source of industrial raw materials and as a market for Western manufactured goods (Duiker & Spielvogel, 1994, 857). Western nations had always engaged in trade with Latin America, Asia, and Africa, but now surplus goods produced in the West were exported to these countries in return for oil, tin, rubber, and other materials needed to fuel the West's growing industrial machine. It became important for the West to find new sources of materials as well as new outlets for their products; otherwise, economic depression would occur.

As the West expanded into other parts of the world, a process called *imperialism* took place. In this context, the word *imperialism* means the efforts of capitalist states to seize markets, cheap raw materials, and lucrative sources for the investment of capital in the countries beyond Western civilization (858). The motives were primarily economic, but they also had political, moral, and self-interest implications: Colonists wanted to gain an advantage over their rivals and to expand their markets and sphere of influence.

Slowly but surely the West made inroads into most parts of the world, sometimes with the assistance of local political elites who saw the advantages that would come to them. Their loyalty was either earned or bought, by economic rewards or by conferring on them positions of authority in the colony. This was a form of *indirect rule* by which the colonial power still pulled the strings of the local officials; a figurehead local authority usually acted on the decisions made by colonial advisers. If there was resistance to this foreign intervention, a new set of officials from the mother country would replace the local authorities (869).

The resistance to colonial rule often came in societies where there was a long tradition of national cohesion and independence, for example, in countries in the central parts of Africa. In those places, the Western colonizers would make every effort to eradicate resistance and to obliterate the local tradition and culture. That resistance still has ramifications today, after most of the colonies have become independent, and the implications continue to be played out in contemporary political entanglements throughout the world.

The philosophy of colonialism followed the "survival of the fittest" ideology and believed that "might makes right." There was also a moral argument to justify colonialism—societies had to adapt to change in order to survive—and thus, the West was morally obligated to assist the "backward" nations of the world to adapt to the challenges of the modern world (869). It was a Social Darwinism in which the colonizers used moral, scientific, and religious arguments to justify their behaviors; they did not try to assimilate with their subjects, but rather, lived as if they were still in their home countries.

Usually a class system developed, with the white elite in positions of power, assisted by an advisory council (also often white Europeans). The wealthy and educated classes were often lighter skinned, and with light skin came higher status and more power. The class system determined who could vote, who would be educated, and who did what work. The local elites of these countries adopted the colonizers' behavior, dress, language, and lifestyles. The middle class developed as foremen, supervisors, and office workers who assisted the functioning of the bureaucracies to help the system run. They, too, often emulated the styles of the colonizers. Usually members of the lower classes and rural dwellers were more likely to continue their traditional cultural practices.

The economic relationship between colonizer and colonized was the most important one. Usually it was in the best interests of the colonizers to export raw materials and import manufactured goods. The system exploited the local peoples because they could not produce the goods that they consumed. Products were made or grown locally for export, while items needed to survive were imported from other countries. Important infrastructures were built, like highways, railroads, communications systems, and power plants, which benefited the colonized, and later became structures that they inherited when they achieved independence. For the most part, however, colonized people ceased feeding their own families.

In action, colonialism varied depending on the colonizers and the countries within which they operated. For example, the French tried to impose a central administrative system much like their own political system, while the British sometimes treated local aristocrats in a colonial society like the landed gentry in Britain (875). Because most colonizers of Africa did not see great economic potential, they invested less there than they did, for example, in Latin America. So there was variation to the pattern of colonization, although there were mostly similarities in the process.

The main colonizers of the West were Spain, Great Britain, Germany, Russia, and the United States, all seeking to enhance their wealth and power. They carved up the world into separate spheres of influence, each country leaving its imprints on the cultures and political structures on the places they colonized. Family life in the colonies was directly impacted by changes in the broader societies; traditional family systems were forced to adapt to new technological advances, and where once the family followed indigenous cultural patterns, it now had to become flexible, to meet the economic needs of the growing capitalist world order.

Latin America

Colonization in Latin America, including Central and South America, was begun by explorers from the Iberian Peninsula as early as 1492 and involved a mix of many cultures and people. Many of the indigenous peoples were killed off either by massacre or disease, or were absorbed into the colonizers' culture through intermarriage. A small number of them did survive to maintain their native cultures. Those who intermarried formed another group, called *mestizo,* who were a mix of Spanish or Portuguese and native peoples of the region. The Spanish and the Portuguese began to colonize as early as the fifteenth century. African slaves were brought to the continent beginning in the sixteenth century; they served in the plantation system as human labor and eventually in the cities as servants, tradesmen, and miners. Colonizers of Spanish origin came in search of precious metals like gold and silver, beginning with the arrival of Fernando Cortes in 1519. The Portuguese colonized Brazil, and Spain established colonies in the rest of Latin America (728). The Spanish colonies lasted from the sixteenth century until the nineteenth, and Brazil even remained a colony of Portugal until its independence in 1822. The Spanish colonial system lasted until 1898, ending in the Spanish American War.

During colonization an oppressed class of wage laborers evolved who worked in agriculture, tending the huge estates of the Spanish and Portuguese landowners.

The *hacienda* system, which is still a feature of Latin America, included the dependent workers, the landowners, and powerless and poor peasants called *campesinos*. Indians worked their own lands as marginal farmers.

The Catholic Church played an important role in Spanish colonialism through the use of missionaries who were first sent to Mexico in 1532 and soon thereafter to other parts of Latin America to convert the native peoples. They built enormous monasteries, convents, universities, and local schools, which were crucial in bringing the Catholic religion to the local peoples and in influencing them to adhere to Western social forms. The Roman Catholic Church had significant power politically; a system of oligarchy (a state governed by just a few people, all connected either by family or friendship) developed and helped determine who was elected and how administration was carried out.

By the late 1800s, Latin America was quite prosperous for the landed classes. Brazil was providing coffee to the West, beef and wheat were exported from Argentina, coffee and bananas were coming from Central America. The economies of the continent were based on export, which made them dependent on Western capitalist nations (Duiker, 1999, 833). Britain and the United States had made inroads through their investments in the region, particularly by the 1880s. However, the poor in these countries were still dominated by rural elites, and newly freed slaves were still at the bottom of the system. Latin America was dependent on foreigners for its economic survival.

By the early 1900s, westernization had been established throughout Latin America. The economy, based on export, led to modernization of the cities; a growing middle class, much as we had seen in the West; and growing numbers of teachers, bureaucrats, and military officers, all employed in service to the economic system that had arisen. Many people of the middle class found the setup comfortable and resisted the revolutionary forces in the region who were agitating for return of the economies and political systems to local rule.

The social and cultural life of Latin America has had a multiplicity of forms, a complex pattern and mixture of European, African, and indigenous peoples. The cultural mold is not rigid; it is a blend of many forces. Individual countries differ in their indigenous cultures, in how colonization took place, and in the reactions of the peoples to colonization. It might look, on the surface, like Latin America has taken on the ways of the West, but the reality, under the surface, is far more complicated.

There are some characteristics that unite Latin American cultures, with family life being one of the most important. In many ways, past patterns, which predated colonialism or have at least survived and thrived in spite of colonialism, are particularly noteworthy.

Family Life in Latin America

Family life in Latin America differs significantly from that of Europe or the United States. The family is one of Latino culture's most central and active institutions, and industrialization and modernization did have not the same effects in Latin America as they did in the West. The model we described in Chapter 4, of a family-based, family-wage, and family-consumer economy, does not quite fit. In Latin America, modern capitalism impacted the people, but the citizens of those places also acted as active agents in the historical process (Smith, 1978, 338).

Upper-Class Families in Latin America

Some historians of Latin America view the family like a corporation, particularly under the colonial era that lasted from the sixteenth through the nineteenth century (Kuznesof & Oppenheimer, 1985). They mean that society was divided into various "corporations," self-contained entities that interacted and cooperated for the sake of the general welfare. These historians see the church, the military, merchants, and artisan groups as corporations, all allowed to regulate their own members and practices (Lockhart & Schwartz, 1983). The family was one of these corporations too. Given the hacienda system and the importance of the church and military in keeping civil order, this description is an appropriate one for early Latin America under colonialism, particularly in the early to late nineteenth century. This is one way the Latino family differs from the Western family.

Another way in which Latino family history differs from the Western model is the concept of *patriarchalism*. Latino families formed hierarchies, social systems with a pecking order, from the youngest person to the senior person, who was in charge of protecting and dominating. The senior person, usually the father or grandfather, controlled the workings of his kindred, and kinship was *bilateral*, meaning that kin could be counted through both sides, the mother's and the father's. The extended kin was crucially important in Latin America; families often lived in close proximity to each other and were integrally involved in members' daily lives.

Ritual kinship was also important in Latino families. Ritual kinship exists when families "adopt" others into their families, even if there is no blood relation. This is an important distinction to remember. As we saw when we discussed Latino immigrants to the United States, people who were not blood kin played necessary roles and took on reciprocal responsibilities for their adoptive family members. *Compadres* (godparents) are crucial in providing economic assistance, encouragement, and even behavior correction to children, and children are easily transferred to other extended family members in times of personal crisis. Adoptive children, taken on without formal legal procedures, are seen as one's own, for whom the extended family has responsibility.

The family is the pillar of society in Latin America, and there is an enormous respect for authority and people in power positions. This follows from the Roman Catholic religion as well as from the hierarchy of the family. All family members are expected to marry and carry on the lineage of the family. For that reason, marriage has been extremely important and has become a responsibility for the church, the state, and the family.

Marriage rites in Latin America were highly elaborate and extremely expensive during the colonial era and through most of the nineteenth and early twentieth centuries (Kuznesof & Oppenheimer, 1985, 217). But quite interestingly, during that period, people postponed marriage until later in life and instead formed consensual unions (similar to living together today). In fact, 30–50 percent of births were children born out of wedlock. When a woman was "deflowered" by a man it was assumed he would marry her, and the expectation was binding. It became his responsibility to be her savior through marriage since he owed her something, having taken her virginity (217).

Under colonialism, parental consent was required for marriage, and parents on either side could refuse if they felt that the marriage would grossly dishonor the family. Disobeying parental authority could lead to disinheritance, but unequal marriages were allowed if the woman's virginity and honor were at stake. In this case the church, which carried enormous clout, could outweigh the objections of the family.

Slowly, industrialization had a major impact on Latin families. By the early 1900s marriages were becoming freer, with people choosing their own partners. Industrialization led to a decline in the use of dowries, which had been a crucial component of marital rituals. It also led to a decline in guaranteed inheritance, which had been an expectation in colonial Latin family life. Guaranteed inheritance was money or property that was handed down upon the death of a parent.

Under colonialism the elites of Latin American families often intermarried in order to consolidate wealth and property or for political gain (219). Women and men were given equal inheritance rights, and all legitimate children, regardless of sex, age, or birth order, received equal amounts. But women's rights were otherwise not equal. Adult males were given more respect and power within the family, with the head of the household having the most power of all. As Western values penetrated Latin society, there was some movement away from this norm, but for the most part, the head of the household and the eldest males still wielded the power over the rest of the family.

The family was crucial in most aspects of Latin American life. Family life influenced the way colonization evolved; it also influenced political life, the government, the church, and even how the urban landscape developed. It influenced the economics of the region, particularly through the rural elites, who wielded enormous power in acquiring property and growing the needed crops and resources for export. In Mexico, for example, ritual kinship ties among the elites had an impact in fostering corruption, with family members providing employment and business for other family members and aided in positioning Mexico as part of the globalizing economy.

One needs to note, when discussing Latin American families, that most of the data used to explain the history comes from family reconstitution methods, through census data and legal archival records. For that reason the history is very much centered on upper-class families; little was written about poorer peasants, Indians, and laborers in the plantation, hacienda system. Thus it is a limited story; the reality is more complex and needs to be viewed with race, class, and gender as part of the picture.

Poor Families in Latin America

Indigenous peoples of Latin America and small landowners were primarily based in the rural areas, where land was leased from wealthy plantation owners.

Poor people would work small plots of land, while others were employed as wage workers or artisans. Many people were unskilled laborers who worked on short-term contracts, and there were many migrants who were poor and homeless. Freed slaves, mulattos, immigrants from Europe, Indians, and other nonwhites were vagrants, roaming in search of day wages. Men were often employed sporadically, and poor women were often forced into prostitution (Pino, 1997).

Freed slaves made up a large portion of the population at the end of the colonial era. In Brazil, for example, slave families had been recognized under Portuguese law, and families maintained a level of organization and stability upon being freed in 1888. Agriculture had been the primary basis for the economy in Latin America, and freed slaves continued to be employed in farming and homesteading. Kinship ties were important to these families, as such ties had been in Africa and on the plantations when they were slaves. Female-headed households were not uncommon, but that was also true for the great majority of women who were not of the upper class. In fact, the great majority of adult free women—white, mulatto, Creole, and African-born—living in rural areas were not married, and as many as 45 percent of all households in the slums of Rio de Janeiro, Brazil, were headed by women (15).

The Impact of Industrialization on Latin American Families

When industrialization came to Latin America, it did not look like it did in the West. First of all, it came later—not until the 1930s. Cities grew, but factories did not, since the economy was still agriculturally based. "The function and structure of the family varied by economic condition" (Pino, 1997, 17), so when families moved to cities they maintained their extended family systems. For the upper classes, that meant that the landed classes controlled the economy, and they used their large extended family systems to obtain jobs for family members. Family connections also remained important for attaining political office.

We might say that the modified extended family became the structure of family life in Latin America. People no longer lived under the same roof, but families remained connected, by telephone and by living nearby. When families moved to the cities, often they maintained family or homes in the rural areas; sometimes individual men migrated, leaving the women behind.

However, for poorer Latin Americans it was not uncommon for men to establish two families, the official one left at home and the city family. In Brazil, for example, this led to the nuclearization of the family, meaning that urban workers began to give up their extended family connections in their search for new jobs in cities. There was no room in the cities for the extended families, and the sense of obligation to family back home eroded (18). Even if they did maintain connections, it was not common to share daily living activities.

It is important to note that the discussion in this chapter has focused on the Latin American family *in history*. Later in the book we look at families in parts of contemporary Latin America. Even if the large extended family has declined historically, the sense of family remains a pillar of Latin American life even today.

Africa

The slave trade, which was the main source of European profit out of Africa during the eighteenth century, was abolished by the 1880s. This form of business had usually been carried out through the use of intermediaries and merchants, using African rulers for trafficking. Slavery had begun centuries earlier, in ancient times, but reached massive proportions in the seventeenth and eighteenth centuries, with millions of slaves removed from their homes and forced onto ships to be exported to the West (Duiker & Spielvogel, 1994, 591). It was the colonization of the Americas that was the primary reason for the increase in slave trade. Workers were needed to cultivate the sugar cane on the plantations. Although Portugal began the practice of slavery, the Spanish soon followed, and then Great Britain and the United States.

Current estimates hold that as many as 10 million slaves were brought to the West from slavery's beginnings in the early sixteenth century until its end in the late nineteenth (592). The mortality rate was high, due to mistreatment of slaves as well as their lack of immunity to certain diseases. Slaves were obtained through a variety of means, as prisoners or war captives, or they were born to people who were already enslaved. Often slaves were kidnapped from their home villages and then traded in large marketplaces for gold, guns, and other European-produced goods. Males brought a higher price than did females, because of their ability to do heavier labor on the plantations.

Slave trade had differing impacts in differing regions of Africa. In areas where the slave trade was heavy, especially along the coasts, it decimated groups of people. In other places it had little impact. As the West penetrated Africa, travelers brought with them corn, peanuts, and manioc, which increased food production. Because African tribal rulers refused to let the Europeans venture beyond the coastal areas, westernization was not as quick nor as significant in the interior as it had been elsewhere on the continent. Africans tended to resist European encroachment, and sometimes tribes allied with each other to resist the West's efforts to take over trade (595).

However, as the slave trade declined, there was an increase in European economic influence, especially along the "slave coast" (West Africa). Westerners began to engage in export and import of natural resources (862). Peanuts, timber, hides, and palm oil were produced in exchange for textiles and Western manufactured goods. With the increase of commerce came the desire on the part of European governments to establish footholds in Africa. Missionaries were sent to convert local peoples, and a growing number of Western-educated Africans became entrepreneurs and middlemen. In fact, historians have described the process by which European culture crept into Africa as an "informal empire" (863).

By the beginning of the 1880s, Africa was still independent, with European rule limited to the fringes, as in Algeria, the West Coast, and South Africa. Nigeria, Senegal, Egypt, and Mozambique were loose protectorates of the West. However, after 1880 there was a scramble to carve up the continent, and by 1900 each area had been claimed by either Britain, Germany, France, or Belgium. Fueled mainly by rivalries among these Western countries, imperialism intensified as they found a new continent on which to work out their nationalistic hostilities.

Missionaries played an important role in the colonization of Africa. Their desire to convert the "pagans" to Christianity led them to convince their governments to take over the regions where they were based. In their ethnocentric bias, the missionaries assumed that it was the responsibility of the "white man" to bring the benefits of Western civilization through the three c's: Christianity, commerce, and civilization (867).

Colonization was going on throughout the world at this time; it was just a matter of time until Africa became part of this global process. With the discovery of natural resources, like gold and diamonds in South Africa, the imperialist battleground was set for yet another continent, this time Africa.

Family Life in Africa

Africa, which is almost four times the size of the United States, is the biggest continent after Asia. It consists of more than 50 independent countries with more than 700 million people and more than 1,000 languages. Africa is also always changing, with people moving to cities and then back again to the rural regions (Ramsay, 1997, 3). It is a much more complex continent than is North America, in that it has a large number of nations, cultures, and tribal affiliations. It is also an enormously diverse continent, with varied household arrangements, kinship systems, and religious beliefs, all of which impact family life. It is in fact unfair to compare the continent of Africa with the country of the United States. Given its complexity, it is not easy to generalize about family life in Africa. For each statement there is an exception.

Past civilizations are extremely important for understanding the family in Africa. They are the source of pride and community, and the past is integrally connected to the present, through ties to ancestors and the land. Ancient kingdoms like Great Zimbabwe, the empires of Mali and Ghana, the Fulani Caliphate of Northern Nigeria, and the Pharaohs of Egypt are but a few of the great cultures that thrived on the continent.

Africa is called the cradle of civilization, and archaeologists have established that it is there that humankind began. The land is where the majority of Africans live; most of Africa is still rural and undeveloped, with major cities, as sophisticated as those of the West, dotting the terrain. The land is where ancestors are buried and where the people have always provided for themselves.

Family is the center of African life. People live in large extended families, based on tribal affiliation. Children are precious, as a continuation of ancient connections and for economic assistance. Loyalty to one's family is valued over all else, and the belief is that "I am because we are." Family life is spiritual as well as social, in that people believe their ancestors influence them. Spiritist religions (worship of nature, animals, and ancestors) coexist with Christianity, Islam, and other religions. The indigenous belief systems involve the use of healers as well as Western medicine, and there is a unique blend of ancient and contemporary religions, art, and music, all of which are central to the social life of Africans.

Virtually no work has been done on the history of homosexuality anywhere in sub-Sahara Africa. There is some anthropological evidence of same-sex sexual

Photo 5.1   Contemporary African siblings. Photographer: Patti Carman

education given prior to marriage among various tribes, but as yet no major piece of work exists to document it. Nonetheless, in South Africa there is some evidence that when, with the coming of the colonists, black workers migrated to mines to find employment to feed their families back in the homelands, there were "mine marriages" (Moodie, Ndatshe, & Sibuyi, 1989, 411). In these temporary relationships, carried on early in the 1900s, "boys" would care for the older men like wives, in exchange for pay and gifts. The relationships were exclusive; thus they were called "mine marriages." The "boys" were expected to be passive sexual recipients, and when they got older, they themselves would become "men" with their own "boys" (418).

Africa was unique in not limiting fertility, often against the wishes of the missionaries. There was very little desire to control female sexuality, and a pro-natal attitude flourished. In other words, procreation and childbearing were encouraged. In addition, there was a strong emphasis on ancestor reverence and a focus on the generational family life (Caldwell, 1997). However, conditions for women deteriorated under the colonialists in Africa (Boserup, 1971, 5–6). The European settlers, administrators, and technical advisors ignored the female agricultural labor force and farming systems that had long been in place when they introduced modern commercial agriculture. Thus they subverted the position of women.

Because Africa is so complex, it would be a mistake to generalize—there may be several concurrent histories operating at once, for each region, for each country, and for each ethnic group of people within the country. Since colonization differed depending on the region, on the resistance to colonization, and on ethnic history, the concepts used in the study of Western history—like family-based, family-wage, and family-consumer—have not been applied to African families. Although the cult of true womanhood might have been relevant to the colonizers' families, it had little impact on the indigenous lives of Africans.

We next discuss two African countries as examples of how colonization, industrialization, and modernization have affected those places. Readers who find these stories of interest may want to explore the richness of African families by further reading about other countries, tribes, or ethnic groups.

Nigerian Families

The Niger River runs through this West African country of 103 million people and has provided a vehicle for communication and trade among the four major tribes—the Hausa, the Fulani, the Igbo, and the Yoruba. It appears that ancient cultures existed in this region, which was rich in oil, minerals, and other natural resources. Pre-colonial Nigeria produced crafts as well as cotton and indigo, and there was a lucrative textile industry.

Slave trade was extensive in this region. With slavery, the country was disrupted by the dislocation of countless men and women. Entire villages were decimated, with slave traders carting off as many as 600 villagers at a time. One estimate was that in a period of 50 years, as many as 500,000 people were sold into slavery (Bascom, 1968, 84, as quoted in Hutter, 1988, 183). Many African Americans today come from Nigerian origins; the southern boundary of Nigeria is the Atlantic Ocean, which shares 500 miles of coastline.

By the time the British arrived in the late nineteenth century, there were already ongoing regional disputes, based on tribal and regional affiliation. When the British conquered Nigeria it chose to divide and rule (Ramsay, 1999, 55). Because of ethnic animosities, Hausas dominated the north, Yorubas the west, and the Igbo the east. The British co-opted the northern Hausas and ruled indirectly through them. In the southwest, the missionaries were encouraged to convert the Yorubas and introduce cocoa cultivation to export to Britain and the West. Meanwhile, the Igbo in the southeast became government employees and traders who moved about the colony more freely.

There are between 200 and 250 ethnic groups in Nigeria, each with distinctive linguistic groupings and dialects as well as political and cultural peculiarities. This diversity makes it difficult to find common ground. Understanding these regional conflicts is crucial to understanding some of the current dilemmas facing Nigeria. Nigeria is in the midst of a grave political crisis, very much based on tribal antagonisms and ethnic strife. Although it is the second richest country in Africa because of its abundant natural resources, it has one of the worst political and human rights records.

Nigeria is 80 percent rural, and family life was and still is based on the land. Traditional families are large and extended, all related by blood, several generations living together. Usually the authority in the family is vested in the eldest male, and everyone's status is defined by seniority. All family members have obligations for economic assistance to kin, even if they move to the city for employment.

It appears that the modified extended form is often the one adopted when some family members move to the city. In the countryside, generations live together, engaged in subsistence farming, child rearing, and typical agrarian tasks. Modernization affected these villages, with the advent of electricity and other innovations; however, for the most part, life continues in the traditional forms, as it has for generations.

In the city, it is not uncommon for nuclear families to form, but kinship networks remain crucial in understanding family relationships. Ties with families back home continue; people raise their families, live with them, and are buried with them, now in the cities rather than the countryside. People marry through the kinship network, and marriage is seen as the joining of two extended families. The nuclear family might be the smallest unit, but it is embedded in the larger extended one. People of the same ethnic group form a kinship network through which individuals find work or further their economic interests.

Because marriage is an alliance between two extended families, it has always been undertaken with great care and negotiation (Nwadiora, 1996, 130). This process has remained throughout historical periods, following the traditions of the culture. Among the Igbo, for example, the process can take months, through the use of a middleperson who does the investigation on both sides. Soothsayers are asked to determine the auspiciousness of the marriage, and if this turns out successfully a dowry is negotiated, as a token of appreciation to the family who raised the bride. After the ceremony of marriage, both families seal the relationships with gifts back and forth. The couple is charged with maintaining moral integrity and the understanding that they are eternally tied. Everyone knows that the family and the community, both living and dead, are watching them (131).

Once children are born, in fact, the mother and her children are considered the bedrock of Nigerian family life. Polygyny is common, and has remained so throughout the colonization period and today. Although not legally sanctioned, it is the ideal for men who see it as a symbol of high status. For example, among the Yoruba in the rural areas, each wife is allotted a room or her own dwelling; the husband has his own room or house, and the children sleep with their mothers. In some compounds there is a general room for the boys (Otite, 1991, 133). Among the Igbo, separate houses are maintained so as to minimize friction between the wives. With urbanization there has been a decline in polygyny in Nigeria, but it still occurs with quite a bit of frequency, with no stigma attached to the practice. Since residence is patrilocal once married, all the members of a compound form one patrilineage.

Women with more sons or first wives are given primacy over other wives, and having a son is a source of power in families. It is sons who have inheritance rights; sons share in the family farmland; sons participate in family discussions and in family decision making, so the mother gains from her sons' shares and involvement (Mere, 1976, 156–157).

Elders have historically mediated conflicts and teach the younger generation ethical and moral values through storytelling and the use of proverbs. The hierarchy of the family consists of the man, the woman, the sons, and then the daughters. Sometimes the eldest son is given the role of the third parent of the family (133). Also among the Igbo, brothers are expected to marry the wives of their late brothers so as to provide for the widow and to honor what the brother held dear.

It is not at all uncommon for Nigerian women to work, to go to school, or to own businesses that support or supplement the family's income. Eldest daughters raise the younger children while the mothers are employed. Women are expected to contribute by providing food, rearing children, and disbursing the proceeds from any of her trades or sales. Children are expected to contribute based on age and abilities. With urbanization there has been a change in the status of women, with greater education and employment opportunities open to them. With greater earning capacity, women have greater freedom and greater say in decision making. Male dominance has also diminished as a result of evolving gender roles.

If a Nigerian family moves to the city, these patterns are still expected of them, although the family size diminishes. Kin will live nearby and be involved in family life, but not live in compounds as they did back home. There is still the intention of returning to the family compound upon retirement, and family members, especially wives and children, return there regularly for visits and family obligations.

The development of a modified extended family seems to be the way the Nigerian families have adapted to historical changes and the effects of westernization upon their traditional culture. In fact, a form of acculturation has occurred, in which the original culture has adapted and changed, and the new culture has also adapted to form a uniquely Nigerian variant of that which exists in Western, core countries. Once again we can see that in Nigeria families have evolved over time but emerge intact.

Zimbabwean Families

Zimbabwe, located in southern Africa, not far from the Indian Ocean, was once the center of a prosperous culture based in trade of gold and other goods. Merchants ventured to the region and interacted with a great civilization, who lived in *zimbabwes*, which are great stone settlements. Slavery did not play an important role here because of the country's distance from the Atlantic Ocean, and the Shona society thrived until the nineteenth century. It was then that invaders from the south came and established a strong Ndebele kingdom. Now the population is 80 percent Shona and 16 percent Ndebele (Ramsay, 1999, 171).

In 1890, Cecil Rhodes, a British entrepreneur based in South Africa, Zimbabwe's southern neighbor, organized an invasion force, and although he encountered fierce resistance, he eventually established a white-run government as part of the British Crown colony. It was called a self-governed colony, but the reality was that the white settlers were in charge, even though they made up only 5 percent of the population.

After the country was proclaimed as Southern Rhodesia (after Cecil Rhodes), the African population was subjected to severe discrimination in schooling, employment, wages, and health care. Nearly 50 percent of all the land, including most of the best land, was confiscated by the state and turned into subsidized white settlers' large-scale commercial farms. Where there were once self-sufficient agricultural households, African men became low-paid migrants and women became unpaid subsistence farmers (Mazur, 1991, 511).

There was a forcible relocation of tens of thousands of African households to the poorest one-half of the land. In fact, 50–75 percent of the men were migrants, forced to search for employment wherever they could. They would occasionally return home and then go out again for work (Mazur & Mhloy, 1988, 1–2). Rhodesia was two nations, black and white and segregated. The economy had become like those in other dependent, periphery countries, in that it was based on export of crops, and two-thirds of the capital was foreign owned. Tobacco, cotton, oil seeds, gold, and nickel became the primary sources of income, with mining and manufacturing developing later.

In 1965 the Rhodesian government severed ties with Britain by proclaiming a Unilateral Declaration of Independence, but whites remained in power. From 1966 to 1980 there was a civil war, with an armed struggle by the African population to overthrow the white, colonial regime. The battles raged, and with war came a white exodus from the country, in fear of the consequences of the independence movement. The war had grave consequences for the rural population as well, because the white government destroyed lives and property in order to contain the guerrillas, whom the rural populations were supporting (Mazur, 1991, 524).

In elections held in 1980, the first African majority took most of the seats, and an independent Zimbabwe was declared. Once-incarcerated dissident Robert Mugabe was elected the first African prime minister.

Colonization and then civil war had significant consequences for families in Zimbabwe. As a result of the forced migration and dislocation during the late nineteenth and early twentieth centuries, families were torn apart, and traditional family patterns had to adapt. Christianity became the main religion, although the indigenous religions persisted, often side by side with Western religions. Spirits and ancestors still play a significant role in family life in Zimbabwe today. Although outwardly, families might have taken on European religious behaviors, behind the scenes traditional practices have remained crucial to family life (Mapondera, 1997, 1). Ancestral spirits are significant forces in guarding the family and ensuring health and well-being.

The traditional family, prior to colonization, centered around the clan, or large extended family. Then, as now, they were primarily rural. Male-headed households have always been the ideal; males have the ultimate decision-making power and control over property, including their wives. Polygyny, not uncommon, places the man at the center, and wives work his land in his name, all in the interests of the patrilineal and patrilocal family (Riphenburg, 1997, 34). For example, other members of the clan refer to father's brothers as fathers, and their children are brothers and sisters. The mother's brothers, on the other hand, are seen as the family's uncles, and their children are cousins.

Under customary law, women had very little in the way of legal rights. Men assumed positions of superiority, with senior women in the clan obtaining power only through the "patriarchically defined powers over junior females" (35). For example, women might have to defer to their husband's sisters, given their role in the patrilineage. Bride price was expected for women upon contracting for marriage, and it was seen as a payment from the husband and his father to the bride's father for her labor. With the payment came the rights to the children she bore, and should she divorce, her children would remain in her husband's family. When a woman married, she was still seen as a member of her own clan; although she lived

Photo 5.2   Contemporary sisters, Zimbabwe. Photographer: Elaine Leeder

and worked with her husband's family, she remained an outsider. Husbands and wives did not usually eat, work, or spend leisure time together (35).

With colonization these patterns endured, although they were severely tested by the migration out of the homelands and the move to cities by men in search of employment. Then, as now, women performed all food-related tasks and were expected to supplement the family income with non-agricultural tasks. Any money a woman earns went to the entire family, and she cannot acquire money for herself, since once a bride price is paid, her labor becomes her husband's possession (Mazur & Mhloy, 1988, 5).

Under the migrant labor system, women were forced to stay behind, relying on sporadic contributions from their husbands. They tended the subsistence farms, still having no access to credit, transportation, or marketing channels. They would supplement their incomes with beer making, sewing, knitting, home craft projects, and raising livestock for sale. Some formed cooperatives, but with no government assistance (7). Families were encouraged to have many children; the hope was that at least one family member would secure a good job and help the rest of the family, or that the large number of contributors might make the family economically viable.

For urban families, life was not much better. Rather than finding meaningful work, many of the men performed day labor or took sporadic employment in mining or commercial farming. Women were marginal workers, self-employed in work that was not self-supporting, or in informal sector employment that was low status and low paying. Because of lack of education, other jobs were not open, especially to women, and if women became pregnant, even their marginal employment would be terminated (8).

Needless to say, there were also class differences in this history. Those who found their way into the middle class under colonial rule had less economic hardship.

They found work as bureaucrats and middle-level managers within the system. As urban dwellers, in a country of primarily rural-based economy, their situation mirrored that of Western families, although the cultural traditions remained intact. There was quite a bit of political repression during the civil war, which led to enormous pain for large numbers of families whose members were either incarcerated or went off to guerrilla camps where they fought in the liberation struggle.

Since independence, many important legal changes have been made in the area of the family. Efforts to enhance women's positions now give them the right to become adults with full rights at the age of 18 (Riphenburg, 1997, 36). However, customary law often rules, even if civil law has granted women equality. Sometimes there are conflicts between civil and customary law, and rural families are more likely to follow what is the custom, either out of ignorance of the civil law or because of fear of antagonizing family members (37). Although laws have been designed to make things more equal and to encourage racial and gender parity, because of global economic need and conditions, poverty and economic hardship remain the primary picture in Zimbabwe today. However, one can easily say that the extended family is the most typical family form, with some modification based on changes in the economy. It is the extended family that remains at the center of life for the Zimbabwean peoples.

Asian Families

Asia is a huge continent, with a wide diversity of peoples and cultures. The continent is often divided for purposes of analysis and description into East Asia, South Asia, Southeast Asia, and the Asian Pacific. China and Japan are the primary forces in East Asia; India, Sri Lanka, Pakistan, Bhutan, Afghanistan, Bangladesh, Nepal, and the Maldive Islands are considered South Asia. Southeast Asia consists of the countries of Vietnam, Cambodia, Malaysia, Philippines, Laos, Myanmar (Burma), Indonesia, and Singapore. The Asian Pacific includes Micronesia, New Guinea, and Fiji, to name a few.

We focus here on China and India, the two largest countries in Asia, to describe the history of the family. The history of these countries is long, involved, and complicated. We consider them in this chapter only since they came into extensive contact with Western society and only since the rise of the industrial and modern era. Of course, the form that families in Asia have taken have ancient precursors. They should be explored in depth by readers who find any of these places interesting and warranting further study.

China: A Very Brief Overview

The history and achievements of Chinese civilization rival Greek and Roman societies at their best. China has a tremendous history of art, music, literature, culture, and sophistication and was a vast empire for centuries. The Chinese developed a written language before 5000 B.C.E. and had a dynastic system in which emperors ruled starting in 221 B.C.E. The dynasties began with Qin and continued until 1911, with the end of the Manchu Dynasty. Under this system, rulers would expand and contract their borders, invading surrounding regions and then fighting off invasions. This resulted in a vast number of ethnic minorities who inhabit the large expanse of what is China today. It also led to the building of the Great Wall, which is more than 2,000 miles across northern China, built to keep "barbarians" out.

Britain attempted to make early inroads into China but was kept at bay until the British began to import opium in the nineteenth century. A war developed between Britain and China, and seems to have led to the beginning of modern China, with the collapse of the dynasty system and the beginning of major Western intervention. The Manchu Dynasty was increasingly corrupt and could not deal with growing agricultural problems and a population explosion. An ancient civil service system made change difficult, and the elite of the country were reluctant to reform. With outside intervention and internal pressures, it was inevitable that the central authority would collapse.

For the next few years chaos reigned, with a failed revolution and various warlords ruling different regions. During the period from 1917 through the 1920s, many Westerners traveled to China, bringing Western ideas, and Chinese intellectuals traveled abroad, bringing back new concepts of democracy and socialism that were spreading throughout other parts of the world.

In 1921 the Communist Party was established, and for a while it united with other political parties to bring China together as one. Finally, in 1934, there was a battle between the communists and the nationalists, with the communists losing and being forced to make what has come to be called the "long march." From 1934 to 1935 they marched 6,000 miles through the interior of China to establish a revolutionary movement. During that time Mao Tse Tung emerged as the leader, and the communists won favor with peasants, who were 85 percent of the population of China.

In 1937, Japan invaded China in the north and east, and the nationalists and communists united, with American assistance, to defeat the Japanese. Finally, when World War II was over, the communists were successful in overthrowing the nationalists and splitting China in two again, with the nationalists moving to Taiwan in 1949.

Since 1949 China has been a communist country, which means that family life changed dramatically from the old "feudal" ways to a more egalitarian society. Feudalism was defined as following the traditional Chinese family structure, as outlined in the next section. However, numerous political movements since communism was introduced have brought further conflict and transformation to the family.

The Traditional Chinese Family

China has always been an agricultural society, with small farmers owning land and only a few wealthy landowners hiring laborers. Daily life for most Chinese remained the same for thousands of years. Farmers and their families lived in millions of villages among rice fields and hillsides (Duiker & Spielvogel, 1994, 915). Lives were governed by the cycle of the seasons, ritual, and tradition. Confucianism, the dominant religion, and the social ethic emphasized harmony and mutual dependence among family members. The traditional Chinese family has always been governed by prescribed roles defined by family hierarchy, obligation, and duties (Lee, 1996, 252).

The traditional Chinese family was patriarchal, with males, particularly eldest sons and fathers, being in the dominant positions. The family was also patrilineal and patrilocal. Filial piety, which emphasized the subordination of the child to the parents and the practice of holding family property in common, was the norm. Rich men often had their sons, wives, and families living in the same compound, as well as concubines who produced children for them. Many generations could be found living under one roof. Marriages were usually arranged, and there was a strict division of labor, with men dealing with the outside world and providing for their families, while women were at home, living separate lives in separate worlds. The spousal relationship was secondary to the parent–child relationship (252).

Homosexuality has been known to exist in China since at least the third century (Ng, 1989, 76). There is evidence of it in early Confucian writings; it was allowed as long as men fulfilled their procreative duties. Male prostitutes existed side by side with females, and during certain eras it was seen as part of the sexual appetite that was rooted in human nature. It was celebrated until the Ming Dynasty clamped down on it in the seventeenth century, when a more strait-laced Confucian ideology was embraced by the leaders and then imposed on the rest of society. Homosexuality was officially eradicated in order to ensure the stability, harmony, and balance that orthodox Confucian doctrine demanded (88).

Under the more conservative Confucian ideology, Chinese mothers were often portrayed as self-sacrificing, and their value was determined by whether or not they produced male offspring. They were expected to obey their in-laws. Girls were seen as temporary family members, since they would marry and leave the family. For this reason they were indulged by their parents, knowing that their lives would be hard upon marriage. Go-betweens who would negotiate, after an investigation was done about the families' backgrounds, arranged the marriages. A girl would marry young, hoping to produce as many male offspring as possible, to please the family and enhance her own position.

Severe discipline was not uncommon, with boys being given harsh training, intellectually and physically. Boys were beaten, and family relationships were based on fear and respect. Every family member knew his or her place and role, and those roles told everyone how to feel, think, and act (88).

Grandparents played significant roles in children's lives, since it was they who ran the family compound; mothers were secondary. In middle- and upper-class families, wet nurses were hired to breast-feed and raise the children. Strong family bonds and obligations indicated that elders would be cared for by their male children in old age (Lee, 1996, 253).

This system was in place for the upper classes until the overthrow of the dynasties. They were only about one-fifth of the population of China, but they set the standard for the rest of the country (Leslie & Korman, 1985, 84). Because Chinese families predated the modern nations of the West, and because there was no strong central government in China until much later, the family clan was the central institution of the society. The *tsu*, or clan, was the way people traced their lineage, got their names. It was how legal matters were determined, and it served the welfare functions that we saw in the Western family-based economy.

For peasants in China, the system was quite different. For those who were poor, work on the land, men and women together, was the norm. Girls were married off early or forced into concubinage, which was legitimate and acceptable, or prostitution. Boys tended the small family plots. The elite family norms were in place for all Chinese families, but economics allowed the peasants some flexibility. Female infanticide was not uncommon, however, because of the need to give the most important children—the boys—preference (Leslie & Korman, 88). There was a chronic shortage of marriageable-age girls among the peasants as a result of prostitution, legitimate concubinage, and female infanticide (92). Also, infanticide took place when famines and poverty made it a necessity, and not just for female children. Poverty also made it impossible for many poor men ever to marry.

But by 1915, the old system was under siege. Youth agitated for change, especially against the ideas of filial piety and the subordination of women. China's isolation from the world was under attack, and as industrial trade increased, the country was infiltrated by Western ideas. Western values of individualism, ideas of political freedom, and revolutionary concepts about education and women's rights led to a decline in the tyranny of the Chinese family. By the 1920s, traditional culture was being influenced heavily by the West, and family life began to modernize. War and civil war had wreaked havoc on the traditional family, with family members torn between the nationalists and the communists and the battles that raged.

The Chinese Family Under Communism

Rather than contact with the technological developments of the West or the rise of industrialization, perhaps the most significant impact on the family came with the Communist Revolution of 1949. One could say that communism has attempted to undermine the traditional family system, but the reality is that the family still has many vestiges of that past firmly intact.

Communism is a political, economic theory that has had a rich and varied history. As you will remember from Chapter 3, Karl Marx developed the ideology extensively through his writings. Revolutionaries in various parts of the world have adopted his ideas and used them to initiate change. In the former Soviet Union, in Cuba, and in China, the ideology was the basis for revolutionary movements that overthrew old traditions and attempted to introduce transformation of all the institutions of society. Although communism has been given a bad name in the West, in other parts of the world it was the source of hope and optimism about the possibility for equality and freedom for people who felt victimized by old regimes. In China, when the Communist Party was victorious, there was hope for land reform, social justice, and peace.

Under communist rule, land was collectivized and efforts were made to mechanize farming. People's communes were established so that no one owned any piece of land; all land was held in common and worked by all. Industry was nationalized, and in one fell swoop, efforts were made to abolish the traditional family system. Mao wanted to see an egalitarian society built as quickly as possible. The impact of collectivization on the family was to make kin less dependent on each other for support, especially in the cities. The communists wanted to undermine kin favoritism in order to build a more equal society.

One of the first programs was called the Great Leap Forward, an economic reform program that was vast in its changes. During this era, urban dwellers were forced, often against their will, to move to collectivized farms to work the land for the revolution. Families suffered greatly, with starvation and the lack of food production. As many as 15 million people may have died from the failure of these plans, and many families were disrupted and destroyed. The Great Leap Forward was a failure because of bad weather, peasant resistance to the system, and administrative problems (Duiker & Spielvogel, 1994, 1104).

In addition there were many reforms of the medical system, especially a program called "barefoot doctors." These lay medical staff were peasants and city dwellers who were trained in basic prevention and simple treatment methods, bringing basic medical care to people who had never received adequate medical care in the past.

Early on, laws were passed to reform the family. By 1950 the Marriage Law was written to give women full equal rights. It outlawed concubinage, allowed free choice of spouses, gave men and women equal inheritance, protected children's rights, allowed divorce by mutual consent, and allowed women to own and control real property (Leslie & Korman, 103). But the structural base of inequality remained, which meant that the traditional family patterns remained. The family was still patrilocal, with women not considered equal to men. In theory, women were allowed education, but the reality was quite different.

From 1966 to 1976, the Great Cultural Revolution disrupted family life in China. During this era Mao, who believed that capitalist values and the old "feudalist" remnants would undermine the fervor of the revolution, argued that China needed to remain in a constant state of change, so as to throw off the past and attain the final stage of utopian communism (Duiker & Spielvogel, 1994, 1105). The party carried out vast economic and educational reforms that eliminated all profit incentives and introduced "The Teachings of Mao Tse Tung." School learning was discouraged, and the most radical elements of society attempted to destroy the vestiges of traditional society.

The Red Guards, as the young radicals were called, rampaged through the country trying to eradicate the "four olds": old thought, old culture, old customs, and old habits (1105). Young family members turned in their elders as "rightists" who were trying to undermine the revolution. Chaos reigned for ten years, while young, uneducated people kept the country in a state of constant revolution. Old allies of Mao and those who felt that this was not the right path were incarcerated or killed. Families were torn by public humiliation of those seen as traitors to the revolution. Many children turned against their parents and reported their elders if they dared criticize the system (1114).

It was not until Mao's death in 1976 that the country entered the industrial and modern age. Through reforms of the next regime, egalitarian policies were reversed, and instead a policy of four modernizations began, in industry, agriculture, technology, and national defense (1106). In that era China made enormous progress in overcoming poverty and underdevelopment; housing and sanitation improved, and education and agricultural output expanded. Life expectancy and nutritional programs increased, and the standard of living for the people greatly improved. Unfortunately, the "fifth modernization" has yet to reach China, that of democracy.

In 1989, students and urban dwellers, those who had contact with the West through education or business dealings, began to agitate for political reform. Mass demonstrations occurred in Tiananmen Square; the more conservative elements of the Communist Party, who run the government, clamped down on them. Tanks and troops took over the square, followed by arrests and killing of the dissidents. What they were agitating for was democratic rule of China and the resignation of the aging party leadership. Those demands remain the hope in China today.

Family life in China has changed quite a bit from feudal days, and yet much remains the same. Because Mao believed that the family was a threat to loyalty to the revolution, much was done to change the family structure. The Marriage Law was important in granting women equality and the right to divorce, and collectivization of agriculture led to favors being granted to individuals rather than to families. But money was given to the head of the household, who remained the patriarch, so in essence the old system was maintained.

The Chinese government initiated a policy of 3 to 12 months paid maternity leave at partial or full pay, in an effort to bolster women's economic position. The result is that often state-run industries refuse to hire women, who are still the primary child caregivers and in charge of the household. Forty percent of the workforce is women, and yet they earn only 74 percent of what men do.

In 1979 China introduced a one-child policy; although originally intended for all Chinese, it seems to have impacted those living in the cities to a greater extent. Rural peasants were able to apply for exemptions. Because of the traditional preference for male children, female infanticide and efforts to have a second child, should the first be a female, have continued. The one-child policy has also led to children being treated quite royally in China. These children are now called "little emperors" because of the overindulgences lavished upon them. The one-child policy, initiated to curb the massive population growth, has been effective in reducing the numbers of children born, but also has led to concern about who will care for aging parents and a lack of girls of marrying age.

Sons are still the preferred children in China, because they are the only ones allowed to perform traditional family rituals and important ancestor worship. Government reforms have attempted to make welfare possible for elders so that they won't rely on their sons in the old age, and there is an effort to have both daughters and sons take the responsibility for caring for aging parents.

The one-child policy has had an important effect on the national minorities of China. Ninety-four percent of the Chinese population is Han Chinese; while only 6 percent are minorities, they occupy 60 percent of China's vast expanse (Ogden, 1997, 14). The Chinese government has made every effort to rid minority groups of what they call "feudal" practices like cultural traditions, family structure, and religion. In an effort to subsume them under the communist government, the one-child policy has been applied to all ethnic groups, far from the Beijing central administration. Mongolians, Tibetans, Muslims are all encouraged, and are often forced through violence, to adhere to the centralized practices followed by the majority.

Photo 5.3   One-child policy, China. Photographer: Patti Carman

The Chinese family under communism is a strange mix of traditional and progressive practices. Forty years of revolution have not eradicated old traditions. Arranged marriages, female infanticide, and patriarchal authority all exist side by side with growing consumerism and ties to the outside world. One cannot call it a nuclear family, nor is it an extended family. In some ways it has evolved into a modified extended family, in that ties to the ancestral family are most important. The Chinese people no longer live in the compounds they once did; now they are crammed into small living quarters, generations living together. Family members remain crucially involved in every aspect of their family's life. There is a large out-migration of the young seeking employment in the West and in Chinese big cities. Social benefits have been cut back, and poverty is on the rise. Urban families are not able to meet the rising expectations. The rise in consumerism is also affecting generational relationships. Today, with the increasingly open markets of China, the family seems to be about to evolve to a new form, the like of which is yet to be determined. The family in China is in a state of flux.

India: A Snapshot

India is the largest country in South Asia and is a place of enormous contrasts. It has one-sixth of the world's population crowded into a landmass only one-third the size of the United States (Norton, 1997, 37). It is 2,000 miles long and 1,000 miles wide, and within its borders are just over a billion people who practice at least five religions, speak 13 major languages and numerous dialects, and are as diverse as any group of people can be. India is also the largest democracy in the world. It was once a glorious empire, but its position on the international trade routes has made it vulnerable to the economic, political, and social forces that have buffeted it. Migrations of peoples, wars, and invasions have all impacted the deep and ancient culture that has thrived there since before the time of recorded history. India has one of the oldest and most continuous civilizations in the world; long before Western influence, it produced a rich heritage of culture, religion, races of people, and languages.

India can appear quite confusing to outsiders. Sometimes its values, lifestyles, foods, religions, climate, and customs seem quite unlike those found in the West; this can lead to misunderstandings and lack of appreciation. With Buddhism, Islam, and religious life in general at the center of daily life, the country is unlike any other. Understanding the Hindu beliefs of tolerance, diversity, and not hurting any living thing plays a crucial role in understanding India.

The British arrived in India as early as the 1600s; they were preceded by the Portuguese, who dominated in trade with the region. The Mughals—Turks from Persia—had conquered the region centuries earlier, but their rule was on the wane, and slowly the West began to make inroads. For a while the Dutch, Danes, and French tried to penetrate the interior of India, but it was the British who prevailed. Through the British East India Trading Company, footholds were gradually established, and by the eighteenth century the British were firmly entrenched there.

India had been primarily Hindu until the Mughals arrived, and with them came the Muslim religion. India became a unique blend of Muslim and Hindu religions and Persian civilization. On top of that is now overlaid a British system that makes India a synthesis of diverse cultures. By the beginning of the nineteenth century, British military power and businesses had blossomed. With colonial rule came the same type of imposition upon local peoples as we saw in Latin America and Africa.

The British colonists established an efficient and centralized government that included a new school system and a means to teach the Indian elites the ways of the British. Using direct and indirect rule, they instituted a bureaucratic structure that permeates Indian society even today. Britain brought with it Western ideas, industry, agricultural practices, culture, and social norms and values. European colonization lasted from the early 1600s until independence in 1947; thus it is hard to separate that which is specifically Indian from that which is a result of colonization.

In 1947 India shook off the yoke of British colonialism through a nonviolent revolution that pressured Britain to grant it independence. Mahatma Gandhi was the significant leader of the revolt, which consisted of massive civil disobedience that urged the British to "quit India." After the revolution the country was divided up between India and Pakistan, with the main determinant being religious separation; Hindus were primarily given India, and Muslims were primarily given Pakistan. Difficulties developed, however, because the countries are not cleanly divided according to religion and ethnicity, leaving groups from each living in the other country. This fact is quite important in understanding the contemporary rivalries and animosities between India and Pakistan. In fact, Gandhi was assassinated soon after independence by nationalists who were angry at him for not wanting a Hindu-dominated India.

Photo 5.4   Brahmin family at home in India. Photographer: Mary Thieme

A crucial factor in understanding the Indian family is to respect the importance of the *caste system,* a legacy of the Hindu religion that pervades all aspects of Indian life. The caste system is a hierarchy of rank that locks individuals into the rank of their parents and is immutable. Where one is born is where one remains. Castes are usually associated with certain occupations and with very clearly defined social boundaries that define whom one will marry, with whom one will have social interactions, and what is proper behavior for each individual. It is very much related to spiritual purity and pollution, with a pecking order of power and privileges. Caste is tied to one's *karma,* the destiny or fate that is determined for you prior to birth. The highest caste are the *Brahmins,* or the priests, and the lowest are the *harijans,* or untouchables. Although outlawed now, the caste system is still firmly in place.

In conjunction with the caste system there is also a class system, based on income and upward mobility. Someone may be of a lower class but of an upper caste, based on his or her ability to earn. The Western concept of race also plays a significant role in understanding the history of Indian family life. In the West the concept of color was much more important than it was in India. However, with the ranking order that took place under colonialism, based on skin color, a mix of race politics interacted with caste and class to further complicate the picture.

The Indian Family

From ancient times until today, the family has played the most important and dominating role in Indian society (Gulati, 1995, 133). Historically, marital life is centered in the family, and the whole society has long been preoccupied with marriage, followed by the birth of children within marriage. Under Hindu law, women have been among the most severely restricted people in the world. The favoritism toward men has been compounded by the Muslim custom of *purdah,* the virtual isolation of women behind veils and in separate compounds. Traditionally restricted to the home and tied to their husbands for life, women's roles in Indian family life have been dictated by custom and expectations. To fight against this system was seen as going against one's karma and was not allowed.

Females received no education and had no inheritance rights. Widows were expected to shave their heads and engage in meditation. In some parts of India there was also the expectation that upon the deaths of their husbands they would immolate themselves on their husbands' funeral pyres (Duiker & Spielvogel, 1994, 1144).

In the patriarchal structure of the Indian Hindu family, all roles and responsibilities, who is in control, and how resources are distributed are determined by one's age, gender, and generation. The man has the power to determine all decisions about his dependents, including when and how many children the family will have. Early marriage was not uncommon, with some matches being made as early as prepuberty; this led to health problems when the girls bore children quite young. It also led to early widowhood, and since widows were not allowed to remarry, the young widow was left without support (Gulati, 1995, 137). Early marriage served the function of preserving virginity and ensuring that children were not born out of wedlock, considered a most horrible fate for a woman.

All families under the Hindu system were expected to have children; to be childless was not considered normal, and the preference at all times was for a male child. Female infanticide was not unusual, especially as the cost of the dowry increased and families faced the cost of raising a daughter who would then leave the family.

The form of the family has tended to vary with caste, religion, and ethnicity. Large extended families were the most common, although single-female-headed households were not unusual for the poorer members of society. Most families in India have been rurally based, with only 26 percent of the population living in cities even today (140). Life in India has always been harsh. The basics of life, like sanitation, education, and health facilities, are not available to all peoples, and as a result families need each other to survive. It is not uncommon for the mainly rural families to have small plots of land that the entire family cultivates for a marginal existence. Assets like cattle and farm implements are often the only property that a family has. Communities share pastures, ponds, water rights, and forests. In fact the model fits that of the family-based economy of Western societies. Since the economy of India was and still is primarily rural, the form that the family seems to take is farm- and family-based.

After independence, a number of major reforms were passed in order to equalize the situation for the lowest caste of society, the harijans, and for the other poorly treated members of society—women. Laws were passed that forbid discrimination based on sex, and employers had to pay equal wages for equal work. *Sati* (throwing oneself on a husband's funeral pyre) was outlawed, and the dowry system was also made illegal. Women were encouraged to attend school and to work. This led to a number of middle-class women getting an education and becoming professionals. Poor women in India had always worked, but now it became acceptable for the upper classes to enter public life. Divorce was legalized for women, and legal reforms made efforts at equalizing their lives.

The harijans, as Gandhi named them, are known as the people of God. The caste has always been known as the "untouchables" or *dalits*. After independence in 1947, laws were passed to outlaw discrimination against them and in fact to make them a protected caste. They were offered admittance to universities and increased professional opportunities (Almeida, 1996, 398). In fact, some of the affirmative action programs for untouchables has led to emigration of some higher-caste professionals even as economic liberalization is seeing the cities emerge as high-tech service centers.

Hindus make up 80 percent of the population of India, and their beliefs about caste and karma impact the other 20 percent. Muslims, Sikhs, Christians, Jews, Buddhists, and Parsis are the religious minorities, and there is an acceptance of these groups and their faiths. Nonetheless, there are conflicts between the Hindus and the Muslims that lead to continuing battles and skirmishes even today. This affects family life through the strict segregation of groups, with little intermarriage, and also through the consequences of periodic riots and uprisings, which cause frequent turmoil and deaths.

Little has changed in family life in India for thousands of years. Arranged marriage is still the norm, with some "love matches" grudgingly allowed. Indian women tend to play a modern role at work but a more traditional one at home. The dowry system, although banned, is in fact still alive and well, and the preference for sons remains.

Recently there has a been a rise once again in female infanticide, and with the advent of high-tech amniocentesis, the sex of a fetus can be determined in utero and female children can be aborted prior to birth. Girl fetuses are aborted at an extremely high rate, and there seems to be a shortage of girls of marrying age because of this phenomenon. The literacy rate for girls is only 40 percent, and even sati is reappearing. Lately, there has been a rise in reported dowry deaths, with young brides mysteriously dying in kitchen fires, because the dowries that they brought are deemed insufficient by the husband's family.

There are some changes in India. For example, there are reforms of laws regarding amniocentesis to determine the sex of the fetus. This was due to the fact that up to 95 percent of the aborted fetuses were female (Interactive Population Center, 2000). Laws have now been passed to outlaw the aborting of a female fetus. Other reforms include the encouragement of education for girls and poorer castes.

Family life in India is difficult to summarize. Since the family is primarily rural, it could be likened to the family-based economy of the West, but colonialism has had an impact, and as a result there is some urbanization. There is also a mixing of the family-wage economy. Poverty plays a crucial role in Indian family life, with fully 43 percent of families living in the countryside falling below the poverty line. There is migration of family members to the cities to find employment, but there is still a strong rural connection for many Indian families. Some argue that the family has become nuclear (Gulati, 1995, 152), but the reality is that families adopt a modified extended family form when they move to cities or immigrate. The bonds and connection to family remain crucially important to Indians, be they rural or urban, Hindu or Muslim, male or female.

Summary

The history of the family in colonized parts of the world is far different from that of the core. Industrialization and modernization came later and had a differing impact, depending on whether or not a place was deemed important to the colonizer. Western influence on Latin America was early and far reaching. Family life changed to follow the norm of the colonizers, so that elites in Latin America took on many of the ways of the Spanish. Families among the poor were more flexible, struggling for survival and taking on more fluid forms. Economic necessity led to less rigid definitions of family expectations. It seems that the modified extended family evolved into a predominant form.

Colonization took longer to reach into the heart of Africa. The African experience was very much related to slavery, the first European involvement on the continent. It gravely impacted family life, especially along the "slave coast." In the south of Africa, colonization came after slavery and had a significant effect on family life, especially through the imposition of white minority rule over the black majority.

Asia, long coveted for its resources, resisted Western advances and was able to maintain cultural autonomy in China for longer than did Latin America and Africa. However, in India the family form seemed to adapt to that of a modified extended family, adjusting to economic needs for mobility. Life in India remains devoted to the family and, although changing, still clings to traditional ways.

From this chapter you can see the complexity of the historical process and how unique each country and its family life is. I hope that in reading this you come to appreciate the special heritages and factors that have contributed to each country reaching its current stage. Families might look the same on the surface, but beneath the exterior linger deep-rooted heritages and cultural histories that make families in each society different and unusual. Given this very brief overview of the "history of the family in the world," my hope is that you will study more about family history, to explore the richness and complexity of the family.

CHAPTER 6

Gender and the Family

For six years, from 1995 to 2001, I led and facilitated a group for transsexual and transgendered people. Once a month, twelve men, all of whom dressed as women, came to my home for socializing, support, and community; they came to discuss what it is like to be cross-dressing and dealing with the outside world. Sometimes these born males brought their heterosexual wives. The wives talked about what it is like to be married to men who prefer to dress as women, who are heterosexual lovers to them, who earn a living and provide for their families, and who seem to be more comfortable in their bodies now that they cross-dress.

When I first started this group, it was to provide a much-needed community service. Now I see the social implications of these men's public actions. They are challenging traditional definitions of gender. Like many others, I had seen trans-genderism as a popular cultural phenomenon. Dennis Rodman, RuPaul, k. d. lang, Annie Lenox, David Bowie, and even Madonna seemed to be all media hype. Or they were people trying to gain fame by being different. My transgendered friends were a bit of a curiosity to me, a sociologist and a person interested in different cultures and peoples.

When I got into that world, I found that it had relevance to me, to my students, and to the world around us. Transgenderism was not just an oddity, a form of deviance, to be understood and tolerated. Instead, the implications of what this growing population is doing are relevant to our understanding of gender and the designation of each of us as male, female, or other. The idea of trangenderism has important implications for family life and for an understanding of socialization and the development of gender identities.

Each of us becomes ourselves through the socialization process, first within the family and then within the other institutions of society. Family plays an important role in our gender identities, as does religion. In this chapter, we see that gender is about performance, about taking on the roles and acts of what a society defines as gender-acceptable behaviors. We explore gender inequality cross-culturally and see that there are many theories about how gender is constructed. Perhaps one of the best ways to illustrate the important role that religion plays in gender identity is to look at current-day Afghanistan and its redefinition of gender as a result of the political and social transformations that are going on there. We look at that later in the chapter. Most of us think we know a lot about gender, about boys being put into blue blankets and girls into pink blankets at birth. However, gender and family life are far more complicated than that.

Transgenderism: Transsexuals, Transvestites, Drag Kings and Queens: The Diversity of Gender Expression

When I first became acquainted with this transgendered world, I was confused about the terms. In fact, I still cannot get them straight, so to speak! That is probably because the "trans" world, as they call themselves, is just defining its own terms. It seems that *transgenderists* have developed a colloquial meaning that is like a catch-all; *transgender* is an

> umbrella term to include everyone who challenges the boundaries of sex and gender. It is also used to draw a distinction between those who reassign the sex they were labeled at birth, and those whose gender expression is considered inappropriate for their sex. (Feinberg, 1996, x)

This group now includes transsexuals, transgenders, transvestites, transgenderists, bigenderists, drag queens, drag kings, cross-dressers, masculine women, feminine men, intersexuals (previously called *hermaphrodites*), androgynes, crossgenders, shape-shifters, passing women, passing men, gender-benders, gender-blenders, bearded women, and women bodybuilders who have crossed the line of what is acceptable for a female body (x).

Transsexuals are people who have had or intend to have sexual reassignment surgery, while some *transgender* people never intend to be reconstructed, but they do blur or bridge the boundaries of their assigned sex. Transsexual usually designates those who feel that their true gender is at variance with their biological sex, and who attempt to "pass" as members of the opposite sex, usually through sex change surgery or through medical treatment (Shapiro, 1991, 249).

As Leslie Feinberg, speaker, author, and activist, has put it, the words are limiting, in that *cross-dresser, bigender, male-to-female*, or any of the other terms assume either/or, two ways to be (xi). In fact, trans people are often many things at the same time and cannot be categorized one way or the other. For example, *transvestite* is a medical term that has fallen out of usage. It once meant sexual fetishism, psychological pathology, and obsession, all of which were seen as unhealthy. The term was used for heterosexual men who liked to dress as women, and sometimes it was a diagnosis given to men who cross-dressed in any way. *Drag queen* tends to refer to gay men who dress as women for performance and entertainment. At other times they dress in gender-appropriate clothing. *Drag kings* are lesbians who dress as men for performance's sake.

It is noteworthy to remind ourselves that *gender expression* differs from *sexual orientation*. One can be a trans person and be either heterosexual or homosexual. Whom one has sex with, in fact, is not necessarily related to how one identifies in gender expression.

The reality is that males, females, and trans can and do sleep with a variety of people. A situation from my transgender group challenged my own understanding of the difference between sexual orientation and gender expression. Two cross-dressed men, previously identified as heterosexual, decided to go home together for a sexual encounter. They continued to wear their wigs and makeup. When I thought of the situation, I described it to myself as a gay interaction. However, when the two of them described it to me, they described themselves as lesbians, because they were dressed as women and felt themselves to be women. It blew my mind. I had previously constructed sexual orientation in one manner and gender expression in another. This showed me the vast variety of possibilities and stretched my thinking to limits I had not previously imagined.

I realized that categories like male, female, transgendered, gay, and straight did not work. The arbitrariness of the construction of gender was too limiting for the people I was encountering. I realized, once again, how socially constructed the concept of gender really is.

Anne Fausto-Sterling has studied people who are *intersexed*. This is the word she uses, taken from medical terminology, to describe people who have a mixture of female and male characteristics (Fausto-Sterling, 1993, 10). These people are true hermaphrodites, a combination of the names Hermes and Aphrodite, the gods who parented Hermaphroditus in Greek mythology. He became half-man and half-woman when his body fused with the body of a nymph he fell in love with. Often the medical establishment, in the name of humanitarianism, chooses at birth which sex a genitally ambiguous child will become, and surgery is performed within days. Fausto-Sterling argues that the surgery and other treatments occur because society cannot deal with the ambiguity and lack of clear distinctions that intersexual people pose. She says,

> Society mandates the control of intersexual bodies because they blur and bridge the great divide, they challenge traditional beliefs about sexual difference. Hermaphrodites have unruly bodies. They do not fall into a binary classification; only a surgical shoehorn can put them there. (10)

The trans world is not just about clothing nor about whom one has sex with. In fact, it is a blurring of all those issues. It is a very postmodern phenomenon. *Postmodernism* is a contemporary theory that looks to "deconstruct, destroy, demythologize and demystify" (Ritzer, 1997) the very concepts and ideas we hold dear in our society. This set of ideas argues that we have moved beyond the view of modernization of the world, and there is now no monolithic explanation of what we are seeing. When the lens is shifted, one might now say that "there is no one way of seeing, there are many ways of seeing" (Laskowitz, private communication, 1998).

In postmodern thinking, we have begun to see that dichotomous thinking—defining things as good and bad, black and white, up and down, male and female, either/or—might well be a dated way of seeing the world. Binary thinking—thinking in these dichotomies—does not account for the variability of human experience. By looking at transgenderists, we might begin to see that the social construction of gender is one of those binary, dichotomous views.

We are encouraged to look to those on the fringe in order to understand what is going on within the fabric, to understand what is the issue for us, who might be more conforming. By looking at transgender as the most extreme form of gender bending, we might be able to understand how the construction of gender is, in fact, *socially constructed and socially defined*. We will look to "decode" why gender is supposed to be so fixed and seek to understand what the hidden message is behind the categorization.

Not many of us would call ourselves transgender, but how many of the women among us have preferred wearing jeans and trousers, and how many men wear earrings and body piercings? How many of the men among us have cross-dressed on Halloween and had a grand old time hamming it up as women for a night? We will see from this discussion that although transgender is an extreme form of gender challenging, many of us have engaged in simpler and less threatening challenges to gender definitions in our everyday life. The definitions of gender are in fact, more amorphous, more changeable than many of us like to admit.

The Paradox of Sex and Gender

Where does all this leave us? When I invite trans people to my classes, students are often impressed by how well some of the male-to-females pass. They swear they could not tell the difference. Some of the men in the classes are grossly uncomfortable, because many of the trans men show pictures of themselves as men who were "normal"-looking for the 1990s. Some were athletes, and many are successful businesspeople who hold reputable jobs and are otherwise quite like the rest of us.

In Chapter 2 we learned that *sex is the biological entity you are when you are born; gender is what you are made into, who you become when you are socialized by your society.* Judith Shapiro (1991) argues that the trans world shows us that a society's gender system is a "trick done with mirrors," but it also builds walls that provide our species with a "very real and only home" (249).

What the whole subject does is to show that gender is, in fact, often about *performance.* It is about how one "acts" out one's gender and how the society defines that act, the role that one should play based on the sex one is alleged to have been born into. These performances determine what we wear and how we use our bodies as a sign of our gender. Gender can be masked, as we saw with transgenderism; it can be parodied; it can be flaunted and played with; and it can be mixed up in any way we desire (Lorber, 1998, 182). As performance, gender is not fixed. However, because of structural arrangements in society, that performance is predetermined for some people and not for others. It is the structure of society, with its hierarchy, that confines and defines those performances.

There is a paradoxical relationship between sex and gender. By seeing that sex does not have to define gender, that gender can be, and often is, a fluid definition, we see gender's mutability. How gender behavior is defined relies upon the establishment of categories, artificial ones at that. We see that this paradox leaves room for change. If one is fluid between one's sex and one's gender identity, one creates a disruptive element. As Marjorie Garber (1992) has argued, there is a space for restructuring and confounding the culture. She sees this not only as a crisis of male and female, but a crisis of categorization itself (17).

Judith Butler (1999) asks us questions that confound the situation even more: Does each sex have a different history? Is there a history of how the duality of sex was established? She even wants to know if gender is socially constructed, is it possible that the very idea of sex is also socially constructed (10)?

Socialization of Gender

The question of who teaches us how to be male and female is initially decided within the family. The parents of an intersex infant are asked to decide at birth whether or not they authorize the surgery, and which sex the child will become. As soon as a clearly born male or female emerges, the socialization begins. I recently visited a friend in the hospital who had just given birth to a son. Her husband had brought, as his first gift, an infant-sized baseball and glove. The child was taken home in a blue blanket.

This fits with a study done in 1974 by Rubin, Provenzano, and Luria, in which they asked parents of 24-hour-old infants to describe the child's characteristics. Parents said that boys were "strong," "aggressive," "athletic" and used other typically American male adjectives. Girls were described as "pretty," "delicate," "sweet," and other typically female words. Interestingly, the researchers then asked hospital workers who did not know what sex the babies were to describe the same children. They found no objective differences among the infants.

In developing what has been called a *gendered self*, children learn early on, no matter what society they are born into, what is expected for them and their gendered behaviors. In another fascinating study, researchers looked at the homes of 120 American children to see how their parents constructed their physical play space. They found that boys had far more sports equipment, and more cars and trucks, and were dressed in blue, red, and white clothing. Girls wore pink and multicolored clothing and were surrounded by typically female toys like dolls, kitchen appliances, typewriters, and softer, more feminine fashion clothing (Pomerleau et al., 1990).

This, of course, is the way white, middle- and upper-class children in the United States are taught their gendered selves. In 1974, Sandra Bem developed a measurement scale of masculinity and femininity based on American cultural definitions of appropriate behaviors for the sexes (Bem, 1974). She found that the highly gender-typed individual, male or female, would internalize society's standards for desirable gender behavior and be motivated to conform to those expectations. An androgynous person would be less sensitive to those definitions and more free from conforming to them.

More recently, a study by Harris (1994) was done using the Bem scale but applying it to African Americans, Anglos, and Latinos. In this study, the author found that concepts of masculinity and femininity differ across cultural groups in the United States and that gender-typed personality traits differ depending on ethnicity. African Americans, for example, were far more able than Anglos and Latinos to consider many of the traits, both masculine and feminine, common to both sexes (for example, assertive, athletic, independent, self-reliant, self-sufficient, gentle). Unfortunately, the Bem scale assumed whiteness as the norm and thus was not really objective in defining male and female characteristics for nonwhite subjects.

Nonetheless, says Harris, an African American child, unlike his or her Anglo or traditional Latino counterpart, does not learn to associate various forms of behavior to one gender alone. Because African American parents teach unity and the bringing together of polar opposites, their children learn that any and all behaviors are appropriate for both sexes. These children do not emphasize dichotomies or gender-specific behaviors. Women can head households, as can men. Women can be aggressive and passive, men can be active and dependent, all at the same time (13–14).

Gender Socialization and the Role of Teachers

Soon after children enter the larger society, they encounter teachers who continue to reinforce gendered behaviors. In one study by Sadker and Sadker (1994), researchers found that teachers construct classrooms to reinforce the inequities. Girls are asked to do typically female activities like water plants, clean the blackboards, and pick up the classroom. Boys are encouraged to run errands and do more male-identified chores. In interactions with the teachers, girls in elementary school are responded to more negatively, while boys are encouraged and given positive reinforcement in their schoolwork and their participation in class. Boys are given more detailed instructions and assistance in learning from their mistakes, while the teachers make the corrections for the girls.

Later in life, college professors continue the inequitable gender socialization. Even female college professors give women subtle messages by ignoring them, discounting their work, using sex-stereotyped examples, calling them "girls," and commenting on their physical appearances rather than their ideas. In what might be called *individual sexism*, behaviors that are performed by individuals accumulate over time to convey important and subtle messages of inferiority.

In other parts of the world, not only how one is treated in the classroom but whether or not one will receive an education is gender determined. For example, in Afghanistan, when the Islamic revolutionary party Taliban took political power, girls over age eight were banned from public education, and even homeschools were closed. Girls were expected to remain at home, as were their mothers and sisters. Women, who once worked in the public sector and had rights similar to those of women in other industrialized countries, were forced to give up any semblance of gender equality (Bad bargain, 1998). As we will see later in the chapter, in Afghanistan, once again women's gender identities are changing.

Gender Socialization and the Media

All around us the media abound. In newspapers, magazines, television, radio, movies, and even in our dress, the external world constructs and teaches us how to perform our gendered behaviors. These cultural artifacts of our society are places where *cultural sexism* takes place. The sexism is inherent in the cultural forms and popular cultural manifestations in our society, such as art, music, dance, dress, and media representations.

Television programs, cartoons, advertisements all reinforce gender roles. Although some change has occurred, mothers are still seen doing housework, or juggling two roles as worker and homemaker. Fathers are occupied in traditional male behaviors, like lawn mowing or car maintenance. Women are portrayed as dependent or in need of male assistance, while males are shown as competent, aggressive, and in control of their lives.

Magazines are another important outlet for gender messaging. *Seventeen* magazine, popular star fan magazines, and girlie magazines oriented to a male audience all encourage dependency and a focus on appearance for women. Women are encouraged to look good, attract men, and hope to find Prince Charming, who will come along on a white horse to sweep them off their feet so they can live happily ever after.

In India, gender socialization follows the same methods as the United States (Bumiller, 1990). Indian films and soap operas are important tools for gender scripting. In highly romantic and often colorful films, women are played as love-crazed, while men are shown as "he-men." Indian feminists have long critiqued the gender differentiation that pervades the society, where women are encouraged to be compliant, passive, conforming, and dependent, and men are trained as active, competitive, and sexually aggressive.

Interestingly, Asians and Asian Americans have had a unique portrayal in the media. Historically, Asian men have been depicted as a sexual danger to virginal white women, especially around the turn of the century, when Asian women were not allowed into the United States. Later, Asian men were depicted as "neuter," which made it easier to discriminate against them. Asian women have been represented as promiscuous and untrustworthy, and as castrating Dragon Ladies who are deceitful and dangerous (Espiritu, 1997). Recently they have been "fetishized" as the embodiment of the perfect woman and the truly exotic feminine (113). Asians are portrayed as threats and model minorities, always maintaining their place as marginalized, and all in the service of maintaining male privilege.

The No Problem Problem

Deborah Rhode, a law professor at Stanford Law School, argued that the perception among Americans is that gender is no longer a problem. She calls it the "no problem problem" (1997, 1). She sees that many individuals fail to recognize the extent of the difficulties still facing women, deny these difficulties by blaming women's own choices and capabilities for the differences, and then deny the need for anyone to take personal responsibility for the problem (3). In denying the difficulties Rhode points to the raw statistics, which are undeniable. For example, she cites a recent study in which men, when surveyed, believed that they shared child rearing equally with their wives. The reality, in terms of reported time devoted to these tasks and the reports of their wives, was much different (7). She quotes Anna Quindlen: "When men do the dishes, it's called helping. When women do dishes, that's called life" (Rhode, 1997, 6).

American workplaces are still gender segregated and gender stratified, with full-time female employees earning less than 77 cents for every dollar earned by men. Latina women college graduates earn lower salaries than white male high school dropouts, and women of color are at the bottom of the occupational hierarchy (7). Women child-care workers earn less than male parking lot attendants (10). Still this is not seen as a problem.

In denying responsibility, we take the tack of individualizing the solutions. Whenever I point out to my students the clear, factual, statistical data documenting gender inequality, they mention cases that are the exceptions. Rather than looking at the aggregate, at the numbers that are irrefutable, students point out how their mothers or friends have broken through the glass ceiling, thus denying the structural condition that keeps gender inequality in place, and making the individual exception the reason they don't have to acknowledge the problem.

Gender as a Structural Condition

In Chapters 1 and 2 we discussed *structural conditions* that exist in societies and make for social inequality and a social stratification system. We learned that how one is treated, one's activities, and how one is seen are defined by one's race, class, ethnicity, sexuality, and gender. To be dominant and subordinate in a society is more than just what the "culture" has defined as acceptable. One needs to see who has the power and how that power is distributed in the society. Power, you'll remember, was defined as the ability to get someone to do something the person would not ordinarily do; it is the ability to control resources and to control one's own fate.

The source of gender inequality is an intersection of race, class, ethnicity, and sexuality that continues patterns of disadvantage for certain groups of people. It is built into the structure of society. In this system, there is a cultural devaluation of women and of men of subordinated racial and ethnic groups (Lorber, 1998, 133). We saw this in the history of the family during the colonial era in other parts of the world, as well as during the immigration eras in the United States. We see it today in the statistics on discrimination against poor women of color in the United States and in the peripheral countries. In fact, there is an intertwined system of oppression that moves along a continuum of advantage and disadvantage (134). The institutions of societies and how they favor the advantaged over the disadvantaged can be called *institutional sexism*. This occurs when the social structure is constructed in such a way as to perpetuate gender inequalities through laws, institutions, and public policies.

With this reminder, one can see that gender is about power, or more specifically who has it and who does not. In the United States, although there has been tremendous progress in the righting of gender inequality, that structural condition remains in place.

A Gendered Analysis

Gender is an important vehicle for conveying the power relationships of a society, but often these relationships are invisible to the family. They are not discussed; they are merely a given, the way things are done. Often gender influences who does what work and how labor is divided. There is men's labor and women's labor, with differing expectations of who should do what and what gets rewarded.

Feminist scholars have divided women's labor into productive versus reproductive activities (Baca-Zinn, 1998, 15). Productive activities are work related, usually out in the marketplace, in industry, in the public sphere of life, like factory work and agricultural labor. Reproductive labor involves activities like birthing, purchasing household goods, preparing and serving food, laundering and repairing clothing, maintaining furnishing and appliances, socializing children, providing emotional and physical care for the elderly, and maintaining kin and community ties (Glenn, 1992, 1). Those two spheres both intersect and show great disparities. It is by looking at production and reproduction that one sees how women's oppression and victimization get played out. As you remember from our first two chapters, it is the *patriarchal* structure of society that constructs gendered behavior and creates and reinforces gender inequities.

As we begin in this chapter to look at some of the gender disparities in the world, and at the consequences of gender inequality, we need always to keep that hierarchy in mind. We must also remember that we are looking at a "no problem problem."

Cross-Cultural Studies on Gender Differences

It is increasingly important that cross-cultural studies on gender differences be undertaken. Much has been done in the core countries, especially in the United States, but few comparisons have been done with other parts of the world. Some research has been done in individual countries. However, when researchers try to understand the similarities and differences of genders cross-culturally, they run into problems trying to define terms and make generalizations.

One study by Smith, Dugan, and Trompenaars (1997) did attempt a pan-cultural description of gender differences. This was done by describing a *locus of control*—whether a person feels in control of his or her own life (internal) or controlled by forces outside of him- or herself (external). Having *agency* is the act of being assertive and controlling one's own behavior. It is about having an internal locus of control.

The assumption behind the study was that men would feel more agency or internal control over their lives than would women. Often achievement is tied to an internal locus of control. Many studies have indicated that in the United States and elsewhere, women more than men believe that control is external (59). Women believed they did not have agency, and that agency was located outside of their control, not within themselves.

By interviewing 4,599 people from 14 countries, all of whom were employees in business organizations, the researchers found that people who lived in less modern countries, like Romania and Mexico, had a higher rating on internal locus of control than did people from more modern countries, like Sweden and the Netherlands. Women in more modern countries believed they had less ability to influence their lives (locus of control); they felt that luck was the reason they were able to achieve at all. The researchers found that men in higher-status (advantaged) occupations exhibited the most internal locus of control, and women in lower-status (disadvantaged) occupations exhibited the most external locus of control, in accordance with their self-perceived potential to influence their own lives. This should come as no surprise to us, given that women as a social group wield less power economically and in the workplace.

In another interesting study that compared gender inequality in the United States, Canada, Australia, Norway, and Sweden, two authors studied how dependence and independence shaped men's and women's gender attitudes (Baxter & Kane, 1995). In looking at these five similar core, capitalist, and industrialized countries, the authors compared employment-related issues, family life, and state policies. They studied women's participation in the labor force and the extent to which their incomes were lower than men's, as well as data on marriage, fertility, and economic dependency within marriage and how some state policies facilitate social and economic equality (195). They found that in countries like Sweden and Norway, women are somewhat more independent, and gender inequality was somewhat less evident in employment, family, and state policies. Women in Canada and the United States are somewhat more dependent on men and experience greater inequality (197).

In this study, the authors argued a crucial point about gender inequality: that men have greater access to social power, prestige, and material resources than do women. At a general level, men benefit from this regardless of whether women are dependent on them at an individual level. They also found that all men maintain some interest in maintaining gender inequality. Further, they discovered that men in the United States report the least egalitarian attitudes of all the countries, with U.S. men and women being the least critical of traditional gender roles and men and women in Scandinavia being the most (204). Canadians and Australians fell roughly between the two. The researchers also found that countries that had policies that encouraged equal opportunity, pay equity, gender-neutral parent leave, and a more equal balance between home and work helped to foster more egalitarian attitudes for both men and women (210–211). The authors' findings are eye-opening, given the idea that in the United States we have a "no problem problem."

As we will see as we look at examples of gender inequality, even in the most advanced and progressive countries of the world, attitudes remain unequal. Although some people believe that women have come a long way in the West, it is obvious that we still have a very long way to go.

Gender Discrimination

Since the UN Decade of Women was launched in 1976, the quality of women's lives in the world, particularly in the periphery countries, has improved in significant ways. Women are living longer, having healthier children, and attending school and participating in the workforce in greater numbers (United Nations Development Fund for Women, 1998). Women now control 50–80 percent of the systems of food production, processing, and marketing. Seventy percent of all small enterprises are run by women, female enrollment in primary and secondary schools has increased from 38 to 78 percent in the past two decades, and the mortality rate of children under five has decreased by more than 50 percent in that time period.

The status of women varies enormously depending on the part of the world they live in. But let us remember a key fact: *Nowhere in the world are women completely equal to men* (Population Crisis Committee, 1988, 1). In the peripheral countries in the Middle East, Asia, Africa, and Latin America, poverty overlaid with long-standing patterns of discrimination create living conditions for women that are almost too harsh for people of the core countries to imagine.

Women still comprise the majority of the world's poor; they continue to lack economic power, even in the core countries; and they are the primary victims of conflict and violence worldwide. The most recent statistics are that women make up 70 percent of the world's 1.3 billion absolute poor, are the sole income earners in 35 percent of the world's households, and hold only 10 percent of parliamentary seats worldwide. Unfortunately, women and their dependents are also 80 percent of the world's 23 million refugees (2).

Women grow half the world's food but own virtually no land; they are one-third of the official paid workforce but are concentrated in the lowest paid occupations. If they work outside of the home they do a double day, usually bearing total responsibility for child care regardless of their contribution to family income (1). In a study of 99 countries in the world, the Population Crisis Committee looked at what amounted to conditions for 2.3 billion women—about 92 percent of the world's female population—to come up with these disturbing statistics.

Agriculture

Severe gender inequities lead women to face significant barriers even to raising food crops to feed their children (International Food Policy Research Institute, 1995, 1). Men seem to receive most of the government-sponsored agricultural extension services and new technologies, even though women are the caretakers of the food supply in developing parts of the world. In Africa, Asia, and Latin America, women spend more of their incomes on feeding their families than do men. But women also spend most of their time fetching water and wood for fuel and grinding grain, rather than in income-generating activities that would contribute to family wealth. Historically, in some hunting and gathering societies and in agricultural communities, women provide the majority of the food.

Photo 6.1   Woman making cow dung patties for cooking, India. Photographer: Mary Thieme

Women in the periphery also account for more than half of the labor needed to produce food in their countries (1). In Africa, women do three-quarters of the labor, while in Asia women work as hired agricultural workers, contributing between 10 and 50 percent of the labor needed to grow various crops. In Latin America, women play a key role in family farming.

But women have weak land rights in these places. Often, they are not granted credit because they do not own the land, due to inheritance rights and laws that bar land ownership by women. They have access to fewer tools should they want to farm. Until recently, newer agricultural technology and machinery were not geared to women's needs. Women were excluded from training programs to teach sustainable agricultural techniques, which were primarily targeted at men (1).

Education

Women are also far less educated than men in most countries. In Asia, 1 out of 2 women is illiterate, and in Africa it is 2 out of 3. Nearly all girls of school age are enrolled in primary or secondary school in North America, Australia, Japan, and much of Western Europe, although in some countries, like the United States, dropout rates are a problem (Population Crisis Committee, 1988, 5). In other regions of the world, figures vary widely, ranging from universal enrollment in Barbados to only 9 percent in Afghanistan. In Latin America the percentage of women enrolled is as high as 80 percent, while in Muslim countries the numbers are much lower: 46 percent of girls are enrolled in oil-rich Saudi Arabia and only

17 percent in Pakistan. The United Nations estimates that a third of developing countries do not have enough schools to educate all their children (6).

When it comes to literacy, there are many more illiterate women than men. In the West literacy seems to be universal, but the largest gap seems to be in Libya, followed by Benin, Syria, Tanzania, and Turkey. Botswana, Lesotho, and Jamaica are the only countries in the world where women's literacy is higher than men's. Even in university enrollment, in the West, men outnumber women (6). Only in the United States are more than 50 percent of people in college women (59 percent). The next highest is Canada, with 46 percent. The rest of the world ranges from 1 percent to 39 percent. The worst enrollment rate seem to be in 12 sub-Saharan countries, but there even men's enrollment in college is low. In Sweden, women are 37 percent of the college enrollees, and in Argentina 39 percent.

Health

Because of the considerable gap in living standards, especially in nutritional status and medical care, life expectancy for both men and women in the world's richest countries is almost twice that in the poorest: 80 years versus 45 years, according to the United Nations (2). In most of the world, women have a longer average life expectancy than men, except in the places in which there is a preference for male children. In those places infanticide of female children is accomplished either through nutritional deprivation after birth, as in China, or through abortion of female embryos after amniocentesis, as in India. In fact, according to UN statistics, as many as 80 million girls seem to be missing from census data (2).

> In families where sons are the preference and there are many children, little girls lose out in the competition for their mother's scarce time. They may also get less to eat. In a significant number of countries men and boys eat first; women and girls eat what is left. In poor families this may be very little. These patterns then are reflected in lowered life expectancies for women. (3)

Women in some of the poorer countries in the world are also up to 200 times more likely to die as a result of complications of pregnancy, abortion, or childbirth, as women in the richest countries. Worldwide, one-half million women die a year because of inadequate reproductive health care. Twenty-five million suffer serious complications in childbirth, such as hemorrhage and infection (3).

Other health-related consequences of gender inequality can be seen in recent statistics on the spread of AIDS in Africa. Data indicates that AIDS is spreading at an alarming rate throughout the continent, with the fastest-growing number of victims being young women in their twenties (Daley, 1998a, A1). In South Africa alone, 3 million people (about 12 percent of the population) are infected with HIV. This number has more than doubled in three years. In South Africa, that is a 1,123 percent increase in five years, and in Nigeria it is a 3,584 percent increase in the same amount of time. AIDS started in Africa among the urban elite, but it has since reached the poor. Men who travel through the region in search of employment have multiple sexual partners, and transmit HIV to women in their villages and where they work (A10).

Birth control is another major health issue. Contraceptive availability varies according to a woman's economic status. In the core countries most women practice family planning, but places like Mali and Afghanistan have the highest fertility rates and the lowest contraceptive use. They also have the lowest educational rates, since there is a direct correlation between increased education and increased birth control use (Population Crisis Committee, 1988, 4). In the core countries, women control the timing and number of children through universal access to contraception and safe abortion. For 250 million women in less developed countries, most pregnancies are not planned, and unplanned ones cannot be safely terminated.

In the United States many women and children are exposed to health risks for financial reasons. The United States was the 17th lowest in infant mortality, just behind Italy and just ahead of Cuba. Even though the United States spends more on health care than most westernized countries, prenatal care lags behind France, where 96 percent of the mothers received such care. In the United States, only 76 percent did (Martin, 1997, 305).

Clearly, health care conditions for women worldwide are abysmal and are not about to change in the immediate future.

Female Genital Mutilation

Another major health-related inequity is the practice of *female circumcision,* in which the victims are either maimed or die (Hosken, 1982). This ritual, carried out in at least 30 countries in southwest Asia and Africa, has become a highly controversial matter. The practice varies from country to country and has been called *female genital mutilation* (FGM). It is estimated that more than 200 million women in the world have had the procedure and that another 2 million undergo it yearly (Leonard, 1996, 255). It is also practiced in countries where immigrants carry the tradition to the new land. There is some argument that the practice is dying out or being adapted for modern times. Nonetheless, the World Health Organization still sees it as a health hazard.

The practice varies from simply causing a drop of blood to flow from the clitoris or labia, called *cutting* (Crossette, 1998b), all the way through removing the tip of the clitoris, or in extreme cases, clitorectomies, in which the clitoris is completely removed. Sometimes this is done without anesthetic or with unsterilized razors or knives. In extremely rare cases clitorectomies include the removal of the labia as well as the whole clitoris and the external genitalia.

There is also the practice of infibulation, in which the clitoris is removed and the labia is scraped and then the lips are sewed together with thread, catgut, or thorns (Hawke, 1995, 1). The vagina is closed except for a small opening created by the insertion of a splinter of wood, which allows menstrual blood to flow. Some research indicates that the women are then opened on their wedding nights and closed up again on a regular basis (Hosken, 1982).

Many reasons are given for the continuation of these practices, including the belief that it increases fertility, increases a woman's beauty, increases the sexual pleasure of the man, as well as preserving virginity or preventing promiscuity. The practice often marks a transition, either from childhood to adulthood, or earlier in a girl's life. It is commonly done from age four to eight but can also be done from the time the girl is just a few days old until after the birth of her first child (Hawke, 1995, 1).

The medical consequences of the practice can lead to trauma, hemorrhage, infections, painful sexual relations, and psychological problems. If a woman is infibulated, it can also lead to difficult childbirth that can cause death in the mother and baby. Often after they give birth the women are reinfibulated.

The United Nations considers this practice a fundamental violation of a child's rights and a form of discrimination against women and girls (1). It is also considered a violation of human rights. There is no call for it in the Koran or the Bible, but in countries where it is common, it is practiced by both Muslims and Christians. Many countries in which the practice occurs have outlawed it. Nonetheless, it continues to be practiced because of traditional beliefs about the social status and role of women, and because of long-standing traditions that lead to fear of ostracism, ridicule, and other social pressures if one does not conform (Leonard, 1996, 261). As an example of the latter, among the Sara of Chad it serves as a part of the essential phase of a girl's education, in which the group's most important lessons about life and morality are conveyed (262). There is a debate going on among activists and feminists as to whether or not the West, or even more westernized segments of a society, should interfere with these practices. The debate centers around whether or not a culture has the right to practice such rituals and whether it should be allowed, using the argument of cultural relativity. Or is it indeed a violation of human rights?

Employment

Another gender inequity appears in women's relationship to the labor market. Women make up a third of the world's labor force, and their numbers have increased dramatically in the past twenty years. Women's participation in paid labor has grown to the point where there is a "feminization" of the labor market (Beneria, 1997). Women's wages remain low, but the globalization of the world economy has opened doors for women to enter the paid workforce. There has been significant progress in the increase of women's wages worldwide. For example, in the United States, women are increasingly in the labor market and can now support themselves, although they are often not able to support their children without male assistance. Sometimes government policies have assisted in the growing importance of women in industrialization, like providing women with grants for their own small businesses (Feldman, 1992).

Yet, women's participation and economic involvement in productive work is often underestimated. In many parts of the world women have small businesses, often in the informal sector, that are not counted in the gross national product of those countries. They also do agricultural work that is not part of their government's statistics.

International structural adjustment policies have had a negative impact on the economic problems of women. There seems to be a gender bias in policies established by the International Monetary Fund, which were set up so that developing countries would begin to pay back some of their debt. The austerity programs that were established resulted in cutbacks of government monies for their own people. Families have experienced great difficulties in feeding their children, and the restructuring has led to the transformation of daily life, with an "unequal burden" being placed on women, who are hard pressed to find jobs and make ends meet. The tariffs placed on imports into those countries also hurt women and have devastated the economies of poor countries, in Latin America especially (Beneria, 1997).

Women play an important economic role in the daily survival of their families and their countries. Sometimes we hear a child say, "My mother doesn't work." The reality of the fact is that women work and work hard; they just do not always get paid for it (Beneria, 1997). Nor are they paid for that work equitably. Men have continued to maintain a big lead over women in employment and in the amount of money they receive (Population Crisis Committee, 1988, 6). Even in the United States, women earn only 77 cents to a man's dollar.

Gender Violence

The final issue of concern about gender inequality is the nature of gender-related violence. There are a number of areas that are included: rape, battery, murder, and neglect, which have been called a "global war against women" (Heise, 1989, 40). Awareness of these problems rose to the forefront in the early 1970s and has reached international proportions, so that the United Nations has made it part of their global platform in dealing with the elimination of all forms of discrimination against women (United Nations Department of Public Information, 1996).

In the United States, 1 out of every 2 women will be hit at least once in a relationship, and 1.4 million women a year are beaten by their male partners. Thirteen hundred women a year are killed by their past or present husbands or boyfriends, which is about 50 percent of all female murders (Kemp, 1998, 232). Current trends indicate that 8–38 percent of girls may be abused by the time they are 18 years old (118). Some authors have argued that there is a continuum of violence: rape, sexual harassment, pornography, physical abuse of women and children, and all the way to genital mutilation and killing of women (called *femicide*) (Radford & Russell, 1992). For example, recently in Jordan there have been a rash of "honor killings," in which brothers, fathers, and uncles have killed young women whom they believe to have had sex, or have even been seen talking to young men against the wishes of their families.

The problem is international in scope, crossing borders and pervading every society in the world. The one thing that all the victims have in common is that they are female, and the abuse is being done by male members of their families, not only by strangers. According to researchers who have studied abuse of women globally, "the patriarchal hierarchy of most, if not all modern societies has led to a culturally legitimized marital hierarchy in which wives are subordinate to their husbands" (Cornell & Gelles, 1983, x). This hierarchy leads to violence to sustain the power. The violence is a form of coercion to keep the women in their "proper" positions.

The United Nations has taken up the issue of rape as a global crime against women. In 1998 evidence was given at the recently formed International Criminal Court to support the recommendation that rape should be considered a war crime because of its widespread incidence during recent ethnic conflicts (Crossette, 1998c, A1). International attention has been focused on this new style of warfare, which attempts to force pregnancy on the civilian population of a region in order to "poison the womb of the enemy" (4). Rape has been an issue before, but its widespread use in Bosnia and Rwanda has raised new pubic awareness. Organizations like Human Rights Watch and the United Nations Commissioner of Refugees have designated rape as such a widespread and horrific tool of warfare that it may soon be elevated to the status of genocide and crimes against humanity. In the United States, rape continues to be a widespread problem with one of the highest rates in the world: 1 in 4 women raped by the age of 21 (Heise, 1989).

The sexual abuse of female children is also an area of concern. The international trafficking in girls for prostitution became a focus when the United Nations Economic and Social Council (UNESCO) took it up in 1983 and called prostitution a form of slavery (Barry & Leidholdt, 1990, 46). In 1985, UNESCO convened a panel of experts in Madrid, Spain, under the Division of Human Rights and Peace to begin to deal with the problem. Their concern is that the sale of women into the sex trade is escalating and leading to the women's deaths or continued sexual exploitation. In the Philippines, for example, women were once transported and sold into prostitution for the gratification of American military personnel. Now they are sold to brothels and sex shows in Japan, Germany, and the United States. The women, because they are penniless, become prisoners of their pimps (46).

In Thailand, a country of 52,000,000 people, 500,000 women are estimated to be in the sex trade industry (Salayakionond, 1985, 23). Small Thai girls are sold as "virgin prostitutes" to European tourists. Japanese and European businessmen can buy "sex vacations" to South Korea and Thailand, where they purchase the services of young women who receive as little as one-thirtieth of what the men pay. Estimates are that one-quarter of all women in South Korea are, or were once, part of this industry. They are called "pleasure girls," and are licensed by the International Trade Federation; they are encouraged "to entertain" visiting tourists from Japan and the West seeking their services (Maniquis, 1985, 23).

Let's remember here that gender is a structural condition. In this case, poor, often desperate families are forced to sell young women into prostitution because they are unable to make money by any other means. The sale of a woman's body becomes a commodity exchange, one between her family and the buyer, and between her pimp and the "john." Sometimes the argument is made that she is selling herself, of her own free will. However, we must remember that there is a global market for her services, and she is part of the world system economy. Her sexuality is not determined by free will but by the economic and social structures that place her in this position. It is not a profession but rather a form of sex discrimination, sexual violence, and the violation of human dignity (Barry & Leidholdt, 1990, 48). It has to be viewed in the context of economic exploitation and the larger framework of poverty suffered in developing parts of the world.

The United Nations is taking an active lead in the battle to eradicate sex tourism (Perpinan, 1985, 22). There have been efforts to control it in the Asia-Pacific region, with governments placing stricter penalties on all those responsible for it. In fact, much is being done around the world to eradicate the other kinds of gender inequality and discrimination that have been documented here.

Theories About Gender Inequality

Is biology destiny? That is a question that has plagued scholars and feminist thinkers for generations. When Darwin did his writing, the answer was "Yes." Now the question is still under debate, with the contemporary answer coming up "No." Does being born male or female determine the rest of one's life? Is the genetic-based explanation for gender differences "proof" of inborn characteristics that can then justify gender inequality? Some people find answers in the Bible or the Koran or other religious writings to explain the differences between the sexes. Others look to primates and other animals to explain, using sociobiology, that human and animal behavior are linked. The answer from a social science approach is that gender inequality might be a mix of all of these ideas: society, biology, psychology, religion, and culture. And feminist scholars argue that it is the patriarchy that leads to women's inequality.

Biological Explanations

People who argue that "biology is destiny" cite evidence from genetics that says that human beings have evolved from other animal species. Using this argument, they say that male baboons, for example, are far more aggressive than females and that human beings are close to baboons on the evolutionary scale. This argument attests to males having more testosterone and females having more estrogen, thus leading to sex differences. Because of testosterone, males are bigger, stronger, and more aggressive. They have stronger sex drives and are better suited to hunting and defense. The power inequities that have evolved are due to biological differentials that give males more physical power, which leads to the development of more political and economic power. Females, because of their reproductive roles—the birthing and nursing of infants—are in a vulnerable position, this argument goes, and are biologically constructed so as to need the care and protection of males. But not all testosterone is male, nor are women purely estrogen. Males and females both carry combinations of hormones and inevitably have differing testosterone-to-estrogen ratios.

The story goes that the gendered division of labor is based on these biological differences. Small pre-industrial societies needed to survive on a subsistence level. Because men could hunt and defend, they went out to track animals, defend against enemies, and protect the females, who remained back at camp to birth, raise infants, gather fruits and vegetables, and hunt small animals.

Of late, little credence is given to this reasoning. Studies done in the 1980s indicate that the belief that all animals behave the same way is a myth (Sperling, 1991).

Newer data indicate that in some animal groupings males are not aggressive. In fact, animals like lemurs and gibbons show no sex differences in dominance. There is plenty of evidence in the animal world of both non-aggressive males and aggressive females. Thus the sociobiological theory has been criticized as not taking important social and cultural factors into consideration.

Social scientists tend not to buy fully the sociobiology explanation. We say that there *are* genetic-based differences, but that cultural influences, socialization, psychological development, and the gendered division of labor are more important in determining inequalities. When we look at different societies and across history, we see that the tasks and duties that are assigned to males and females vary, and that male and female behaviors are defined by the society and culture in which one lives. To say it is all biological is far too easy and does not account for human complexity.

Sociocultural Explanations

Most women and men in industrial and post-industrial societies, like the United States and much of the contemporary world, have a more fluid definition of the division of labor than the one just described. Women do not spend their time only having babies and rearing them. Most women work at both paid and unpaid labor, take care of their children, and contribute to the family upkeep with food, clothing, and shelter (Lorber, 1998, 6). Men can and do care for children while laboring at paid work. Human beings have a more complicated system of gender relations than do animals. Biology might play an important role, but it is interfaced with society's expectations and its gendered behaviors.

Major social and cultural institutions, like religion, the media, and families, support the system of gender inequality. It is built into the organization of marriage and relationships, work and economic life, politics, religion, the arts, and the language that we speak (7). Every society decides how the division of labor shall be constructed and then provides the socialization and institutions that keep that system in place.

Conflict theory would say that gender inequalities are based on the unequal distribution of wealth, power, and control. Women, without the locus of power, are one of the subordinated groups in society and are in conflict with males, who hold the status positions that grant them the privileges associated with being male. The argument is that political and economic factors keep women in subordinate positions and that the two groups are in conflict, battling to change the power relations between them.

Religious arguments are also given for gender differentials. Religious arguments seem to follow a structural functionalist perspective, believing that inequality and inferior positions of women serve to keep the social system going and ordered. Certainly many religions teach that men are superior to women. Islamic, Jewish, Hindu, Buddhist, and Christian dogma are interpreted as alleging women's inferiority. Under the argument that God's primary creation is man, not woman, women become secondary and derivative from men. They are also created *for* men, not only *from* men, and they are alleged to be the primary agents of evil and sin (Hassan, 1989, 11).

Patriarchal ideology has given rise to the idea that there is legitimate evidence in religious writings of man's superiority, which justifies casting women into subservient positions. The Bible, the Koran, the Book of Mormon, and other religious tracts are given as evidence that male superiority to women is God-given. Religious rituals are organized and conducted by men, and ancient spiritual myths about the creation are tied to a belief in the superiority of men. Religious explanations continue to hold credence in contemporary society. These patriarchal ideologies explain and justify inequities between men and women in a number of places in the world.

Feminist Theories

Feminist thinkers have spent a great deal of time attempting to explain gender differentials. Much of their work has added a depth of understanding to the complexity of gender relations and might help the reader make sense out of the inequality between men and women. Feminists are "not satisfied with the explanation that it is natural, God-given, or necessary because women get pregnant and give birth and men do not" (Lorber, 1998, 7). Some feminists have given a psychological spin to explaining differences, while others have more of an economic, racial, and social analysis. We'll begin with the analysis that seems to be the most currently accepted and with the discussions going on among feminist scholars today. This section is based on the excellent explication done by feminist scholar Judith Lorber (1998).

Psychoanalytic Theory

Nancy Chodorow (1978) has had a significant influence on contemporary thinking about gender differences. Taking off on the work of Sigmund Freud, who primarily studied male personality development during the rise of capitalism and the early European patriarchal family structure, Chodorow argues that the source of men's domination is their unconscious ambivalent need for women and women's emotionality. Simultaneously, men reject women as potential castrators (Lorber, 1998, 104). Women submit to men because of their own unconscious desires for emotional connectedness. These gendered identities come out of the *Oedipal complex,* the psychological separation from the mother as the child develops a sense of individual identity.

According to Freudian theory, infants bond with the mother because she is usually the primary parent. Boys learn that they must separate from her and identify with their fathers to establish their masculinity. This leads them to become independent, objective, and rational, with strong ego boundaries, which is highly valued in Western society (Lorber, 1998, 104). Women are seen as a threat to men because they remind them of their dependence on the mother. However, men also need women for their emotionality and intimacy, which men cannot give to each other. The ambivalence leads to a love-hate relationship (104).

Girls continue to identify with their mothers and develop more fluid ego boundaries that make them empathic, sensitive, and emotional. These are the capacities that make them potentially good mothers and able to handle men's emotional needs. But since men are not available emotionally, women want to have children so as to have someone with whom to bond; thus they have children and reproduce the psychological gendering of society (104).

Although well accepted, this theory is not without its flaws. Certainly it is based on the white, middle-class, Western family we read about in Chapter 4. It assumes that all men are emotionally distant and that all families are heterosexual, neither of which is the case. In other parts of the world, fathers are more involved in parenting, and more men are doing so in the West. Chodorow's theory also assumes that all men in the West are misogynist (woman hating) and that all women are nurturing and desirous of having children, neither of which is the case (Lorber, 1998, 111).

This theory also does not account for the economic and social manifestations of gender inequality. It is primarily a psychological explanation, which in and of itself cannot totally explain the vast differences between men's and women's access to resources and the phenomenon of inequality between countries in the West and developing parts of the world. Nor does it explain the differences between men and women in other cultures, where the socialization process might differ from the one this theory establishes as the norm. It has a Western bias that needs critiquing.

Development Theory

The next set of theories tries to make visible the pervasiveness of overt discriminatory practices, both formal and informal, that lead to inequality. Although there are a few theories that fit under this rubric, like Marxist feminism and liberal feminism, which we studied in Chapter 3, here I focus on development theory because of its international orientation and its emphasis on human rights for women.

Development feminism argues that during the Industrial Revolution, when the production of commodities moved out of the home and into the factory, men and women, as well as children, had to go out to work (remember the history of the family in Chapters 4 and 5). Men who could support their families completely were the factory owners; their wives could stay home and raise the children with the help of servants. The rest of society—immigrants, working-class people, racial and ethnic minorities—had to struggle to make a living, and lives for women were particularly difficult because they had to juggle work and home life to keep their families alive.

Marxist feminist theory, as you might remember, argued that men's labor is primarily in paid production and women's in the family. Women are exploited because they work at production and reproduction in the home and in low-paying jobs outside the home as well. Marxist feminists used as the model for their study the Western, capitalist family.

Development feminists take that idea further and say that economic exploitation of women in countries on the way to developing is even greater. They show that women in Latin America, the Caribbean, Asia, and Africa are paid less than male workers, whether they work in factories or in piecework at home. They grow food and earn money in any way possible to supplement what their migrant husbands send them (Lorber, 1998, 46). This theory talks about the global economy that links

Photo 6.2   Women as the "last colony," washing clothes and children in a tent city in India. Photographer: Mary Thieme

countries whose economies focus on service, information, and finance, with manufacturing sites and the sources of raw materials in other countries.

Development theory is based on the analysis of the world system we studied in Chapters 2 and 3. Theorists argue that the gendered division of labor in developing countries is the result of centuries of colonization and imperialism. Women's traditional contribution to food production was undermined in favor of exportable crops like coffee. Male workers were favored in mining and large-scale agriculture, but workers were not paid living wages to support their families. Women had to provide, as best they could, on land that was poor and unsustainable.

Since achieving independence, many of these countries have sought business investments and financial help from the West. However, because of the consequent restructuring of the economies, women have suffered further. Women, when hired, receive lower wages than men. Men, since they are considered heads of households, obtain the higher-status jobs or get the government monies for agricultural development. Married women have to use all their money to feed their children and are paid the least of all. Some of these theorists have called poor women "the last colony" (47).

Development theory has gained much credence during the past ten years and seems to be the one that international organizations are adopting in understanding conditions for women. It might not explain the initial causes of women's oppression, but it does begin with the late 1800s and provides reasons for the vast data that show women's subjugation economically, in health, in education, and through gender violence (51). We have used development theory frequently in describing the conditions for women in developing parts of the world in this book.

Multiracial Theory

The next theories try to destabilize that which many people think is normal and natural and moral. They attempt to develop new ideas for family life, for gender relationships, and for work. They are rebellious because they "question the dominant paradigm" and threaten the status quo, because they ask us to think outside of the hegemonic ways we have been taught to think and to become creative in our own gendered lives.

Multiracial theory, also called multiethnic or multicultural feminism, talks about the *intersectionality* of gender, race, ethnicity, and social class (Lorber, 1998, 134). It says you cannot look at any one of those issues alone; there is an interaction that is "synergistic: together they construct a social location. Some locations are more oppressive than others because they are the result of multiple systems of domination" (134). Thus gender inequality is rooted in this intersectionality.

Gender, race, class, and ethnicity create a hierarchy of stratification that puts white, upper-class men at the top and lower-class women and men who are disadvantaged at the bottom. Race, ethnicity, and class are located along a continuum from advantage to disadvantage, but gender is a dichotomy. By this they mean that "the social location of a man and a woman of the same racial, ethnic or social class status differs" (134). Men of a lower status group may be oppressed in different ways than women of the same group. A woman may not be more disadvantaged than a man, especially the lower in status the group is. For example, black men and women in the United States are both of low status, but black women are more able to earn money and move up socioeconomically than are black men.

This theory discusses *social maps* that chart a person's position and life chances, values, identities, and consciousness of self, depending on position in the social structure. These theorists also give evidence about the domination in politics and social agendas of the most advantaged groups and how those advantages play out in funding and in marginalizing these groups. They show that since the norm against which such groups are measured is set by those who are advantaged, the disadvantaged groups are defined as problems and as deviant from the norm of white. This feminist theory says that most of the problems are structural but there are cultural variables that play out as well. Thus there are no such things as "male and female." There are white women, black women, white men, black men, and a variety of other social statuses that make up the hierarchy. It is that multiple system of domination that must be used to explain gender complexity and inequalities.

Social Constructionist Theory

This theory sees gender as a social institution that is built into all organizations in society. As an institution it teaches us to be our gendered selves, with unequal power, privileges, and economic resources (160). The family is the prime site for the social construction of gender, which leads to differences in male and female characteristics and produces gender inequality. In other words, we "do gender" and then think that is the way it has to be. *Inequality is the core of gender; it has to be done this way.* Men and women become socially differentiated, and then this is justified so as to continue the unequal treatment. It is an invisible process in which we all collude. This theory argues that the dichotomies we discussed earlier, like male and female, are in fact social constructions that could be set up differently. We can see that genital and hormonal ambiguities and similar abilities between men and women are gender blurring that points to other possible social constructions. There is a gender continuum along which we all fall; the argument is that most of the time we "do" gender, allowing the differences and the inequities to continue (172). We collude with the continuing inequalities.

Postmodern and Queer Theory

This is a new historical era, one in which those who are on the edges, on the margins, at the fringe are causing a shift in the thinking of theorists to include the marginalized. That is why it is necessary to have texts about the family in the world, with the full understanding that one cannot even begin to explain the family in all its complexity or to make any universal statements about its nature. There are no longer any universal truths. In fact, there is no rationality; all is relative, depending on who you are and where you are coming from. There is no grand narrative, no grand explanation. There is no one voice; there are many voices. This is postmodern thinking.

The best way to explain postmodernism is to describe it visually and musically. Imagine contemporary hip-hop or hard rock music. Think of music that you might hear on the radio, a pop music station. For the most part the music is dissonant. To some it sounds raucous and harsh. This is the postmodern world. There might be a few words you can understand, there might be a melody that comes through once in a while, but for the most part it mirrors our daily lives—postmodern, busy, loud, and challenging. It is not harmonious, it is not lyrical or poetic, as in the Romantic era. It is not measured or regular, like rock and roll of the '60s and '70s. Like our contemporary world, it is completely off center and unexplainable, except to the people who understand it.

Now imagine a new building. The base is of a classical Greco-Roman design with arches, in the middle it moves to a Victorian form of architecture, and at the top is a modern, contemporary skyscraper. The building itself is a joke. That is the essence of postmodernism. It is about fragmentation, about the uncertainty of life, about the fact that the "core" might disappear, that there no longer needs to be a center; that we need to shift the center, to build on the foundations of the past, while including the voices of those formerly excluded from the center.

Although similar to social construction feminism, queer theory and postmodern theory take the points further in challenging gender categories and gender inequalities. They argue that there really is no male or female, that they are merely categories that dichotomize people into two sexes, two sexualities, and two genders. Equality will come when there are so many sexes, sexualities, and genders that one cannot win over the others (174).

Using terms like *deconstruct, destroy, demythologize,* queer and postmodern theorists argue that one must read the "texts." In all cultural artifacts, like art, music, literature, movies, and newspapers, embedded hidden messages represent the dominant viewpoint of the time. A film made during a conservative era will be different than one made during a time of social change (181). The audience also constructs the text by its own interpretations. Our job is to tease out the hidden messages in the text and debunk or at least demystify them, make them conscious and clear. It is these texts that perpetuate gender dichotomies and maintain the dominant social order. The challenge is to change that.

An example would be country and western music. Are the lyrics telling us something about male and female behaviors, about relationships, about the nature of what is good and bad, right and wrong, how to be and how to act out our gendered selves? What about TV soap operas? What do they tell you about males and females in early twenty-first-century America? What do they tell you about how you should be living your life? How does commercial television construct gendered identities? This is what postmodern feminists ask.

Queer theory goes beyond cultural productions to look at sexuality. Queer theory argues that we are "performing" gender. How we carry our bodies, what we wear, how we display ourselves are all gender self-creations. Queer theorists argue that we can defy these gendered prescriptions. They want us all to be rebels and "queers" in everyday life, to smash the social proscriptions and create freer social definitions of gender. They might not provide us with an explanation of why the genders are so different, but they do provide us with a tool for changing gender differences.

Where Does This Leave Us?

Let's look at a contemporary issue and try to apply some of these theories. Women and men in Afghanistan had been living lives similar to many Americans, with industrialization and modernization equalizing the differentials between men and women. Then the Taliban revolution occurred, and the construction of gender was completely up for grabs. This story shows how easily gender is constructed, then changed and then reconstructed again. It provides a vivid example about the nature of gender relations today.

Gender Construction in Afghanistan

The story of gender in Afghanistan is the story of how gender is socially constructed. In the course of twenty years, the roles and definitions of what is acceptable for men and women have changed a number of times. In 1973, after two centuries of monarchy, the king was ousted in a military takeover that lasted until 1979, when the Soviets invaded and instituted a communist regime. From 1979 until the Soviets' final withdrawal in 1989, many new social reforms were imposed, following the Soviet communist model. Many Afghanis fled the country, seeking refuge in Iran and Pakistan. Then in 1992 civil war broke out, and rival factions struggled for power. Again millions of refugees fled, uprooted from their ancestral homes by the fighting. After that time, the Taliban, a fundamentalist Islamic faction, gained a foothold in a large portion of the country. With them came another social transformation, this time in the form of a return to fundamentalist interpretations of the Koran (Culville, 1997, 3–9). Then, as we know, September 11 occurred in the United States, and President George W. Bush declared war on terrorists, attacking Afghanistan in search for Osama bin Laden. With that war came another shift, when a Western-backed government was put into power.

The Afghanis' story as it relates to gender is most enlightening. Under the monarchy, after World War II, many women entered the workforce. Although Afghanistan is an Islamic society, there was a liberal interpretation of the Koran during that era. Many legal and constitutional reforms were instituted that gave women the right to vote, freedom of movement, and education and employment rights.

There was always the belief that men are superior to women, but standards of acceptable behavior varied greatly among Afghanistan's very diverse populations. The rural interpretations required that men keep strict control over women, while urban interpretations emphasized another spirit in Islam: equality, justice, and education for both men and women. In the cities, women went to work, entered the marketplace to become sole breadwinners, especially in families where the husbands had been killed in the fighting of the previous twenty years. It was similar to the Western pattern, in which women went out to work, many becoming professionals, surgeons, doctors, lawyers, accountants, and civil servants.

Under the communist rule of the Soviets, liberalization was forced on the rural populations, too; they had been reluctant to grant their daughters the kind of freedom that existed in the cities. Women, who had once worn the *burka* (a complete body covering that goes from head to toe and has a lattice grill over the eyes), took on Western garb or began to wear the *chador* (a scarf that covers most of the face but not the eyes). Young women were sent to schools, under Soviet orders, and there was considerable resentment among the rural population for having to liberalize their gender roles.

Then the Taliban began to win. The Taliban were a rural-based, generally uneducated group of young men who were concerned with security and with preserving their traditions, and who had a far more fundamentalist interpretation of the Koran than either the Soviets or the monarchy that preceded them. Now gender roles took on a whole new look. All women in the parts of Afghanistan under their rule were required to wear the burka. With few exceptions, women were forbidden to work outside of the home. Girls were banned from schools and universities, and all the freedoms and flexibility that were possible in the gendered selves of Afghanis were withdrawn. If a woman was seen without her burka, even if she was in a chador, she would be beaten publicly for breaking the law. Women who were once teachers, doctors, civil servants, and in the public sector were told they could not go to work. Schools were closed, not only for girls but for boys, too, since most of the teachers were women. Afghani women lost most of the freedoms it took a century to win.

Life dramatically changed for men, too. When gender roles are redefined, it has implications for everyone. Prohibitions, sometimes issued at the rate of two a week, ordered that men could not shave or even trim their beards. Men could not listen to music, and Taliban checkpoints were covered with the innards of music cassettes. No one could watch television, and they could not have any photographs of living creatures.

Not all Afghanis opposed this regime. Many rural peasants were pleased that the reforms were being instituted. They believed that their society had become too lax and Western and that gender roles were far too liberal, not following the tenets of the Koran. The Taliban were forcibly imposing their rural culture and politics on the cities, and the clash is remarkable. The Taliban faced much criticism, including criticism from other Islamic countries, about the reforms, and prior to the war there was some loosening on the education issue. Nonetheless, women were still not allowed to register for classes, and women teachers were not allowed into class-rooms with male students. Because there was restriction on their movement, women could not receive medical care, which was quite problematic, since Afghanistan already had a very high maternal and infant mortality.

Once the war on terrorism in Afghanistan occurred, and a Western-backed gov-ernment was installed, things changed back slowly. Women are now able to go with-out the burka, although many are afraid to take it off, in fear that the Taliban will return. Schools have opened for women; women are back in positions as doctors and ministers in the government. Although there is much yet to be accomplished, the definition of what gender is remains malleable in Afghanistan, and is still being determined.

In a matter of months, what was expected, how one was to act, move, and be was completely redefined. Because of the political conditions, overlaid with religious patriarchal ideology, gender behaviors were redefined to fit the expectations of those who were in positions of power. In most other parts of the world, gendered behaviors and definitions are not as quickly altered. Nonetheless, the example helps us understand how the structural conditions of a society play out in gender and the family. By seeing this changing of gender roles and the resultant inequalities, we see that gender is very much a social construction.

Summary

In this chapter we began by investigating the concept of transgenderism and the interplay between gender expression and the social construction of male and female behaviors. We saw that gender can be viewed through the lens of performance. From there we studied how gender is a socialized phenomenon, taught first by the family, and reinforced and continued by teachers, the media, and other institutions of society. We were again shown that gender is a structural condition that promotes inequality, and we investigated the "no problem problem" of inequality and why it is not seen as an issue in American society.

We looked at sexism—individual, cultural, and institutional—and were urged to make a gendered analysis, noting that gender is about power relationships. By looking cross-culturally through studies, we saw that inequality between the gen-ders exists everywhere in the world, and we looked at data that corroborated that point extensively. We studied agriculture, health, education, employment, and gender-related violence to cite the gender inequalities and the forms of discrimination that occur based on which sex one is born into.

Finally, we looked at a number of theories employed to explain these differences. By looking at biological and at sociocultural explanations, which included religion and patriarchal ideology, we saw that there are many ways to explain gender-related disparities.

We focused in on the feminist theories that have delved deeply into these differences and learned about feminist psychoanalytic theory, development theory, multiracial theory, social constructionist, and postmodern and queer theory. Last, we studied the definition, redefinition, and further defining of gender that is occurring in current-day Afghanistan, to illustrate gender as a social construction.

CHAPTER 7

Race, Class, Ethnicity, Caste, and Family Life

Race, class, ethnic background, and caste—like gender—are structural conditions that impact how family life plays out. These variables are ordained by a society, are determined to be important, and then are acted upon behaviorally, resulting in ranking differences among people. In this chapter I use observations and information gained on my most recent trip with Semester at Sea, which was filmed by *Road Rules* and shown on MTV in the summer and fall of 1999. I visited the Bahamas, Cuba, Brazil, South Africa, Kenya, India, Malaysia, Vietnam, China, and Japan. It became painfully obvious on that trip that every society has a pecking order and sets up its own hierarchy of inequality. Societies use skin color, income, historically accrued wealth, ethnic background, or birth-ascribed rank to determine where a family fits within its system. In every part of the world, people make ranking distinctions among themselves and others. Sometimes those rankings are benign; however, other times these distinctions lead to war, genocide, and cruel discrimination that can be severe enough to cause death.

When I returned from circumnavigating the world, I drove down the coast of Washington, Oregon, and California. One night I stopped in a motel nestled in the redwoods of California. In the office I found the owner, a fortyish man of Indian origin. I was surprised to find someone who looked so similar to the people I had just encountered on my travels through India. I learned that this man was part of a subcaste from the Gujarti region of India; his people were of the Hindu religion and served as *vaishyas* or traders. Back in India they had once been employed to calculate tithes that were owed to medieval kings by farmers in their region near the Arabian Sea. Upon their arrival in the United States, through the pattern of chain migration of immigrants, they gradually bought up 50 percent of all motels in the United States, although they make up only 1 percent of the American population (Varadarajan, 1999, 36–37).

What this encounter showed me is that although we think there is no caste system in the United States, in fact, vestiges of the uniquely Indian-based stratification system have found their way into American society. I realized that caste, like race, class, ethnicity, and gender, is a way we divide people. I saw, too, that lives are lived following preconceived paths set out by the structural conditions of one's society. Needless to say, family life is impacted by these structures. I saw this man and his wife raising their two daughters far from India, still following Indian traditions while living the American dream.

The Indian caste system is based upon a *jati* (a verb meaning "to be born"), just as one is born into a family. A jati extends the concept of family to a larger social group of cousins, potential in-laws, and acquaintances whom one can expect to marry. There are several thousand jatis, or caste communities, throughout India (Elder, 1996, 49).

You will remember from Chapter 5 that *caste* is a hierarchy of rank that locks individuals into the grouping of their parents, and is immutable. Where one is born, one remains. It is also an inequitable system, as certain castes are usually associated with certain occupations. For example, the dalits are those who were once called "untouchables" because they were associated with polluting roles in Hindu society. Untouchables were given the jobs of dealing with human waste, cleaning latrines, sweeping streets, and removing the dead carcasses of animals. They were to be avoided because they might demean those of higher castes, especially the Brahmins, or priestly caste. Mahatma Gandhi crusaded on their behalf, and the name was changed to *harijans*, or children of God. Now they are known as *dalits*, or the "oppressed," a name that reflects their attempt to seek recognition as equal members of Indian society.

While I was in India I visited a dalit village and saw abysmal accommodations and squalor that shocked me. Poor families were jammed into small huts, no latrines or running water were evident, and children were emaciated, struggling to survive. Across the road was a village of higher castes who refused to talk or interact with their neighbors for fear of contamination. Although my hosts said that the government had done much to eliminate the discrimination against the dalits, it was obvious that more was needed.

In contrast, I visited the home of a high-ranking Brahmin. There I saw what looked like a typical American homelife. The family had TV, a home entertainment system, a microwave, many rooms for only four people, and a sense of entitlement and power that came of their rank. It was clear that caste, although said by some to be diminishing in importance, still remains a method of division in Indian society. Every society has such divisions. In the United States, the divisions are based on race and class. In Brazil, it might be class, and in South Africa it is generally race.

These distinctions among people, the creation of the hierarchy of social order, is known by social scientists as *social stratification*.

Social Stratification

Stratification is a common feature of systems of shared social inequality. It is a set of socially ranked categories, whether given at birth or not. If it is given at birth, as

Photo 7.1   Social stratification in India: street scene of contemporary lower castes.
Photographer: Mary Thieme

in the Indian castes, then the ranking is traditionally defined. For example, a society will indicate that some people are intrinsically worth more than others, will rationalize this difference by developing a myth of the origin of this difference, and will legitimate the system that keeps the differences in place (Berreman, 1999, 40). A society will also say what behaviors are acceptable for each group and give different rewards to each group. Then each group is given "different access to goods, services, livelihood, respect, self-determination, peace of mind, pleasure and other valued things including nourishment, shelter, health, independence, justice, security and long life" (41).

We know that in the United States, for example, people on welfare receive poorer health care, are looked down upon by other groups, live in poor housing, and have less money available for leisure and fun activities. They receive inferior education and can't buy as much as wealthier people. That is what is meant by differing rewards and access. Every society decides who will be on the top and who will be on the bottom, whether it is determined by skin color, money, upbringing, sex, or ethnic background. Family life reflects these differences, since families are embedded within these social structures. The unequal distribution of opportunities also has consequences in terms of life expectancy and basic quality of life.

Now we will look at some of the kinds of divisions that societies make, looking specifically at countries that exhibit a more exaggerated delineation than we may see at home. It is important to remember that in the United States we have these distinctions, but because of our false consciousness we tend to ignore them when they are close to us. I challenge you to use these examples to consider how we make distinctions at home and how they are similar or different in other places.

Fluidity of Race and Ethnicity Definitions

Race is, in fact, a very complicated concept. Although in the United States we like to think we know what race is—black, white, Latino, biracial, Asian—the reality is that these are arbitrary social constructions that change over time and place. What was once called black or white, even in the United States, has changed. We know that "a person defined as white in the year 2002 might have been defined as black or Irish or Italian at various times in American history" (Gallagher, 1999, 1). Race, and the often-used term *ethnicity*, are social constructions, because their meanings develop through a focus on characteristics that a given society deems as socially important. Gallagher says that they are social products that are based on cultural values, not on scientific facts.

Racial and ethnic definitions are based on the physical traits a society chooses to value or devalue. In fact, each society's values are based on a different set of historical experiences, cultural circumstances, and political definitions. Thus ideas about race and ethnicity can vary both between and within countries. Usually people think of race as *the sharing of inherited characteristics, something that is defined as shared physical distinctions*. Racial groups are thought of as separate and see themselves, or others see them, as unique. Ethnicity, on the other hand, is often defined as *the sharing of a common origin or a separate subculture*. The distinction is not about physical characteristics but about sharing a culture that is transmitted through language, religion, and history.

I'll give you some examples of the fluidity of racial and ethnic delineations. In the United States, people who are of mixed black and white backgrounds are now defined as *biracial* by the U.S. Census Bureau. However, under apartheid, until 1994, the same people would have been called *African* in South Africa. In the United States, under antimiscegenation laws, families were sometimes parted by the attempted "passing" as white of a lighter-skinned family member. This led to the breakup of families and a denial of ancestral origins.

A person of Indian origin in the United States would be defined as Asian, while in South Africa that person would be called *colored*, a term we would find offensive if used in the United States. In Britain people who are not white are called *black*, whether they are from Africa, India, or any other nonwhite country of origin. In the United States, someone born black in the South might have tried to pass as white in the North if he or she was light-skinned. In Brazil, where there is much less of a racially defined hierarchy, children of the same family can be categorized through intermediate racial groupings. Thus sisters and brothers in the same family might be placed in different categories, all of which would come under the main category Brazilian (Omi & Winant, 1999, 11). Needless to say, this can have traumatic consequences for people within the same family. The race you belong to depends on where you live, your family, and the historical era you live in. Race and ethnicity, like gender, are social constructions.

Social constructions are created by people, and they can change, depending on the social historical moment. When Jews, Irish, and Italians first came to the United States, they were not called white; they were in a racially ambiguous state. Now they are all considered white. This illustrates the social construction of race: definitions are constantly changing, and with the changes come different opportunity structures and access to resources.

Race

In 1992, I had the honor of spending two weeks with Archbishop Desmond Tutu while we sailed from Brazil to South Africa. During that remarkable time I was able to have a private audience with the man I see as a cross between Mother Teresa and Martin Luther King, Jr. Tutu was the recipient of the Nobel Peace Prize in 1984 and later went on to establish the Truth and Reconciliation Commission in South Africa after the end of apartheid.

During my meeting with him, I asked a question I had long been trying to answer for myself. "Why is it," I asked, "that people do not want to deal with issues of race? And how is it best to approach the topic as a teacher?" He gave a deep sigh and told me that this was one of the hardest questions he, too, had ever confronted. But his answer was about *fear*. "People," he said, "are afraid of what they might lose and what might happen to them when they confront others of a different race." In South Africa, whites were afraid of retaliation by blacks at the end of apartheid. It has not come. In the United States we fear the unknown and we fear difference. He urged me to continue to reach students on the subject and not to run away from this most difficult subject just because people do not want to deal with it.

I tell you this story because, as a colleague of mine once said, "Racism is like a serpent living in the ceiling of our house. One day the serpent will emerge again and we will have to slay it" (Scott, 1999). In other parts of the world it is at the forefront of the discourse, while in the United States, where race has been an issue since this country began, we don't like to talk about it. Yet as W. E. B. Du Bois, famed early civil rights leader and educator, put it, "The color line is still with us" (Zinn, 1999, 4).

In South Africa, the Truth and Reconciliation Commission, organized in 1994, met for years to hear about the racial atrocities committed there under apartheid. The commission, headed by Tutu, heard testimony from both blacks and whites about their participation in brutality and atrocities during that era. Linked to the telling was application for amnesty, which was determined after the party told the whole truth. The idea was that truth and amnesty would be linked to reconciliation and would move the country beyond racial divisions (Jones, 1998, 204). It was a unique approach to dealing with horrific behaviors on both sides. Rather than prosecute the criminal acts, the commission decided to hear the truths and then forgive those who committed them. In only a few cases have they decided to bring criminal charges against the perpetrators. Although the testimony was sometimes difficult to hear for those who were the victims, ultimately it is hoped that this approach will be effective in healing the racial divisions and transitioning the country to harmony between the races (Asmal, Asmal, & Roberts, 1996).

The situation in South Africa is the most blatant example of the worst that can happen as a result of racial distinctions. Even today, much work has to be done to heal the racial wounds. The impact of this trauma was great on family life in South Africa, injuring families who lost fathers, mothers, sons, and daughters who disappeared into prisons, some never to return. Now another impact is taking place as families begin to hear the truth about what occurred to their loved ones who were brutalized under apartheid. Some are forgiving of those who murdered and maimed their family members. The economy in South Africa was divided into two countries, one for whites, which resembled the First World, another for blacks and coloreds (mixed-race peoples), whose life was like those in other Third World countries. Let's take a look at apartheid in South Africa and its impact on family life.

South Africa and Race

White supremacy in South Africa began with the Dutch settlement at Cape Town in 1652. For three and a half centuries, the white minority expanded and built its racial hegemony over the nonwhite majority (Ramsay, 1999, 159). Through a gradual process of enslaving, creating servitude, and taking over of land, the whites were able to move the indigenous Khoisan and Bantu-speaking peoples out of their homelands and impose a system of domination that lives on even today. The Boers, originally Dutch-speaking farmers, evolved a language known as Afrikaans, a form of Cape Dutch. Gradually they moved north, seeking good farmland. They did so also to move away from the British, who were slowly arriving in the region. The Boers killed many Zulus and other local peoples along the way. By the 1860s, whites were growing in numbers and putting indigenous Africans on reservations in order to continue their expansion.

Although the British took over rule of Cape Colony in the nineteenth century and treated the Africans somewhat better, the lines of racial stratification were well entrenched. By early in the twentieth century, the British and Boers fought a war in which Boers, blacks, and coloreds were interned in concentration camps. By 1910, when the war ended, an independent country of South Africa was formed, primarily made up of former British settlements and Afrikaner republics. The Bantu-speaking peoples (the linguistic groups of the region) were relegated to subservient positions.

By 1948 the Afrikaners were voted into office and formalized apartheid, a separation of peoples. New laws of segregation were enacted, which imposed pass laws, under which black peoples were forced to carry "passbooks" at all times to prove that they lived in certain areas. If they needed to go somewhere else, they had to apply for permission. Under the Group Areas Act, more than 80 percent of South Africa was reserved for whites, who were no more than 14 percent of the population (Ramsay, 1999, 160). Blacks were confined to townships or on white-owned farms. Ten homelands were established in poor, rural parts of the country, where blacks were required to live unless they had work near the cities or on the white farms. These homelands were called "nations" and spread black citizens out so that there was no black majority in any one area, leaving the whites in control. Coloreds and Asians were never given any clear status; they remained ambiguous, never quite white and not black either. All groups were pitted against each other, with job classifications established to reserve the best jobs for whites, the middle-level positions for Asians and coloreds, and unskilled positions for blacks (160).

Consequences of Apartheid on Families

"While for whites apartheid was an ideology of mass delusion, for Blacks it meant continuous suffering" (160). Large numbers of blacks were forcibly moved when they squatted in white areas, seeking jobs there to feed their families. In the squatter camps and townships, the blacks lived in fear of raids by police coming to check on their passbooks. The camps themselves were hovels, with one spigot of running water for thousands of people. They were ringed by barbed wire and surrounded by tanks, with white soldiers patrolling the periphery. Children lived in terror that their parents would be rounded up for not having the right passbooks or for being members of radical organizations. Terror and fear were constant emotions under apartheid.

I visited the squatter camps and townships in 1992 and 1999, and was appalled to see, in the richest country in Africa, thousands of people living in horrific conditions. Many of my students and I were physically sickened by the squalor, the sadness, and the poverty. Education was second-rate, people traveled countless miles to white areas for employment, when they could find it, and conditions were overcrowded, with numerous health hazards.

Resistance to white domination by blacks has been a significant part of South African history, and impacts family life greatly. Blacks have fought against whites since 1659, continuing up to the present time. The African National Congress, which was founded in 1912 to focus on black liberation, was long an outlawed black association. Many of its leaders were incarcerated for years because of their political activity against the white government. In 1960 there was a massacre of 60 persons in Sharpeville during a peaceful protest against the passbooks. In the 1960s, Nelson Mandela was incarcerated for what ended up being 22 years because of his political activity as part of the militant branch of the ANC. In 1976 there were riots in Soweto, a Johannesburg township, when students protested the unequal educational system. The Black Consciousness Movement, led by Steven Biko, urged the unification of all black peoples in South Africa. Biko was killed in 1977 at the hands of the dreaded security police.

Because of increased agitation by the ANC, coupled with worldwide sanctions against the South African government, by 1990 the then-president of the white supremacist party (the National Party), F. W. deKlerk, released Nelson Mandela from prison and began the process of dismantling apartheid. In 1994 Mandela was elected the first black president of South Africa, and the painful and difficult process of rebuilding a country with deep racial hatreds began.

South Africa suffered greatly under apartheid. Whites argued that they knew little about what the government was doing. Most whites knew blacks only as servants, and blacks often saw whites as the devil and as their enemies. Family life was deeply affected by these separations. In a moving tale of life under apartheid, Mark Mathabane writes in his book, *Kaffir Boy* (1986), about the humiliation and dehumanization that he experienced. He watched his father being dragged away in the middle of night during a raid. He described begging for food, fearing the first white people he ever laid eyes on, and being insulted and beaten because of his skin color. His mother struggled to feed the children and keep them in school, paying for the fees and the clothing with her meager savings.

Photo 7.2   Young man in Africa building family home with straw and mud.
Photographer: Elaine Leeder

Interestingly, when Mathabane came to the United States, after receiving a tennis scholarship, he said that he found much the same situation here. Although, he said, the signs of apartheid were more subtle in the United States, it was only less physically obvious that discrimination was rampant.

Under apartheid, family life was significantly impacted by the movement of adult males to the cities or to mine areas seeking employment. Old people, some women, and children remained in the rural regions, keeping the family plots of land and living off the money sent home by the adults. This strategy existed to keep wages low for the workers, offloading the costs of human reproduction and maintenance. It might be useful to use a Marxist or a conflict theoretical perspective to explain what happened in South Africa and why the races were kept apart, by understanding that it was economically expedient to create the separation and inequality. If we understand that it paid off for whites, we see why the apartheid system lasted so long and was so effective.

Life in South Africa is somewhat better now, since the end of apartheid. Public health and educational facilities were desegregated, and a national constitution has made South Africa one of the most equitable in the world, at least on paper. Unfortunately, centuries of inequity are not undone in just a few years. There are still parties committed to white supremacy; the government does not have enough money to complete all the projects necessary to bring blacks to parity with whites; education is still poor for blacks; there is a huge unemployment rate; there are competing black nationalist parties vying to take over the reins of government. Nelson Mandela stepped down as president in 1999, and President Thabo Mbeki is faced with enormous political and economic challenges as the second black president of the country.

Family life in South Africa is still problematic because of the consequences of apartheid. Life expectancy is low, with men living until 54 and women until 58. The literacy rate is 82 percent. And South Africa is currently the most murderous country in the world, with the highest rates of homicide (Ramsay, 1999, 158). AIDS is on the rise in alarming proportions. Between 1990 and 1995 the infection rate increased by 1,123 percent (Daley, 1998b). Today almost 3 million South Africans, about 12 percent of all adults, are infected with HIV. This leaves children orphaned at a young age, many of them left to care for their siblings. Money that might have gone to AIDS prevention went instead to the apartheid battle.

Under apartheid, a system known as the "dop" was established, under which black and colored workers in the wine industry were given a weekly allotment of wine as part of their salary. The purpose was to addict laborers to alcohol and to keep them working for virtually nothing (Daley, 1998b, A1). The consequence is that now, once the allotment has been curtailed, researchers at the University of Cape Town Foundation for Alcohol Related Research are finding that the incidence of fetal alcohol syndrome is quite high. In the United States the rate is 0.2 percent; even among Native Americans, whose rate of alcoholism has been documented to be quite high, the rate of fetal alcohol syndrome is 2.0 percent. In South Africa the rate is 11 percent among children of the vineyard farm workers.

South Africa is also experiencing a rise in child abuse and child sexual abuse. Government officials are concerned about the situation and are forming task forces to recommend new laws to deal with the incidence (Jacobson, 1999). Rapes, both marital and stranger rapes, are also on the rise. Other studies indicate that the fact that family members have to migrate for work has had a destructive effect on the family life. Family members have shown migration-related stresses, and have developed a state of being in chronic crisis. Their children show emotional distress through behavior problems (Steyn & Viljoen, 1996).

Clearly the demise of apartheid has not ended the difficulties. Family life in South Africa, particularly for blacks, has been problematic since before apartheid; it just got worse under that system. South Africa remains one of the most fascinating countries in the world to follow and watch. Because of its long history of entrenched and legalized racism, and now with a new era of attempted reconciliation, it could serve as a model for the rest of the world in overcoming and healing deep racial wounds.

Race in the United States

The situation in the United States bears many similarities to racial conditions in South Africa. Remember what Mathabane said, that the situations in both countries are quite similar, only the signs saying "Whites Only" are down in the United States. The situation is just a hundred years beyond the time of the signs coming down.

Historically, blacks entered the United States through force—slavery. As early as the mid-1600s, settlers needed cheap labor to grow food for subsistence and tobacco for export. Because they could not force the Indians to work for them, fearing retaliation, and could not import white servants in sufficient numbers, they turned to slaves (Zinn, 1999, 34-45). Africans were torn from their families, marched thousands of miles in chains, were sold at auction and placed on slave ships in spaces no bigger than coffins. Many died, with up to 50 million perishing in what is now called the "middle passage," the stage between freedom and slavery. Estimates are that by 1800, between 10 and 15 million people came to the United States under these conditions (38).

Once here, the situation they found was one of antagonism and mistreatment, much like conditions between whites and blacks in South Africa. As Zinn has pointed out, the color black has always been distasteful to whites. As early as 1600, English dictionaries define *black* as being deeply stained with dirt, soiled, dirty, or foul (40). However, when blacks and whites of similar economic conditions interacted, they often had cordial relations, so much so that laws had to be enforced to separate the races.

As the plantation system grew, so did slavery and family life. With the growth came the need for new slaves imported from Africa. On plantations in the South of the United States there are similarities in housing accommodations between those homes and housing seen in Africa. Africans brought their cultures with them and formed new families, emulating the family systems they had left behind. Different groups of people—Igbo from Nigeria, Ghanians, individuals from Sierra Leone, Angolans, Congolese, Senegalese, Gambians, people from Guinea-Bissau, Liberians, all from the "slave coast of Africa" and all thousands of miles from home—formed new family groupings, slowly losing some of their heritage, but holding on to some vestiges from the past.

For example, to this day, on the coast of South Carolina and Georgia, a dialect known as "Gullah" is spoken, and food is cooked that emulates the traditions of the African slave coast. These peoples, brought from Sierra Leone, came to work in the rice and cotton fields. Slaves were brought to the upper colonies like Pennsylvania and Rhode Island as artisans and craftsmen. In the southern colonies they were brought to be agriculturalists. Grazing patterns for herding animals, for example, emulate those of Africa rather than European patterns (Elliot, 1999).

Racial slavery was possible because whites considered blacks heathen savages who needed to be civilized and believed that blacks lacked a civilization of their own. In fact, some believed they were doing blacks a favor, since they would now be Christianized and have a religion. Justification was even found in the biblical story of Ham. The slavers believed nonwhites were enslaveable due to their legal and cultural vulnerability. Of course, we now know that enslaved peoples had their own ancient civilizations and religions, which were not recognized. Once here, these people had no legal rights, and, deprived of their culture, were open to victimization (Elliot, 1999). In fact, a Marxist or conflict theory analysis would argue that it was necessary to maintain the idea of blacks as heathen savages because it was then acceptable to exploit them for their labor and not feel guilt. It became merely an economic arrangement, using chattel who are less than human.

Classic American racism developed in the 1800s, when the debate over slavery coincided with U.S. expansion westward (Jaret, 1995, 131). Massachusetts had outlawed slavery as early as 1783, when a slave argued that the state constitution said all men were free and equal, and the courts agreed with him. But the need for slaves for cotton production superseded the spirit of the Declaration of Independence, and slave owners argued that the right to private property (slaves) had priority over slaves' rights to freedom (132). Soon thereafter, proslavery forces developed a dehumanizing racist ideology that blacks were biologically inferior to whites and therefore not really human, more like beasts, and therefore enslaveable.

The territorial expansion also gave rise to racism. This was mainly directed at Native Americans, who were seen as savages and unable to be "civilized." The spirit of Manifest Destiny ordained that whites were to bring factories, buildings, growth, and "progress" to the world, and justified the killing of Native peoples who stood in the way. Mexicans were viewed as lazy, dirty, violent, and cruel, which also justified taking over the land they held in the Southwest (133).

Social Darwinism is the belief that the "survival of the fittest" of the human species justified the domination of superior groups over inferior ones. Although it did not come into existence until later in the century, it served as a justification for whites being defined as having the right to judge and subjugate others. The idea of the "White Man's Burden" was another way to justify distinctions and classification of peoples. According to this argument, the "higher" races' job was to uplift the "backward" races and to Americanize them to follow the norm set by white, Anglo-Saxon, Protestant Americans.

Interestingly, we are now seeing a rise of such thinking once again. This time it is in the form of white supremacist groups such as the Aryan Nation, the White Patriot Party, and the Ku Klux Klan, all of which espouse hatred of any group other than whites. They do so out of fear that their social status, economic condition, and political influence are declining (138). Hate group members tend to be working-class, blue-collar workers and others whose lives are not economically stable. There is often a correlation between economically difficult times and the rise of hate group activity.

Consequences of Racism in the United States

Many students in my classes argue that slavery ended a hundred years ago and that they are not responsible for the inequities of the past. They also allege that blacks now have equal opportunity under the law and that affirmative action programs and legislation have eradicated the differences between blacks and whites. Unfortunately, this is another "no problem problem," like the one we discussed in Chapter 6 when we were looking at gender. You'll remember Deborah Rhode, Professor of Law at Stanford, argued that many Americans fail to see the problems faced by women, blame women for their own problems, and deny the need for anyone to take personal responsibility for the problem (Rhode, 1997, 1). We have a similar situation with race. We can see the consequences of racism in South Africa, but it is harder for us to perceive when it is close to home. A few examples make my point.

For five years I volunteered at a maximum security state prison in Elmira, New York. There I ran a college lecture series for inmates who have high school diplomas or have obtained a GED. That experience was quite eye-opening. For one thing, the men are primarily black and Latino, with a few white, working-class participants. They are somewhat atypical from other inmates who have not attained the GED. All of these inmates are extremely well read, articulate, and very street smart. In fact, the class was far more challenging and exciting intellectually than my usual college-level classes. Many of the inmates are there because they have committed felonies, including murder, robbery, burglary, and rape. All are serving long sentences. I was often struck with the intelligence of this group. They put information together in fascinating and creative ways and asked provocative questions that kept me on my toes. I found myself doing lots of homework after class. I was distressed at the waste of the inmates' talents and knowledge as they languish in prison. New York State does not fund higher education for inmates, and none of these men is able to obtain a college degree because of this. In fact no state in the country funds such education.

Why, you might ask, are these intelligent men locked away? I asked them that very question and got some fascinating answers. Many of them said they were smart in school, but some had been humiliated by teachers early on. Others did well but found no jobs after completing high school, and turned to crime. Others said that they did not want to be criminals but found no other work in their neighborhoods. One white man described coming from a middle-class family and hanging out with bikers, who taught him to be a criminal. Another described doing well in a private school, but then finding no job or money to go to college. All describe experiences of racism, especially in the criminal justice system.

In what has been described as a "culture of discrimination" (Minority troopers, 1999, B2) in the criminal justice system, black state police officers in New Jersey have alleged racial mistreatment of both drivers on the road and minorities on the police force. They describe a culture that condones racist remarks, racial profiling in which minorities are regularly pulled over and searched because of their skin color, and ridicule and harassment of officers who complained. Racial profiling is a phenomenon that is receiving more attention at the policy levels of government, since it appears to be a common pattern among police forces.

The discriminatory application of capital punishment is also noteworthy. Wolfgang and Riedel (1973) found that blacks are more likely than whites to be executed for the same crimes, and that people who can afford good lawyers are far more likely to escape execution than those who lack the means to hire the best legal defenders.

Life for blacks who are not in prison is plagued with inequity as well. This gravely impacts family life on a daily basis. Many social scientists who study the problem argue that the older patterns of racism and discrimination impact the present situation and lead to a continuation of inequality. Blacks in the United States face more prejudice and discrimination than any other group, partly because they are more easily identifiable. The legacy of slavery labeled them as inferior, and that labeling continues to this day. Job discrimination and changes in the economic sectors keep blacks out of the labor force to a greater degree than any other group. The unemployment rate for black males is twice that for white males. Without a high school degree, the rate rises to three times higher than for white men (Oliver & Shapiro, 1990). Fifty-four percent of all black men between 18 and 29 are unemployed (Massey & Denton, 1999, 316). More than one-half of black households report assets of $5,000 or less, and 30 percent say they have no assets at all, while only 9 percent of all white families report having no assets. The median net worth of black households is $4,169, while white households are worth $43,279.

It is true that some blacks are now in the middle class, but the majority of black workers remain in manual labor and lower-end service jobs. Only 16 percent of black households earn more than $50,000, while 47 percent of white households do. And even in the middle class, black Americans report hundreds of instances of blatant and subtle bias in their daily lives (Feagin, 1991). Thirty-four out of every 100 white men have college degrees, while only 11 out of every 100 black men do. Black families suffer as a result of technological advances that have put black men out of jobs. For example, black men began losing jobs between the 1950s and the 1970s, and now there is little employment available for African American men (Billingsley, 1992, 132). Still employed as blue-collar workers, with diminishing job opportunities open to them, black men are often blamed for being unemployable, when in fact, there might be fewer jobs available.

Black women die in childbirth at a rate four times higher than that of white women, and black babies have twice the infant mortality rate as white; black babies die at 17.6 per 1,000 versus 8.5 for white live births. Blacks are also employed in the most dangerous jobs, where they face a 37 percent greater chance of occupational injury and a 20 percent greater chance of death. Blacks live to an average of 69.2 years, whites to 75.6 years. Black families benefit less from the positive consequences of technological changes that seem to benefit whites (Billingsley, 1992, 131). For example, since the turn of the twentieth century, white infant mortality was reduced from 43 per 1,000 births to 10, while blacks' infant mortality is the same level that it was for whites two decades ago (131). The AIDS death rate is three times higher for blacks than it is for whites. Clearly, family life is impacted daily by the consequences of racism in the United States today.

Black children have a 30 percent higher chance of dying before the age of 14 than do white children. While blacks make up only 12 percent of the population, they are 45 percent of the people killed by police officers. The average sentence for a juvenile delinquent who is white is two years and six weeks, while black youth receive average sentences of five years and seven months.

The number of black households headed by single black women with children grew in the 40 years between the 1950s and the late 1990s (Kaplan, 1997). The rates were 25 percent in the '50s and up to 61 percent in the '90s. Of these families, more than half will have daughters who were or will become single mothers themselves. Birthrates for single black women have climbed in those 40 years two to three times more than for white women of the same ages, which was 17 years old or lower (3). There are a number of theories about why this rate has risen so dramatically, including the one idea stated by Elaine Bell Kaplan, that black single mothers are seen as social deviants and that they choose to reproduce more of their own kind as a slap in the face of America's "family values" (5). Other theories include the belief that there are no jobs available to such women and that the economy's structure makes it difficult for black mothers to find a place for themselves in the upwardly mobile society (6).

Family life is severely affected by the racism that blacks experience in American society. In a study done in 1998, the authors found that black families tend to rely on their kin to help cope with the daily racism they experience at work and in public (St. Jean & Feagin, 1998, 297). The family spirit seems to help them but also transfers the pain of bigotry to family members, leading to an emotional price paid by the whole family for the racism they experience. But it also helps with a collective memory; by facing adversity a sense of family is preserved. Both black men and women are aware of the history of victimization and the current inequities based on race and deal with it on a daily basis, with their families helping them to cope with it.

Prejudice + Discrimination = Racism

Why are there such enormous differences between the races? Why do people dislike others? Why do we look down on people or think they are inferior to us? Here it will be useful to define our terms and to understand that as much as each of us might like to allege that we are bias-free, we all carry within us some of the internalized attitudes that pervade our culture. We carry values that have been taught to us by our families, the media, and the dominant society. None of us is pure enough to have missed or overcome that learning. Sometimes we act on those attitudes; sometimes we carry them quietly within us. The problem is that they impact family life and lead to difficulties for real people trying to live and raise their children.

Prejudice is the belief that another group is inferior. It is an attitude and a prejudgment made based solely on the basis of membership in a category. It is a thought. Prejudice presumes that an individual has objectionable qualities that have been ascribed to his or her group. In fact, a truly prejudiced person will go on making incorrect judgments even in the face of contradictory information. Sometimes prejudice can view another group favorably, but for the most part social scientists argue that prejudice is a negative prejudgment.

Prejudice is usually based on misinformation and is taught through socialization and programming by those around you. We have to be taught to hate and fear; they are not innate and genetic. They are not voluntary, either; it is merely the best thinking the person has at the moment. Usually no one has educated the prejudiced person to be aware of biases. We all display prejudice to some extent, when we cross the street to avoid someone of a different group, when we dislike their music or wince at their behaviors, when we don't listen, when we discredit and discount another. When we stereotype another group, we are carrying on the prejudice.

Examples of a prejudice might be saying that all blacks can dance, all Jews are cheap, that all Native Americans are alcoholics, or that people on welfare "breed like jackrabbits." Think about some of your own prejudices; we all have them.

Many times we have prejudicial ideas but do not show them because we know that it is unacceptable to do so. *Discrimination is the acting out of prejudice.* It is the behavior that follows the attitude, the overt action that is taken. Discrimination is the active expression of the negative attitude that leads to unfair treatment.

Racism is the combination of both thought and behavior. *It is the ingrained set of attitudes and actions that has an ideology that justifies the subjugating of others.* It is usually justified on a variety of grounds, like religious or scientific, and then the belief is acted upon. Those of us in the social sciences argue that racism is perpetrated by the dominant group in a society upon the minority group. It is about who is in power and how that power is manifested. Racism denies the minority group full participation in the society. We can show our racism individually, toward people. We can also show that racism through our institutions, which continue to perpetuate the inequality.

You might ask why I include this information about prejudice, discrimination, and racism when discussing the family. These three phenomena impact family life greatly. When a child in a family is more likely to die, the quality of life is compromised. When a mother dies of AIDS, the children of that family suffer. When a head of household cannot earn a living, that situation is devastating to the family. The structural condition of race is profoundly important to the quality of family life.

Patricia Hill Collins, a noted black sociologist, has pointed out, for example, that the increasing rates of black single mothers is a structural, racial construction. It is the result of racism. She notes that it is the industrial mix that characterizes the employment base of an area that articulate the family organization (1998). For example, where there are heavy industries such as oil refineries, families will remain intact, with men staying home and working. If men have to leave for employment, or if women go to places where there are female-labor-dependent jobs, like garment work, then the family life will become more female headed. Thus family structures are impacted by the structures of society that perpetuate racism and discrimination.

Ethnicity

Earlier I made the distinction between race and ethnicity. Ethnicity, as I said before, is shared cultural heritage; race is often thought of as shared physical characteristics. The cultural factors are transmitted through language, religion, national origin, and a sense of common history. Some ethnic groups share no common physical traits and exist only because they conceive of themselves as a group. They may believe they share a common ancestry and are bound together by nationality or culture. Nowadays race and ethnicity are used together (Berreman, 1972, 41).

Ethnicity is birth-ascribed: you are defined as part of an ethnic group when you are born into it. Some (Jaret, 1995, 51) define *ethnicity* as a sense of "peoplehood," the sense of attachment one has to a group, a "we" feeling that is a consciousness of being the same kind. It is about being part of a community, even if you are of differing sex, socioeconomic class, and age. The term *ethnic* comes from the Greek word *ethnos* or *ethnikos*, which means "nation" or "people" (66). Examples might be American Jews who feel a peoplehood and ethnic bond with Jews in Israel, or Southern Italians or people of Irish extraction, all of whom feel an affinity for people of the same background. You can't change your ethnic affiliation, although you can change how strongly you identify with that group.

Ethnicity is as important in influencing family life as is race. The language one speaks, the food one eats, the holidays one celebrates, the religion one practices are all ethnically related. Think about your own ethnic background. How does it impact your life and the life of your family? It's usually most important at holidays, family events, and crucial life passages such as weddings and funerals.

Ethnicity has had a large impact on family life worldwide. Recently the war in Kosovo was related to ethnic differences between the Albanians and the Kosovars. More often than not, wars are fought because of ethnic conflict. Ethnic differences can lead to genocide, which is the killing of groups of people, as in the "ethnic cleansing" of Albanians. It can also lead to *ecocide,* which is the destruction of the environment surrounding a group of people. An example of that might be the destruction of the rainforest in Brazil and the resultant loss of life of the indigenous peoples who live there. There is also *ethnocide,* which is the destruction of the culture of an ethnic group. A contemporary example might be the destruction of the Tibetan Buddhist religion through the intermarriage with Han Chinese settlers in current-day Tibet.

Ethnic Cleansing and Genocide in Rwanda

As an example of the consequences of ethnicity on family life I describe what occurred in Rwanda in 1994. Many of my students have been shocked to learn of this horror, wondering why it had never come to their attention before. They had heard about Kosovo and knew about the ethnic conflicts there, but had never learned about an equally horrific tragedy in Africa. They wondered why the world did not intervene in this incident the way NATO chose to in Kosovo. I leave you to answer that question for yourself.

Rwanda is a small country about the size of Maryland that sits in East Africa, neighboring Burundi, Uganda, the Central African Republic of the Congo, and Tanzania. All of its citizens are black African except for a very small white, expatriate community. The ethnic composition is 89 percent Hutu, 10 percent Tutsi, and 1 percent Twa (Ramsay, 1999, 122–123). These ethnic differences have been based historically on what kind of work the groups do. They all share the same language and look the same physically, although the Tutsi are supposedly somewhat taller. Hutu are primarily pastoralists, meaning they are farmers and herders. Tutsi and Hutu had gotten along well, and there was intermarriage between the two main groups. In the traditional social order, the Twa were considered the outcasts, the Hutu were the servants, and the Tutsi were the aristocrats. The Hutu cared for the cattle and served the Tutsi, who protected them.

During the colonial era, the old order of things was changed, and the Hutu became coffee growers, through the encouragement of the German and Belgian colonists. Because of Western concepts of ethnicity, distinctions were made between the groups, with the Tutsi being favored by the colonists, who saw them as lighter skinned. Discontent grew because land was crowded, and by the 1950s conflict developed between the groups. The Hutu began to rebel against the Tutsi aristocracy, and by 1962, the traditionally Tutsi-dominated government shifted to Hutu. From the 1960s until today, there has been continued interethnic competition for power. The Tutsi have sought independence, wanting to establish their own country, and formed a revolutionary group based in neighboring Uganda.

On April 6, 1994, the Hutu president of the country and the president of neighboring Burundi, who was also Hutu, were shot down in their plane. Within half an hour of their deaths, a slaughter of Tutsi began, urged on by Hutu extremists who alleged that Tutsi had killed the president. Death lists were prepared by local Hutu chiefs, and within a few months more than 500,000 Tutsi were massacred. One newspaper article described Tutsi huddled in a church, seeking asylum, being turned over to the Hutu, who systematically slaughtered a few thousand in a matter of hours. In neighboring Tanzania, bodies were found floating down the river at a rate of 80 an hour, entering Lake Victoria almost 100 miles from the Rwandan border (122). Estimates of total number killed are now between 500,000 and 800,000 (Krulfeld, 1999).

Plans for the genocide had been going on for quite a while before the killing of the Hutu president (Ramsay, 1999, 122). Death squads had already begun slaughtering Tutsi months earlier. The United Nations was already there as a peacekeeping force, but took no action during this crisis; in fact, UN soldiers were evacuated to protect them from harm. Over one-third of the Tutsi population was killed. Then those who survived began to retaliate. In all, more than 3 million Rwandans, both Tutsi and Hutu, fled in panic across the borders of other countries, all trying to save their lives and the lives of their children. To this day there are more than 1 million refugees still in Burundi, Tanzania, and Uganda, all waiting to go home and barred from doing so by the Hutu-dominated government. The situation remains tense and contentious.

How does this affect family life? Families were destroyed. Children watched their parents being maimed and killed. Babies were taken from their pregnant mothers' bellies. Young men who'd had their hands cut off, but were left alive so they would carry the story out, were traumatized by their experiences and unable to work or feed their families. Families were in flight. They became refugees, homeless and struggling. They lived in desolate and overcrowded camps, searching for their loved ones and struggling to survive. Families that might have had a Tutsi wife and a Hutu husband were forced to break up, and the country and families were in chaos. Needless to say, there were countless orphans as well. Many of those children were homeless and had to be taken in by relatives or even strangers. Many of the children had to fend for themselves and raise their younger siblings. All this because of ethnic differences.

Ethnic conflict is the source of social upheaval and directly impacts family life in tremendous ways. Although it might appear that ethnicity is about people hating members of different ethnic groups, sometimes it is deeper than that. Often what appears to be ethnic conflict is really political conflict. For example, the issue of ethnicity in Rwanda is about who is in political power there. The minority Tutsi ran the country; the Hutu took over, the Tutsi wanted independence, and the Hutu slaughtered them because of their desire to maintain political power without having to cede money and territory to them. What was once no difference at all became culturally constructed difference that led to war and genocide. The economy was suffering from this political process, and eventually war ensued. What we find in situations like this is that transnational migrations are taking place because of these culturally constructed ethnic differences.

Transnational Migrations and Family Life

Transnational migrations are movements of people, populations who move because conditions within their homelands are forcing them to go (Krulfeld, 1999). Immigrants may decide to leave their homes because economic conditions are such that they are seeking to better themselves. Many of your grandparents and great-grandparents came to the United States for this reason. Migrants travel because they are seeking work; they cross borders to avoid starvation and move with the seasons, seeking any employment they can find. Sometimes migrants are legal, allowed into a country for a season and then forced to leave. Some are also illegal, coming across borders hoping to hide and blend into the new homeland. Refugees flee because of political repression or war; they flee for a specific reason: fear of political persecution (Krulfeld, 1999).

The point is that, although borders between countries appear permanent, in fact, they are permeable. They are crossed regularly and are not as effective as we might like to think. Think, for example, how Rwanda's neighbors were impacted by the civil war there. There has been a regular ebb and flow of peoples across the borders, taxing the economies of the neighbors. Sometimes there is a cyclical migration, with people going back and forth, when the danger passes or the economy changes. Communities are not bounded entities—they move, change, and reformulate. For example, sometimes refugees are joined by their immigrant family members, and thus become both refugee and immigrant families. The process is a globally dynamic one. In fact, it is a whole world system in which various ethnic and racial groups move from their homelands to take up residence in new places. It happens all the time.

In the recent past as many as 16–20 million people a year have had to flee their homelands (Krulfeld, 1999). Often the reason for the displacement is ethnicity and race. Decisions about whose rights are denied are usually racially or ethnically based. This displacement necessitates creativity of the human spirit. Families must deal with where to go, what they do with themselves, and how to survive in the face of such trauma. They are forced to be quite versatile, learning to live in refugee camps, then in new homes where they probably do not speak the language. Children often become the interpreters for families. Where once traditional expectations of behavior prevailed, now children are in positions of authority. Roles are challenged, and families are forced to adapt and change in ways they might never have thought imaginable.

From this discussion, you can imagine the significant consequences ethnicity and race have on family life. They sometimes determine whether you will live or die. They impact employment, education, mortality rates, mental and physical health. In a study of Cambodian refugees living in Thailand, almost half of the 993 family members experienced symptoms of post-traumatic stress disorder and major depression. Many had seen the killing of their families and forced labor. The result of that trauma to their families has had lasting effects in their lives (Mollica, Donelan, Tor, Lavelle, Elais, Frankel, & Blendon, 1993). Clearly race and ethnicity have significant influence on how life will be lived, on the quality of life, and on lifestyle. They are important structural conditions that cannot be overlooked.

Class Differences

Equally important to family life is one's class background. Class is another part of the socio-structural system, determining where one fits, this time in terms of socioeconomic status. How class is determined is a complicated process. It is not just about how much money one earns, nor about educational level or occupation. Current work on *class* indicates that the term refers to *access to power (or lack thereof), consciousness about one's position in life, the ability to pass the status on to one's children, one's educational level, and the actual control that one has over his or her life* (Barker, 1991). It also has to do with culture, values, norms, and worldview. One's social origins play an important role in determining one's class.

For a woman, class involves other factors as well. A woman's class status might be defined by her husband's or partner's earnings. There is a dynamic interaction that comes as a result of the class one is born into, the class of one's partner, and one's current income. People are more mobile into or out of different classes than they are in race, ethnicity, or caste. One can leave one's class origins through marriage, education, or training. People also move down in class, depending on availability of opportunities. However, the reality is that very few people move up or down in any significant numbers. It tends to be something of a myth that people can get rich and change their lifestyles.

In the United States, many people would claim that they are middle class, no matter how much they earn. In one of my classes I regularly do a median distribution of students' families' annual income. I ask the students what class they belong to. Then I chart the income distribution for the class. About three-quarters of the students say they are of the middle class. However, when we look at the spread of income alone—not including family wealth, which involves acquired assets like stocks and property—we find that the lowest income is approximately $15,000 and the highest is $3 million a year. The median distribution is more than $80,000, well over the approximate national median of $45,000 in the United States. Yet nearly all of the students have told me that they are middle class.

Among the core countries, the United States has the widest gap between rich and poor. The richest 10 percent own almost 80 percent of real estate, more than 90 percent of securities (stocks and bonds), and about 60 percent of all the money in bank accounts. The situation has gotten worse since the 1970s. The incomes of the richest one-fifth of the population are increasing, while those of the poorest one-fifth are decreasing at a rate of 0.78 per year. Ninety percent of all American families own only 28 percent of the wealth in the United States (Mantsiso, 1996, 98).

In the United States, we tend to identify four classes: the upper class, the middle class, the working class, and the poor. We talked briefly about these divisions in Chapter 4 when we discussed the history of family life in the core countries. The upper class is generally considered to be of two types: the old rich and the new rich. The old rich are people like the Rockefellers and DuPonts, those people who have had wealth in their families for generations and have established lifestyles that many of us envy. Old money usually means expensive private education for their children, affluent homes and social clubs, and secluded communities. The new rich are people who have recently earned large amounts of money, perhaps from investment or technology, but have not yet attained the prestige associated with old wealth. But they live well. They make up about 8 percent of the U.S. population (164).

Those who are "super-rich," be it from new or old money, include about 420,000 households in the United States. The average value of their wealth is $8.9 million (Mantsiso, 1996, 98). Family life for them emulates life on *Lifestyles of the Rich and Famous,* although not without emotional trauma and difficulties, too. For example, wife battering, child abuse, and sexual abuse still occur within upper-class families, even with the insulation of money surrounding them.

The middle class is made up of educated professionals, small business owners, and bureaucrats in the service sectors. Their lifestyles are more moderate; they tend to live in the suburbs and share the American value of upward mobility and affluence. They tend to spend more than they earn, and their patterns of consumption have been described as "conspicuous." They make up about 43 percent of the population (164). Worldwide, the idea of being middle class is spreading. For example, in Brazil there is the recent (since 1960) emergence of the democratic middle-class family, who resembles the American middle-class family in many ways (Westfield, 1997). There tend to be more egalitarian relationships developing between men and women; there is a belief in individual liberty, the ability of a child to express his or her true feelings to the parents, and the increasing possibility of divorce in the case of an unhappy marriage (30).

The working class are those people who are employed in skilled, semi-skilled, or unskilled labor. They are the "working people" who belong to labor unions, and "blue-collar workers" who live close to the edge economically. There is more racial and ethnic diversity in the working class than in the other classes, in that new immigrants to the United States are likely to begin in this class when they arrive (Mantsiso, 166). Lillian Rubin (1994) has studied working-class families in America and notes that there are greater similarities than differences among black, Asian, and white working-class families. She found that the working class are hidden from view and have an enormous struggle in making ends meet. She noted that "when the economy falters, families tremble" (223) and that working-class families, regardless of race or ethnicity, share common worries and difficulties raising their families. Their lifestyles are not that different from one another.

The poor make up only 11.8 percent of the population, and are "down on their luck." Currently there are 32.3 million people in the United States who are considered poor. These are folks who are in poverty, either the working poor or those receiving public assistance. Sometimes they are called lower class. Any family of four earning less than $17,029 is considered poor by government calculations (United States Census Bureau, 2000b). Many are working poor who do not make enough money to raise themselves above the poverty line, even though one of the partners in the home may have a full-time job. Low wages are often the cause of poverty. In 1999, 2 million Americans worked full-time throughout the year and were still poor.

Contrary to public opinion, not all poor people are on public assistance, nor do people stay on public assistance for generations. Gottschalk, McLanahan, and Sandefur (1994) found that people are in poverty temporarily, with only 12 percent of people on public assistance for five or more years and only 5 percent having spells of poverty when they are forced to receive public assistance for seven or more years. So much for the myth of generational dependence on public assistance. This research began charting families from 1968, so the new welfare laws of 1996 played no role in these low numbers.

With differences in class come differences in quality of life and quality of family life. Hunger, for example, is alive and well in the United States, with 20 million poor Americans experiencing hunger for at least some period of time each month (Mantsiso, 1996, 97). More than 2 million poor people live in New York City alone, and 1 in 8 Americans lives in poverty. Parents are unable to feed their children. There is a direct connection between socioeconomic status and health. The United States is 19th in the world in infant deaths, at 10.6 per 1,000 live births. This places us behind Spain, Singapore, and Hong Kong (99). If you look at poor blacks, the rate rises to 18.2, placing the United States in 28th position, behind Bulgaria and equal to Costa Rica. Family life is directly impacted by poverty and hunger.

Class is directly correlated with deaths from cancer, chronic disease, and surgical and medical complications. The rate of health problems in poor neighborhoods is several times greater than in wealthy neighborhoods. These numbers are related to inadequate nutrition, exposure to occupational and environmental health hazards, and access to health care. The poor cannot afford common hospital procedures that people with medical insurance receive.

Matrix of Domination

Class is a position that people are placed in because of the social stratification system; it is a product of being limited and confined by the opportunity structure. Adding race and gender to the matrix increases the chances of poverty and of lower-class standing (103). Patricia Hill Collins (1998) argues that race, class, and gender are categories of analysis that are essential in understanding the structural bases of domination and subordination. In other words, there is no hierarchy of victimization. These three variables weave together to create a system of systematic inequities. So black women have less opportunity to make money or obtain education than do white males, for example. It is this intersection of race, class, and gender that impacts family life differentially depending on one's position in the structure. If one is a middle-class black, one will experience racism differently than will a poor black American, for example. Sexism is experienced differently by an upper-class white woman than by a woman of color. It is this matrix of domination that allows for understanding the differential experiences of people within similar systems. Members of groups holding minority status in the United States, for example, must get their children ready to participate and survive in a society that is stratified along racial and ethnic lines. They are forced to teach their children about the consequences of racism, while still trying to help them develop positive self-images and to function in a racist society (Arendell, 1997).

Let's look at family life in Brazil, for another example.

Brazil and Class

Perhaps one of the most inequitable societies in the world, in terms of class disparities, is Brazil. Brazil's population is the largest in Latin America and is as ethnically diverse as any in the world. African slaves were imported to Brazil beginning in the sixteenth century, after the Europeans displaced the indigenous peoples and labor was needed to work the land. Today most Brazilians are descendants of Indians, Africans, and Portuguese. There are also new immigrants who come from Europe, the Middle East, and Asia. The Brazilian culture is a mix of all these influences.

Because Brazil has had military dictatorships, mass uprisings, and political upheavals, it is a newly emerging market economically and experiences extreme poverty, violence, and disturbing exploitation of its poor. Nonetheless, it has become the 10th-largest economy in the world, primarily through the exploitation of its vast resources. Recently Brazilians opened the largest industrial park in the developing world (McMullen, 1999), and the country has been considered a miracle in terms of its quick economic growth. Unfortunately the growth primarily benefited the upper classes, who enjoyed the consumer goods that came along with the boom. Agriculture was neglected, and the country could not feed itself and had to import food. The poor have suffered.

Class membership in Brazil is based chiefly on income, family history and connections, education, social behavior, tastes in housing, food, and dress, as well as personality, appearance, and talent (Goodwin, 1998). Some scholars argue that what looks like racial difficulties seem to be class-based problems. By this I mean that poverty and the great disparities between rich and poor are what divides the country, not skin color. However, it is also important to mention that in Brazil, darker skinned people earn 40 percent less than whites who are in the same profession. So there seem to be some racial inequities present, even if most people in the country say they have no racial problems. In fact, class is the biggest division in Brazil.

Anthropologist Nancy Scheper-Hughes (1992a) studied family life in the *favelas* of Brazil. Favelas are slum shantytowns that dot the Brazilian cities, built by rural-urban migrants in search of employment. They are squatter villages, often rigged with electricity stolen by using cords strung across yards and shanties. I have visited favelas and found them squalid, a maze of narrow streets, with latrines and water spigots placed sporadically around the area for public use.

Living in these favelas, Scheper-Hughes found that life was marked by violence. Women were beaten regularly by their partners, and death was ever-present. "Mother love and child death" were the experiences of families there. With a 25 percent infant mortality rate, many of those babies died because of inadequate diets. Mothers would know which babies would live or die, and they developed a sense of "mortal neglect," which was a fatalistic withholding of nourishment and maternal care. They maintained a distance from their children because conditions were so distressing that they had to protect themselves from the inevitable and regular loss. The political/economic situation had put them there, and they had no way to protect their children from the inevitability of death. In fact, Scheper-Hughes's book is called *Death Without Weeping*. In Brazil, class membership is life-giving and life-taking. To be poor in Brazil means to die earlier and often to see the deaths of one's children.

Interestingly, lower-income families in Brazil also tend to be more mother-centered than upper-class families (Fonseca, 1991). Because women are often the heads of households in the Brazilian slums, they become the center of the economic and decision-making coalition with their children. There is strong solidarity among groups of women, daughters and daughters' children, because it provides continuity and security. Often, if there is any employment at all, the women work as domestics, cooks, washerwomen, or seamstresses. Although men are not frequently at home, the women come to rely on their male blood relatives in time of need or for protection. Blood becomes far more important than marriage, and deep-bonded kinship patterns serve as the basis for family life in the favelas of Brazil (154–155).

Why?

For generations scholars have been trying to explain why the inequities of social stratification exist. Why is there racism, elitism, anti-ethnic bias? As I noted Chapter 3, on theory, there are two schools of thought about social problems: the structural functionalist (or order approach) and the social conflict model.

If you remember, the structural functionalists (I called them the consensus makers) believe that the world is harmonious and ordered. They argue that humankind is basically good and that people can achieve whatever they set out to do because society is integrated, whole, and for the most part, at peace. These people accent patterns of inclusion, of the orderly integration and assimilation of racial and ethnic groups into the dominant society.

The social conflict theorists say that the world is a struggle between groups of people in a hierarchical system, and all are vying for scarce resources and power. They give more attention to the persisting inequality that leads to an unequal distribution of resources associated with racial and ethnic subordination (Feagin & Feagin, 1993, 26). It is from this social conflict model that I provide an explanation for social inequality.

Social Conflict Explanations of Inequality

Some social theorists think that there is a caste system of inequality. Early in this chapter we defined *caste* as a hierarchy of rank that locks individuals into the grouping of their parents and is immutable (unchanging). It is said that the United States has a caste system much like India's, and that a system of institutionalized discrimination perpetuates it. In fact, social theorists have even used the term "American apartheid," just like South African apartheid (keeping separate).

W. E. B. Du Bois, an important African American social theorist and civil rights activist, said that racial oppression was really about class oppression that comes from capitalism. He argued that as long as black workers were excluded from full citizenship by those who owned the workplaces and other dominant capitalists, there would be no racial equality. Another black thinker, Oliver Cox, argued that slavery was about the need to find cheap labor for the plantations, and had little to do with skin color. The search for cheap labor by a profit-oriented capitalist class led to a system of racial subordination that continues to this day (Feagin, 1991, 35). These two thinkers believe that race and class oppression are one and the same.

Some theorists argue that race and class oppression are separate but related systems. In Chapter 3, we discussed internal colonial theory, which says that current inequalities are due to a long history of exploitation of workers who were needed to fuel capitalism. This led to slavery and to the exploitation of Native American, Mexicans, and later Asians in the United States. Exploitation was based on the colonists engaging first in external colonialism in other parts of the world, but then needing laborers here as well. Thus it was in the interest of whites to keep low-wage paid laborers so that whites can reap enormous profits (36). These theorists argue that the government has played a role in legitimating the exploitation of minorities, and say that African Americans, in particular, are still a "colony" in the United States.

Such theories also have relevance in other parts of the world where the elite still need the poor and ethnic minorities to do the labor. Thus, the elite in Brazil need the poor in the favelas for their low-paid work. As we have seen throughout this book, this has daily impact on the way that family life is lived in these places.

Asians and Asian Americans are another group of people whose situations can be explained by the conflict theory. Espiritu (1997) has argued that Asians are constructed as neither "black" nor "white" (109). As an intermediary group between blacks and whites, they are the "nonwhite other," who receive special opportunities but also experience unique disabilities. They are in an alien status: historically, they were above blacks in the hierarchy of domination, but were able to take over work that blacks could do. Now they hold "model minority" status, in which they are almost, but not quite, white (109).

Contemporary conflict theorists say that race and class are intertwined; they are not one and the same thing, nor are they separate. Instead they are like threads woven together; you need to pull out the threads and look at each one closely to understand why groups are oppressed. It is an interactive system.

For conflict theorists, there are four classes. First are the capitalists who own and control capital investments and buy the labor of others. Then there are the managers, who administer the capitalists' investments and have gained control over the work of others; the petit bourgeoisie, who are the small group of merchants who own businesses and work for themselves; and finally the working class, the largest group, who sell their labor to employers in return for wages and salaries (37). The dominant class in the political-economic system is the capitalist class, who subordinate all the rest of us, be we white or nonwhite, for their own profit. But the nonwhite workers suffer from structural discrimination for being workers and also from being workers of color. In this process of first class and then racial exploitation, two threads are intertwined to create a crosscut of race and class discrimination.

Some examples will make this more understandable. If you are from the working class, you make less money than the capitalists or the managers, and if you are a person of color, you make less money than a white worker. As we know from earlier statistics, this impacts your life and the life of your family quite a bit. So it is important to real people, and it means that family life will be easier or harder depending on your race or class position.

In Brazil, for example, if you are poor and black, you might lose your child to malnutrition at a young age. In the United States, you might get sick and not have health care because of your race and class position. If you are richer and of an ethnic group that has been well assimilated, your life chances are better.

Let's Add Gender to the Mix: Gendered Racism

Feminist theorists have added gender to the system of oppression, and some have said, as Patricia Hill Collins did, that racism has many gendered forms. Black women are exploited both as blacks and as women, and the racism they suffer differs from what men experience. For example, under slavery, women were sex objects for white men. White women are still the standard of beauty that black women try to live up to and judge themselves by. Black women are disproportionately found in lower-paying jobs as secretaries or domestics. These are examples of gendered racism. Other feminist theorists have pointed out triple oppressions: race, class, and gender, all of which have cumulative effects that put women of color, like our Brazilian example, in subordinate positions to men of color and to the majority of the white population (43).

Summary

Race, ethnicity, class, and caste are all social constructions. With these constructions come differences in family life that are called structural arrangements. Rather than blaming individual poor or black or minority groups for their conditions, we understand that the way a society is set up creates these problems. Then families have to adapt, change, and respond to these social constructions. Thus race, class, caste, and ethnicity disparities have an external cause and are part of the fabric within which families have to operate.

In this chapter we looked at the concept of caste and saw that it was a hierarchy of rank based on the level at which a person is born. Some thinkers believe that we have a caste system in the United States. Social stratification was defined as the social ranking and categorization of people, determining the inherent worth of individuals based on a social category. We looked at the fluid definitions of race and ethnicity, realizing that people can be called a race at one point in time and an ethnic group at another. We defined the terms *race* and *ethnicity*—race being alleged physical differences, while ethnicity is more culturally and historically defined.

We looked at the history of apartheid in South Africa and saw some of the consequences on families. Then, by looking at the history and statistics of race relations in the United States, we saw the consequences of racial differences here. We defined *social Darwinism* and saw that racism, prejudice, and discrimination in the United States have their roots in the debate over slavery and the territorial expansion to the West.

Ethnicity was then addressed, and we saw that ethnicity is a sense of peoplehood and a shared cultural heritage. We looked at Rwanda and the ethnic cleansing that took place there in 1994, understanding the painful consequences that ethnic differences can take. We discussed transnational migrations and refugees, immigrants and migrant workers and their family lives, and learned that many transnational migrations take place because of racial and ethnic conflicts.

We looked class and saw it as a fluid category, sometimes meaning how much money one earns, but also reflecting level of education, inherited wealth, and with whom one associates. Then we discussed the matrix of domination and the intersection of race, class, ethnicity, and gender, using Brazilian families as an example.

Finally we looked at the social theorists and their explanations as to why people treat others differently. Focusing primarily on the social conflict theorists, we saw that race and ethnic differences are really class differences, and that capitalist arrangements are at the root of difficulties among people.

Gendered racism was the final form we dissected. Here we saw that there is differential discrimination based on an interplay among race, gender, ethnicity, and class. As much as we might like to tease out the differences for argument's sake, people's lives, especially women's and children's lives, are made more difficult because of their place in the social stratification system.

But it really isn't all so bad as it seems. Family lives are hard, depending on these variables, but remarkably, people go on, and even thrive, in the face of enormous difficulties. In the next few chapters we look at the joys of family life. When families form, when people partner, marry, decide to have and raise children, and even when and if they break up, there is a vitality and a resilience. We turn to family formation, marriages and partnering, raising children, and intergenerational relationships to see the elasticity and staying power that family life has.

Once again we continue on our journey around the world. I have seen many of these examples firsthand; I have spoken with people and I have been in their homes. I ask you to continue this journey with me, into the homes and lives of families in the world.

CHAPTER 8

Intimate Relationships

Love, Marriage, and Their Dissolution

I n 1989 I was stuck in Lusaka, Zambia, for four days, waiting for a plane to leave the country. Trying to find a way to keep myself busy, I wandered the streets and the marketplaces. One day I came upon a public building where I noticed groups of people waiting in the courtyard. I ventured into the building and found a hall filled with crowds of celebrants patiently lined up, waiting to be called before the official for what appeared to be wedding ceremonies. I took a seat in the back of the huge room and ended up staying there the entire day. What I saw was truly fascinating.

Everyone was joyous. Feelings of festivity permeated the room. The brides were in fantastic white wedding dresses. They had long trains, flowers, tiaras, the whole works. Near them were the future husbands, some of them in suits, tuxedos, or the traditional African garb of their ethnic groups. Also nearby were family members—children, elders, siblings, cousins, aunts, uncles, parents. There were huge numbers of people with each couple, all gleeful to be present at such an occasion.

The ceremonies themselves were quite simple. A state or government official officiated at a brief ritual. Each ceremony lasted only a few minutes. But when it was over the exuberance was remarkable. Each group would burst into song and dance, as their respective family members were pronounced husband and wife. Some of the attendants were dressed in traditional ethnic clothing; some of the men carried drums and began drumming as the ceremony ended. Then they would file out, and another group would step forth.

I spoke with some people who were waiting and learned that this was the first of at least two ceremonies that each couple would have. This was the state-sanctioned event, which looked more Western, with white gowns and government officials.

Photo 8.1   White wedding in Zambia. In this photo the bride is wearing the Western white gown. Later she will change into the more traditional garb of her tribe. Photographer: Elaine Leeder

Later the couple would return to their village, and another ceremony would take place, one that followed the traditions of the couple's ancestors. Sometimes— among those families that were more urbanized and educated—the "white weddings" would include some element of the traditional, tribal weddings. But for the most part, the state and the tribal ceremonies were very different events. Most couples had these two ceremonies, as well as a huge party with all their friends and relatives present, with song, food, and dance. The parties would take place after the two official events. Walking away from that day, I felt that I had been privileged to participate in such a fascinating cultural phenomenon. It made me think seriously about partnering, ceremonies, weddings, and families.

White Weddings

After I got home, I began to read about weddings and discovered that they are more than they seem at face value. In a fascinating book that deconstructs what weddings mean in a society, Ingraham (1999) argues that weddings help to institutionalize heterosexuality and make it compulsory. She says that "weddings are one of the major events which signal readiness and prepare heterosexuals for membership in marriage as an organizing practice for the institution of heterosexuality" (4). She points out that weddings are big business, especially in the United States, and that American families can spend as much as $19,000 per wedding. Weddings are part of a mystique that seems to grab the attention of most everyone in our society. In fact, few people don't like a good wedding. Look at me, I sat in Lusaka for hours enjoying the events.

The point Ingraham makes is that weddings are taken-for-granted events that mask hidden power relations, actually regulating sexuality and controlling behavior. She coins the term "the wedding industrial complex," (16) much like the military industrial complex that allegedly controls our foreign policy and runs the war machine. This wedding industry makes more than $32 billion a year in the United States. But beyond the fact that weddings make money, the real issue, she says, is what they conceal.

Ingraham believes that the romance of weddings hides a belief system that relies on romantic and sacred notions of heterosexuality in order to create and maintain the illusion of social well-being. In other words, weddings have hidden within them the compulsion to be straight. Weddings romanticize heterosexuality. But more than that, they leave unquestioned the gendered behaviors that people play out in weddings, and they preserve race, class, and sexual hierarchies as well (18). Weddings are part of the system that helps to keep inequalities in place. By having a white wedding, we say, "That is just the way it is"—that's how weddings take place. And most of us also say we want one. In fact, quite a few lesbian and gay couples have tried to emulate the heterosexual world by having commitment ceremonies and weddings, to make acceptable their relationships.

I'll bet some of you are angrily asking, Why does she have to critique such a wonderful institution? And why do I have to bring it to your attention, you might ask? I do so because weddings cross cultures. They happen everywhere. And they are not benign and painless institutions. What weddings do is *codify dominant social arrangements in a society and give privilege to some and not to others.* Since we are going to look at partnering and weddings in other societies, I want you to be critical, to suspend your judgments, and to learn, once again, that what you see at face value is *not* all there is. To be critical means that you expose the hidden meanings behind things; once you reveal the "taken-for-granted order," there is the possibility for change (26).

Patriarchy, says Ingraham, is institutionalized by weddings and creates a hierarchy of privilege of men over women (24). Take fathers walking their daughters down the aisle and handing them over to the husband at the altar. This is one example of patriarchy at work.

Patriarchy structures social practices and deems them natural and universal; we don't even question them. As other feminist theorists have said, patriarchy positions men in hierarchical opposition to women and differentially in relation to other structures like race, class, and ethnicity. Now Ingraham adds that patriarchy's continued success depends on maintaining these systems of difference among people. It needs to keep the structure in place to perpetuate itself. Like in the film *Aliens,* the monster keeps planting its seeds in the bodies of the hosts, to ensure the continuation of its line.

This critique of weddings may be useful for you as you look at intimate relationships. At face value they seem benign, non-injurious to the parties involved. Intimate relationships are fun. We all want to be in them; they give life sustenance and meaning. However, when we employ a critical consciousness, as traveling social scientists, we must remember there is more than what we see. There are hidden relationships that reflect structural conditions that differ for those involved. Few applications of this critique have found their way to studies on marriages in other parts of the globe, but certainly it is a relevant analysis as we look at the construction of marriages globally.

Love

Love is a universal phenomenon, but its meaning differs cross-culturally. Though individuals have different expectations for loving and meeting a mate, there are clear patterns of ideologies in different regions of the world. Some of us might be appalled at the idea of arranged marriages, as happens in India. Yet the divorce rate for this type of marriage is far lower than it is in the United States, where 20 per 1,000 married women will divorce per year (Cherlin, 1996, 353). People who marry through arrangement in India say that the love they feel grows over time; it is not necessarily romantic, but it is love. Conceptions of love have changed over time and differ in various places. Love, like all the other concepts we have looked at so far, is socially and historically constructed.

Historical and Social Construction of Love

Perhaps the best way to understand how love and marriage became tied together is to look at the early stages of Christianity in Europe. Early Christian faith placed a high value on the marriage bond, when two people took a marriage vow that said that God recognized their relationship. It was only then that virginity could end and a family could begin. There was also an ascetic morality attached to sex and love. Sex was seen as evil and shameful. Abstinence was the best behavior, but if one could not abstain, then sex should be limited to procreation within marriage (Murstein, 1974).

There was also a high value placed on the eternal permanence of the marriage bond. In Christian theology, it is reported by Mark that Jesus said, "Whosoever shall put away his wife, and marry another committeth adultery against her. And if a woman shall put away her husband, and be married to another, she committeth adultery" (100).

During the Middle Ages, love and lust were separated. Under the pattern of chivalry, distinctions were made between courtly love, the love of knights and their ladies, and lust. Love was about purity, the romantic ideal, and obsession with the beauty and character of the loved one. It was usually asexual and occurred outside of marriage (Hutter, 1998).

Lust, on the other hand, was for sexual relations. It was inferior to romantic love and usually took place within marriage. But romantic love was still the ideal, the courtly adoration for one you could not have. Marriages became business arrangements, the place where two families joined their business dealings—their lands, loyalties, and production of heirs. "Romantic love thus offered an alternative to the mundane relationships of marriage" (211).

With this distinction between courtly or romantic love and lustful, sometimes adulterous love came the concept of the "good" versus the "bad" woman. Good women would refrain from sexual activities prior to marriage, and even restrain themselves in marriage, while bad women would be available to satisfy men's sexual needs outside of marriage. This distinction continues even to this day. The good woman was placed on a pedestal, revered for her pure qualities, while the bad woman was the slut, the evil, the whore (216).

The early views of Christianity, especially among the upper classes, have shaped many of today's Western ideals about marriage. But romantic ideals of love put it in conflict with the marriage contract. Romantic and courtly love is spontaneous and includes the freedom of choice. Conversely, marriage is a fixed contract that sets the relationship in formal vows within a religion. Many people feel that love dies in marriage without this romantic element. Thus, divorce is an inevitable correlate to love matches. When and if love vanishes, the partner must be replaced by a new love, because romantic love is still the ideal. This is not the way it is in other parts of the world, in societies that are not based on Christianity and that come out of different historical roots.

Love in the United States

You remember that in Chapter 4 we traced the history of the family in the West, particularly the United States, and noted the importance of the late 1800s as formative in determining how the family looks today. During that era the woman was seen as the man's moral superior, but legal and social power belonged to the man. Eventually, love became the basis for marriage. As individualism rose, so too rose the idea that one should marry for happiness. Marriage was still an economic arrangement, but less for the merging of two family economic units and more for the division of labor between men and women, which kept the family functioning and serving the economic order.

Courtship in the United States moved into dating, in which individuals were allowed to choose their own partners. Rather than families choosing one's partner, people were now allowed to decide for themselves who they would marry, usually as long as it was someone who was socially approved of by the parents. Dating became the practice by which people tried on different types of partners and relationships as a prelude to marrying.

Today, people not only date, they also live together prior to marrying. In the United States, cohabitation is on the rise. Many of the people who live together are young people, some of whom are divorced. In 1970, 523,000 people lived together. In 1996, 3.96 million did so. That is a 600 percent increase (United States Bureau of Census, 1997). Some people suggest that cohabitation is a prelude to marriage, sort of a new courtship pattern. Others suggest that it has become an alternative to marriage, a new family structure. Nonetheless, in the United States we are still a very marrying society. Ninety percent of all Americans eventually marry, even if they do so later in life.

Marriage in the United States

Although one-quarter of all Americans live alone, three-quarters of the population live with others. Fifty-four percent of all households in the United States are reported as married couples, with or without children (United States Bureau of Census, 1995). We are a marrying society, and with those marriages generally come children. Although Americans are having fewer children than in the past (3.67 in 1960 and 3.17 in 1990), we still believe in having them. We are also devoted to relationships. In fact, those who marry and then divorce are likely to remarry, with 40 percent of all marriages in the United States involving at least one partner who was previously married (Taylor, 74). People who marry are doing so later, with men marrying at 26.5 years old and women at 24.5 in 1993; in 1975 it was 23.5 for men and 21.1 for women (Taylor, 1997). This trend of marrying later has to do with higher rates of people working and higher educational attainment (71).

There are also significant racial differences among people who never marry. For example, in 1993, for women under 30 years old, the highest proportion who never married was black women (71). At ages 30–34, 43 percent of black women had not yet married, compared to 16 percent of white women and 18 percent of Latino women. By ages 55–64, only 9 percent of black women never married, compared to 4 percent of whites and 7 percent of Latinos. In fact, if the trend continues, it is estimated that fewer than 3 of 4 black women will ever marry, compared to 9 of 10 white women (71).

People who marry seem to be healthier. In studies done in the 1990s (Horowitz, White, & Howell-White, 1996), indications are that people who are married engage in less risky behavior than do nonmarrieds; they drink less, have fewer sexual partners, and do less drinking and driving. Marrieds, especially men, also have better mental health and are likely to live longer than those who are unmarried. They also have more assets and economic resources. Interestingly, women do not fare as well. For example, young married women are showing declining rates on marital happiness, especially those who are employed (Wolf, 1996, 180). However, it is clear that although marrying behavior has changed in the United States, there are still many rewards to settling down and having a family.

Marriage in the United States has a *normative definition* (Nock, 1998, 6). By this we mean that there are certain ideals for a marriage: Marriage is a personal choice; maturity is presumed to be present in order to be married; marriage is a heterosexual relationship; the husband is the head of the household and principal wage earner; sexual fidelity and monogamy are the norm; and marriage typically involves children (6). Certainly many of these norms are changing, but they are still part of the basic fabric and expectation of those who enter a marriage.

Americans know what they want in a marriage: erotic love, sympathetic love, passionate love, tender and nurturing love, and they want it for their entire adult lives (Blakeslee & Wallerstein, 1995). In fact, American couples hold marriage in the highest esteem. They value it over friends, jobs, and money (5). They also want a partner to be a friend who is compassionate, encouraging, who understands them and appreciates them, not only for what they do, but for what they try to do and fail. People who marry want someone who sees them as unique and irreplaceable (5). A good marriage seems to be able to offset the loneliness of life and provides a refuge from the pressures of work. In a good marriage, each person feels sustenance and a sense of being in an oasis, with sex, humor, and play all rolled into one person. People in lasting marriages that include children seek a connection with the past and an interest in the future, which provides purpose and identity.

A marriage must endure a great deal of complexity that can lead to differing ways of dealing with stress. A fascinating study done in the early 1960s but still relevant today is the work of Cuber and Haroff (1963), in which they studied the relationships of upper-class American couples. They identified a typology of relationships in which they described five kinds of couples: the vital, devitalized, conflict-habituated, passive congenial, and the total relationship. The *vital* couples are those who are alive, excited, energized by the company of the other and who continue to enjoy each other's company long into the relationship. The *devitalized* couple once felt similar to the vital couple, but have lost the spark, and continue together because of the history and connection. The *conflict-habituated* couples are always arguing, and actually seem to form the connection with each other through the difficulties that hold them together. The *passive congenial* couple is nice to each other, pleasant and kind, but there is not much of a spark. The *total relationship* is reflected in a couple who spend a great deal of time together; they may even begin to look like the other after years of being together. The total relationship is often what one might want early in a marriage, but it does not often last as the years evolve. Often these different types of couples are easily identified once one is familiar with this typology with which to analyze relationships.

American marriages tend to go through a series of stages. In the first stage, the individuals are still becoming adults, and they spend time getting to know each other sexually, emotionally, and psychologically (Blakeslee & Wallerstein, 1995). With the birth of the first child, the marriage is revamped as the couple steps into a major life commitment. As the children grow, they find themselves busier than ever in their lives (25). The children's needs are central to the couple's focus, and as the children become adolescents, turbulence ensues. At about this time comes the stages of dependency and illness of the couple's aging parents. The couple becomes part of the "sandwich generation," caring both for one generation older and for one generation younger. In the later part of the couple's journey comes the retirement period, with one or the other becoming dependent and ill. Once again the marriage is changed, but now the couple faces the loss of one or the other to death (25). A long-term marriage has many stages and phases through which a couple learns to deal with all of life's vagaries.

Love in India

Marriage is the norm in other parts of the world as well as in the United States; other cultures just do it differently and have differing statistics. Let's look at India as an example.

Many Indians find the American belief in dating, romance, and living happily ever after as strange as we might find the idea of arranged marriage. Indians fault

Americans for not taking marriage seriously enough. They believe that Americans fall in love, and then when love ends and the fun is over, divorce ensues. In India, what matters is that an individual makes a decision and sticks to it. It is an underlying assumption in Indian marriages that there is a shared commitment from which love will build. Instead of worrying about whether they made the right decision, or whether love will last, married couples work to love each other and see their love grow. Needless to say, however, sometimes the "shared commitment" comes as a result of the lack of alternative options. Thus sticking it out becomes the only choice.

An estimated 95 percent of all marriages in India are arranged (Bumiller, 1990, 24). However, a growing number of people marry for love—some educated professionals in India are now choosing their own partners—and Indians are not strangers to the ideal of love. They have their own conceptions of caring and togetherness and how they are important in life. Indian ideologies of love and marriage are influenced by Hinduism, by the caste system, and by Indian society in general.

According to the Hindu religion, the fate of a person's life is predestined by his or her karma. *Karma* is the sum of all the person's previous actions in this life and in previous lives. Thus, the union of two people is believed to come as it will, regardless of the decisions of the individuals involved. Indians accept arranged marriages because they do not want to take the chance of altering what was meant to be.

Before the courtship of two Indian youths can be approved, both sets of parents consult an astrologer, who looks at the couple's compatibility in accordance with their zodiac signs and the psychological energy that the pair possess (Leviton, 1993). Much emphasis is placed on Mars and where it sits in the individuals' astrological houses. Since marriage is the joining of two families, not just two individuals, careful consideration is given to making a proper match; according to Hindu beliefs, two people living harmoniously together enable each other and their families to reach liberation from the cycle of rebirth (40).

Dowry and marriage go hand in hand in India. Even in today's advanced Indian society, women are seen as important commodities in a family's economic arrangement. A woman must bring wealth to her future in-laws, and it is an economic responsibility for her family to provide her with a suitable dowry, depending on her class and caste background. A woman is valued for her net worth and for the caste from which she comes. Given the substantial monetary value placed on a woman in India, negotiation for marriage is a long and drawn-out affair that often leaves the father of the bride in serious debt.

You may remember from Chapter 1 that the dowry is a tradition in which the wife's family provides monetary reward and often gifts to the groom's family. Although dowries have been outlawed in India, they are still customary practice. Dowry differs from bride price, which is monies given by the groom's family to the bride's, often as compensation for raising her or for removing her earning capabilities from her family of origin. Both are negotiated family to family and do not usually involve the woman herself.

It might be hard for romantics to understand arranged marriages, because they precede the development of love. However, marriage is a social act that ties in with status and family. Indian couples do come to love each other, for the most part. For

Indians, love does not have a simple definition. It is a combination of contradictory ideologies: oneness and separateness, equality and domination. Some have described love as a private, unexpressed devotion. It lies deeper than the physical, in a mutual loyalty and shared concern for the unity and integrity of the family. It grows over time, through the experience of the positive and negative aspects of life (Jung, 1990, 11).

Indian marriages are a mixture of togetherness and separation. There is an emphasis on the union of two people into one bond, like two hands on the same body. It is said that one spouse is not complete without the other. Like hands on a body, spouses are separate in the context of a larger togetherness.

Unfortunately, the ancient image of two hands suggests an ideal of equality that conflicts with the religious and social realities of male and female relationships in India. Because of the belief that women are primarily important for bearing children and serving men, the reality is that some relationships are not as equal as the ideal might suggest. Life for Indian women, especially of the poorer classes, is difficult. In later chapters we will discuss the consequences of the dowry system, including extortion and dowry deaths of young wives.

Weddings in India

Marriages in India are strongly influenced by the caste system. Marriage is usually to members of the same caste; different castes perform various different ceremonies prior to the actual wedding day. Wedding ceremonies in India are wondrous sights to behold, far more colorful than in the United States. The Brahmins, the highest caste in India, start their ceremonies a week prior to the wedding with a ritual known as the *phera*. This ritual begins with a priest reciting a prayer over the couple; then a symbol is painted on their foreheads. In the bride's village, a cow dung–smeared circle is prepared, which will later serve as a place where the sacred wedding fire will be made (Leviton, 1993, 81).

Hindus believe that marriage is the last of twelve purification rites to cleanse the bad karma from one's parents. Thus, prior to the wedding day, the couple stays in hiding, not bathing or changing their clothes, in order to maintain their energetic bodies against evil influences. Rituals are conducted by kinswomen on the couple's behalf, such as rubbing the bride's and groom's bodies with turmeric and staining their palms red to cleanse them (82).

Mundas, a middle-range caste beneath the Brahmins, likewise perform similar pre-wedding ceremonies. They prepare a pulpit made of mud, with seven trees smeared with rice-flour paste and cotton thread, in a courtyard, beneath which the couple sit and receive guests. They are smeared with turmeric and mustard oil to help them maintain an energetic body shield to ward off invisible evil influences, and on the eve of the wedding turmeric-dyed clothes are placed on the couple and a blessing ceremony is performed (81–83). Often on the day of the wedding the bride will "marry" an inanimate object, like a plant or a water pitcher, for the purpose of tricking the spirits of previous wives from other lives (92), in an attempt to keep the previous wives away from the current husband-to-be.

Interestingly, the ritual of throwing rice at Western weddings comes from this school of thought. The throwing of rice was seen as a way to pay homage to past spirits to appease them and encourage them to depart (92).

Child Marriage in India

India has other fascinating (and shocking to Westerners) aspects to its marriage rituals. Using a feminist analysis, we can see that some of them are related to the idea of women and children as property under patriarchy. For example, there is the phenomenon of child marriage. Although outlawed in 1978 through the Child Marriage Restraint Act, which established a required age of 18 for women and 21 for men, the reality is that child marriage, occurring mainly in the North, where 40 percent of the Indian population lives, is common (Burns, 1998, 148). In one province, Rajasthan, out of 5,000 women surveyed in 1996, 56 percent were married before age 18. It is not uncommon for girls as young as 4 and boys as young as 12 to be married.

Since such a union is obviously not about love, it is interesting to ponder the causes. Once again it is important to look at history rather than to judge by Western standards. Remember to employ cultural relativity, rather than ethnocentrism, in thinking about this. During the Muslim invasions, more than 1,000 years ago, unmarried young girls were raped by the invaders or carried off as booty. Among the Gujjars and other groups in this northern region, the solution was to marry off their young daughters almost from birth, to protect them. Today the thinking is that one should marry off any girl before she reaches puberty, because otherwise she might fall prey to sexual exploitation. Many men in the region believe that having sex with a "fresh" girl can cure syphilis, gonorrhea, and even the virus that causes AIDS (148). Again, a feminist interpretation would argue that this is exploitative and detrimental to the girls and treats them as sexual commodities.

It is also argued that there are economic reasons for the practice. Poverty is rampant in India, so to secure a marriage for a daughter early in life means that a father will not have to be responsible for her financially. If he can pay off the dowry early, he has freed himself from those obligations. For the groom's side, there is also economic gain. If the groom's family chooses to have the child bride come to live with them early, there is an extra set of hands to help as servant or field hand (148). Even if they allow the bride to remain with her own family until puberty, they know that eventually this young girl will aid them in work, as well as eventually bearing children to assist the family. Clearly, in India, child marriage is an economic arrangement that suits both families.

Unfortunately, there are many negative consequences to child marriage. In Rajasthan, of the 5,000 women studied (not all of them child brides), barely 18 percent were literate, and only 3 percent used any form of birth control other than sterilization. The result was large families and poor health. That survey showed that of every 1,000 births, 73 children died in infancy and 103 died before they reached age five. Sixty-three percent of the children under age four were malnourished, and the average life expectancy for the women was 58. The numbers were among the worst

Photo 8.2   Contemporary wedding in Indonesia. Photographer: Mary Thieme

in India. Often the husbands tire of these marriages after multiple births of children. There is alcoholism, domestic violence, and killings of wives and of husbands by the wives who tire of being beaten (148). Clearly, early unions of children are one of the more challenging aspects of love and marriage in India. It is the downside of what should be a joyous and happy phenomenon. It also reflects the continuing evidence of the patriarchal nature of family life in India.

Love and Marriage in China

Arranged marriages, much like those in India, were the dominant tradition in China for all classes for centuries (Xiaohe & White, 1998). Because the couple never even laid eyes on each other until the day of the wedding, there were often serious consequences, including suicide. However, after the revolution in 1949 in the People's Republic of China, and as a result of the increasing wage labor in mainland China's towns and cities and the growing Western influence, love-marriages became the norm. Prior to the revolution, parents were involved in determining whom their children married as much as 60–70 percent of the time (122). Now parents are involved in only 10 percent of the mate selections. Those arranged marriages usually occur in the rural areas.

One research project tried to determine if greater freedom in mate selection produced more or less satisfactory marital relations. In China, unlike in the United States, marriage quality is very much influenced not only by relationship to spouse and children but to also others in the family, like in-laws and grandchildren (127). Young women who have a say in whom they marry seem to feel better about their marriages than do women who experienced arranged marriages (129). Although people who argued against love matches believed that they would lead to greater marital disharmony and even more divorce, the findings are that they did not. However, love matches are thought to be disruptive to lineage patterns and to weaken kinship lines. The reality of the situation is that as a society modernizes and becomes more westernized, love matches seem to become the norm. In societies that emphasize the importance of kinship links, like in India, arranged marriages remain important.

Weddings in China

Traditional Chinese weddings still reflect the Confucian vestiges of a patriarchal society, however. These traditional weddings occur more in Taiwan than in the People's Republic. The process of marriage begins with a proposal by the groom to the parents of the bride-to-be. Before this match can be agreed upon, an astrologer looks to the stars for guidance about the partnership (Leviton, 1993, 29). Once it has been agreed upon that the two young people are compatible, the parents of each sit down to a bargaining session. The groom's family brings gifts and money to the bride's family. Cakes are distributed to the bride's relatives and friends, signifying the importance of each person to the bride. This is actually done to entice the friends and relatives to give generous gifts to the couple. The bride also comes with a dowry, often practical gifts of pots, pans, and money.

The wedding ceremony itself is relatively simple. The Chinese prefer a small ceremony, either at the family altar, if there is one, or at the local government office. If it happens at the altar, homage is paid to heaven and earth with two lotus seeds and two red dates (45). The seeds symbolize fertility, peace, harmony, and unity. The procession to the altar is led by a woman from the groom's family, carrying the bride from her village to the groom's village. Firecrackers and noise are used to ward off evil spirits who might lurk in the distance (48). The bride is dressed in red silk, with an elaborate headdress. The groom also wears a wedding cap, which is red, the symbolic color of joy. Fertility and children are wished for on the wedding day, and a special bed is installed in the groom's home the day of the wedding, with children placed on the bed to encourage fertility. The festivities are colorful, loud, and joyous. There is much food, music, and laughter as the families celebrate the newest cycle of life. As with the white weddings in the United States, however, traditional Chinese weddings symbolize and codify heterosexual normative behavior. Recent studies indicate that greater affluence has raised the expectation that parents will spend a lot of money on the wedding, and they are beginning to emulate the West in ostentatiousness.

Love, Marriage, and Weddings Elsewhere

Latin America

Popular culture in Brazil and other parts of Latin America emphasizes a Western style of marriage ceremonies and traditions. Because of the popularity of

Catholicism, and with the emergence of evangelical, Pentecostal religions, Brazilian weddings tend to look similar to American weddings. Brazilian popular culture emphasizes love and courtship in marriage. For the sake of illustration, we will single out a specific ethnic group in Brazil as an example. One Amazonian people, the Mehinaku, choose to marry only out of economic necessity, not for love matches (Gregor, 1985). For them, the concept of love is foreign, and even dangerous and damaging to a marriage (22). Upon reaching puberty, boys are secluded from girls for almost three years, while the girls are developing their menses. Then they are allowed to have sex, but once a girl is of marriageable age, a match is made for her.

Marriage is looked upon as a way of life that assists the man in his undertakings. Thus, on the day of the wedding, he brings the best fish home, while the bride prepares manioc, a Brazilian staple. Alone, neither of these foods would be enough for a meal; together, the nutrients are healthy. The meal is symbolic of the newly formed union and of the husband's prowess in supplying the basics to meet their needs.

Interestingly, extramarital affairs are the norm in this society (25). On average, men have 3–4 girlfriends outside of the marriage, and the women are often seduced by men in common areas like bathing rivers and community gardens. In this society, there is no connection between romantic love and marriage. Erotic encounters with the opposite sex are accepted and on many levels expected. They are public and acknowledged.

South Africa

In South Africa, the fall of apartheid has changed the nature of weddings and marriage, although not necessarily how one loves. Under apartheid, marriages following local traditions were denied state sanction. Tribal weddings were widely practiced, and the woman became the ward of her husband when she married him (Daley, 1998a).

Once a woman married under apartheid, she had no claim to the couple's assets, and her husband could even take another wife without her consent. The white government favored the needs of other whites, those who married with a license, and had a ceremony that was performed by someone authorized by the state. In 1998 the law changed so that tribal marriages were recognized, and attempts have been made to bring them in line with the new constitution that guarantees equal rights to women (A8).

The new law allows a wife to own property and gives her half the assets should the couple divorce. If there is only a tribal marriage, the man is still allowed to take another wife as long as the first wife agrees, and she is guaranteed ownership of her property through a formal inventory.

Although some in the United States might see problems with this system, because of the polygamy as well as the unequal status of women under the law, this is an improvement over the old system of marriages. Tribal marriages are on the wane, and an interesting mix of Christian, tribal, and state-sanctioned marriages are becoming the norm, much as I saw in Zambia.

In a Zulu practice, for example, after the church wedding another tribal ceremony takes place. A cow is slaughtered by the men of the groom's family, while the women cook. Then gifts are given to both families, to honor the union. In earlier times, a bride price, called the *lobola*, was negotiated. It consisted of money and gifts paid by the groom's family for the woman. Currently, in South Africa, the discussion of bride price is negotiated in terms of cows and then converted into cash, because the basis of the culture was agrarian and how many cows one had were long considered a sign of wealth (A8). Lobola was seen as an insurance policy; if the marriage broke up, the woman would be able to go back to her family, who would take her in and support her.

Other parts of the traditional ceremonies include members of the bride's family being allowed to ask for more gifts and a playful episode of doing skits, to tell the groom to treat his wife well. Marriage ceremonies among the Zulu in South Africa are elaborate and expensive affairs, reflecting the mix of tribal, Christian, and now state-sanctioned events.

Clearly, there is a diversity of ways that love, marriage, and weddings play themselves out worldwide. Different societies have different expectations of how people will love, marry, and wed. There is no one way to be; there are many ways.

Gays and Lesbians

A discussion on the diversity of forms of love and marriage would not be complete without a discussion of gay and lesbian intimate relationships. Not too long ago, it would have seemed strange to talk about gay and lesbian families. Stereotypes would have prevailed, with the assumption that all gays wanted was sex anyway and that love had little to do with it. The stereotypes also prevailed that there were no gay families, and that marriage and weddings between people of the same sex was a ridiculous idea. Those times have changed, especially in the Western world.

It is obvious that gay relationships are here, and here to stay. Since the Stonewall rebellion of 1969, in which transvestites, drag queens, gay men, and lesbians took a public stand against police harassment in New York City, the gay rights movement has grown and thrived. Many communities throughout the United States and the world have passed gay rights ordinances, barring discrimination based on sexual orientation. Other communities have enacted domestic partnership laws that allow gays and lesbians to register as partners, to receive benefits, in some cases, like heterosexual couples—including medical insurance, hospital visiting rights, and pension benefits. Some states are seriously debating whether or not to allow gays and lesbians to "marry," just as straight couples do.

There are now as many as 1.6 million same-sex couples living together in the United States (Seligmann, 1990). Within these relationships, gays seem to confront many of the same issues as heterosexual couples: division of labor, power, and authority and emotional obligations. But because of many people's homophobia (fear of gays), gays are not allowed to show their affection in public and often have to hide their sexual preferences.

Although there is a growing atmosphere of acceptance of gays, they still face much antagonism, including hate crimes like the killing of Matthew Shepherd in 1998. In 1999 a gay couple was killed in their bed in a small town in northern California. The two suspects in the case were brothers who grew up in a fundamentalist household with an eccentric and tyrannical father. They were members of the World Church of the Creator, whose members have committed other hate crimes.

Conservative groups have mobilized politically against gay rights, going so far as passing a bill in the Montana senate requiring that people convicted of having homosexual sex register as violent sex offenders (Stacey, 1999). Other anti-gay legislative efforts are regularly proposed by conservatives who are against granting gays equal rights.

Gays and lesbians are quite different from each other in the way they live their lives. This fact is usually unknown to their heterosexual colleagues. For example, lesbians are more likely to partner earlier and stay in long-term relationships, compared to gay men, who partner up later in life (Bell & Weinberg, 1978).

Popular estimates of how many gays and lesbians there are average between 4 and 10 percent of the population. It is hard to say how many people are gay because often a person's sexuality is fluid, depending on stage of life, availability of partners, or levels of persecution. Conservative estimates of the numbers of lesbians and gays are that 5 percent of the U.S. population live in such families (Stacey, 1998).

Some gays and lesbians are eager to get on the wedding band wagon. Jewish rabbis, Protestant ministers, Quaker meetings, and even some Catholic priests have performed gay and lesbian commitment ceremonies, and they have even been depicted in the popular media (168). Scenes of same-sex couples kissing have made it onto national television. In Vermont, legislators have voted to allow same-sex couples to form consensual unions under state law.

In other parts of the world, there are differing reactions to gay and lesbian intimate relationships. In South Africa, the new constitution gives full rights to gays and lesbians, in parity with all other citizens of the country. Although there is still much to be done there in terms of overcoming the stigma attached to a gay lifestyle, policymakers have decided to go on record as according gays and lesbians full equality under the law (Jacobson, 1999). In fact, when I recently visited South Africa, I encountered a white, lesbian couple who had been the first to publicly have a commitment ceremony and had recently adopted two black children, breaking a number of taboos all at the same time.

In the Netherlands, the Dutch parliament approved legislation designed to sanction gay marriage and give lesbian and gay couples the right to adopt children. In 1997, the Dutch justice minister argued against the proposal, but the progressive Parliament overcame the objections, arguing that the rights of children in homosexual relationships had to be better regulated. Polls there indicate that 7 out of 10 Dutch citizens believe that gays and lesbians should be able to have families (Datalounge, 1997, October 29).

In Ecuador, until 1997, it was illegal for gays to have sex. Consensual sex between adults of the same sex was a crime punishable by up to eight years in prison (Datalounge, 1997, December 17b). However, activists lobbied the government and won their case after Ecuadorian police raided a bar and arrested 14 men on charges of crimes against morality. In Cuba there is growing acceptance of gays. President Fidel Castro went on record as saying that homosexuality was "a natural human tendency that simply must be respected" (Datalounge, 1998, February 18). Since 1992, several arrests have led only to fines, rather than incarceration. There seems to be an increasing tolerance for gay entertainers and others who choose to be more public about their lifestyles. When I visited Cuba recently, gay citizens were careful about showing their preference in public, but seemed to participate in private activities and were pushing the limits of official tolerance.

However, there are many places in the world that resist gay reform. In the Bahamas, an ex-British colony, pressure is being brought to bear by the British government to change the laws against homosexual acts between consenting adults. The laws currently say that homosexual acts are illegal; the British government has attempted to make them legal. However, the British Virgin Islands, the Turks and Caicos Islands, Anguilla, Montserrat, and the Cayman Islands are all resisting London's wishes. Citing religious objections, officials in those places argue that their "deeply rooted Christian traditions" do not allow them to sanction such behavior (Datalounge, 1998, February 20).

In New Zealand, a court of appeals rejected the right of gays and lesbians to marry under the state's Marriage Act of 1955. The justices found that there was nothing discriminatory about not allowing them to marry because gay marriage did not fit conventionally acceptable modes of behavior (Datalounge, 1997, December 17a). However, a dissenting justice argued that gays and lesbians were effectively being excluded from full membership in society.

And in many parts of the world, not only are gays and lesbians not accepted, they are harassed and vilified. In the Middle East country of Qatar, a peninsula state bordering Saudi Arabia, 20 suspected gay Filipinos were deported because of their sexuality. They were all legal workers in the clothing and barber shop industry, but officials alleged that they were sex workers, involved in a lucrative illegal sex trade industry in that country (Datalounge, 1997, November 3).

It is clear that as much as the gay lifestyle may be accepted in some parts of the world, others react with hostility to the very presence of homosexuals. The process of acceptance is a long and arduous one. However, there seem to have been some dramatic developments since the beginnings of the gay rights movement 30 years ago. With this change comes a gradual acceptance of gay and lesbian intimate relationships and family life.

Dissolution of Intimate Relationships

Often when we think of the end of intimate relationships we think of divorce rates. But that is just part of the picture, and a limited one at that. Divorce rates are not very useful indicators of relationship dissolution; they say nothing about relationship satisfaction and happiness. Many people stay married or partnered in painful and difficult relationships, and that data never shows up in the statistics. Intimate relationships also end because of death of a partner, hospitalization of one partner, or partners living apart even when they never formally dissolve their union.

We start with the statistics on divorce in the United States, and compare them to statistics from other parts of the world. Then we take a look at the internal dynamics of families and relationships, to determine the positive and negative consequences of such terminations. It is also important to look at parts of the world where termination of relationships is either not an option or is done differently than in the United States. This gives us a basis for comparison and helps us to see that termination is not always the most successful resolution to difficulties.

Divorce in the United States

The United States leads the 19 major industrial nations in divorce (Sorrentino, 1990). Since nearly one-half of all marriages end this way, the U.S. rate is two-and-a-half times greater than Germany, the Netherlands, and France and 10 times greater than that of Italy. But the divorce rate in the United States has slowed recently, while it is increasing dramatically in Canada, the Netherlands, Sweden, and the United Kingdom. In fact, the U.S. rate has been declining since 1981. Because people are living longer, marriages today could last as much as three times longer than those of 200 years ago. So even though there are large numbers of people who are divorcing, so too there are large numbers of people staying together for long periods of time (Coontz, 1997, 31).

The average marriage that ends in divorce in the United States lasts only 6.3 years. Coontz argues in her book, *The Way We Really Are: Coming to Terms with America's Changing Families,* that there are currently in the United States what could be referred to as "long term, healthy relationships" and "short term, medium to low quality relationships" (31–32). She also points out that highly educated and highly paid women have a greater chance of divorcing than women with lower earnings and education. But it is interesting to note that these educated and highly paid women are more likely to have married in the first place, because women with lower earnings and education have lower prospects of getting married (82). The lower the income, it seems, the higher the divorce rates.

How early one marries also affects divorce rates. People who marry under the age of 20 are far more likely to divorce than those who marry later (Price & McKenry, 1988, 17). Whether or not one has children also influences the rate. People who have up to three children tend to have more marital stability than do those who have five or more children, and those who have no children are more likely to divorce than those who have one child (Heaton, 1990).

Divorce rates also vary with race. Blacks have twice the rate of divorce of whites and Latinos in the United States, and interracial couples are more likely to divorce than are those who marry within the same race (Cherlin, 1996). Religion also seems to play a role, with those of no religious affiliation more likely to divorce than those who are affiliated with a religion (359). Protestants divorce more than Catholics, and Jews less than Catholics. Interreligious couples divorce more than those of the same religions (361). Women of Spanish origin of all ages are the least likely to have been divorced (Taylor, 1997, 73).

There are numerous explanations as to why people divorce. Some argue that because women have greater employment opportunities than in the past, it is more possible for wives to terminate marriages that once might have survived (74). There are changing attitudes toward marriage and divorce, as well liberalization of divorce laws, such as no-fault divorce, that make it easier to end a marriage (74). Certainly no one answer explains why people terminate long-term relationships.

Divorce seems to have a varying impact on family members. Most researchers study what divorce does to the children. You might find the results surprising. Findings seem to indicate that a large proportion of children from divorced families do well on achievement and adjustment tests. Contrary to popular opinion, only 20–25 percent of children from divorced families have behavior problems, about twice as many as the 10 percent from nondivorced families who have such problems. But that means that 75–80 percent of children from divorced families are not having problems, and are doing quite well (Coontz, 1997, 100). Coontz points out that adolescent self-image seems to be lowest for teens in two-parent families in which the fathers show little interest in the children, and in which the children internalize the problem with self-blame. It seems that for some children, being in a difficult two-parent family is worse than being in a divorced family. A critical factor in long- and short-term adjustment to divorce seems to be how effectively the mother, as the usual custodial parent, handles the breakup and how well she parents (Furstenberg & Cherlin, 1991, 71).

Women experience a substantial decline in their standard of living upon divorcing (Ahrons, 1994). This occurs because they usually have custody of the children, and a large proportion of single fathers do not pay child support. Although the women work upon divorcing, they tend to work part-time and make less money (416). In fact, on average, divorced women and the minor children in their homes experience a 73 percent decline in their standard of living in the first year after divorce, while their former husbands experience a 42 percent rise in their standard of living (Weitzman, 1985).

The stigma attached to divorce has lessened over time, but divorced individuals find a diminishment of social support upon ending their marriages. Because of the demands of employment, household management, and child care, divorced people in the United States find little time to develop social networks. Men tend to remarry more quickly than women and seem to have somewhat fewer problems in social adjustment than do women (Ahrons, 1994, 419).

Most people in the United States experience emotional distress upon terminating a relationship, but over time their emotional well-being gradually returns (420). There also seems to be a better adjustment to breakups when couples demonstrate better education, income, labor force participation, young age, few children, short length of marriage, social support, and nontraditional attitudes and emotional adjustment to divorce (422).

In fact, it is not uncommon for divorced couples to end up as friends, or at least cooperative. In a fascinating piece of work done by Ahrons (1994), she discovered that not all couples who divorce become embittered. According to her research, there are four kinds of divorced couples: the perfect pals, the cooperative colleagues, the angry associates, and the fiery foes. The perfect pals made up 12 percent of the sample; they had not remarried and still got along very well. They had joint custody and even spent time together. The cooperative colleagues were 38 percent of the couples studied, and they had a moderate level of interaction. They were cordial and mostly focused on their children. The angry associates were 25 percent of the sample; their relationships were filled with conflict. The fiery foes were 25 percent of the population; they never interacted and were openly hostile to their former partners. In fact, they only communicated through their children.

It appears that eventually those who experience divorce in the United States adjust well to it and move on. This seems to be the case in other westernized countries as well.

Dissolution of Relationships in Sweden

When studying the issue of dissolution of relationships, researchers often look to Sweden, because contemporary family change in that country seems to be an extension of the global family trend underway in all modernizing countries, with shifts away from the extended and toward the nuclear family form (Popenoe, 1988, 167). Swedish marriage rates have been low since the 1960s, especially among young people. Swedes are more likely to live in a nonmarital cohabitation relationship; in other words, they live together rather than marrying.

Living together is an old custom in Sweden, where there is a long history of permissive sexuality and open attitudes about relationships (170). As early as 1917, Sweden dropped the idea that children can be illegitimate, believing that children of all unions should have the same rights as children of married unions. Because so many Swedes do not marry, it is impossible to use divorce rates to look at breakup. Instead, researchers look to see how many couples with children dissolve their unions. The rate seems to be high, with Sweden having "the highest rate of family dissolution in the world" (174).

Nonetheless, while the number of "broken homes" may be increasing rapidly, most Swedish children still live in intact families (174). Swedes still favor living in relationships, just not married ones. They do not choose voluntary singlehood, living alone, or even nonexclusive sexual relationships. In fact, Swedes have less extramarital sex than do Americans (179). In the '60s Kinsey found that 90 percent of Swedes did not accept extramarital affairs, and to this day there is far less recreational sex in Sweden than there is in the United States (179).

In Sweden, the government provides a family allowance plan that guarantees a minimum amount of support to all parents with children (Weitzman, 1985, 309). After divorce, the custodial parent continues to receive the allowance directly from the state. The amount of child support to be paid by the noncustodial parent is established by judicial procedure, not by an individual judge as is done in the United States. The state advances that amount to the custodial parent and then assumes responsibility for collecting payment from the noncustodial parent. There is a minimum amount stipulated for child support awards so that each child is guaranteed an adequate standard of living. If the court-ordered support is less than this minimum, the government goes the extra mile to make up the difference (310).

Divorce in Japan

Although statistics show that divorce rates in Japan are beginning to rise from where they have been historically, Japan still has a fairly low divorce rate compared to the United States (Hutter, 1998, 505). It is one of the lowest in the world. Divorce and family breakup is a scandal in Japan; it even impacts marriage prospects for the children of the divorce. Marriages in Japan were once negotiated by go-betweens in a form of arranged marriage; however, since the modernization and industrialization that occurred after World War II, there have been more freedom of choice and love-marriages.

Women have gained more rights in Japan during the past 50 years, but there is still much inequality between men and women. For example, there is no alimony or child support in Japan, and women have little recourse to public assistance or social services (506). A divorced woman bears a stigma, and she is expected to return to her family of origin. Often the divorced woman's income is less than one-half of the national average for heads of households (Condon, as quoted in Hutter, 1998, 506). Women earn less than men, so it is particularly difficult for them to divorce and then support themselves and their children. In Japan, it is far more likely that a woman will decide to stay in a difficult marriage because it is easier than facing the alternative.

Divorce in Non-Western Countries

In Chapter 1 we talked about how difficult it is to find information on family life cross-culturally so that we can have a comprehensive picture of families around the world. When we try to compare the dissolution or breakup of intimate relationships, the complexity becomes glaringly apparent: there is very little data available on cross-cultural comparisons of divorce in non-Western and developing countries. Much of what we are learning comes from emerging literature that is sporadic at best. Often we get anecdotal information—a short article here describing conditions in one country, a statistical piece there comparing a few places. What I convey to you here is once again a mosaic, a few pieces of the puzzle, placed together in hopes that you get a sense of the complexity of the whole. I try to put together a few snapshots, so you get a piece of the picture.

Divorce in India

Little is known about divorce among groups other than Hindus in India; remember that there are Muslims, Jains, Sikhs, and Christians as well living there. Divorce is becoming more common, due to changes in legislation and the larger

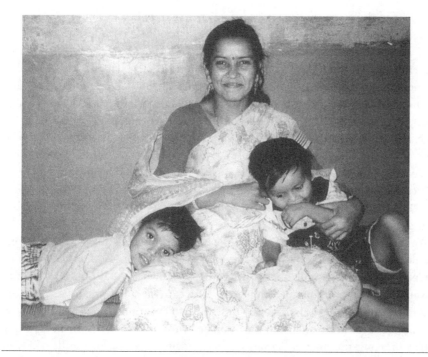

Photo 8.3   Divorce in India, mother and children. Photographer: Mary Thieme

society (Amato, 1998, 414). There is a joint family system, with a man, his sons, and their dependents (wives and children) all living in the same home. Sometimes, as we know, this is called the extended family. Most Indians spend at least some portion of their lives in a joint family, and most marriages are arranged. Only 14 percent of adult females work outside of the home; generally Indian women bear four children in their lifetimes (415).

Recently the rise in divorce rates indicates that the ratio of divorced to married adults increased by 19 percent for men and 35 percent for women (415). The divorces seem to take place, much like in the United States, in the early years of the marriage, and custody of children is usually given to the women. Unfortunately, fathers rarely pay adequate levels of child support, and women do not receive a share of the matrimonial property when they divorce. It is assumed that they belong to the husband and his family (417).

Some states in India allow public assistance for divorced women, but the amounts are quite little, barely enough to live on. Initially most women turn to their kin for help, but eventually they must try to establish their own homes and become self-sufficient. Families generally feel they have discharged their obligations once they give a daughter a dowry when she marries; often they are poor themselves and cannot afford to help her for long (417). It is very difficult for Indian women to find work in the labor force because they have few skills or education, and unfortunately, few divorced women in India remarry because of the stigma attached to divorce. Many resign themselves to being single for the rest of their lives (417).

Divorced women, but not men, experience economic hardship upon severing their marital ties. They are blamed by others when their relationships fail, in the belief that it is the woman's responsibility to keep the marriage alive. This is true even if there is infidelity or abuse (419). Although both men and women receive emotional support from their families, men remain within their joint families and are surrounded by people who will take their side. When a woman returns home to her family, the status of the family may suffer; this may even compromise the chances for other daughters' marriages. Thus the woman is not welcomed with open arms. She is often given the most menial and unpleasant tasks to perform, and she has few people who are of her status—divorced woman—which means fewer friends. Often these women report loneliness (420).

In India, people who divorce have been found to feel more dissatisfied, irritable, insecure, and generally more maladjusted than those who are married (421). Women also seem to experience more emotional problems than do men. Many report thoughts of suicide, depression, and sleep disorders. In one study, women reported feeling like failures and believed that their lives had ended (421). Rarely do women seek divorce, and then only in the most extreme situations. Divorce is more common among those of the upper classes, if it occurs at all. Rearing children is also a major source of stress for divorced women, with 71 percent of women reporting that bringing up children alone was hard, mainly because of the demands of employment and housework.

But many find that divorce has its benefits as well. Some women were relieved that the unhappy marriage was over; some had an increase in self-confidence and feelings of competence in dealing with the everyday demands of life, and many decided to get further education, which increases self-worth (422).

The difficulties facing those who are divorced in India are tied to the fact that in that country women are economically dependent on men (423). They are dependent first on their fathers, then on their husbands, and eventually on their sons. Girls generally do not inherit property, and although there are dowries, they become the property of the husband and his family and are not returned upon divorce (423). Because there are few economic resources to draw on, Indian women are much more trapped than are American women. An unhappily married woman is expected to accept her destiny—it is predestined, following Hindu belief.

The patriarchal joint family puts Indian women at a disadvantage and men at an advantage in divorce. Men live continuously with their mothers, fathers, and brothers. The wife is the outsider in the household; her husband's responsibility is to his family, not to her. When she leaves his home, her family does not want her, nor are there legitimate opportunities for her elsewhere. In fact, it appears that in India we can see that the greater the inequity between men and women in a society, the more detrimental the impact of divorce on women (424).

Divorce in Iran

The rate of divorce is rising in Iran, and with it comes dramatic changes in a society steeped in tradition. Iran is a fundamentalist Islamic country that has seen much political turmoil in the past 40 years. Mohammed Reza Shah Pahlavi was the reigning monarch until February 1979, when radical fundamentalist Sh'ite militants took over the government and turned it into a country that uses the Koran as the basis for its practices. Under the Shah, the country had been westernizing and modernizing, quickly becoming a developed nation because of its vast resources of oil (Hutter, 1998, 507). Unfortunately, under the Shah there was also political persecution, foreign domination, and wasting of financial gains. Popular opinion was against the Shah, and the holy men *(ayatollahs)* and priests *(mullahs)* came to embody Iranian nationalism, integrity, and selflessness (507).

The Koran contains three assumptions about male and female relationships that rest on the idea of men's superiority to women (Hassan, 1989, 11). The first belief is that God's primary creation is man, not woman; woman is secondary, since she was created from his rib. Second, the Koran maintains that woman, not man, is the reason both were expelled from the Garden of Eden; thus all women, as the "daughters of Eve," are to be regarded with hatred, suspicion, and contempt. Third, there is the belief that women were created *for* men, as well as *from* men. A woman's life is to be instrumental to a man's needs, not because of her own fundamental importance. You will note that these beliefs bear a strong resemblance to Judeo-Christian ideologies.

After the fall of the Shah, the country changed its practices around the family; with this came changes in marriage and divorce. Before the Shah, Iran had a very high divorce rate; a man could simply declare himself divorced in front of two witnesses and it was accomplished. Under the Shah, the laws changed to require court proceedings and mutual consent (507). However, under the fundamentalist government, divorce is easy again, with a man needing to file at a notary public office, with two witnesses. The couple must be mutually consenting, but women can easily be forced to consent.

The Iranian family is traditionally patriarchal, and the woman often gives up her dowry upon divorcing (508). Although the Koran does not stipulate that a woman should provide a dowry, it has become a common practice in Iran as well as in other fundamentalist Muslim countries. Fortunately, in 1994 laws were passed to give a divorced woman the right to monetary compensation for the years she worked in her husband's home as wife and mother (Esfandiari, 1997, 43).

The government has also developed a written model contract to be used at the time of marriage (43). In it a divorced woman is given the right to half the property acquired during the marriage, providing she does not seek the divorce herself and it is not her fault that the husband seeks the divorce. Another part of the contract gives the wife the power of attorney to divorce should her husband fail to provide proper maintenance, desert her for five or more years, become insane, or develop an incurable disease.

Iran allows polygyny, and the consequences for women are variable. When a man takes another wife, he must inform the future second wife of the first wife's existence, but the first wife has no say in whether or not he takes another. Muslim law permits a man to have four wives, although in the lower classes the men tend to divorce the earlier wife at the time of subsequent marriages. If divorced and no longer young, the woman has little chance of remarrying. Often the divorced woman returns to her family of origin, although they rarely can afford to support her.

Putting women behind the veil has been an important aspect of life in Iran. Shops and restaurants refuse to serve women not wearing a *hejab*, or dark scarf pulled over the forehead, with a baggy dark smock and loose trousers, and in all government offices officials check to see if women are properly attired. Women also are attacked if not properly dressed. The return of the veil was a cornerstone of the revolution, and women were expected to cover their faces and hands to show their revolutionary zeal. Although there were protests against this imposition, the rule prevails 25 years later.

Women are considered minors, and their testimony is considered half equal to men's; evidence must be given by two women to equal that of one man in court cases, and often a woman is considered to be lying and liable to slander punishment if she is found wrong. Women had been excluded from the workforce, especially from traditionally male occupations. However, since the war between Iran and Iraq, which occurred from 1980 to 1988, women have been allowed to temporarily return to the workforce.

Iran's political changes have had a significant impact on middle-class families (508). People who were once similar in lifestyle to Westerners have had to hide their sophistication. To be Western is to be suspect. However, many women have embraced the changes. Some women, for example, prefer the veil because it keeps them safe from the prying eyes of men.

Recent events in Iran indicate that young college students are dismayed with the slow pace of the reform of some of these laws that has been promised by religious leaders. Riots, demonstrations, and police retaliation have begun to occur, once again with people seeking changes to this traditional fundamentalist regime. It is yet unforeseeable just what changes will take place there.

Summary

You can see that there is more to marital breakup than divorce. There are many different ways of ending a partnership without going through legal procedures. Family life and its forms around the world are complex and do not always look the way they do to us at home. It also appears that as extended families diminish, there is an increased need for social networks, social support, and some social intervention into family life. There are growing solutions that come out of the changing social context of family dissolution, such as economic support for broken families, like child support, welfare acts, and even safety nets for the elderly. Those are areas we will deal with in the chapters to come.

In this chapter we looked at the nature of intimate relationships, discovering that love, marriage, and their endings are socially constructed. We critiqued the concept of "white weddings," seeing that they were means for institutionalizing compulsory heterosexuality and keeping the patriarchy alive. Using a feminist approach, we noted that love has many meanings, depending on one's cultural and historical context. After comparing love and marriage in the United States, we moved on to India, where we saw that arranged marriages are the norm and that love grows over time; it is not romantic, as we in the West might call it. We took a look at weddings in

India and at the concept of child marriage there. Later we studied love and marriage in China, then Latin America, and South Africa.

Studying partnership between same-sex couples, we saw that different parts of the world handled the issue in various ways. We found that dissolution of intimate relationships also seemed dependent on historical and social forces, with divorce rates falling in the United States but increasing in other parts of the world. We learned that there are many ways to end relationships without having to divorce. Throughout this chapter, we took a feminist theoretical perspective to understand that women have fared more poorly in intimate relationships than have men.

CHAPTER 9

Intergenerational Relationships

Years ago, I worked with a Nigerian woman who had her Ph.D. and was teaching at my college. I was invited home to meet her family and was amazed to find out that she had 12 children, all between the ages of 18 and 2. She worked full-time, volunteered in the community, and was a respected churchgoer. When I asked her how she was able to accomplish so much while still being a mother, she told me that it was because her three eldest daughters, ages 14, 16, and 18, were at home to raise the younger children. She said that this freed up her time to do her professional and community work. Although she was at home every evening to put the smallest children to bed, the rest of her day was free for other activities. I realized how different parenting was for her, raised Igbo in Nigeria, where family responsibilities and expectations were so unlike those for American-born women like myself.

Years later I traveled to Zimbabwe, Kenya, South Africa, and Zambia, and discovered an aspect of sibling relationships similar to that of my colleague's family. Siblings played an important role in the raising of kin. It was very unlike that with which I was familiar.

On another trip, to China, I found myself out and about one morning. In Beijing, I saw parents taking their children to school on bicycles and then bustling off to work. Later in the day I saw aged grandparents with the smallest children, caring for them and entertaining them. These same grandparents met the school-aged children after school and brought them home, caring for them until the parents came home, as well as tending the home and doing the housework. Once again I was struck with how dissimilar this was to the way things were done back home. I realized that parenting and child rearing truly differed depending on where one lived, and I decided to do some research to study the differing dynamics of intergenerational relationships and how other societies handled those intimate interactions.

Photo 9.1   Intergenerational family selling red pepper paste in Turkey.
Photographer: Mary Thieme

In modern societies such as those in the West, "family relationships are characterized primarily for their emotional content and by the degree of psychological satisfaction and support which they offer their members" (Hareven, 1976, 202). This is not necessarily true in more traditional societies, where the division of tasks for the management of the family's economic well-being is more crucial. Family members may be valued for the labor that they provide within the family and for their respective economic contributions. Thus we can see the value of daughters and elders in raising children. They are important child-care providers, allowing the parents to go out to work to support the family. In addition, children are viewed not just as emotional extensions of their parents, but also as a form of social security, since in the future they will care for their aged parents (203).

Families in developing parts of the world are more likely to see family members as part of a work unit, one in which the careers of the individual members are enmeshed with the economic activities of the rest of the kin. This is particularly true for working-class families who need the assistance of all family members to survive. But they still involve psychological and emotional satisfaction as well.

In this chapter we explore the nature of intergenerational relationships: the internal structure of family life and the differences that occur as a result of social change. Where once there may have been traditional ways for families to interact, changes in power dynamics and hierarchy have come about as societies move toward a Western and industrialized model. Globalization is changing the traditional models of family interaction. Some societies hold on to old patterns, struggling to maintain some semblance of the old social order in the roles of parents, mothering and fathering, relationships to elders, and sibling relational patterns. These generational relationships determine people's interactions with others; people in different roles have differing expectations of others' behavior. These generational interactions are very much tied to how societies conceive of childhood and adolescence. We discuss how we in the United States handle various intergenerational relationships, then focus on a few other countries, to compare families in the United States to those in places with patterns dissimilar to our own. Let's start with parenting.

Parenting

Parenting is a term that is used generically to describe the broad category of relationships between children and their birth or adoptive child rearers. In this section, I describe those relationships in broad terms; mothering and fathering are discussed more specifically later in the chapter. Parenting differs in various parts of the globe, with the roles and expectations of those people who are parents being quite diverse, depending on the culture.

Parenting in the United States

Parenting in the United States has changed over time. Early in the history of the United States, when children were expected to be involved in agriculture, as soon as children were old enough to help out it became their responsibility to do so. Everyone contributed to the family upkeep, because all hands were needed in the household. Mothers and fathers worked, usually in the home (as discussed in Chapter 4), and everyone cared for the children. All family members were counted on for their contributions; even the youngest child would do what he or she could to keep the family-based economy going. During this time, fathers were authoritarian and had primary power in family decision making.

Then came the move to the factories, under the family-wage economy. Fathers went out to work and left mothers at home to raise the children and care for the homes. Gradually fathers became less involved with their children's lives because they were out of the home; the mother became the arbiter of justice and the primary caregiver.

Now we are in a family-consumer economy, in which both parents must work out of the home to meet the increased costs of raising a family and succeeding economically. An increase in consumerism in general makes it necessary for all adults in a family to work. Remarkably, some single-parent mothers are able to make it on one income. Three-quarters of all mothers are employed outside of the home, and it is common for children to go to child care or preschool and then to public school.

The job of being a parent has evolved as the economy and history have demanded. Along with these changes has come the conceptualization of childhood and other stages and roles according to age. As parenting changes, so do the definitions of childhood, adolescence, adulthood, and old age. These all evolve depending on cultural relativity and historical period.

The demographic patterns of parenting have evolved as well. The rate of fertility, or childbearing rate, has diminished significantly in the United States in the past

200 years. For example, in 1800, women bore an average of eight children; now the norm is two per woman (Baca-Zinn & Eitzen, 1999, 290). One of the many reasons for the lower fertility rate is that women marry later and bear children at a later age. Women who marry late have fewer years ahead of them during which they can bear children. There is also more divorce, so the length of time that women can have children within marriage is shortened. Because the economy demands two incomes for survival, there are more women in the labor force, and staying home to care for children is less likely to be an option (291). Also, women and men are choosing to work because their work is seen as important and interesting. The rates for fertility in the United States differ depending on race and ethnicity, with whites and Asians having the lowest rates, African Americans next, and Latinos the highest (294).

Nearly half of all American children live apart from one or more of their parents, and 15 percent live in stepfamilies (297). The traditional family structure of the past—two parents with children—has changed; now 1 in 3 children live with a single mother (298). There are also more people living in multigenerational homes, with an increased number of children living with their grandparents, who have become primary caregivers, or with adult children living with their aged parents as caregivers. There is also a rise in sons continuing to live with their parents into adulthood: 15–20 percent of adult children aged 20–30, and nearly 10 percent aged 30 and above, live with their parents (299). This is usually due to economic hardship. There are a growing number of women having children out of wedlock, as well as increased levels of divorce, which are leading to more children than ever spending at least parts of their childhoods in single-parent families (Taylor, 1997).

During the late twentieth and early twenty-first centuries, there has also been a rise in the numbers of gays and lesbians who are parenting. There are estimates of between 6 million and 14 million children living with gay parents (84). Most of those children are from previous marriages, but there are a growing number of gay men and lesbians becoming parents through artificial insemination, adoption, heterosexual intercourse, surrogate parenting, and co-parenting (85). Lesbian mothers are the fastest-growing segment of gay parenting, due to the use of artificial insemination; there is a "lesbian baby boom" going on, especially on the west coast (85). With greater tolerance for a gay lifestyle and single parenting, as well as a supportive environment for lesbian and gay couples, the numbers seem to be rising. However, there is still resistance to such parenting styles in the United States, and very few states recognize the parental rights of same-sex parents (85).

There are many benefits as well as costs to parenting in the United States. Children help parents feel that there is meaning and purpose in their lives, and children help family members become more connected with their families of origin and others in their communities. However, the consequences are quite significant as well. For example, the transition to becoming a parent is highly stressful due to the irrevocability of the decision, the lack of experience in having a child in the home, and the isolation that sometimes occurs if the parent is living apart from family and friends. The stresses of parenting continue throughout the child's life: concern over the child's health, the need to educate the child, and worry about the child's economic and emotional future. All these concerns and joys cause parenting to be one of the most intense experiences of an adult's life.

Parenting in Japan

Although many aspects of parenting elsewhere in the world are similar to the United States, there are also differences. All parents birth children; we have that in common. But what happens next is up for grabs. Let's take Japan as an example. Japan has few natural physical resources; what the Japanese do have is "human capital": the attitudes, values, health, and intelligence of its people (Zinsmeister, 1990, 53). In contrast to American children, a full 95 percent of Japanese children live in two-parent homes, with a third of these also living with a grandparent in the house. Japanese divorce rates are 25 percent lower than those in the United States (54).

In Japan, marriage is a rite of passage to adulthood, and a person's highest calling is to be a parent. Between one-quarter and one-half of all marriages are arranged; marrying age is 25 for women and slightly older for men. But interestingly, although romantic love is gaining popularity in Japan, the "basic social unit in Japan is the coalition of the mother and child, rather than the husband-wife coalition of the west" (54). The family is primarily child-centered, with the child sleeping with the mother, tightly bound to her back when they go out, and breast-fed as old as age six.

Surprisingly to us in the West, child-centeredness in parenting in Japan seems to produce some healthy consequences. Crime is very low, with fewer than 2,000 instances each of homicide, robbery, and rape. And that is in a country of 120 million people (54). Behavioral problems like juvenile delinquency are low, and there are much lower arrest rates for rape, assault, and battery among teens, too. While crime is on the rise in the rest of the world, it is diminishing in Japan.

Japan also has lower fertility rates than the United States. The rate is 1.8 children per woman—below the "replacement rate" of two parents having two children to replace themselves—so that in the near future there will be more older Japanese living than younger people. In the early 2000s, Japan has a productive peak of people in the workforce, with 70 percent of its population in the market. But the ranks of older retirees will expand rapidly (55). Also, Japanese now live longer than any other people in the world, with 78 the average age of death (56). Japanese health care costs are less than half those of the United States, and the later years of their lives seem to be spent with their children, particularly their eldest sons.

There is quite a bit of stress in parents' lives in Japan. The pressures of the educational system place a burden on parents who want to produce high-achieving children. Japan is a "credential society," which means that one's individual social mobility is limited by the particulars of one's formal education (58). There are many suicides and self-image problems because of this pressure. Parents are continually striving to help their children study for exams and deal with the "examination war" or "examination hell" that has become a form of Japanese social trauma (58).

Life in Japan is so stressful that drinking and suicide are high among people who are in the workforce. A recent survey found that two-thirds of Japanese men get drunk at least once a week, and 1 in 8 does so daily (58). Interestingly, each year 1 office worker in 3 in Tokyo needs treatment for a mental disorder, stress, or alcohol-related disease (59). This certainly has an impact on family life and the role parents play in their children's lives.

Japan is a congested place, with one-quarter of all Japanese living within a 30-mile radius in Tokyo. Housing is so expensive that people have to commute long hours to work. These stresses take their toll on parenting in Japan. Fathers, in particular, spend long hours at work, leaving the home early and returning late. The mothers tend to be at home, caring for all ages of their children.

Japanese workers work six days a week, with an average worker racking up 2,110 hours a year—about 500 hours more than West Germans and 200 more than Americans (59). They get only three days off a year for annual leave, with a total of only 17 days off a year. Japanese workers have a greater commitment to their jobs than they do to their families. They socialize with each other after work, often late into the night, with extended drinking and informal business transactions taking place. I remember many an evening walking in the streets of Osaka and Kobe watching drunken businessmen staggering to the subway, making their way home. Japanese men are married to their jobs, while wives are isolated in their homes with their children.

Surprisingly, dedication to one's work is encouraged by family members in Japan. As a collectivist society in which the identity of the individual is found in interaction with others, the group is far more important than the individual. In the United States, the concept of the self, or what a person is, defines our sense of reality. Here we see ourselves as independent beings, separate in our own skins, in our own minds. The "I" is behind our faces. We have individual identities and are taught this from birth. From day one, parents speak to their baby and tell the child to look inside, to focus on the inner individual self (Fessler, 1999).

In Japan, as in other parts of Asia, the mind, body, and world are more interactive, which creates a collective identity in the person. Whereas in the United States the child is separated from the parents and placed in a crib, or even in another room, this would be considered barbaric in Japan, where the mother and baby sleep together. In the United States we are brought up to want our separate space, our separate rooms or offices. We want to be ourselves, to express ourselves in isolation, independent of the group. We guard our property; this is "mine" versus this is "ours," or the group's. In Japan, one's identity, as taught by parents, is to the collective. Individualism is not encouraged, and conformity is the norm. This collectivism leads to a different approach to parenting and to the form that family life takes.

The current situation—fathers off at work and mothers isolated at home—reflects great changes in what was once considered normal family life in Japan. In traditional Japan, the wife moved to her husband's home, and families resembled the premodern, Confucian-based ones we saw when we studied Chinese families: women as subordinate, with the father as the patriarch, the head of the family. He looked more like the head of a business than like the absentee father of today. But with the growth of the economy after World War II and the move to urbanization and industrialized cities, this family form evolved to what we see today. With these changes came new forms of parenting and resultant stress. However, most families are quite comfortable with these changes: 88 percent of wives surveyed said that they preferred to spend their leisure time away from their husbands and with their children, relaxing in their homes when their husbands are not there (Collinwood, 1997, 19).

Photo 9.2   Contemporary schoolchildren in Japan, a collectivist "we" society.
Photographer: Patti Carman

Parenting in Malaysia

I use Malaysia as an example of evolving parenting because of the uniqueness of its ethnic composition, and because I was fortunate enough to visit there in 1992 and 1999, when I saw dramatic growth and changes. Malaysia is a magnificent tropical peninsula set in the South China Sea, between Singapore and Thailand. What is most interesting about it is its ethnic diversity: 59 percent of the population is ethnic Malay and other indigenous peoples, 32 percent is Chinese, and 9 percent is Indian and Pakistani (64). It is said to be a fragmented nation because part of its territory is on the main peninsula, while part is 400 miles away on the island of North Borneo. Because of these territorial and ethnic divisions, Malaysia is a complex place, and family life, with resultant parenting patterns, reflects that diversity.

The ethnic Malays are Muslim, following Islam and customary practices that adhere to the Koran. The edicts of the religion specify how family life and parenting are carried out. However, Malaysia has also experienced very quick economic growth, as one of the "little tigers" of Asia: expansion and investment have resulted in changes to the economy. With those changes came Western influence through the mass media. I found it so interesting to walk through the streets of Penang, seeing women in veils, wearing jeans, and listening to Western music through headphones. On one side of the street would be high-rise apartment buildings, and across from or even beside them would be small, dank, and dark old-style hovels, now unlived in.

So what does parenting look like in Malaysia? It is a mix of it all. The family is still the basic social unit, with Islamic family codes being followed. Behavior is regulated by traditional values of etiquette and language. Proper behavior is expected to be displayed in private, and different behavior is expected in public. For example, a young woman should be modest and quiet in public, but may be outspoken and freer in private. There is a strong sense of morality and ethical behavior: a hierarchy of power exists, with the elders in charge. People still use traditional manners of address to the elders. But the intergenerational equality and permissiveness portrayed in the media have provided an alternative for Malay children to follow (Kling, 1995, 16).

There is a youth culture, with contemporary television and music. Parents tend to fall back on traditional and religious teachings for guidance in the face of what they see as "bad influences" and a fear that the family is in decay. Traditional family networks are changing as a result of economic growth and the resulting migration and behavior evolution. One recent study of young people between the ages of 13 and 21 found that 71 percent smoked, 40 percent watched pornographic videos, 28 percent gambled, and 14 percent took hard drugs (Vatikiotis, 1996, 39). Divorce rates in Kuala Lumpur, the capital, have risen. Migration to the cities has left children at home in the care of their grandparents, as absentee parents are forced to find employment far from home. The global economy has had a direct and immediate impact on family life there.

It appears that the traditional extended family of the Malays is giving way to the dominance of the nuclear family, and with it come changes away from the more authoritarian traditional parenting styles. Urbanization, rising incomes, greater geographical mobility, and greater exposure to global culture are changing the nature of being a parent and also changing the intergenerational relationships that have long been dominant in Malaysia. There are many more single-parent families than ever before (Vatikiotis, 1996, 39).

Parenting in West Germany

One might think that family and parenting patterns in Germany, an industrialized and westernized country, would resemble patterns in the United States. However, families in Germany seem to differ from those we are familiar with, especially when caring for children. Almost all women in Germany remain employed, although part-time, after marriage and the birth of children. However, studies find that despite the increasing integration of women into the workforce, they still do most of the housework and child rearing (Rerrich, 1996, 28). It seems that the traditional division of labor is still in place, despite the changes in the economy and social order. The family, although nuclear, has not made the roles of men and women more equal in terms of household work or time spent parenting. State policies in Germany still discourage employment for women.

One study found that the extent to which women could go out to work depended on their ability to find other women on whom they could rely to "substitute" for them at home (29). These other women, be they grandmothers, neighbors, friends, or paid child-care workers, became surrogate parents, while the mothers joined the labor force.

German work life differs from that in the United States. Three out of 4 workers keep hours that do not conform to the Monday-through-Friday, morning-to-evening schedule: they work shifts, they work regularly on weekends, and they have some sort of flexible work schedules (29). There is little in the way of subsidized child care, and young children go to school for only four hours a day. Parents are expected to meet the children after school, arrange extracurricular activities, and chauffeur them around. Thus these patterns of parenting have led to parents hiring people to substitute for them or arranging for others to take over some of their responsibilities. The mothers act as the coordinators and organizers for these schedules, arranging a complex network of cooperation with many people involved, usually other women (30).

In Germany, those who help out tend to be class-specific: if one is poor, extended family members help out, for no pay. If one is middle class, paid help extends the support network. In some ways this is similar to the practices of dual-career families in the United States. However, it differs from the United States in that the job of finding the help and coordinating it is the woman's responsibility alone, thus keeping the hierarchy of women and men's work separate. In the United States, we have seen a shift to men and women sharing some of those responsibilities.

In the United States, as in Germany, women do more of the household work than do men. Arlie Hochschild (1989) found that women are doing a "second shift" when they come home from work. She found that in her 50 sample couples, the women were doing up to an extra month a year of work in household chores. However, other researchers have argued that men—especially those with higher education—are doing more child-care work. This seems unlike the findings for West Germany. We should also add here that although white men in the United States may allege to do work around the home, it is actually black and Latino men who do more housework (Baca-Zinn & Eitzen, 1999, 203). This is due to the fact that they earn less and their families are less able to hire help.

What we have in both Germany and the United States is a discontinuity in parenting responsibilities. In both places women spend more time in parenting and doing the daily work of bringing up the children. This is not the case in all westernized countries. Denmark, as we shall see, has a more egalitarian method of parenting and gives us yet another cross-cultural example of how parenting differs throughout the world.

Parenting in Denmark

One study done quite a number of years ago and yet still relevant today was a comparison of internal family structures in Denmark and the United States. In that study the authors tried to contrast parental power, how decisions are made about parenting of adolescents, as it was negotiated by the two parents (Kandel & Lesser, 1972). The researchers looked at authority patterns of parenting, trying to understand communication, emotional quality, and modeling behavior of those parents, and focused on three specific patterns:

1. *Authoritarian:* The parent makes all the decisions relevant to the adolescent. This type of parenting is far more autocratic, with a rigidity in the way the family does business.

2. *Democratic:* The decisions are made jointly by the parent and the adolescent, and the children take on responsibility appropriate to their age.

3. *Permissive:* The adolescent has more influence in decision making than the parent, with the parent taking little responsibility in the child rearing (73).

The results were noteworthy, in that the Danes were more likely than Americans to report that husbands and wives shared equally in making a variety of family decisions (73). They also found that the discipline of the adolescent was more often the equal responsibility of both parents in Denmark than it is in the United States, and that if there was a disagreement it is less likely that one parent would consistently win (74). Danish parents were also more likely than American parents to engage the child actively in the decision-making process that directly related to that child. The general parenting pattern was more egalitarian in Denmark than in the United States, and there was more maternal domination in the United States (75).

In both countries it was found that the more permissive parenting style seemed to lead to a greater distance between parents and children (79). Parents who were permissive gave more detailed explanations to their children, but the children did not feel close to their parents and did not give positive answers to questions about family life. The most interesting finding was that children of democratic parents viewed their parents more favorably than those who lived with the other two parenting styles; democratic families were more open, more trusting, and warmer, and there was a better relationship between the adolescents and their parents (79). The authors found that parents can reject their children in one of two ways: either by controlling them too much (authoritarian) or ignoring them (permissive) (79).

What we can see from these various examples of parenting around the world is that although there are many similarities in parenting methods, there are also major differences in how different cultures handle the basics of raising children. Parenting is socially constructed by the society in which it is being done. Although families must give birth, raise children, socialize them, and train them to be productive members of society, the form that this takes changes, depending on the historical era and the social context. As the concept of parenting differs, so do the definitions of motherhood, fatherhood, childhood, adolescence, sibling relations, and being elderly. Let's take a look at how we construct those stages of life in the United States and contrast them with other places.

Motherhood

Motherhood in the United States

The modern notion of mothering in the United States began, as I mentioned earlier, during the late 1800s. It is a notion that assumes white women as the norm and does not include alternative constructions of motherhood. During that era, motherhood, for white women, became glorified as a sacred act, one in which the woman's main task was to care for the children physically, preserve their moral innocence, protect them from evil influences, and inspire them with spiritual values (Hoffnung, 1998). Before that time, mothering had been synthesized into the other activities of life and work; it was not women's most important task. When America became an industrial power, that kind of family life was disrupted, and the separate spheres of influence came into existence: men went out to work, and women were expected to stay home. It was then that women's jobs began to be considered nonproducing housework, and "motherwork" became the center of middle- and upper-class women's lives (279).

> In contrast to the economic value of women's work in the past, today a woman's devotion to "women's work" makes her dependent on the people she tends. It results in an economic dependence on her husband—a man chosen for love—and a psychological dependence on her children as products of her mothering. (279)

This statement tends to sum up the conditions for mothering in the early twenty-first century in the United States. Although women are well integrated into the workforce and have made great strides in entering the political arena, it is still expected that women will mother and that a woman's place is essentially in the home, even if she is working too (280).

In the United States we have a "motherhood mystique," the assumption that it is natural to mother and that to mother is an unchanging phenomenon (282). It is thought that mothering is the ultimate fulfillment for a woman, that the majority of this work should fall to the woman, that women must like the work of mothering, and that a mother's intense devotion to her children is good for those children. In reality, this is not always true. These ideas are part of the mystique and social construction of motherhood. These are the ideologies, or dominant ideas, that help create and perpetuate our thinking about motherhood.

Motherhood is really a mixed bag—good and bad, fun and difficult, challenging and rewarding. The real problem is that most women want to be mothers and want to have at least two children, but they do not always appreciate the reality of the undertaking. Motherhood is actually a conflictual part of a woman's life in the United States, because of the challenges of work and child rearing, the fact that giving birth is not always the ultimate fulfillment, that there are difficulties related to housework and child care, and that it alters the marital relationship, not always for the better (283–284). Motherwork is also not as highly valued in the United States as it is in other parts of the world.

Mothers of Color

For women of color in the United States, motherwork is even harder than for women of the majority. Their children face infant mortality two times higher than do white children, and mothers are faced with having to provide for children while living in poverty (Collins, 1994). While living in rural areas or in urban centers, one-third of Latino children and one-half of African American children will be poor and face drugs, crime, industrial pollutants, and violence, which threaten their survival (49). Mothers in these environments are often separated from their children for long periods of time while they are out working. Often there are community "other-mothers" or grandmothers who assist them in parenting, which serves as a balancing force for the children (55). Mothers of color must deal with the tensions inherent in trying to foster meaningful racial identities for children within a society that denigrates their color (57). However, many peoples of color, through their mothers, have passed on a sense of personal identity and a collective sense of peoplehood.

Mothers of African American, Latin, and Asian American backgrounds nearly always have had to work, often as cheap labor, so their roles as workers took precedence over their roles as mothers (Glenn, 1994). They were not expected to be full-time mothers, and they moved back and forth between public and private labor (6). There is clearly a racial division of mothering, with women of color doing the hard "mother" work for women of privilege. Often they have had to neglect the responsibilities of caring for their own children while caring for the children of others. They do so because of a lack of other choices in their lives (7).

Interestingly, in a study done by Denise Segura (1994), the author found that women who are Mexican immigrants to the United States *(Chicanas)* have a different view of working out of the home than do Mexican women who continue to live in Mexico. Chicanas prefer the idealized images of motherhood, in which the mothers stay home with their children, while Mexicanas understand the family-wage economy, in which all members of the family work at productive, paying tasks. Here the definition of motherhood differs depending on the social context in which the motherhood is being done. For Chicanas who are surrounded by the Anglo definition of motherhood, staying home seems like the right thing to do; for Mexicanas, who see all members of the family contributing to the family upkeep, working seems to be acceptable, even while still being a mother (224).

Unfortunately, undocumented Latinas (women without the proper immigration documentation) are put at a great risk should they attempt to get proper documentation in order to seek legal status and legal employment (Chang, 1996). These new employable mothers serve an important purpose in the United States, in that they are often domestic workers and child-care providers, especially in California and other border states. They are needed to care for children whose white mothers seek paid employment in the workforce, but should the undocumented immigrants register, they are in jeopardy of deportation. The double bind is a challenging one, as these women need to find work to be able to feed their own families (265).

Another group facing difficulties in the motherhood role is Filipinas. Many of these women come to the United States from their native Philippines to seek employment. "The mental image of Filipinas leaving their children, spouses and families behind to care for others around the world is a powerful one. Leaving one's own children goes against popular notions in this country of what it means to be a 'good mother'" (Tung, 2000). However, these women see themselves as good mothers because they are acting as breadwinners and providers for their children left at home. They "mother from afar" by extending their families' living standard, and they are better mothers by being better able to provide financially for their families (65). In fact, 34–54 percent of the Filipino population is sent money from these migrant workers (Salazar Parrenas, 2002, 39). There are 1.4 million Filipino Americans in the United States right now, and 80 percent of them are women. Many of these women are employed as caregivers to the elderly, although their actual numbers are hard to estimate (62).

Children in this situation miss the contact with their mothers, but they are not delinquent, nor do their families see themselves as "broken families" (51). The families are highly adaptive and learn to make do and sacrifice in order to have the income the mothers provide, and they attempt to maintain close bonds with their mothers from a great distance.

Lesbian Mothers

For lesbian mothers also, parenting is quite complicated. For example, when mothers who are lesbians seek custody of their children in divorce proceedings, the courts tend to view homosexuality as "unnatural" and the mothers as unfit to parent because of a moral flaw (Lewin, 1994). The mothers' task is often to demonstrate that they have the "natural" attributes needed to parent. Because heterosexuality is the norm, lesbian parenting is seen as deviant behavior, and as such, women who are lesbian mothers have to overcome negative stereotypes of themselves as bad parents. Often these women share the parenting with another woman, her partner, or with men (either gay or straight) who have been the adoptive "fathers" or sperm donors. Lesbian mothers are shaping their identities and renegotiating the meaning of being a lesbian and a mother at every turn, trying to "reinvent themselves as they make their way in a difficult world" (350).

The reality is that in very few places in the world is motherhood assigned to just one person, the way it is done in the United States. Let's take a look at how motherhood is conceptualized elsewhere, in contrast to what we know goes on here.

Motherhood in Japan

The Western, ethnocentric idea would hold that, now that Japan is industrialized and modernized, mothers in Japan should look like mothers in the United States. As we saw earlier in the chapter, this very modern country has different patterns and forms of parenting. Japan is undeniably economically successful and developed, but the shapes of people's lives, the sources of satisfaction and meaning for men and women differ; there is no single, ideal model (White, 1987).

Women in Japan perceive their work as wives and mothers as important because it is socially valued there (153). To be a good wife and a wise mother is of the highest value, and it is as a mother that a woman is known. At home she manages her husband's money, gives him an allowance, manages the children's daily life, purchases all the clothing, gets involved in her children's activities, and is at home as much as possible to tend the children's needs. If she does work, it is after the child has gone to school, part-time, and later in her life, perhaps full-time (154).

The Japanese mother is stereotypically gentle, obedient, and compliant. Divorce is rare, and sometimes the mother becomes over-invested in the child's educational success. Because the focus is primarily on the children, Japanese mothers postpone their own independence until later in life. Although this might seem problematic to us in the West, given that Japan is a collectivist society, Japanese women do not find this a sacrifice. Because a woman's self-worth is tied to her children's accomplishments, she is willing and pleased to wait until the children have grown to begin other activities (159).

Motherhood in Japan can teach us a number of cross-cultural lessons. For one, what might appear limiting to one society may be self-enhancing to another (159). We also see the diversity of motherhood patterns in the world as well as the fact that in a collectivist society, the ideals of individualism and self-growth are not highly valued or acted upon. In collectivist societies, the greater good is the group, the family, the society—not the person, the individual, or the self. Let's take a look at another collectivist society to see the further contrasts to the United States.

Motherhood in China

Elsewhere in this book we have looked at China through a number of lenses—traditional Chinese families, the effects of the revolution on family life, marriage, and weddings. But one of the more fascinating aspects of contemporary China is the one-child policy. With a population of 1.2 billion people, the nation's economic development was being burdened. You'll remember that in 1979, the People's Republic of China introduced a policy that limited the Chinese population to having one child per family unless they had twins or a baby with birth defects (Strom, Strom, & Xie, 1996). In the cities, more than 90 percent of the population favor the policy. In the countryside, fewer people follow the policy or agree with it. In 1988 the policy was amended to take into account differing economic needs in different regions, as well as traditions around the country. Nonetheless, the policy has been quite successful, with the average number of children per family dropping from 4.0 to 2.4 in those two decades (40).

The impact of this policy on parenting, and most especially on the role of mothers, has been great. In China traditionally, motherhood had been one of women's few defining identities. With the revolution, women were given far more options, including working and participating in the social change process. Women are well integrated into the workforce in China and have full equality under the law. However, given the historical and cultural pattern of valuing boys over girls, there is still a bias against having girl children, particularly in the countryside. With sonogram technology, prospective parents can more easily identify and abort female fetuses (40). One survey found that in Liaoning Province in northeast China, 80 percent of miscarried babies were female. Couples in urban areas do not seem to care whether they have male or female children. In those places, with access to government programs, the economic reasons for parental preference for sons have diminished.

Parenting has changed now that there is only one child in the family. Mothers are challenged by the fact that the children are becoming overindulged, overprotected, over-cared for, overloved, and over-expected to achieve (41). They call it the 4–2–1 syndrome: four grandparents, two parents, lavishing attention on one child. Single children are such a treasure that they have become less respectful to adults and exhibit more temper tantrums.

When I was in China in 1999, I heard the phrase "the little emperors" to describe these overindulged children. It was fascinating to be out on the streets, watching large numbers of adults accompanied by beautifully dressed and overly watched small children. The families were particularly proud of their offspring, flattered by and encouraging my picture taking and appreciation of their children. The children, too, seemed to beam under the attention, often hamming it up for the adults.

Mothering in China presents a number of other challenges. Because women are in the workforce to such a great degree, it is the grandparents who primarily raise these single children. This responsibility leads to conflict over who is in charge and who is primary caregiver. With filial piety and respect for elders so ingrained in the society, the role of motherhood is seriously challenged by this development. Can a mother question the word of the caregiving grandparent? We see that in China raising a child is a collective responsibility, shared with grandparents, and to an increasing extent, with the fathers as well. This leads to an evolving definition of the role of motherhood in China.

Historically, Chinese motherhood is supposed to be associated with hard work and long suffering (Hare-Mustin & Hare, 1986). Mothers are often seen as doing heavy work in the home and having a tolerance for drudgery. They suffer from the burdens of motherhood and are at the very core of the family as decision makers, motivators, and keepers of the family harmony (74). Most frequently, mothers are seen as caregivers for the children, even if the grandparent is doing the daily work. A mother should be loving and kind; she should worry about her children and be protecting and comforting. Mothers are supposed to be rich in the spirit of self-sacrifice, and most of all, responsible for their children's moral development (75).

Motherhood in China is associated with care for the family, even over-concern for the nation and the revolution (75). Although mothers should work for the society, their loyalty is first to their family and their children, then to the neighborhood and society. But the emphasis is on the collective, the family, the group, and not the individual or her own self-development. Even in the policy of having one child, we see that the will of the individual, be it the mother or her family, is subsumed in the needs of the group, the larger society. The one-child policy is an interesting window into China's values and belief system. It teaches us once again how different parenting can look, how the definition of motherhood reflects the values of a society, and how history and social context changes the definitions of these simple words.

Fatherhood

Fatherhood in the United States

To be a father in the United States is no easy task. Earlier the roles were quite clear: in a family-based economy, fathers worked on the farms and were active in all aspects of the child's life—nurturing and educating. Fathers played other important roles like taking care of the family correspondence and handling dealings with the public. Then, under the family-wage economy, the father's active role at home diminished and his job became that of the "breadwinner." He was to provide for his children on a material and physical level. Fathers were out in the marketplace and spent little time with their children at home; mothers were in charge of child care. If and when fathers were involved, it was in the role of disciplinarian or moral role model. Unfortunately for men, this also meant a distancing of emotional involvement in the children's lives. With the division of the spheres of influence into male and female came the assignment of the affective role—doing the emotional jobs of the family, like nurturing children or tending elders—to the woman, and the instrumental role—doing the outside work that brings home the money—to the father.

Male identity became associated with being a good provider for the family, and that identity maintained itself until very recently. In fact, fathers were so absent from family life that for years they were not even studied by sociologists. It is only recently that any research has been done on the role of fathers in their children's lives. Fathers were in the workforce, developing their identities through their success on the job, how much money they made, and their acquisition of property and wealth. Fathers were like *Leave It to Beaver* dads on TV, or like the father in the '90s movie *Pleasantville*. In those shows, the fathers played roles in which they were gone all day, and smiling and loving but aloof upon their return home. Their interactions with their children were as firm, gentle yet tough adults who were present late in the day, before the kids went to bed.

Today fathers in the United States are increasingly involved in raising their children, although certainly not to the extent of women; they provide approximately 25 percent of the care for preschool children while mothers work. Since the 1970s, fathers have played an increasingly involved role in the direct care of their children. When my daughter was born in 1972, my husband was a stay-at-home dad. He cared for her while I went out to work. At the time he was a rarity, so much so that local merchants would offer to watch the child while he shopped, thinking he could not handle child care while shopping too. Nowadays this model of fathering is not unusual at all. Often one sees men carrying babies, leading toddlers down the street, and shopping with children, without a woman present.

Fatherhood in contemporary America includes men now taking time off work for parental leave upon the birth of their children. Fathers are also making a commitment to emotionally and physically caring for their children (Newman, 1999, 276). However, even though fathers *are* more involved, roles are still not equal in terms of who does the parenting. Men are *helping out* more. In one study, in two-parent families with employed mothers, fathers spent about 33 percent as much time as mothers engaged in one-to-one interaction with their children, and about 65 percent as much time as mothers being accessible (275–276). Mothers still carry 90 percent of the responsibility for the kids, like going to the doctor or getting clothes ready. It appears that as a society we talk a lot about fathers' participation in child rearing, but the reality is that fathers do not do as much as mothers.

For African American men in the United States, the story is a different one. McAdoo and McAdoo (1998) studied black fathers and found a great level of involvement in their children's lives. A black father's involvement in parenting seems to depend on the resources that he brings in: fathers who bring in greater resources are more involved in the daily decision making of family life. Fathers seemed to share equally with their wives the major decisions on child rearing, purchases, health care, and jobs (378). Looking at middle-class and working-class men, one study found that both groups were involved equally in disciplining children, grocery shopping, selecting doctors, and deciding where to live (Jackson as cited in McAdoo & McAdoo, 1998, 378). In another study of economically self-sufficient African American men, fathers were seen as warm and loving toward their children, seemed to have high expectations for their behavior, and spent time providing explanations to their children regarding unacceptable behavior (379).

Many unemployed and underemployed black men have also been found to interact positively with their children (379). Their employment status did not seem to block their ability to relate to their kids and to provide some input in their children's lives. Many times African American fathers also play a significant kinship role with their sisters' children as well as their own children. They act as role models and disciplinarians, serving in that capacity for family members as well as neighborhood children. The kinship system plays an important role in the way that African American men father in the United States.

Fatherhood in China

Interestingly, fathers' roles in China are changing significantly since the one-child policy was introduced. It appears that changes in economic forces, governmental intervention, and exposure to the West are influencing a once very traditional definition of fatherhood (Abbott, Ming, & Meredith, 1992). Historically, fatherhood in China was defined by Confucian philosophy, which established the father as the undisputed patriarchal head of the family. For 2,000 years fathers had nearly complete authority over wives, children, and subordinate family members (46).

Filial piety, you'll remember, is the devotion and respect given to parents by their children, and has been the dominant rule in China for role behavior. In adulthood, sons were to provide for the material well-being of their parents and to perform the ceremonial tasks of ancestor worship. Fathers were to be educators and disciplinarians, with little in the way of daily interaction with their children (46). In fact, fathers only became involved with their children when they were old enough to be instructed or disciplined. The Chinese father's main role was to provide the moral and temporal education of his sons, and he was allowed to use force and violence to ensure respect and subservience. As I said earlier, it was a harsh form of parenting.

Contemporary China is quite different. The communist revolution tried to change that fatherhood relationship. Laws were passed to equalize parental roles, there were campaigns against corporal punishment, and massive parent education programs were established on child development and child psychology to enhance children's self-esteem (47). By the 1980s it appeared that fathers were beginning to subscribe to a more contemporary view of their roles. They expected less filial piety and subservience and more emphasis on children developing independence, creativity, and self-respect (47).

In a study done in 1992, findings indicated that Chinese fathers are sharing in the duties and responsibilities of parenting; they just emphasize different aspects (50). Fathers in China do not provide much physical care for the children, but they do play with them. They prefer to engage in recreational activities when the children are old enough. They also still see themselves as the disciplinarians and teachers, as they did in the past. They are concerned with their children's schoolwork and think they should help with school and encourage higher education.

Obedience is still a strong cultural component of the father role in China. Fathers are concerned with children's disobedience and their lack of respect for parents and other adults. Spanking, hitting, and striking children is infrequent nowadays in China, but fathers still are firm and coercive in the way they handle their children (51). Many Chinese fathers are authoritarian in their interactions with their children; they threaten, scold, shame, and punish in order to teach their lessons (51).

Like American fathers, dads in China enjoy watching their children grow up, and they love to teach and help their children. They enjoy the companionship and the feeling of being loved and needed; it gives their lives purpose and meaning. Chinese fathers also look forward to grandparenthood and have high expectations that their adult children will care for them in old age (51). For them the main reason to have children is to ensure that they will be looked after in old age.

For Chinese fathers the primary relationship in their lives is the parent-child bond, not the marital relationship. This differs significantly from American fathers, who are disturbed when the parental role interferes with the marital bond. In China this is expected and acceptable (51). With more Chinese women in the workforce and with there being fewer children, fatherhood in China is undergoing transformation. What was once a traditional, authoritarian, and patriarchal system seems to be evolving toward a more egalitarian model of parenting. With these changes, the way a father behaves in China is slowly moving toward more involvement in his child's life.

Childhood

Childhood in Western Societies

The conceptualization of childhood has changed over time, and like other concepts, depends on where you are in the world. We can say that childhood is a social construction (are you getting tired of hearing that?). It is considered a natural stage of development; after all, we all are born and then have to grow up. But how it is done is culturally and historically relative. Ideas about childhood are tied to a society's social structure and what that society needs from those children and their parents. If children are needed to work, they grow up early and leave childhood behind. If, as in an economy like the United States, they are not needed for income generation, childhood and later adolescence can be extended, and these children do not become adults for quite a while.

According to some historians, the concept of childhood did not even exist before the sixteenth century (Aries, 1962). From the Middle Ages on, children were merely miniature versions of adults, without specific needs. Children were not emotionally important to their parents; they were workers who could assist their families. Children in the sixteenth century quickly became part of the adult world. People lacked the understanding that children might have emotional needs specific to childhood. Children were expected to carry out whatever work their parents did, to the best of their physical abilities. Parents did not become too attached to their children, since infant mortality was high. The children were not given special treatment, and they were expected to "earn their keep" (Newman, 1999, 292). During this era, children were beaten as common practice, since they were viewed as inherently evil and it was necessary to teach them right and wrong.

Aries argued that conceptions of children reflected what families looked like during different historical eras. As the family became more private, such as happened during the rise of the industrial era, ideas of childhood changed. So, for example, in the seventeenth century, children were considered to be in a period of training to become adults. They were treated differently than adults; they were coddled and loved, but they were still being readied for the workplace (375).

The rise of the private family led to the moving inward of family life, into the home and out of the community. With these changes came more contemporary conceptions of childhood. Rather than being raised by a community, as was the case in the Middle Ages, children were now raised by their parents, a movement toward the privatization of the family. Children became dependent on their families, especially their nuclear families. For middle-class families, childhood became a more emotional and affectionate stage of life. By the mid-nineteenth century, children were viewed as innocent and needing protection from the outside world. With this change, away from children as contributors to the family economy, came the idea of children being one's property. During the family-wage economy, children were potential wage earners. These children would eventually bring in income, and raising a child was an investment for the future.

Contemporary Western conceptualization of childhood has changed once again. Now families view their children as emotional investments rather than financial ones (297). Children are costly and provide no economic benefit. We are in a family-consumer economy, and children are terrific consumers. Parents focus on the importance of the parent–child bond and often find the emotional intimacy they are seeking through their children. In fact, childhood is being extended, with children remaining at home far longer than they did during the two previous historical eras. In fact, Western society has become more child-centered, with much emotional attachment placed on having and rearing children. Children have become the center of family life in the West, in a way that is not always the case elsewhere.

Today there are two views of childhood (Hutter, 1998, 422). One side argues that children are no longer allowed to be children; they are being forced to grow up and become involved in adult-like concerns, and far too soon. Because both parents need to work outside of the home, children are forced to grow up fast, wearing adult clothing, and doing homemaking tasks that mothers once did (422). Although children are still living within the private sphere of the family, internal family life is forcing them into early adulthood and all its related problems. The other side argues that the increase of responsibility in childhood is, in fact, a positive development, because it leads to increased productivity and a sense of contribution and importance in family life. It teaches children independence, dependability, and maturity, all of which have a positive impact on children's sense of self.

It appears that the conception of childhood is once again at a crossroad: Is the child a full participant in family life and economy, or is a child an appendage and economic burden? What do you think? Where is childhood heading? Are kids growing up too fast, or do you believe that children are learning how to be contributing members of society early?

Childhood in Other Parts of the World

Ruth Benedict (1983), an anthropologist, studied literate and preliterate societies and found that in societies such as ours, childhood is difficult because there are discontinuities, or breaks between stages of life, that make for hard transitions. She says it is a challenge for children to become adults because they are not really part of adult life. For us, children's lives are organized around play, with little connection to adult work. Adults are expected to work and be sexually active; children are expected to play and be pure. This is a disjuncture or discontinuity—there is not an easy transition from one stage to the other.

She argues that in preliterate societies, there is ease in this transition because children participate in adult activities and responsibilities. Children might see sexual activity and not find it embarrassing or negative, because their societies see nothing wrong with it. They participate in activities that the rest of the community engages in; for example, boys go on hunting trips, girls help their mothers in skinning the animals. In other words, the jobs of childhood are culturally relative and are neither clear-cut nor universal. They differ according to place and time. And with these differing roles come easier transitions from childhood to adulthood.

In my many travels I saw children engaging in work that was hard for me to imagine American kids doing. For example, I saw boy children in Africa helping to side a mud house with their fathers and uncles. They would mash the mud into a malleable mass so that the adults could apply the mixture to the wooden framing of the house. I saw little girls carrying heavy cans of water on their heads, following their mothers back to their homes, bringing the daily water supply back to their families. I saw little children helping their parents in the gardens outside of their homes, hauling water, and bending in the hot sun, weeding the plants.

In Brazil I saw young boys driving tractors, with their fathers proudly watching and assisting, as need be. There I also saw little girls minding even littler children so that their mothers could work in the fields. In fact, in many parts of the world little girls watch their siblings so that their parents are free to labor without encumbrance. Children seem to be small workers, expected to participate as much as they can to the well-being of their families.

In many parts of the world, including Brazil, Venezuela, Dominican Republic, Zambia, Kenya, India, and Vietnam, I have seen countless children out on the

Photo 9.3   Street children in a village in India. Photographer: Mary Thieme

streets begging or trying to sell small items in an effort to bring home some income to their families. In Vietnam they are called "children of the dust," because they live in the dirt, trying hard to survive. These children know that they must contribute to the family economy; if they do not, other family members will not eat. It becomes their responsibility to do as much as they can to help out, as best they can. Here childhood is short, with the need for money putting children out on the streets as soon as they can go. In South Africa, the street children are usually African boys who have lived on the streets for as many as three years or longer. They are there because of family violence, alcohol abuse, and poverty, which have forced them to the streets (LeRoux, 1996).

In Latin America, street children have become a major social welfare problem, with growing numbers of children and adolescents seeking to survive on the city streets. The numbers seem to be increasing, with millions of children being forced to fend for themselves. There seem to be three types of street children in Latin America (Raffaelli, 1997). The first is the group who work in the streets, doing jobs like shining shoes, selling candy, or washing cars. They return to their families at night or on the weekends. The second group is the homeless youth, who have no place to go; they too live in the streets. The final group is part of the street families who live in family groups in public locations because of the lack of adequate and affordable housing (90). At a time of growing poverty in developing parts of the world, there is no solution to this grave problem of children being forced to fend for themselves.

In one study of Egyptian family life (Dickerscheid, 1990), the author describes a scene that is familiar to me from my travels and my observations from many parts of the developing world. She says

It is quite common to see girls as young as five or six years old carrying water from the canal, gathering fuel, cleaning the house, preparing food, and doing

Photo 9.4   Girls carrying hay in India. Photographer: Mary Thieme

laundry around the house. In addition, they begin caring for younger siblings almost as soon as they, themselves, can toddle. By the time they are 10 or so, there is little or no time for play. (7)

Childhood in developing parts of the world resembles childhood during the family-based economy era of the United States. Children grow up fast, participate in many aspects of family life, and contribute as much as they can and as soon as they can to the family upkeep. Because of economic necessity, it becomes imperative for them to go out to work to keep the family alive. There is no time for the luxury of indulging their childhoods, because every cent is needed to feed the family, and the children's labor is crucial to family survival. Children are also becoming more expensive in the less-developed countries. There are increasing school fees as well as rising consumer expectations, particularly in the cities. Nonetheless, children in developing parts of the world still contribute greatly to their family's upkeep.

Adolescence

Just as childhood is a social construction, so too is adolescence. Adolescence, or puberty, is a new phenomenon, again originating in the late nineteenth century in the West. Social and economic changes extended childhood dependency on the family into the teen years, because children were not necessary in the paid labor market. There were social movements that developed to keep children and young

Photo 9.5   Adolescent schoolgirls in Turkey. Photographer: Mary Thieme

people safe in the workplace, and child labor laws were put in place to control their exploitation.

Compulsory education came into existence at this time, and the length of time that children spent in school now increased into their teen years. These social changes created a new, recognizable stage of life—teens, those who were no longer children and yet were not ready for the full-time workforce. They were not children and they were not adults; they were adolescents.

By the beginning of the twentieth century, the idea of adolescence had taken hold in our society. Now it is a major phenomenon, with a vast segment of the popular culture and the economy dedicated to the needs of this age set. MTV, movies, clothing, and music are all geared to the desires and demands of this newly created age group. Today, adolescents are not producers, as were youth in the past. They are consumers. And they are often viewed as people who are going through a difficult time because of their age: in the past it was called the "storm and stress" of adolescence (Hutter, 1998, 406).

The picture is often painted of a group in trouble: drugs, alcohol, violence, and sex all dominate the news, telling us that teens are problematic. The reality is that in much of the world, and even in the West, teens are for the most part healthy, trusting, and loving human beings (Newman, 1999, 301). Nonetheless, things have changed for adolescents since the late 1800s. For one thing, they have sex younger than they once did. In 1970, only 4.6 percent of girls ages 15 to 20 were sexually active; in 1999, 70 percent of girls have had at least one sexual experience by the age of 20 (301). The number of teens having children has decreased since the 1950s, especially among African Americans (302); however, more of those who have children are not married, so we have more out-of-wedlock babies than in the past. Many attribute the deferring of marriage, especially among black women, with the dearth of marriageable young males due to high rates of incarceration, unemployment, and homicide (Taylor, 1991, 219).

Adolescence in the West differs significantly from its conception elsewhere. Many parts of the world hold initiation rites that mark the passage from childhood to adulthood, leaving adolescence out completely. In the West, we might take a young man out for a beer, or get him drunk when he reaches the right age. Or we might have a religious service, like a bar mitzvah or a confirmation, but the person honored is still an adolescent. Elsewhere, the ritual means that the child is now a full member of society.

Adolescence Among the Maasai

An interesting contrast to adolescence in the West is found among the Maasai, an ethnic group living on the savannas of Kenya and Tanzania. The Maasai are a small tile in a mosaic of African peoples; they are tall, thin pastoralists who can be spotted miles away by their signature red clothing. Their lives are simple; they depend on their cattle and their families, living closely with the earth. Wealth is measured by the number of cattle and children a man has, and the economy is a family-based one, in which all contribute to the family's well-being. It is a patriarchal and polygynous society; the men are in charge, primarily protecting the village and caring for the animals. The Maasai hold a ritual in which young men are circumcised in order for them to become warriors, a most respected age group (Saitoti, 1986, 110).

Women build the houses, collect wood, cook, clean, milk the cows, and raise the children. The men are expected to be fearless and have great physical courage. By the age of five the children are out caring for the animals. Girls are circumcised by age thirteen, marking their availability for marriage.

For the men the passage to adulthood is a long and rigorous process. Early on a boy is assigned to a *moran*, the group of warriors with whom he will be associated, his age mates. The moran is divided into junior and senior groups as well as the specific group the boy will be circumcised with. Male circumcision takes place between the ages of thirteen and seventeen; some boys do not have younger brothers old enough to take their place caring for the animals, so they stay behind to help with the cattle until a younger brother is ready. When the circumcision takes place the young man is not allowed to cry or yell; to do so leads to disrespect for his entire family. His parents could be beaten by members of the entire village for raising such a coward.

Once boys are circumcised, they become junior warriors and live with their age mates in a special dwelling set aside for them. The mother accompanies her son, adorning herself with elaborate beaded ear ornaments that show everyone she is the mother of a warrior. She builds a house for him while he roams about freely with his moran, having sex with women, hunting, growing his hair long, and decorating elaborate headdresses. The moran becomes so close that they even urinate together;

these men are now brothers and share everything in life, even their wives when they later take them.

When the junior morans age they become senior warriors, and the life of the community is centered on them. They direct the stock, are in charge of defense and security, and occasionally deal with the local government. They are hunters and are allowed to do so by the Kenyan government, although only to a limited extent. Theirs is a most important position in that society, and the young men are now fully adults.

From this example one can see that adolescence as we know it at home in the United States does not exist in all cultures. Instead, being a moran and being circumcised prepares a young man in the Maasai for his coming role in society. There is no delineation as a teen; the young man is a warrior in training and thus is fully respected and important to his society. He is responsible, and his job is crucial to the survival of his society.

Sibling Relationships

Sibling Relationships in the United States

Perhaps one of the least understood intimate relationships in family life is that among siblings. Siblings can be very influential in personality formation and in providing the guidance and support one needs in growing up. Nonetheless, except for a few books, most research focuses on sibling rivalry and the belief that sibling relationships are inherently negative. My experience as a therapist, traveler, and teacher has taught me that this is not always the case. In fact, siblings are important to the life of a family and can impact every aspect of a child's life. Sibling relationships are also important as one ages and as one loses one's parents in adulthood.

One author believes that the sibling connection is one of the most vital and yet the most overlooked of all relationships (Markowitz, 1999). She notes that at the beginning of our lives we

> orbit our parents like planets vying for the position closest to the sun. They are our primary source of light, warmth and love, but we have to compete with omnipresent siblings who at times eclipse us, collide with us, and even at odd moments, awkwardly love us. (124)

These relationships are often portrayed as ambivalent ones, dramatic in their extremes of loyalty and hate. She cites the Bible, in which Cain slays Abel and Joseph is sold into slavery by his brothers. And in *King Lear,* Cordelia's older sisters manipulate her to get their father's kingdom, then delight in her banishment. But eventually Joseph forgives his brothers and saves them from the famine, and we also have Hansel taking Gretel's hand and saving her from the witch. The ambivalence is noteworthy (124).

In the West, Freud's ideas about siblings have had a significant impact on how we view our brothers and sisters. He postulated the idea of sibling rivalry, with children naturally feeling envy, aggression, and competitiveness with siblings as they fight for parental love (124). However, there have been critiques of the view that children feel only negative emotions about their siblings. Feminist scholars have pointed out that women, whose personalities are forged in forming affiliations and warm relationships, form loving and lasting relationships with their sisters. These are called *horizontal ties,* connections between people of the same generation (Sandmaier, 1995).

African American scholars have also critiqued Freud, and point out that sibling rivalry is *not* the primary force among siblings in other cultures. In some African societies, as we shall see, both material and emotional support come from one's siblings. They argue that "not all families in our society operate exclusively from Eurocentric values of individualism" (Markowitz, 1999, 125). They cite, for example, that in contemporary African American families, siblings and parents often pour all their resources and energy into one child who carries the family torch into mainstream success. That child is then expected to send money back and help the others, to repay this debt (125).

Siblings are crucially important to one another. The relationship has been described as planets orbiting one another; each has a pull that shapes the others' courses. Siblings share the same family, the same history and culture and genetic material. There is no escaping the mutual influence. Freud said that a child's position in the birth order had an impact on later life, and others have studied that area, finding that older siblings are more responsible and tend to be over-controlling; only children tend to be loners; and women who are not fond of children tend to be younger siblings (125). Later-born children never have the attention of their parents as exclusively as the eldest did; thus, they tend to be more impulsive, less cautious, and more involved in physically dangerous activities. They also appear more peer-conscious and more willing to challenge authority (Kagan, 1977). In industrialized societies, older siblings have significant influence on younger sibs' cognitive, social, and emotional development. They serve as models, teachers, counselors, and confidants (Cicirelli, 1995). The older sibs may also assume the position of leadership in the family as adults (75).

Some siblings grow up to be best of friends; others are quite distant from each other. Some see each other as far-off enemies, to be avoided, while others use their siblings as measuring rods against whom to measure their own success (Kagan, 124). In mid-life often the sibling relationship is brought back to full view, when siblings are forced to deal with aging and dying parents. Since these times evoke fears of death and mortality, it is a time of crisis, added to by the need to collaborate with siblings, sometimes after years of mutual alienation (126). These are times, when faced with "huge existential issues, it is easier to fall back on picking on one another, feeding the illusion that they will be children forever instead of accepting terminal adulthood" (126).

Interestingly, sometimes with the death of parents, relationships with siblings are allowed to change. Often the pull is to remain connected somehow, even in the face of earlier conflict. Siblings realize that, given the many losses they experience later in life, it is comforting that one's sibling remembers how it was when they were children, since they share so much history. Markowitz argues that there is a paradox in sibling relationships: siblings are our connection to the past, but it is sometimes a painful past. She says,

> Our siblings hold up a mirror before us, forcing us to look at an image of our-selves that may be either comforting or devastating, perhaps evoking self-acceptance and pride, perhaps shame and humiliation. (127)

Sibling relationships, especially in the United States, are thorny. Our siblings walk with us through most of our lives; they are fellow travelers, and they are bridges to our past. In a study done on adult siblings, a national survey found that siblings in the United States who had living sisters felt significantly more contact, affection, and perceived and actual support from siblings; women without sisters were particularly disadvantaged in perceived social support from sibs (White & Riedmann, 1992, 99). The authors also found that higher education and family income were related to more contact and exchange among sibs. For black families there was more contact among sibs, although not necessarily more reliance or feel-ings of closeness (100). It appears that in the United States, sibs are the second tier of family ties, after one's parents or one's own children and spouses (100).

In the United States, a child is quite likely to live in a blended family in which there is at least one stepparent, stepsibling, and/or half-siblings (Taylor, 1997, 77). These sibling relationships represent a full 15 percent of all children, with African American children somewhat more likely to live in such a situation, compared with white children and Latino children (77). These relationships are fraught with much of the turmoil described in relation with other siblings.

In other parts of the world, sibling relationships are not so tumultuous nor as distant. As we shall see, in places like Brazil, the Philippines, and in Africa, siblings are crucial for survival and provide life-sustaining assistance in the journey. It is also true that in much of the world, when siblings do not marry or have children of their own, they are more closely tied to their siblings.

Sibling Relationships in Other Parts of the World

Sibling relationships in other parts of the world do not seem to have the same angst attached to them as they do in the United States. Especially in the developing parts of the world, the periphery, relations between brothers and sisters, sisters and sisters, and brothers and brothers take on significant importance and are some of the most important blood ties.

Sibling Relationships in Brazil

In Brazil, for example, one study of a Brazilian slum near Porto Alegre found that two-thirds of their sample had connections with their siblings in the neigh-borhood (Fonseca, 1991). In this community, the author found that brother-to-sister bonds were as important as sister-to-sister bonds in helping families deal with the poverty and challenges of slum life. Siblings often lodged in their kin's homes,

Photo 9.6   Siblings and cousins in India. Photographer: Mary Thieme

and male siblings were often the people to whom sisters would turn in case of need, both financial and emotional (144).

In Brazil, if a woman is living with her male partner, she does not have access to money. He holds the purse strings. Thus, if she needs help, her female siblings cannot help her the way her brothers can. She may ask her brother for money, or in case of trouble, move in with him (144). Her role as sister is also very important to the brother. He can turn to her for advice and a place to live, if need be. Often a companionship develops that is sometimes greater than the marital bond (149). Because siblings do not live together for too long in adulthood, they do not suffer the tensions of co-residence. The link between brother and sister is a lasting one because there are no permanent, defined material obligations. He helps her when she needs him, and vice versa. Many brothers and sisters visit each other regularly in middle age, and there is much value in showing physical affection.

In case of physical violence, as in wife battering, it is the brother who comes to his sister's assistance (151). The most effective protection a woman has against her husband is the presence of a male blood relative. Perhaps it is physical brawn, or his male honor, but a brother is able to protect his sister from a husband's absolute authority over her.

The sister's major contribution is the performance of needed feminine tasks should her brother not have a wife, or if the wife is not doing those tasks (153). She may wash his clothes, but she is also there to provide affection and moral support. She may run administrative errands for him and could provide a potential home for her brother's offspring (153). Whatever support siblings can provide for each other in Brazil is quite unconditional, and a sister has moral sway over a brother in a way that other family members do not. She is able to control his violent behavior, and she also takes in his children should he decide to remove them from the care of their mother (154).

Obviously, sibling bonds in Brazil have a huge impact on the quality of family life. For some readers, what I have described may seem unfamiliar. And yet, for some communities in our country, like the Latino or African American community, what I have described in Brazil is not unlike what happens in the United States.

Sibling Relationships in the Philippines

In the Philippines, life is similar to that in Brazil. Family life is filled with an enormous number of relatives, since lineage is bilateral, meaning that it is traced through both mother and father. Therefore, siblings abound, and there is a huge extended kinship network. All the siblings and their children are considered family. With this huge network, daily life consists of many interactions with kin. During times of adversity, the siblings are crucial to the family's survival (Hirtz, 1992). People turn first to kin, then to their work groups with whom they share land, or to neighborhood stores and religious organizations. There is a vast array of reciprocal relationships, all of whom serve as non-informal alliances that take the place of state-provided social services (77).

Sometimes, if the families are poor, they are not able to provide financial assistance to their members. However, they are there emotionally and provide what they can. Nobody dies of hunger in the Philippines because it is such a fertile place, especially in the rural areas.

Families in the Philippines tend to be egalitarian (Miralao, 1992). There is an increasing number of female-headed households, as men die or leave to find work in the cities. There is a related rise in women living with their relatives, especially their siblings, upon dissolution of their marriages. In Filipino families, the eldest child gets more schooling relative to his or her siblings (Quisumbing, 1994). This is consistent with the idea, as we saw with African American families, that he or she will contribute to the education of the younger siblings when it is their turn (182). It appears that in the Philippines, having siblings and other extended family kin provides the safety net that families need in times of strife. Siblings seem to be the unacknowledged force that keeps many families afloat.

Sibling Relationships in Africa

In Africa, also, siblings are particularly important in family life. In Tanzania, for example, siblings are responsible for the care of younger sibs as well as for the socialization of those children (Omari, 1991). There are few day care centers, and most socialization takes place in the home, where older siblings act as role models and contribute to the care and feeding of others. Every family member is expected to contribute to the well-being of the family, much as we saw in the family-based economy in the West. With more members of the family, more work can be handled, and thus more production can be generated. Particularly in rural regions, siblings are crucial in lending their hands to the family work, as well as caring for siblings while the parents are working on production for the family (64).

Later in life, siblings in Tanzania serve as counselors in case of marital discord. They are available to provide financial assistance and a place to live should divorce, which is rare, occur (66). Tanzania is a collectivist society, with many tribal variations. But nonetheless, the emphasis is on kin helping kin, and in this schema siblings play a crucial relationship in keeping families functioning.

In Nigeria the situation is similar. Siblings are important in the raising of children but also later in life. Should a husband die, it becomes the responsibility of his brother to take in and assist the husband's wife and family. In what is called *levirate marriage,* brothers will even take their brothers' widows as their second or third wives, to provide a home and support for them (Otite, 1991). Extended families, with siblings playing a most important role, are responsible for supporting the aged, aunts and uncles, nieces and nephews, educating their siblings' children, contributing to one another's marriage payments, caring for the needy and the infirm of their families, and taking in the orphans and the elderly (47). The family, with siblings in a key role, acts like a corporate unit in matters of funeral and naming ceremonies and anniversaries. Families also act like voluntary associations, sometimes meeting monthly to discuss family matters.

In Zimbabwe, siblings are so important that should there be conflict outside of the family, all the siblings will unite to turn and fight the outsider (Mapondera, 1995). The attitude is that one may argue with siblings, but that this should never separate families, because they are still needed. The sibling bond is considered one of the primary relationships in the kinship network (2). Siblings' children are considered to be one's own children, and all are called sons and daughters, with the terms *nieces* and *nephews* rarely used.

In all parts of the globe, older brothers have the greatest seniority or status, followed by the oldest sister, and finally the younger sibs (Cicirelli, 1995, 75). All younger siblings are taught to respect older siblings and obey them as they would a parent. Although inheritance customs vary from culture to culture, it is often the oldest brother or sister who is in charge of distributing the wealth to the others (75).

From these descriptions, you can see that sibling relationships are a vast unchartered terrain that needs further exploration. The role of siblings in all of our lives is far greater than has been acknowledged thus far. Sibling relationships, whether in the United States or in other parts of the world, seem to provide the invisible glue that holds families together. Our siblings are crucial for our material and psychic growth and development. As we will see in the next section when we explore relations with the elderly, the sibling bond plays an important role in caring for and responsibility for the elderly.

Aging and Grandparenting

As we age, the roles and responsibilities of family life change. No longer is the responsibility of adults solely parenting and wage earning. Many societies have new jobs for the elders in the society. With people living longer, there are more old people in our societies, and more of those old people tend to be women, since women live longer than men (Tepperman & Wilson, 1993). Because people are living longer, they have longer periods of unemployment and retirement. How they use that time depends on the culture they live in: some have different responsibilities depending on the needs of their children. Others have no responsibilities to anyone but themselves and live in individual retirement. Societies also tend to have differing attitudes toward their aged populations, with some having great respect for their elders, while others ignore or marginalize them.

In my travels, and on this journey we are taking together, there are different snapshots of aging and family life. In China, one can often see older people tending their grandchildren while both parents are out working. Grandparents take the children to the market, to school on bicycles, to after-school cultural programs (called "children's palaces"), and just to sit in the city square and watch the daily activities. In Vietnam, one can see elders working in the fields, tending the rice paddies, working alongside their children; when they die, they are buried in vaults right there in the paddy, close to the family. In India, elders do the daily work of life, sweeping the streets, watching the children at home, or carrying heavy stones as they help to build their communities. Elderly life in the non-Western world is quite variable. Old people do not live in retirement communities, far from their families and their original homes. That is a uniquely Western phenomenon.

Aging and Grandparenting in the United States

In the United States, to many people, aging has a negative connotation. Some people in our society see people over age 65 as "out to pasture," as nonproductive members of society. We place a lot of emphasis on chronological age, and when people reach 65, for the most part, they are considered old and ready for retirement. In phrases like "over the hill" and "old fogey," we see the stigma that our society places on people who are no longer productive in the economy. We establish retirement homes for people who are able to care for themselves, and nursing homes for those who are not. Sometimes there is the "out of sight, out of mind" phenomenon, in which the aged are removed from the family and seen only on holidays, if at all.

In the United States, perhaps one of the most significant stages in the aging process is becoming a grandparent. In earlier times, women gave birth to as many as fourteen children and were still raising their younger children when their eldest became parents. Grandparenting as a stage did not last as long, because people did not live as long, nor did it provide as much of a separate identity as it does today (Newman, 1999, 433). Grandparents did not play a significant role in the daily raising of their grandchildren; they were busy with their own children. Now grandparents have more money, time, and leisure, giving them ample time to be involved with their grandchildren. They are also younger, often not more than middle-aged when their first grandchildren are born, and as grandparents they are healthier and more fit and active. Except for immigrants and minority groups, we do not see many grandparents living with their extended families. Elders seem to enjoy their independence and the autonomous lives that they have carved out, post-"empty nest."

Photo 9.7   Grandfather and child going to school, China. Photographer: Patti Carman

We do see ethnic variation in grandparenting in the United States. African American, Latino, and Native American grandparents, as well as those in recent immigrant families, have more daily involvement with their grandchildren (435). They play a critical role in raising these children and are highly influential as role models and daily caregivers. This is especially true for African American grandmothers, who are integrally involved in the raising of their grandchildren. In fact, this emulates the process in Africa, where grandmothers and multigenerational families are actively involved in the day-to-day process of teaching and caring for the grandchildren. In Native American culture, it is also common for the grandmothers to be the primary caretakers of the children. This follows a long tradition in which mothers are freed up to participate in "the economics of the tribal community; . . . [and there is] the belief that old age represents the culmination of cultural experience" (436). Elders are the ones thought to be the best people to convey tribal beliefs to the children. There is a greater tendency, relative to whites, of blacks, Asians, and Latinos to live in extended family arrangements, which means that these grandparents are more involved with and exercise more authority in the upbringing of their grandchildren at all income and class levels (Taylor, 1997, 80).

There seems to be some variation in gender as to how grandparents play their roles. Grandmothers have been found to be more nurturant, having warm relations with their grandchildren (Hagestad, 1981, as quoted in Hutter, 1998, 456). Grandfathers are the repositories of family wisdom and seem to favor their grandsons, while grandmothers tend to be more equal in their affection. In other words, we continue playing our gender-specific roles even into grandparenthood. This really comes as no surprise.

When elders become incapacitated, it is often a challenge to their adult children to decide what will become of their elderly parents. Should they go to a nursing home, should they come to live with a family member, should they stay in their own homes and get some help? It is usually the daughter who cares for the aged parents and elderly kin. These women are part of "the sandwich generation," caught between their parents and their own children and responding to the needs and demands of both. Even when they choose nursing home placement, women are still integrally involved in the management aspects of their elders' lives. Women in the United States spend approximately 17 years of their lives caring for children and 18 years caring for aged parents (Martin, 1997, 315). This heavy workload is stressful to women. In one study in Portland, Oregon, it was found that women with responsibilities for both children and elderly experienced more stress and were absent more from work than workers who did not have such responsibilities (316).

In other societies this is also the case, with the caretaking responsibility placed on the women. Let's take a look at what aging and grandparenting look like in other parts of the globe.

Aging and Grandparenting Internationally

It appears that worldwide, the family is the primary caregiver for the elderly; that fact seems to transcend politics, culture, and economics (Kendig, Hashimoto, & Coppard, 1992). There seems to be no other alternative in developing parts of the world, where nursing homes and other living arrangements are not available. In a study done for the World Health Organization, 21 countries were surveyed and seemed to represent the full spectrum: English-speaking and European countries, the Middle East and Africa, Latin America, Asia, and the Pacific.

According to the authors of the study, the families in the West live within a modified extended family system. As you'll remember from earlier chapters, that is a system in which family members are integrally involved with each other but maintain separate dwellings, because they can afford to do so. They maintain close contact on a regular basis (32). The countries that use this structure also provide a considerable amount of state monies to assist the elderly, like Medicare and Medicaid in the United States.

People in developing parts of the world do not have these economic assets; they care for their elderly through the extended family. Most older people not in the West do not have a pension or Social Security and must depend on their offspring for support. This makes it possible for the elderly to help raise the children, saves what limited money the family does have, and permits the whole family to be involved in the decisions of family life. In fact, this is the main difference between families in the developed parts of the world and those that are developing (32).

For example, in countries in Scandinavia, where there are many economic resources as well as extensive support services, a high proportion of the frail elderly are institutionalized or live alone, but with assistance. In contrast, in countries like India and Ghana, there are no social security systems to assist the elderly (32). Thus they live with their families. But Japan once again is an aberration. Even though the Japanese have achieved significant economic growth, their cultural traditions preclude placing elders out of the home, and thus, the elderly continue to reside with their families.

Although in many parts of the world the economies are changing, with more women going out into the workforce, cultural patterns of caring for the elderly do not seem to be changing dramatically. Because of the strength of the extended family in developing parts of the world, the authors of the study think that the pattern we have in the West, "the intimacy at a distance" phenomenon, will not take place there (Kendig, Hashimoto, & Coppard, 1992, 33).

In Mexico, for example, where it is forecast that the aging population will exceed 12 million by the year 2025, the appreciation of the aged is so ancient and deep-rooted that obligation to the elderly is integral to the culture. Old men are seen as responsible for preserving and communicating traditions, and old women are the custodians of the family unit. In fact, God is seen as a God who is both father *and* mother (33).

Regardless of social class, three-generation families are the norm in Mexico. Poorer families may reside in adjacent buildings, sharing water and other resources. Wealthier families look for houses near one another and spend all their time together. Families share a sense of solidarity. In the upper classes, this takes the form of loyalty to the family businesses and mutual economic undertakings between fathers and sons. Among the poor, this means sharing food, clothing, and shelter. Family solidarity always means parents and siblings, as well as sons and daughters. In fact, 93 percent of all elderly in Mexico are integrated with their families. Only 15 percent of the elderly live alone with their spouses (34). And only 3 percent of men and 9 percent of women live alone.

In Brazil, things are somewhat different. In one study, only 28 percent lived in three-generation households, while 32 percent lived in one-generation homes, 28 percent in two-generation homes, and 12 percent lived alone. It was more common for poorer people and for those from rural regions to live in a multigenerational setting (35). But nearly 90 percent of older people had some kind of domestic help coming in to aid them, and a vast majority of those people had care provided by family members, even if they did not live with them.

In Japan, the elderly are also important, with the same respect shown them through the belief in filial piety that exists in China and other Asian countries.

Japan even has an annual Respect for the Elders Day, and there is employment provided to retired workers, just to keep them productive in their society (Newman, 1999, 437). In Japan, aging is respected because of the hierarchical structure of that society. The Japanese believe that those above them in the hierarchy, through age, seniority, gender, and other status positions, should be shown respect for their greater power and knowledge. Responsibility for care of the elderly still resides with women, but increasingly other family members assist because of women's need to go outside the home to work. Nonetheless, even with increasing social change, elders are expected to live with their extended families, caring for the children and remaining there until death.

Finally, in the Philippines, co-residence with children is the norm for elders (Domingo & Asis, 1995). Most live with their family members. This arrangement is mutually beneficial. Even though some elderly may prefer to live alone, they often stay with their families to provide needed assistance to the younger generations. They give money, moral support, and advice, run errands, and deal with the daily details of life, as well as receiving the benefit of being with their families (49). Although we like to think that the family is doing the elder a favor, in fact, having her or him in the house provides valuable assistance to all the family. Intergenerational co-residence is a benefit to all concerned.

In situations in which children of the elders have moved to other parts of the globe, it is not at all uncommon for the children to send money home to maintain and assist the elder in meeting expenses and living comfortably.

Summary

In this chapter we took a look at intergenerational relationships. We began with the history of parenting in the West and then looked at some demographic patterns of parenting, particularly in the United States. We compared parenting in Japan to that of the West and saw different value systems and patterns of parenting, especially that of child-centeredness in Japan. We then looked at parenting in Malaysia, particularly among Muslim Malays. We saw the impact of traditional religious values on parenting styles. When looking at parenting in West Germany, we saw it is similar to parenting in the United States in some ways, but also that it is dissimilar in some patterns, like the reliance on other women to help mothers in parenting. In Denmark, we saw a style of democratic parenting that seemed to turn out healthier children than did the authoritarian or permissive style.

When looking at mothering, we saw that this role, too, is socially constructed. We contrasted motherhood in the United States to motherhood in Japan, and then again contrasted with China and the impact of the one-child policy on mothering. Fatherhood was also put under the microscope, and we considered the difficulties of fathering in the United States. Then we looked at fatherhood in China.

Later in the chapter we looked at the constructions of childhood and adolescence in the West, and contrasted the Western concept of childhood to that in other parts of the world, where that stage of life is not as marked and delineated so clearly.

We looked at adolescence among the Maasai as an example of how another society marks the transition into adulthood.

We looked at the nature of sibling relationships and the importance they play in family life. Siblings play key social roles in the United States and elsewhere, and in this chapter how siblings behave in Brazil, the Philippines, and Africa. Finally, we looked at aging and grandparenthood as the final stage of intimate relationships. We saw how these stages are constructed in the West, and then contrasted this with developing parts of the world, noting that in most places elders live with their children and help raise the grandchildren.

Family life is a complex web and tangle of interpersonal relationships. It is not easy to explain it and put it simply. In Chapter 10, we look at the family in trouble, particularly at what happens when family life confronts conflict and violence.

CHAPTER 10

Violence and the Family

For the past 25 years I have worked in the field of domestic violence. I started by teaching a course on battered women, which has since expanded to include family violence, covering child abuse, wife battering, sexual abuse, sibling violence, parricide and marricide (the killing of parents), and elder abuse. I also teach a seminar in the treatment and prevention of family violence, as well as a course on international domestic violence. It all started for me when I was involved as a supporter in a local court case in which a woman was convicted of killing her battering husband and was given a sentence of 25 years to life by the court. Since that time, I have been a student of the field and look at the world through the lens of violence. In 1994, I published a book on my work with battering and violent American families (Leeder, 1994).

For the past few years I have focused my attention on the movements in other countries that are working to prevent or reduce domestic violence. Much work has been done in the past 20 years to make people aware of the incidence and prevalence of family aggression. Programs exist all over the world; Internet communication goes on across nations; conferences take place all the time, with people trying to help each other find ways of coping with this worldwide phenomenon.

Since I first began my studies, the academic field of domestic violence has blossomed, and many people are now aware of the severity of the problem and the fact that violence is all around us. The American family is rife with wife abuse, but violence is abundant outside of the family, too. The violence we experience in our family life merely reflects what our society holds in high value—violence and aggression. America is a violent society, with a wide acceptance of corporal punishment, aggressive sports, and violent video games, violence shown extensively in the media, laws that sanction the use of violence, and the easy availability of guns and other weapons. As a society, we have become desensitized to the levels of aggression going on around us. Thus, family violence comes as no shock to those of us who study American society; it is a reflection of our society's values and norms.

However, what I have also found in my studies is that domestic violence exists everywhere in the world. My cross-cultural visits have shown me that every society in the world, except for the few I cite later in the chapter, has some level of violence in the home. Be it child abuse, wife battering, elder abuse. or homicide, we see the prevalence of aggression in intimate relationships almost everywhere. In this chapter I discuss some of the problems as well as some of the solutions that are being developed. I give you a window into some of the societies we have studied so far, but through a new lens: violence in intimate relationships.

In this chapter, we look at programs that have been established to help families cope with violence. We know that both war and battering are not healthy: they hurt all concerned. It is important to find creative ways for dealing with these problems. Some countries have found methods for curtailing, or at least educating, their populaces about the consequences of violence. We discuss some of those programs and how well they work.

Not only is violence present within individual families, but violence and war in societies have a direct impact on family life. In Chapter 7, I discussed the problem of ethnic conflict—when one ethnic group tries to "cleanse" a society of another group—and its impact on families. We were talking about war and its consequences on family life. War has an enormous impact on families: it breaks them up, it uproots them from their homes, it kills family members, it destroys economies. War is one of the primary agents of devastation of families, and we need to study how families cope with as well as how they survive such difficulties. At the end of the chapter, we direct our attention to families and war.

Domestic Violence in the United States

Domestic violence is a nice way of saying "the beating of loved ones." It is a sanitized term that takes the sting out of the fact that it is women, children, and elders who are for the most part the victims of male family members. It was for a long time legal for violence to occur between family members. In colonial times, there was the "rule of thumb," which allowed men to beat their wives with a rod "no thicker than the thumb"; children could be killed if the father found them to be incorrigible and too difficult to control (Gelles & Straus, 1988). A commonly used phrase was "Spare the rod and spoil the child." Family or domestic violence is any act that is carried out with the intent or the perceived intent of causing physical pain or injury to a family member. It is true that the laws have changed, with the intent to control the problem. However, domestic violence still occurs, and on a frequent and frightening level. Let me cite some shocking statistics for you.

Sixty percent of all American families use violence on a regular basis, including hitting, biting, or using a hard object (Straus, 1994). Ninety percent of all American children are spanked by the age of five. While not all children who are spanked are abused, researchers who work in the field argue that the use of corporal punishment interferes with optimal child development and teaches children that "might makes right," that it is normal for people who love you to hit you. It also teaches a child to tolerate aggression and has been found to contribute to physical aggression later in life. In fact, it has been found to lead to higher delinquency rates, low self-esteem, and depression in adulthood (Straus, 1994). Spanking has been known to lead to harsher forms of punishment, and it does not work in terms of teaching acceptable behavior. What it does teach is fear of the perpetrator. The continuum of family violence begins with spanking and can lead all the way to death.

Further statistics indicate that 1 in 4 young American women will be raped, and 50 percent of all women will be beaten at least once in a relationship. Yearly, 1.8 million women are beaten by their partners. These beatings are severe enough to require medical attention, and beating by an intimate occurs more than muggings and other physical crimes (Kemp, 1998). A woman in the United States is beaten every 9 seconds, with 42 percent of all murdered women being killed by their partners. Ninety women a week are killed, and 55 percent of all women who are separating from their partners report that abuse is the reason for the departure. In fact, in 92–95 percent of divorces, the alleged grounds for divorce is violence, particularly toward the female.

In the United States, 2,000 children a year are killed at the hands of their parents or guardians. The estimates of physical child abuse are between 200,000 and 2.8 million a year, with nearly 1 million substantiated reports of abuse (Martin, 1997, 307). This disparity of numbers indicates the discrepancy between reported cases and estimates of what actually occurs. For example, often the government numbers are far lower than random survey results, which are not based only on reports coming into official channels. In fact, there is some evidence that the numbers may be on the rise: in 1983 there were 1.4 million cases reported, and in 1993 there were 2.8 million. This may reflect more of a willingness to report violence (Crosson-Tower, 1999).

A National Center on Child Abuse and Neglect study found that 80 percent of the damage to children is done by parents. Fifty-three percent of the children they studied suffered neglect, 26 percent were physically abused, 5 percent were emotionally abused, 22 percent had multiple kinds of abuse, and sexual abuse accounted for 14 percent of the reported cases (Kemp, 1998).

Sexual abuse estimates range from 130,000 to 1.3 million cases a year (Lewin, 1995). Generally, the reported cases of sexual abuse predominantly involve young girls, although a growing number of boys are victims also. The estimates are that 1 in 3 girls and 1 in 5 boys will be sexually abused by the age of 18. Most of the sexual abuse is done by fathers and stepfathers, primarily heterosexual men.

Children who are not victims themselves but who view violence are also at risk: 3.3 million children see violence in their homes, and children who do so are 10 times more likely to assault a non-family member than kids from non-abusive homes. In 70 percent of families in which there is a battered wife, there is also an abused child. And 75 percent of men who batter report having witnessed their fathers abusing their mothers (Kemp, 1998).

Sixty-two percent of all homicides are done by persons known to the victim, and 1 in 4 female suicide attempts were by women who had been battered. When a victim tries to leave the battering situation, it is likely that she will be followed and harassed, which increases the likelihood of further violence. In fact, the government passed a law in 1994 making it a federal crime for someone to kidnap his wife or ex-wife and transport her across state borders.

There has also been much controversy about the nature of battered husbands. Men are in fact hit frequently in domestic relations. Statistics indicate the numbers are about equal to women's, but what is *not* equal is the damage that is done. Men are generally larger than women and do greater bodily damage when they are aggressive (Gelles & Straus, 1988, 90). Thus, even though the statistics are similar, the damage is not. Women are less likely to initiate the violence, and are more likely to hit in self-defense or retaliation. A woman who beats is more likely to have been beaten. In fact, only 11.3 percent of all violent crimes in the United States are committed by women, and only 18 percent of all arrests are of women. Eighty-eight percent of those arrested for violent crimes are men, and men comprise 82 percent of those arrested for all crimes (Laskowitz, 1998).

In 1994 the United States developed legislation through the Violence Against Women Act. This act makes some domestic violence offenses a federal crime and provides funding for public education and treatment programs for offenders. By so doing, the government placed domestic violence on the federal agenda for the first time (Martin, 1997, 307).

And, believe it or not, we also abuse our elderly. The elderly are sexually abused as well as being killed. We neglect them, either by ignoring their needs or by actively withholding care from them, thus leading to their eventual demise. Estimates are that 2–4 elder deaths per 100 are caused by neglect, and that is an underreported estimate (Pillemer, 1998). It is estimated that in 1996, a total of 449,924 persons aged 60 or over experienced abuse and/or neglect in domestic settings. These numbers reflect only reports; the real numbers are certainly much higher than these reflect.

As you can see, we are a violent society; we hit and even kill our family members. The family is a paradox; it is the most loving institution in our society, and yet it is also one of the most dangerous. It is the third most violent institution in our society, with rates of injuries following only those done to police officers and to the military in times of war. The family has been called "a haven in a heartless world" (Lasch, 1977); yet, for some members, it is a violent and scary place in which to reside. Certainly, until we make some significant changes in our society, the violence will continue. We are not able to socially re-engineer the family. Nor are we able to reduce the economic stressors, but we might be able to discourage aggression by making weapons less available, teaching conflict resolution, reducing the importance of contact sports, especially in high school, and perhaps reducing the depiction of violence on television.

In Chapter 6 we discussed gender violence, and noted that most of the violence done in families is perpetrated against women, children, and the elderly. It is interesting that women, who are still the primary caretakers of children, commit only 50 percent of the abuse against children (Breiner & Gordon, 1999, 504). If we controlled for the amount of time that fathers actually spend with their children, the numbers would be disproportionately higher than they are now. In other words, the percentage would be higher if the time fathers spent with their children (which is much less than mothers do) was factored in. The violence in U.S. society is primarily male violence. Women participate in aggression, as we have seen, but not to the same extent as males. For now it is a gender problem, with men being disproportionately the perpetrators of the aggression in our society.

Family Violence Among Ethnic
and Racial Minorities in the United States

Recently there has been a growing body of research on violence among black, Latino, and immigrant families in the United States. Early studies, starting 25 years ago, focused on white families and then generalized to other groups. There was little data with which to compare racial and ethnic minorities to the white majority. In fact, many of the statistics presented earlier in the chapter were aggregates, meaning they did not separate out percentages for race or ethnic background. Fortunately, we are now gathering more evidence about different groups in the United States.

For example, although a common stereotype holds that African American homes are more violent than white homes, the reality is that violence is not greater. For example, over time, child abuse rates are staying the same. Studies conducted by Gelles and Straus (1988) and Hampton (1987) found that "survey data have not supported the contention derived from official child abuse and neglect report data that black parents are more abusive than white parents. . . . [There was] little difference between blacks and whites in the rate of severe violence toward children (15 percent for black families and 14 percent for white families)" (Hampton, Gelles, & Harrop, 1989, 4). Children in poor black homes are reported as being abused more than children from more affluent and majority homes (4). However, while in this survey child abuse rates in the majority population appeared to be decreasing, the authors found that between 1975 and 1985 the rate stayed the same in the black family (4).

The survey also found that within the general population, wife battering has remained constant, while in the black family wife abuse has decreased (8). One explanation for this decline is that black women are increasingly in the workforce; thus they have benefited economically and are able to stand up for themselves more, decreasing the likelihood of abuse. There is definitely a correlation between abuse and income levels for blacks. Generally, the higher the income, the lower the level of abuse reported (Cazenave & Straus, 1979). Working-class blacks are more likely to abuse than are middle-class blacks, which is also true of the white majority in the United States. This does not adequately explain, however, why child abuse rates among black families have stayed the same.

For Latinos, who are the fastest-growing minority population in the United States, there is little data that indicates that they abuse their children any more than the rest of the population (Zayas, 1992). Whether one looks at Puerto Ricans, Mexican Americans, or generic groups of Hispanics or Latinos, the rates do not differ. Even though, due to recent immigration, the Latino population is generally poorer than the general population, they do not abuse their children more. One explanation for this is the *familism* we discussed in earlier chapters—the emphasis on family unity and the fact that there are kin present who act as intermediaries or buffers in case of trouble and stress (302). Latino families who want to protect their children from the negativities of life and teach them to respect authority do use corporal punishment, but avoid any hitting that could be misinterpreted as abuse (304).

Interestingly, the rates for child sexual abuse among Latina girls is about the same as for white girls (Arroyo, Simpson, & Aragon, 1997). Although one study reported that Latina women suffered more serious abuse in terms of how old they were when it occurred or how physically intrusive the abuse was, the emotional response and the frequency was almost equal to that of white girls (57). A significantly greater proportion of Latina women reported that the perpetrators of the abuse were extended family members, while the white women reported nuclear family or extrafamilial perpetrators. And the white women were less likely to report that something happened. In another study that compared young black, white, and Latina American women, the author found that all of them had similar rates of symptoms after the abuse, and they were similar to each other in knowledge of the identity of the perpetrator, the age when abuse occurred, and the kind of abuse. The only difference among the three groups was that white girls experienced longer periods of abuse than the Latina or the African American subjects (Mennan, 1994).

In a study of Asian American immigrants, Ho (1990) looked at various groups of Southeast Asian women immigrants to determine the incidence of wife battering and resistance to it. She studied Chinese, Vietnamese, Laotian, and Cambodian Khmer women and found that the level of male domination and wife battering differed among the groups. Chinese men seemed to give their wives more freedom, although they did maintain the final authority and power in the family. These women suffered less violence than the other groups. The Vietnamese women were more openly dominated, and their husbands claimed "ownership" of them. The Laotian and Khmer women's status was even lower than the other two groups, and all of them raised their own daughters to be obedient and subservient (141). All groups, except Chinese, used physical discipline to train their children, with the Khmer and Laotians using small sticks. The Chinese did not believe in using physical force to train their children, unlike the other Asian groups (142).

Chinese women were far less accepting of violence against them than were the other three groups. Researchers estimated that 20–30 percent of the Chinese women were hit by their partners, while the Vietnamese were far more tolerant of the abuse against them. Ho thinks this might be due to the fact that in Vietnam, Laos, and Cambodia there are fewer prohibitions against the use of violence. Finally, she found that all of the Asian women were afraid to leave their abusers for fear of losing their children, or because of limited finances and fear of discrimination by the dominant society (143). Asian women are also handicapped in seeking help because of their social values, which stress secrecy and submission to authority. We mentioned in earlier chapters that Asian women are supposed to be submissive and to keep the family harmony at all costs. Suffering seems to be an integral part of Asian women's experience.

Another study found that Korean immigrant women had the highest rate of wife battering compared to the other Asian American populations and compared to other ethnic populations (Rhee, 1997). This author points out that Korean immigration to the United States has been sizeable since the 1970s, and that the Korean community is well organized and cohesive, establishing business and ethnic organizations for its members. The Korean immigrants are well educated and well employed. Nonetheless, Korean culture is patrilineal, and patriarchal male dominance defines the traditional family unit (66). Upon arrival in the United States, the traditional family structure is challenged, with women going out to work and becoming more independent. This study found that 60 percent of the women surveyed were battered at least once in their marriages. This is double the U.S. rate (68). The findings were that, in the previous year, 35 percent of women had been hit; the national average for all women per year is 12 percent. According to this study, wife battering seems to be rampant in the Korean immigrant community. We can compare this to black women, who are also in the workforce in great numbers but have a far lower incidence of battering. In Korean culture, a woman's earning money does not necessarily enhance her status in the family (70).

You can see that domestic violence is alive and well in the United States. It exists in the dominant, majority society as well as in ethnic and racial minority and immigrant communities. But there is variability and complexity in it all. In some communities wife battering is prevalent, while in others child abuse and child sexual abuse dominate. Now we look at other societies to see how well they fare.

Family Violence in a Cross-Cultural Perspective

Having seen how pervasive domestic violence is in our own society, we can begin to look elsewhere, realizing that the United States is no better and no worse than other places in the world. We are certainly not beacons of enlightenment in the area of family violence. In one important study, David Levinson's book *Family Violence in Cross-Cultural Perspective*—done in 1989 but based on work done in 1949 by anthropologist George Murdock—looks at data on 90 societies around the world. He found that 15 of the 90 had little or no family violence (Levinson, 1989).

Levinson found that the groups of women who are least abused worldwide are those who have a sense of support from other members of their communities (Levinson, 1989). This can be in the form of groups walking to and from the water source daily, or tending the crops, or selling in the marketplace. Support and safety can come in many different forms and can be a result of different factors. Levinson says that "it appears that the presence of exclusively female work groups, whether an indicator of female solidarity or of female economic power, or both, serves to control or prevent wife beating" (Levinson, 1989, 58). He also found that domestic violence was much less prevalent in societies that had monogamous marriages and economic equality between the man and the woman, and where there was equal access to divorce. What theory do you think he was using to explain these findings?

Levinson also found that in societies in which there were alternative caretakers available to help with children, and where community and kinship networks were in place, there was less domestic violence. In such societies there were norms in place that encouraged the nonviolent resolution of disputes inside and outside of the home. For example, among some Latino cultures, other family members, like uncles, will go into the home and find a way to solve the problem, encouraging the abuser to not hit the partner. In other places with strong community bonds, men in the villages may go into the home and communicate with the potential abuser to resolve the conflict.

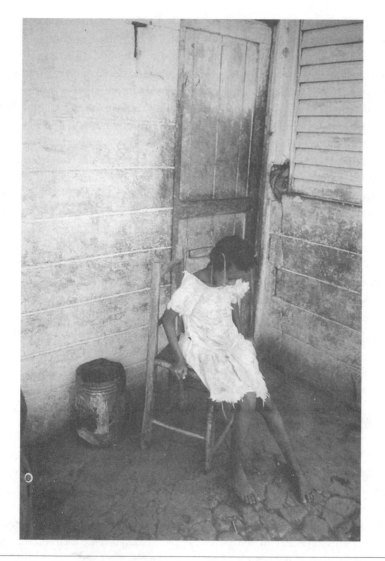

Photo 10.1   Poor and abused child in Dominican Republic. Photographer: Elaine
Leeder

Much research has been done on domestic violence in Western countries, but
thus far, little has focused on developing parts of the world. Abuse is a global concern, however, and it is certain to become a major area of intervention cross-
nationally in the twenty-first century (Segal, 1995). Just as abuse is common in the
United States, so too it appears to be elsewhere in the world.

There are major plans in the works to research and do global comparisons of the
incidence and prevalence of domestic violence worldwide. This is a hard job, since
what is abuse in one place might not be considered abuse in another, making it
problematic to devise questionnaires and instruments that could test the data.
Researchers from all over the world, in collaboration with the Family Research
Laboratory at University of New Hampshire, are working to find a way to do so.

For now, what we have are findings from individual countries. The information on specific countries presented in this chapter is by no means comprehensive. It represents some of the latest research, but that research itself is spotty, with more work being done in some places and less in others. It also is spotty in terms of the kind of abuse studied. For example, there is more information on wife battering and child abuse in India, but there is little on child abuse in other parts of the world. I emphasize that this information is anecdotal and is by no means comprehensive or exhaustive. It is perhaps just the tip of the iceberg.

For a number of years I have participated in an Internet discussion list through the United Nations; it was originally established to prepare for a UN video satellite conference on domestic violence worldwide. The discussion list provides information shared by organizations and individuals in such diverse countries as Norway, Namibia, India, the Bahamas, Belize, Croatia, and Russia, to name just a few. I share with you some of that information, as well as recent literature and research from India, Vietnam, China, Malaysia, Japan, Nigeria, and Zimbabwe. This is not representative of many parts of the globe; nonetheless it represents the state-of-the-art research in the field. The least violent countries, particularly in terms of child abuse, seem to be those in which economic conditions are favorable and there is little social change, such as the Scandinavian countries. Countries that are industrializing and becoming more modern have more social disruptions, and thus more violence. India is a good case in point.

Family Violence in India

The Indian government and feminist organizations are concerned about wife battering, child abuse and neglect, and infanticide, which occur quite regularly there. In Chapter 5 I mentioned bride burnings in India, called "dowry deaths," which occur as a result of rising demands for the dowry given from the bride's side to the groom's family. I also briefly mentioned female infanticide. Those are extreme forms of gender violence. However, in this chapter we focus on the regular and daily patterns of domestic violence that take place in India.

Many forms of domestic violence in India occur as a result of rising industrialization and modernization. Families have rising economic expectations, and the problems are acted out at home. Wife battering is a fairly common occurrence (Rao, 1997). Mild forms of wife beating are commonplace, and many men and women admit freely in interviews that it is justified if the woman does not "behave herself" (1171). Interestingly, though, in one study only 22 percent of the women admitted on surveys to having been beaten; it is unacceptable to admit abuse, yet it seems to be such a common practice that it is not considered worthy of mention (1172). Only women for whom abuse is a serious or chronic problem are willing to admit it. Otherwise it is such an everyday affair that it is not considered a problem.

In rural India, women believe that alcohol and inadequate dowries provoke the abuse. Some drunken husbands beat their wives without provocation, and women who are beaten complain that the problem is exacerbated by the drunken fits of their husbands (1172). Alcohol is widely available, as it is in the United States, and

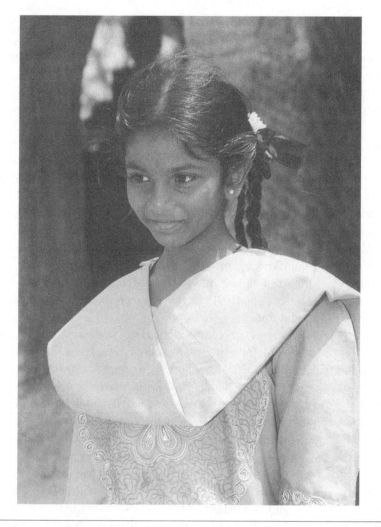

Photo 10.2   Child in India for whom dowry will be required. Photographer: Patti
Carman

many of the men say that their drinking is due to a feeling of hopelessness caused
by poverty. Their lack of options for breaking out of poverty leads them to drink to
"forget their troubles."

Also, as dowry demands have escalated in the past 20 years, many parents have
been unable to keep up with the inflation. Some girls are kept hostage by their in-
laws in an attempt to extract larger amounts of money from the girls' parents
(1173). When those demands are not met, the young bride is beaten, often living in
terror of what might become of her. Her power is also diminished in the home after
she has been beaten. Sometimes "family resources are transferred away from the
wife and her children to other members of the household . . . and the husband and
wife are unable to construct a strong marital bond" (1173).

It appears that if women have male children they are less likely to be beaten.
Having fulfilled societal expectations seems to provide a deterrent to abuse. A rural

woman is more likely to be beaten if she has been sterilized. Sterilization is a major form of birth control in rural India; after bearing enough children, a woman often chooses it as contraception. It appears that a man feels freer to beat a woman who has been sterilized, perhaps out of fear of her infidelity (1175).

In rural India, abuse is tolerated under certain circumstances, which include dowry problems, a wife's infidelity, her neglect of household duties, or her disobedience to her husband's dictates. Abuse is also tolerated if a husband beats his wife when he is drunk but is otherwise a good husband. But if a man batters his wife beyond levels considered tolerable for the village, or if he beats her for reasons not considered legitimate by the village, then a village elder or a local monk will intervene to stop the violence (1174).

Finally, we should mention that living outside of marriage is not an option for an Indian woman. There are no alternatives to marriage for Indian women at this time. Although many women work outside of the home, the types of jobs available are limited, pay is quite low, and marriage is considered the norm.

Clearly, wife battering is a prevalent and "normal" family dynamic in India. It is part of the social fabric, so much so that it is not even commented on unless it is extreme. So too is child abuse.

Child abuse has occurred since time immemorial and exists across cultures. Usually it is the poorer classes who get the attention of public health and welfare services. But middle-class practices are more reflective of whether or not abuse is common in a society. In India middle-class families have experienced a greater amount of stress as the country modernizes and industrializes. India is becoming more urban, and this points to a rise in child abuse among Indian families (Segal, 1995, 219). There is intense competition and effort at upward mobility. This also puts stress on the family. In addition, there is a well-established pattern of corporal punishment in raising children. Children are socialized to obey their parents, and there is strict discipline, even though infants are highly indulged (219). The family is highly hierarchical, and now that families are moving away from the joint family, there is less support for raising children and sharing household tasks. All these factors create an environment that's ripe for an increase in child abuse rates.

The use of corporal punishment is so well entrenched in Indian society that even the middle and upper classes admit to using it. In one study of 319 highly educated, college-graduate parents in three cities in India, a full 56.9 percent reported having used "acceptable" forms of violence, while 41.9 percent engaged in "abusive" violence, and 2.9 percent admitted using "extreme" violence on their children (217). Unfortunately we have no specific studies of middle- and upper-class parents in the United States with which to compare this data. Suffice it to say that in the United States we have comparably high rates of child abuse, too (Gelles & Straus, 1986). Remember that in the United States *at least* a million children are abused a year.

Female infanticide and child neglect are also major child abuse issues in India, particularly in rural villages. Barbara Miller (1987) has spent years studying abuse in rural north India and has found significant discrimination against girl children there. There is a strong preference for sons. Boys are needed as economic assets, for farming, and for the money they send home if they move away. They are more likely to stay with their families after marriage and maintain their parents in old age. Girls

Photo 10.3   Contemporary women in India, veiled. Photographer: Mary Thieme

move away when they marry and cannot contribute to the family upkeep. Sons bring dowries and perform rituals among the Hindus when the father dies; therefore boys are important to the maintenance of family life, while girls are seen as a drain economically. This strong preference for sons has led to disappointment when a girl is born, withholding of medical care for girls, and preferential feeding of boy children (424).

Infanticide is the killing of a child under one year old, and is the most extreme form of child abuse. *Neonaticide* is the killing of an infant up to 24 hours old, and *feticide* is the abortion of a baby in utero, particularly when it is done as sex selection (425). After a child is 12 months old, the killing is considered a homicide. In north India, the killing of female infants is quite an old phenomenon. The British discovered it as early as 1789 and outlawed it by 1870. In some parts of India during that time, the sex ratio was 118 men to 100 women (426). Nowadays, systematic, indirect female infanticide still exists. Girls are not actively killed; they are just neglected so badly that they die from lack of care. The numbers seem to cross class and caste, with even wealthier families preferring sons. This is also true for well-educated families (427–428).

In India there is also sex-selective abortion. Although there is a lack of definitive data, anecdotal evidence indicates that it is quite widespread. One study found that in one hospital, of the 700 amniocenteses done, 250 were male and 450 were female. A full 430 of the 450 females were aborted, while all the male fetuses were brought to full term (429).

Now that I have presented this data, I urge a suspension of any ethnocentric value judgments. It is true that these figures are disturbing and certainly are contrary to Western-based humanistic values. Let's try to keep a view that is culturally relative, to understand why people would engage in such behavior. Understanding why it is done, and being aware of one's own bias, might lead us to think of what can be done about it. There are groups working in India and through the United Nations who have declared this problem a public health issue and are trying to prevent or reduce the incidence of these practices.

Wife Battering in Japan

Now let's focus our lens on another part of Asia, this time Japan. In previous chapters we talked about the way the Japanese family is organized, and how unlike it is to families in the United States, even though both countries are highly industrialized. In Japan the incidence of wife battering is quite high. In one study (Yoshihama & Sorenson, 1994), a survey was done of 796 married women, in which more than three-fourths reported at least one type of violence perpetrated by a male intimate partner. This ranged from a slap to an assault with a deadly weapon, from verbal ridicule to restriction of social activities, and from incompliance with contraception to forced, violent sex. About two-thirds of the most serious physically violent incidents resulted in injury (63).

Unlike the United States, Japan has no specific laws against wife battering as a crime, and there is no governmental funding for services that address the problem. Often, if women get help, it is through services intended for other purposes, like homes established under child welfare laws. Fully one-third of the women who use other services, like shelters that protect prostitutes, were actually battered women seeking protection from their abusers (64). A husband's violence is one of the primary reasons women list when they are seeking divorce, and contrary to the myths of the quiet, passive Japanese man, violence is an integral part of family life in Japanese society.

Often, when a woman seeks to end a violent marriage, the violence does not end. This is true in the United States as well as Japan (71). Violence often escalates during the process of separation and divorce. It is as if the man does not want to let go of his property, holding tighter and becoming more abusive as he fears the loss. Male violence in Japan seems to cross all socioeconomic strata and can lead to serious consequences. Women report broken bones, lacerations requiring stitches, ruptured eardrums, and other injuries requiring medical care (72).

Domestic violence in Japan is still an unrecognized problem. There is not even a word for it in Japanese; language has been adapted from the English to refer to it (74). An increasing level of media attention is being focused on the problem at the time of the publication of this book, but the level is far below that with which we are familiar in the West. This is a problem that bears watching closely, to see how well Japan deals with a problem that many countries are starting to grapple with.

Family Violence in Hong Kong

In an interesting study on wife battering in Hong Kong, So-kum Tang (1994) provided data for other Asian countries as well. She cited that in 1992 there were

8,906 incidents of dowry deaths in India, that 99 percent of the housewives and 77 percent of the women workers in Pakistan were beaten in that year by their husbands, and that there were high levels of wife battering in Iran, India, and Taiwan (347–348). In rural China and Taiwan, wife battering seems to be related to sexual jealousy of the husband, the failure of wives to bear male offspring, and punishment for wives who engage in what seems to the husbands to be improper conduct (348). In urban cities in Taiwan and in Hong Kong, the reasons given are hot temperament, family finance, discipline of the children, extramarital affairs, gambling and alcoholism, and the patriarchal nature of the family. By studying 246 women and 136 men who were college students, the author sought to find out about the levels of violence that their parents displayed (349).

She found that various forms of spouse aggression among Chinese families in Hong Kong were more frequent than is reflected in official statistics. Seventy-five percent of her sample reported the use of verbal and nonverbal acts by their parents to threaten or symbolically hurt each other. Fourteen percent actually hit each other; this is comparable to the U.S. data (354). And similar to rural China, fathers engaged in more violence toward their wives than vice versa. Women also engaged in violent activities, like beating or threatening with knives, but as in the United States, this was often done as retaliation, fighting back, and self-defense (354). The majority of the cases were unreported and undetected, and were part of the so-called "normal violence" of married life in Hong Kong.

So-kum Tang also studied adolescent abuse in Hong Kong Chinese families (1996). She used the same sample of college students that she used for the spousal violence study, and asked them about the amount of verbal abuse, minor violence, and severe violence that they experienced at the hands of their parents. The students were 17- and 18-year-olds. The author found that spouse abuse and adolescent abuse are closely related. Sixty-two percent of her sample were verbally abused, 13.2 percent experienced minor physical violence, and 8.5 percent had severe physical abuse at the hands of their parents in the previous year (877). She compared this to U.S. rates, and found that it was lower for milder forms of physical abuse but comparable for severe violence. She said that filial piety plays a role in abuse of adolescents in Hong Kong, obligating parents to assert authority and inflict punishment on their children so that they will obey and support their parents in later life. Chinese parents often use strict discipline with their children to maintain their authority over them, as well as to push children toward high academic achievement and moral attainment (877). This is particularly true for adolescent sons, who are to carry on the family name and bring honor to the family.

This is a good place to caution you against drawing the conclusion that, because studies indicate there is violence in families in Hong Kong, there is more family violence there than in other places. It just means that there are researchers studying family violence in Hong Kong.

Elder abuse is also a phenomenon in Hong Kong. As you remember, in China the elderly have long been revered, respected, and cared for in old age by their sons. They are seen as people with great wisdom and high status in the traditional family. There is reverence for longevity, and filial piety is one of the dominant obligations of that society. So what is happening?

Hong Kong is in a period of transition from traditional family systems to a new form, perhaps more nuclear in nature. Homes are smaller due to crowding, and parents are being left behind in deteriorating residential areas in the city center. The elderly are no longer as respected as they once were. Hong Kong is extremely prosperous in the global economy; it is booming and growing. However, there is an increasing suicide rate among the elderly, who see that there is no longer any place for them in the family (69).

An increasing number of elderly are being abandoned by their families at local hospitals. Data from research also shows that 22.6 percent of the elderly population in Hong Kong are at risk of abuse, and that these are primarily female, widowed, poorly educated, 70 years old or older, and financially dependent on a family caregiver (72). The Hong Kong findings may be shocking, but they are not unlike those in the United States, where financial exploitation, neglect, and abandonment are part of the patterns of elder abuse.

Unfortunately, in the twenty-first century the problem of elder abuse is one that will increase. By the year 2025, there are projected to be more than a billion people over 60 years old living in the world. Of those, more than 70 percent will be living in developing regions (Yui-huen Kwan, 1995). With the aging of the population and with the diminishment in family size and resources, we will be seeing more elder abuse in the West as well as in other parts of the developing world.

Abuse in Malaysia

Another place where abuse has been studied and seems to be prevalent is Malaysia. In Chapter 9 I described Malaysia as one of the newly emerging "little tigers" of Asia, where the economy has been growing at a rapid rate; it has moved from being a "developing country" (or periphery) to a "newly developed one" (semiperiphery). Although Malaysia has a very low unemployment rate, with only 6 percent of the population unemployed at any given time, the country unfortunately is starting to emulate some of the disturbing social problems found in the West.

In one study of 119 cases of reported physical abuse in Kuala Lumpur, the capital of Malaysia, the authors compared the Malay, Indian, and Chinese populations and looked at whether the abuse was mild or severe (Kassim, Shafie, & Cheah, 1994). They found that abuse was more prevalent among the Malay and Indian populations of that country than among the Chinese (405). This was especially true for those children who were severely abused. The authors attributed this to the fact that the Malays and Indians move to the cities and give up the extended families who assisted them in raising the children. The Chinese in Malaysia tend to stay in extended families, even in the cities, thereby providing help in child rearing.

The findings also indicate that the children who are more severely abused are younger, with 64.8 percent of them being under age five. The abusers tend to be fathers, quite unlike findings in other parts of the world, where mothers are the primary caretakers and thus have more "face time" with their children. The high rates of abuse by fathers might be due to the fact that fathers are left at home to care for the children while the mothers go out to work and do not do well in the child-caring role (406). Most of the fathers had low-paying and menial jobs, which seems to play a role in the abuse as well. Recently, a new Child Protection Act was passed in Malaysia, which is attempting to deal with the increasing numbers of child abuse cases reported in the country.

In Malaysia there is also a preference for male children, particularly among the Chinese. Malay and Indian parents do not seem to have a preference, but Chinese parents, following the traditions we have been studying, continue to prefer boys over girls (Pong, 1994). This is interesting information, considering that in India, families prefer male children, particularly in rural areas. Why, then, in Malaysia is it only the Chinese who prefer boys? The Indians in Malaysia are from south India, where there is not a strong preference for boys; when they immigrate to Malaysia they maintain their cultural values. Thus, they demonstrate less sex preference than do the Chinese (139).

In Malaysia, the Chinese are Taoists, Christians, and Buddhists. The Indians are primarily Hindu, and the Malays are Muslim. Intermarriage between the groups is rare except among the highly educated. It is a truly multicultural society, and all ethnic groups seem to live harmoniously. Each group carries on its own traditions, with the Chinese continuing their values of filial piety, patriarchal family structures, and patrilocalism. The Muslims are matrilineal in some regions and bilateral in terms of kinship patterns (kin from both sides of the family are important). Lately, Malay elders are living more with their daughters than their sons, and sometimes girls are even preferred over sons because they are proving to be more reliable for their parents in old age (139).

A Malay married woman of childbearing age is almost equal to a man in status. Women travel by themselves, smoke in public, control the family budget, make financial decisions, and even engage in conversation directly with men (139). This is significant, given that they are Muslim women. In Malaysia, Muslim women have more independence than other women living under Islam, although there has been a resurgence of fundamentalism, following a pattern similar to that of Muslim countries like Iran and Afghanistan. We'll have to see what happens when this fundamentalism becomes more firmly entrenched. Will Malaysian families begin to desire primarily male children?

Domestic Violence in Vietnam

Vietnam is a fascinating country not far from Malaysia. I was there in 1999 and quote here a bumper sticker I saw while visiting: "Vietnam, a Country Not a War."

The Socialist Republic of Vietnam is rich in culture, deep in religion, and ancient yet modern. It is beautiful, with pristine beaches, huge rivers, and rice paddies galore. Eighty percent of the population lives in the rural areas, and it has a 94 percent literacy rate. We in the United States think that Vietnam is a place of war, and it was, in fact, for most of the past century. In 1945 Vietnam became independent of France, fought for its freedom, and then fought against the Americans, who established their presence there after the French pulled out.

The war has had a significant impact on family life in Vietnam. With the revolution in 1945 came the first attempts to change the inferior position of women there. Laws were passed to equalize the rights, positions, and interests of women. Unfortunately, today the vestiges of Confucian ideology still linger. Men act as kings in their homes even while the women in the workforce make more money than their husbands (Quy, 1996). Women are employed in the labor market in great numbers, but still do the "second shift" that's common in the United States. After work at the factory, Vietnamese women spend five to six hours a night on housework at home. This has been called the "invisible violence" of Vietnam, because while there may not be physical violence between men and women, intimidation and fear drive the relationships (266). This inequity occurs for both urban educated and rural poor women. Many women feel that their situation is predestined, in accordance with Confucian ideology.

Then there is the "visible violence" that recently has led to a large number of divorces in Vietnam. One report indicates that as many as 87.5 percent of the divorces in 1992 were a result of violence or violence-related causes (267). There are numerous injuries and deaths related to violence in the home, although exact numbers are not available. What is known is that 17.5 percent of the deaths in Vietnam in 1992 were caused by family violence (271).

One of the reasons given for this problem is low socioeconomic status. Poor men, in particular, feel that it is permissible to take out their frustration and anger on their wives and children (268). Another reason given is the "feudal attitude": the old Confucian ideas of "thinking highly of men and slightly of women" seem to inform beliefs about hitting one's wife (268). Sometimes men take lovers, or even concubines, who come to live in the home with the wife, against the wife's will.

Other reasons for violence are drinking, gambling, adultery, and jealousy (269). Although there are no numbers available on this, the researcher conducted interviews with battered wives who attributed the abusive behavior to a few of these factors. Another reason given was what we would call the "intra-individual theory": that there is "mad blood" in the perpetrator (270). In Vietnam this means that there are people who always feel anxious and angry and tend to shift the blame onto others, especially their next of kin.

In Vietnamese law, men and women are considered equal. Violence toward wives and children is specifically prohibited and is considered a violation of human rights (272), and the government has established a series of local and state programs for intervention. There are also laws against the preference for male children, although as we will see, these have certainly not had much of an impact. Interestingly, however, the incidence of rape in Vietnam seems to be low, specifically as compared with the United States (Goodstein, 1996). The Vietnamese Women's Union plays a role at the local level, watching out for the rights of women (Johnson, 1996).

As in many parts of the world, preference for a son remains strong in Vietnam, especially in light of the family planning policy there, which recommends only two children per family (Haughton & Haughton, 1995). Payments must be made to the government should a family have more than two children, although the sanctions are not as strict as they are in neighboring China. Following the Confucian model, in Vietnam there is still the belief that a son will care for you in old age and that a son is an investment, while a daughter will leave. Even though women in Vietnam are well educated (remember, the literacy rate is 94 percent) and well integrated into the workforce, the Vietnamese still prefer male children.

Another problem related to violence in Vietnam is the trafficking in women (Barry, 1996). Vietnam's traditional values, like fate and filial piety, shape the culture and make it ripe for exploitation by the "sex work" industry. Other countries in the region, like Japan, Thailand, and Australia, have well-established sex industries that have begun moving into Vietnam as the country moves toward economic development (153). Vietnam has a history of sexual exploitation of women, most notably during the Vietnam War, when more than 500,000 women served as prostitutes to the U.S. troops (149). Many were rape victims or war widows needing to earn a living. Now many women are being forced into prostitution as part of the growing sex trade industry. Because prostitution provides immediate cash incentives for the women when other work is not available, it is becoming an increasingly viable option as the country moves toward a more westernized model of economics (153).

Vietnam, although a socialist country with some new elements of capitalism, seems to have similar domestic violence problems as other parts of the world: violence against wives, son sex preference, and a growing sex trade. It appears that not many places in the world are free of domestic violence.

Domestic Violence in Africa

Some of the information that follows comes from international Internet communications networks that have been established so that people who work in the field of domestic violence can "talk" with each other, to determine what is being done and how to establish international networks. The information is not comprehensive and merely reflects what some people have written. It also represents people who have computers and Internet access as well as access to the international listservs.

One interesting piece of information comes from Uganda in east Africa. In Uganda, violence against one's wife is accepted as legitimate; when it is mentioned, most men just shrug and say, "It's our culture" (Doro, 1999). If a woman attacks her husband, the violence is considered criminal. The U.S. Department of State Uganda Report on Human Rights Practices for 1998 says that violence against women, including rape, is quite common. There are no specific laws against wife battering, although a law passed in 1997 provides protection for families, including wives and children. But it is hard to implement the law since law enforcement officials view the problem the way the public does, as not a problem.

Families in Uganda endure violence in silence, and violence is worse in the countryside than it is in the city (1). According to the Human Rights Report, the pattern is similar in other African countries, too. Women have few rights, neighbors don't want to get involved, and the women lie about their injuries if asked about them at medical facilities.

Several women's organizations in coalition are actively pursuing reform and holding public workshops to lobby for a revision of the Domestic Relations Act.

Most of the trouble in getting anything done is related to lack of funding. Many of the countries in Africa do not have adequate funds to handle the many social problems they have, like AIDS, and they have put domestic violence issues on the back burner, because they think, after all, "It is our culture."

Other studies done in Africa are also not comprehensive. One study of domestic violence in Nigeria found that polygamy lends itself more to wife battering than do monogamous marriages (Efoghe, 1990). In this study, more polygamous marriages were violent than were monogamous marriages. Another study, of child sexual abuse in Zimbabwe, found that sexual abuse of children is not as prevalent there as it is internationally, with only about 10 percent of the population being victims of this kind of abuse (Khan, 1995). The authors of the study wonder whether this discrepancy reflects underreporting, or if sexual abuse of children is really not a big problem in Zimbabwe.

Finally, let's remember that Africa and parts of Southwest Asia perform ritual circumcision of girls. In Somalia, Kenya, the Sudan, Tanzania, Ethiopia, Egypt, Uganda, Chad, Mali, Senegal, Cameroon, Zaire, Nigeria, to name just a few, girls are cut and scraped to make their bodies more attractive and marriageable. This practice has been framed as a human rights abuse, as well as a form of child abuse that is being taken up as a problem by the United Nations and the World Health Organization.

Programs for Dealing with Domestic Violence

There are many ways that countries have begun to deal with the problem of domestic violence. Since I began working in this field 25 years ago, there has been an amazing growth in awareness about the problem as well as a vast number of new programs established worldwide to educate and eradicate violence in the family. Countries are passing laws, programs are being established, organizations are forming to combat the issue worldwide.

In my two trips on Semester at Sea, I made it a point to visit several domestic violence programs that had recently been established. In one, in Salvador, Bahia, Brazil, I visited a police precinct that was founded by the federal government and funded to arrest and prosecute batterers. They made it mandatory that arrest take place should the woman swear out a complaint. Within 30 days a full report is made, and then prosecution proceeds.

In Malaysia I visited a women's center that was modeled on a Western approach to dealing with wife battering and rape. There all three major ethnic groups—Malay, Chinese, and Indian—worked at the shelter to help each other. They had received funding for four years of programming from a Canadian foundation, and planned that they eventually would be self-sufficient.

In Zimbabwe I visited a program called the Musasa Project, a four-bedroom house for women fleeing domestic and sexual abuse. Since 1996, 300 women have stayed there, utilizing the services of the staff counselors and legal advisors during a two-month stay. As we saw earlier, women in Zimbabwe often say, "Well, that's how marriage is." Women are beaten for suspected infidelities, for being childless, for not bearing enough sons, and for more trivial reasons (Matetakufa, 1997). In Zimbabwe, 59 percent of the 249 women murdered in one year were killed by their partners. Police reports indicate that 20 women a day are assaulted by their spouses, and that is considered an underreport. They have also found that women who are beaten when pregnant tend to miscarry, have stillbirths, or low-birthweight babies (1). Marital rape is also a concern in Zimbabwe, particularly because of the concern about the rise of AIDS there. Fully 15–25 percent of Zimbabwean adults are infected with HIV. There is an effort afoot to criminalize domestic violence; right now if a man is arrested for abusing his wife, he commonly gets away with a $10 fine.

In 1999 a campaign was launched in Zimbabwe to educate people about violence. They held 16 days of public education about making people responsible and accountable for violence against women and girls. They held outreach programs, meetings to share research findings on perpetrators of child sexual abuse, media training programs, and fieldwork training for people wanting to learn how to intervene. Zimbabwe seems to be taking this problem seriously.

In South Africa, violence within the family is also a serious problem, one compounded by the atrocities performed against women during South Africa's history of apartheid. It appears that in South Africa, women are prone to experiencing violence. For example, in the province of Kwa Zulu Natal reports are that 1 in 35 women report domestic violence, but that the actual numbers are far greater than that. South Africa has one of the highest rape rates in the world. In March 1998, at a conference held in South Africa, participants developed a Declaration on the Prevention and Eradication of Violence Against Women and Children. A Domestic Violence Bill has also been debated in the National Assembly and is close to ratification. Unfortunately, because of limited resources, domestic violence is low on the priority list for services, with basics like housing and education coming first.

Also in Africa there are countless nongovernmental organizations working to combat domestic violence. One such group is Femmes Africa Solidarity (FAS), which is based in Geneva, Switzerland, but serves as advisor to the Organization of African Unity and the Economic Commission for Africa on issues to related to violence and conflict (End-Violence listserv Nov 1998). They have found from their field experience in such countries as Liberia, Sierra Leone, Gambia, Burundi, and Rwanda that women are the foremost victims of conflict. Women often bear the brunt of war and conflict, suffering such things as sexual slavery, rape, and other grave social injustices.

There are so many programs and policies on domestic violence developing or in place in so many countries that it is impossible to fully cover even a few of them. Suffice it to say that awareness is growing. Unfortunately, eradication does not always follow awareness. Many attitudes, values, and norms in places where domestic violence occurs still enforce and encourage abuse. We may have "come a long way, baby," but we sure have a long way yet to go to eradicate domestic violence.

War and Family Life

So far in this chapter we have focused on domestic violence as the primary form of violence encountered in family life. However, war is a major form of violence experienced by families also. In so many places in the world—Kosovo, Rwanda, the Democratic Republic of the Congo, Afghanistan, Iraq, and Iran, to name just a few—families' daily lives are disrupted, often by forces far beyond their control. The emotional and physical costs of war on family life are almost unimaginable. Think of what it must be like to have one's home burned, or one's family members taken away, never to return. Think of life in a refugee camp. Think of walking miles to a safe place and then being uprooted again. Think of moving to a new land, where you do not speak the language and where you do not understand the customs or even the street signs. These are some of the situations that war victims and refugees must face.

A current issue facing families confronted by war is that of children serving as regular soldiers, guerrilla fighters, spies, porters, cooks, sexual slaves, and even suicide bombers in 50 nations in the world where there are armed conflicts (Miller & Lewis, 1999, 14). The United Nations Children's Fund (UNICEF) estimates that worldwide 300,000 children have been recruited or coerced into combat. In addition, during the past decade more than 2 million children have died, with 6 million maimed or disabled, as well as 1 million orphaned and 10 million suffering serious psychological trauma. In fact, children make up one-half of the world's 24 million refugees (14).

Efforts are afoot by the United Nations to raise the age of soldiers to 18, but the United States, Britain, and a few others are against this because they want to be able to recruit young high school graduates to the military. Right now, the minimum age for recruitment is 15, which was established in 1989 under the UN Convention on the Rights of the Child, based on the request of the United States and Britain (14).

A number of countries have agreed to stop using children as soldiers and even grant special care and protection to children from the ravages of war. However, because weapons have become lighter to carry, more children are being recruited to war, especially as older soldiers are less available. Children, unfortunately, make good killers. They are willing to follow orders and are highly malleable.

Graphic stories abound of children who are soldiers and have their hands cut off by the enemy, leaving them to a life of pain and suffering. Countries like Sri Lanka, Sudan, Burundi, and Angola are all willing to stop using children as soldiers and are taking steps to do so. The United Nations has limited funds but has authorized a special post, answerable to the Secretary General, to deal with the problem. This is quite a thorny issue, since war is often an uncontrollable phenomenon and not one that lends itself easily to outside intervention.

War leads to social disorganization. War migrants are uprooted from their homes and places of origin. In their homes they had a semblance of respect and recognition that is lost when war occurs. Perhaps the extended family provided economic security, with farming or small businesses being run by family members. With war comes a complete disruption of normality. Many times family members must quickly move away and sometimes end up in different refugee camps and different cities or even countries after the war.

The experience of war is typically one of loss for families. Families lose their homes, loved ones, material possessions, status, culture, language, employment, a sense of the future, and their human rights (Williams, 1993). Individual loss occurs, as well as collective loss. For example, one may lose one's parents specifically, but the whole family is altered when a mother or father dies. Who then takes care of the children? Who earns the money? Who is responsible? This is the collective loss, as well as the individual loss of one's kin.

War also makes grieving difficult, since one's grief might have to be put on hold while the family makes its way to safety. Numbing can occur, as well as apathy, detachment, and an inability to relate at all (251). But sometimes war brings out the best in people. Strengths emerge as one confronts the most traumatic of life events. People are amazingly resilient, overcoming losses and facing the worst to emerge as survivors. My own experience as the child of a Holocaust survivor has taught me about the inherent strength of humankind, in the face of enormous adversity, to overcome the worst inhumanity and to emerge with strength and dignity.

The social disorganization of family life through war can lead to family breakup and other problems. For example, divorce can occur, as well as domestic violence, alcohol abuse, desertions, and utter exhaustion. Families can make it through the worst of times, only to find when they reach safety that the whole family system has fallen apart. Research indicates that if the woman of the family adapts well, the rest of the family will also cope (252). Because women still have to raise their children and feed their families, they seem to have a job to do that helps them survive. Women also seem to cope better on a day-to-day basis and can organize their lives around simple household tasks (252). Because men lose their jobs as breadwinners through war, they seem to have a harder time adjusting, which leads to depression and apathy.

But women suffer greatly from war, too. For women there is the personal violence that takes place as they move from place to place and camp to camp. They become victims of rape, abduction, and violent sexual abuse. Sometimes women prostitute themselves to obtain food, but often it is done against their will and is a form of war atrocity.

Children also suffer from the tensions related to family reorganization (253). With parents who are no longer employed, with roles reversed, with the boredom of daily life in camps, children see all the negatives associated with being in war-torn families. Their own growth and development is hampered, and they often experience cognitive delays like language and learning problems (254). They are subjected to psychological trauma, having witnessed violence against their family members. Often they experience fear and terror that can lead to night terrors and nightmares in later life. Children who are able to stay with close family members tend to fare better than children who are separated from those ties (254).

Children are forced to grow up fast when they are in wars. They might have to take over caretaking roles for the other children; they may have to scavenge to feed their families. They may assume adult roles that are difficult to give up when the family settles down again (254). The consequences of being in a war have reverberations that can last for generations. Paranoia, fear, feelings of retribution and anger can become part of the fabric of a family's psychic life, leaving marks for generations to come.

Summary

In this chapter we looked at the dark side of family life. Exploring first the nature of domestic violence in the United States, we saw that violence is an integral part of the fabric of life for many Americans. We beat our wives, children, and elders. We neglect and emotionally abuse them, too. We looked at the differences and similarities in abuse among racial and ethnic minorities. We discussed family violence in a cross-cultural perspective and looked at the kinds of societies that were the least violent. Then we began to look globally, starting with India, then Japan, Hong Kong, Malaysia, and Vietnam.

Leaving Asia, we looked at violence in Africa, including Uganda, South Africa, and Zimbabwe. We discussed programs and policies that have been evolving to cope with the growing awareness of domestic violence in the world, including nongovernmental organizations, grassroots programs, and governmental legislation.

Finally we looked briefly at the effects of war on family life, particularly children as soldiers, women as rape victims, and family disorganization and disruption.

Families are ravaged by violence, both internally and externally. The effects of these assaults are deep and far ranging. Families cope with these stressors in a variety of ways. What is truly remarkable is that families are able to survive and sometimes even thrive after the ravages of war and internal violence.

CHAPTER 11

The Future of the Family in Global Perspective

A s we move though the twenty-first century, family life will be greatly affected by the globalization and homogenization processes that began in the previous era. Throughout this book we have discussed how the expansion and change of capitalism have impacted whole countries and trickled down to family life. As economies change, as global capital moves from country to country, permeating boundaries in a way that has never been seen before, family life once again will have to adapt and maintain the flexibility and elasticity that has been its hallmark.

Goods, people, and technology move faster than they ever have before, and with this comes a new global culture, in which all countries in the world look similar. This also leads to a "mixture of experimentation and innovation" in which societies learn and benefit from each other, bringing about new forms of social adaptation (Swerdlow, 1999).

English is now spoken in almost one-fifth of the world; it continues to spread and to be adapted in each of the places it is spoken. Some would argue that this is an example of neo-colonialism (a new kind of colonialism), that the world is being taken over by Western technology, language, and ideas, and that it will lead to cultural genocide, or to the destruction of culturally specific practices and groups of people (Mies, 1999). Mies says that wars are fought for economic reasons, to promote globalized free trade, and end up triggering conflicts between groups of people who once lived in peace. Post-colonial societies seem to be emulating the first onslaught of colonialism that took place hundreds of years ago, only in new forms.

Let's look at family life and see what we think. Is globalization positive, negative, or just the way it is? Is it a conspiracy or is it progress? What impact will the process have on families at the day-to-day level of their lives?

Globalization

The world is becoming more uniform and standardized, more homogenized, as a result of the spread of technology, commerce, and Western cultural forms. In fact, the spread of Western culture is the essence of globalization; with it comes the loss of traditional cultures and the loss of information about and knowledge of those cultures. The reality is that globalization is already upon us. The foods we eat, the clothes we wear, the technology and concepts we use are all the results of this global process. The process is one of dynamic diffusion, however; artifacts and ideas from various parts of the world also find their way to other places.

In 1936, Ralph Linton wrote a description of globalization. What he said then is even more true today. He described a typical U.S. day, during which we rise from a bed that came from the Near East via northern Europe; the sheets are cotton from India, or silk from China. The pajamas are from India. Shaving is a ritual for men adopted from Egypt. The custom of wearing neckties comes from seventeenth-century Croatia; umbrellas were invented in Southeast Asia, coins in ancient Lydia. While eating breakfast, the typical American eats from plates that were invented in China, uses knives from southern India, forks from Italy, and spoons from the Romans. The orange came from the eastern Mediterranean, the cantaloupe from Persia, coffee from ancient Abyssinia. The after-breakfast cigarette comes from Mexico, with tobacco originating in Brazil. We read newspapers printed in type invented in Germany, and finally we thank a Hebrew deity in an Indo-European language that we are 100 percent American.

What happens today is that goods, ideas, and peoples move fast and far, using technology to quickly spread the newest information. Globalization, according to the International Monetary Fund, is the "growing economic interdependence of countries worldwide through the increasing volume and variety of cross-border transactions in good and services and of international capital flows, and also through the more rapid and widespread diffusion of technology" (Wolf, 2000, 9). It is a reality; we no longer have a choice whether or not to accept these ideas. The cultural assault is everywhere. McDonald's, Gap jeans, Marlboro cigarettes, SONY technology, Reebok sneakers, Coke, Nike, and MTV are brands and products available throughout the world. This globalization deeply impacts family life on a daily basis. Who will be hired to work for the multinationals? Who becomes the breadwinner in the family? How is authority negotiated when the children are the English speakers in the family? All of these intimate questions have an immediate impact on the day-to-day life of families.

Global Culture

Although there is a global culture, there is also cultural resilience; people are unpredictable and resourceful in what they accept and what they refuse to make parts of their lives. A strange process of adaptation is occurring, in which parts of the global culture impart their characteristics through adaptation with local culture. Let me give a few examples. In India, some men wear *lungis*, the traditional male equivalent of a sari. Today, however, some men wear white tailored shirts, while others wear Western T-shirts, on top of their lungis. That is an adaptation, combining local culture with global culture.

There are other examples. In most parts of the world, McDonald's serves its regular American fare, but will add foods to the menu to serve local tastes, like teriyaki in Japan. In China, *Sesame Street* was adapted to teach Chinese values and traditions. Mehendi, the art of henna dying of the skin in India, has found its way into U.S. culture, with workshops being offered in countless locations. Revlon has developed cosmetics that fit the color palette of Indian skin tones, and MTV has an Indian-dedicated network (Zwingle, 1999, 30). Even therapy and self-help concepts are now included in globalized marketing.

According to Alvin Toffler (1999), who wrote of the big changes we are experiencing in global culture, the old cultures of the past are changing, maintaining some of their old ways, but evolving to adapt to the technological challenges. He describes the world as divided into the agrarian nations on the bottom, the smokestack nations in the middle, and the knowledge-based economies on top (30). His typology is similar to Wallerstein's ideas about the core, the semi-periphery, and the periphery. In the United States we have moved from a manufacturing economy to an economy based on information and services, while other parts of the world manufacture and still others grow what we need to eat. Toffler also said that we will continue to see big changes in the worldwide blending of cultures, with TV helping us to reach and understand large and disparate groups of people.

The Role of Transnational Corporations

In order to grasp what is happening culturally, we have to understand that economic forces are driving most of these changes. Even the World Trade Organization and the International Monetary Fund, which seem to be the main organizations behind the growth of globalization, are influenced by corporations that know no boundaries. Transnational corporations are business operations that transcend national borders. While they may be located in one country, they impact on and do business in many. Their goal is to produce commodities that can be sold anywhere; the ideology underlying it all is that *consumerism* is the driving force of the economy. The executives of such corporations tend to be people who come from different countries, "citizens of the world" with luxurious lifestyles. They are not just the owners of corporations; they are a "transnational capitalist class" (Sklair, 2000). This class also includes state bureaucrats who help the corporations gain a foothold in their countries, politicians and professionals who support globalization, and consumer elites like merchants and the media who set the trends in the countries.

The transnational corporations have great influence—often greater than the governments of the countries in which they operate—in that they can replace local practices and policies with practices that are followed globally. They have been called the "lords of the global village" (67). These corporations strive to control global capital and material resources, and they use the media to push consumerism, so that the world becomes tightly woven into a political-social-economic hegemony that keeps us all buying, trading, selling, and participating in a commercialized and commodified system of interaction. The companies also play a major role in influencing family lifestyles and goals, and contribute to the structural forces that transform family life. Needless to say, child labor and the sweatshops that are established to serve these corporations have significant implications for family life in the parts of the world where they exist.

The Role of Governments

In this era of the growing global economy, it has been argued that the role of states (or governments, as we call them in the United States) is in demise. By this I mean that while states or governments were once sovereign, defended themselves, maintained internal order, and ran the show—deciding how their countries would operate and how business would be done—in these times of globalization, governments play less of a role in many important aspects of their citizens' lives. Some transnational corporations make far more money than do individual countries. With growing social problems like pollution and terrorism, national borders and governmental actions are far less able to control the fates of their citizens. Because of this, the transnationals have a direct impact on family life. They determine who they need for workers, how many workers are necessary, in which countries they will locate, and how business practices will be undertaken.

Governments continue to determine educational policies, social welfare practices, health care, and foreign policy and military defense (Lechner & Boli, 2000, 195-196). Thus both transnationals and governments are important to the future of the family. This dynamic interaction among business, governments, and the global economy is a complicated process that is inextricable in its impact on real people's lives.

Governmental Policies on the Family

Government policies on the family fall under the heading of "social policies" *that exist to provide basic services for people's social needs. Social policies are actions and plans designed to alleviate a social problem.* Some countries, those with more money and that are more individualist in orientation, provide more social programs than do poorer countries, where families traditionally assist needy members. Social policies have direct impact on family life, in that their focus is on the social fabric of the society. Policies are usually created to deal with negative feedback that a government has received. Such programs can change how families operate, impact their daily welfare, and influence the quality of family life.

In the United States, national family policies tend to provide cash benefits to supplement the incomes of adults who are unemployed, the aged, and the disabled, with some benefits directed to educational needs. We lack a comprehensive health care system, and as such, health care in this country is in crisis. Some argue that there is also a crisis in family policy, which lags behind the new needs of American families, and that the government hasn't developed a comprehensive plan to deal with the recurrent problems that contemporary families face (Martin, 1997).

For example, in the United States, the people who are most vulnerable to changing economic conditions are caregivers, caregivers' children, the unemployed, and the aged. Social rights accrue to workers, but not to people who stay home to care for others or have no opportunity to work. In 1995, a study found that poor children in the United States were poorer than those in 15 other nations. In fact, 23 percent of all American children live below the poverty line (295).

In 1996 a new law was passed that ended the federal guarantee for cash assistance to poor children. The Personal Responsibility and Work Opportunity Reconciliation Act terminated Aid to Families with Dependent Children (AFDC), which had guaranteed a safety net for all poor people with children. Instead it put in place a *workfare* program that required welfare recipients to perform work in exchange for benefits. Unfortunately, workfare has not measurably reduced poverty because of the lack of available, decent paying jobs (300). The program was aimed to "end welfare as we know it," but the goal of self-sufficiency has been quite elusive. For example, it has made mothers and children more vulnerable to hunger and homelessness (Lens, 2002), and food pantries throughout the country are reporting an increase in people requesting food. People are being evicted from their homes, and there are numerous barriers to poor mothers' success in obtaining education and then work (287).

The United States does not have a comprehensive full-employment policy; instead, interim reforms have been developed to help families who, to survive financially, need to have both parents in the workforce. Flextime is one policy that helps people who need child care cobble together a way to work. It allows workers to put in their required hours at flexible times, and it reduces absenteeism. Parental leaves are being developed for working parents who need to take time off for family health reasons. Although we have no comprehensive policy in the United States on this, individual employers are developing policies to compensate families in such situations (Martin, 1997, 303). The U.S. government is moving toward decentralization of family policy, and at this time the family is a low priority (320).

What the government in the United States does do is provide services and programs for the elderly. On a per-capita basis, government expenditure on the elderly has increased, while monies for the younger generations have been diminishing (Chapa, Hayes-Bautista, & Schink, 1988). Nationally, educational benefits have been dropping, and as a result the young are less well educated now than they were 30 years ago (52). In fact, the needs of the young are being left to the family, while the expensive needs of the elderly are increasingly being assumed by the public (53).

There are more than 35 million Medicare-eligible adults over 65 living in the United States; they form almost 13 percent of the population (Peck, 2002). The yearly payments to elders now exceeds $5,550 per capita in Medicare costs. That is 17 percent of the total government health expenditures. By 2011, when the elder population reaches nearly 40 million, the total cost will be close to $2 billion (3). It is the older elders, aged 85 and above, who cost the government the most, almost three times more than those aged 65–69. Fortunately, as health technology has improved, more elders are able to live at home, with assistance, so that the numbers of elders in nursing homes has diminished to 18 percent of elders over 85, compared to 25 percent in 1990 (4).

Life expectancy in the United States is now 84 years for women and 81 years for men (4). However, although people are living longer, they are also vulnerable to debilitating illnesses and diseases that require medical attention. Such maladies as heart disease (21 percent), hypertension (45 percent), and arthritis (70 percent) require medication, much of which is covered by Medicare (4). These costs continue to rise. Since 1970, the costs have tripled, and in real dollars Medicare spending has seen more than a 600 percent increase (4). It appears that the costs associated with aging have occupied our policymakers; they are spending more on our elders and not as much on other groups.

Besides physical health issues, mental health issues related to aging also impact policy. Treatment for depression among the elderly costs the United States $43.7 billion annually (4). And dementia suffered by the elderly is also costly. For example, the annual cost of care per patient with Alzheimer's disease exceeds $12,000. Medicare pays approximately $1,500 of that; the rest must be covered by the family caregivers.

Clearly, caregiving to elders is a major policy area that needs attention. The oldest old (those over age 85) are growing in numbers, and it becomes a policy dilemma to determine who will care for those who become frail. The United States has not developed a comprehensive policy on aging, leaving caregiving to the daughters or daughters-in-law, who become members of the sandwich generation, caring for both aging parents and their own children and/or grandchildren. These matters will need attention in the coming decades, as the numbers of such dependents rise.

Despite the amount of money spent, when Social Security and Medicare are excluded from federal allocations, only about 4 percent of the total federal budget goes to programs for elders (Hooyman & Kiyak, 2002). Most services for elders are fragmented, duplicated, and often do not get to the people who need them most (507). Even with growing allocations, the U.S. government lacks an integrated, comprehensive, and effective policy for older adults. Although the elderly are the most well-covered service group, U.S. policy on the elderly is as inadequate as its policy on the family.

Since the United States lacks a well-thought-out and integrated set of policies on the family, it's interesting to see what other countries have done. For the most part, family policies in other nations have four cornerstones: cash benefits to supplement the incomes of adults who raise children, comprehensive health services for pregnant women and for children, paid work leaves for parents who care for newborns and ill family members, and a child care program. Some countries are more comprehensive than others, especially the "welfare states" such as Sweden and other Scandinavian countries (Martin, 1997, 289).

Sweden

In 1979, Sweden introduced a social policy whose impact on family life is seen even today. Sweden was the first country in the world to prohibit the use of corporal punishment in the home and in the classroom (Corporal Punishment of Children, 1998). The Swedish government views children's rights as so important that it made the law part of the parental codes of its country's constitution. The law is not easily prosecutable, but it has become part of the social fabric, part of the country's norms for behavior.

Sweden is a constitutional monarchy, with a democratic parliamentary system. Prior to the passing of the law, policymakers determined that beatings of children were on the rise, even though children had been granted protection of equal rights, much like adults, under an earlier law (Durrant & Olsen, 1997). But in 1979 all forms of physical punishment were outlawed. The policymakers were trying to make the environment violence-free, including strongly urging Swedish toymakers to cease marketing violent toys and instigating a ban on renting or selling violent videos to children under 15. They also designed car-free housing developments and better packaging to make appliances and merchandise safer (444). Those changes, coupled with providing parents with leave and reduced workdays until the child is seven years old, have led to a diminishment of the child abuse rate (448). Clearly, governmental policies have had a dramatic impact on the way families operate in Sweden. Families are no longer permitted to physically reprimand their children, and the society is increasingly becoming less violent.

What would such a policy do in the United States? In Chapter 10 we discussed the problem of violence in the family, and the fact that parents in the United States have permission to employ corporal punishment of their children (Straus, 1994). Because in America we have a history of allowing violence to occur all around us, with little intervention in family life until recently, a policy of no physical punishment at all might appear outrageous to some. However, such a policy has been proposed by scholars who are concerned with the growing violence in our society. Straus, for example, has argued that a society that brings up children by caring, humane, and nonviolent methods is likely to be less violent, and more likely to be healthier and wealthier (188). He sees that we are at a stage of social change where the elimination of corporal punishment is imminent and would have profound and far-reaching benefits for humanity.

Cuba

The next country we look at is Cuba, a place I visited in 1999 and found most fascinating. Cuba is a communist country just 90 miles off the coast of Florida. Whatever you might think of the politics there, Cuba has a remarkably advanced health care system. Yet, prior to the communist revolution in 1959, health care in Cuba was abysmal. The country was among the poorest in Latin America and was plagued with political corruption, illiteracy, economic inequality, and social injustice (Iatridis, 1990).

Cuban health policy has been part of the fabric of that society since 1959, when the constitution was adopted. Since that time the system has become more sophisticated and comprehensive. For example, the incidence of child malnutrition in Cuba for children aged 1–15 is 0.7 percent, while in the United States it is 5 percent (30).

Universal health care benefits have been significant in diminishing the numbers of severe illness in that country, even with a poor economy and political difficulties.

Cubans believe that guaranteed health care is a human right, and therefore provide care to all citizens. There are national hospitals, provincial and municipal specialized treatment centers, local clinics, and even area and sector clinics where people can go see a doctor, free and right in their neighborhoods (Ochoa, Rojas, & Lopez, 1997). The Cuban government provides food for people who are unable to afford it, as part of their health policy to provide daily nutrition to all citizens. Since medical education in Cuba is free, new doctors go to many parts of the world, on behalf of the Cuban government, to administer medical care. They have become known far and wide, particularly in the developing world, as sources of sound medical treatment.

Unfortunately the U.S. embargo, which began soon after Castro took over in 1959, has had a significant effect on medical care in Cuba. Many countries that once did business with Cuba and provided medical supplies have stopped doing so because of threatened sanctions from the U.S. government. Before the tightening of the embargo under the Clinton administration, the Cuban health policy was admired and emulated in many parts of the world.

But global politics and economic concerns, particularly as a result of U.S. intervention, have led to a slow demise of a once extensive and highly viable medical system. We can see from this that the transnational nature of politics and economics can play a role in the internal policies of a country. Consequently, daily family life is dramatically impacted by politics far beyond the individual's control.

The Czech Republic

The last country we cover is the Czech Republic, which split from the Slovak Republic in 1993; previously the two republics had constituted Czechoslovakia. It was once part of the former Eastern Bloc, and was primarily a collectivist society that provided services and programs for all its citizens under the communist model. For 41 years communism was the form of government, and with it came guaranteed health care, housing, jobs, and a completely nationalized property system. With the fall of the Soviet Union in 1989, the whole system changed, becoming democratized through a parliament, the privatization of property, the establishment of a stock market, and a rapidly developed industrialized system. What is so interesting about the Czech Republic is that since the fall of communism, the birth rate of the country has dropped dramatically. Couples are reluctant to marry, and the marriage rate is diminishing yearly. In 1974 there were 195,000 children born in the Czech Republic, while in 1996 there were only 90,000 (Embassy of the Czech Republic, 1999). It appears that these changes are similar in all of the Eastern Bloc countries.

Why, one might ask, have these changes taken place? The changes seem to be related, once again, to economics and politics, the structural conditions of a country. Life in the Czech Republic has become difficult. Where once housing and jobs were widely available, through guarantees from the state government, families are now forced to seek housing from already limited accommodations. Jobs are in the private sector, not state controlled. There are not enough jobs for everyone, and people do not have a guaranteed income; thus they fear marrying, having children, and starting families. The future of the family in this country is very much tied to macro-level, structural factors, far beyond the control of individual family life.

When we hypothesize about the future of the family, there is much to take into consideration: the internal economics of a country, its politics, transnational economic interests, global culture, religion, demographics, technology, and many other structural variables. However, there are a number of trends that seem to be emerging. We summarize them next, to give you a hint of what I think is yet to come.

Gender

It is clear that gender behavior will be a major area of change in families in the future. Worldwide, women are increasingly in the labor market. Although women have always worked, both at home and at earning money, as global changes continue, more workers will be needed to fuel the economic machine. Working women are slowly moving into male-dominated sectors, and the patriarchy is being challenged to deal with the growing demands of women. Some institutions, including some religions, are not eager to make these changes. Nonetheless, given how much women's roles changed during the twentieth century, it is safe to predict that those changes will continue to reach farther and wider.

The women's movement, which has had a profound impact on attitudinal changes and demands in the United States, is now reaching worldwide. Organizations exist throughout the world to combat gender inequity and gender violence. The United Nations and other international groups count gender as one of their major focuses. There are many areas yet to be battled, like the issues of abortion, domestic violence, health care, equal pay for equal work (women still only make 77 cents to every man's dollar, even in the most industrialized countries), and child care.

Another area that bears watching is that of slavery. The trafficking of human beings is a phenomenon that has existed for centuries and continues to this day. In all parts of the globe, from Albania to Zimbabwe and countries in between, including the United States, people are being sold and transported for profit (Cockburn, 2003). These twenty-first-century slaves are sold for sex, service as indentured servants in agriculture, as diamond workers and for countless other tasks. This phenomenon is being monitored by the United Nations and other human rights groups and will be dealt with in this century. It is particularly a gender issue, since many of the slaves are women and children, powerless to free themselves from these painful lives.

Parenting is another gendered behavior that will see transformation in the twenty-first century. Historically, and in all parts of the globe, parenting has been done disproportionately by mothers. Maternal child rearing leads to women working double shifts, caring for their families, and then doing their paid labor. There

Photo 11.1   Hindu women in India. Photographer: Mary Thieme

have been some changes in the West, with men increasing their contributions to household and child-rearing tasks. However, more is certainly indicated as women join the labor market in increasing numbers.

We have seen that since the beginnings of the first wave of feminism, much has improved for women in many areas. The twenty-first century will continue to see dramatic transformation. Although fundamentalist religions are generally not conducive to change in women's roles, even in countries taken over by such ideologies we see the rise of women's movements, created to bring about transformation within the strictures of those religions. Women's movements are networking globally, meeting in various parts of the world, sharing strategies and ideas for change, and supporting each other in confronting the dominant patriarchal social structures that control power. These global feminisms began in the nineteenth century, flowered in the twentieth century, and are fast moving and vitally important for the twenty-first.

Religion

Changes in the family are also tied to the role that religion plays in family life. With the rise of fundamentalist religions, there has been in some places a return to the traditional family. In many parts of the world, fundamentalism is taking over countries that were once progressive and westernized. With fundamentalism comes the pressure for women to return to subservient positions, to reinstate the father as the breadwinner and the children as his possessions, and to adhere to a strict orthodoxy of behavior (as in the Taliban).

Religion also plays a role in a country's birth rate. When countries adhere to a rigid fundamentalism, birth control is often discouraged, and birth rates rise. In countries where religion is less of a focus, there are fewer births. Thus, more strictly fundamentalist cultures will have early marriages, larger families, and few divorces. Families in those places will look less like they do in the West.

Religion also emphasizes reliance on the large extended family. Traditional families are more likely to have multiple generations nearby and involved in daily family life. With the rise of fundamentalism, family life impacts the roles of women and their relationships to their husbands, marriage, and children. For example, Islamic family law remained relatively unchanged throughout the twentieth century; now, in the twenty-first, there are calls to "reform" suggested by people who are challenging those in power; those calls are resisted by others, who see such reform as a capitulation to the West (Haeri, 2000). Obedience is the cornerstone of the Islamic vision of a solid society; even the word *Islam* means submission and obedience (351). The goal is to maintain the status quo and to make a hierarchy of social relationships, with a wife having no legal autonomy and a man never being obedient to a woman.

Veiling is a good example of the obedience and submission that is expected of women as a result of fundamentalist Muslim beliefs. Not all Muslim countries require veiling as a part of women's garb, but the requirement is growing as fundamentalism takes root in more countries. In fact, many countries are clamping down on any expressions of women's autonomy in how they would veil. For example, in Iran the regime is passing directives on the way a veil is worn, the specific colors chosen, and the arena within which women can appear and work (356).

It will be most interesting to watch how the roles of women and the edicts of the fundamentalist regimes play out in the coming era. Clearly, there is a dynamic tension between the forces for social change and those desiring maintenance of the status quo.

As we have seen, many families in the world, even those that are westernized, are following a modified extended family structure, in which the primary couple and children live together, but the rest of the family lives in close proximity or within easy reach by phone or plane. Although many researchers argue that the nuclear family is dominant, my travels and research indicate that most folks in the world seem to feel comfortable with the modified extended family.

The nature of family relationships will inevitably change as we move forward. In the West, as the Baby Boom generation ages, their children will be forced to care for them. Life expectancy is increasing in most countries in the world, and with that will come more responsibility for the care of the aged. That will invariably affect relationships within family systems. Who will care for these people? What social institutions will arise to meet that growing need?

And the question yet to be answered is, "What will become of the family?" Can the family, especially the extended kinship systems, survive the changes brought about by the hegemony of the World Trade Organization and the global corporations? Will the form of the family emulate that of the West? Obviously no one knows the answers, but the questions are worth pondering.

Demographics

It is useful to note that changing demographics, or population trends, also will impact the future of the family. In the twenty-first century, minorities, especially blacks, Latinos, and Asians, will outnumber whites in the United States. When this occurs, those who were in power, the white majority, will become the minority. It is hard to say exactly how that will affect political and economic power, but there will almost certainly be a dramatic shift in how those groups see themselves. Given that minority groups, especially blacks and Latinos, earn far less money than does the white majority, it is possible that changes will occur in the distribution of wealth. If not, there will likely be demands for a reallocation of wealth. This could lead to further agitation or efforts at social change.

In other parts of the world, such disparities are even more apparent. It is yet to be seen whether this will lead to efforts at redistribution of wealth. We do know that income disparities will increase the tensions between the countries that "have" and those that "have not." We have already seen how such tensions have led to social upheaval in places like Indonesia, in the fall of the Soviet Union, and in demonstrations against the World Trade Organization meetings in Seattle in 1999. What will come next is yet to be seen.

Other demographic issues include the growing divorce and remarriage rates, the decreasing fertility rates, and the fact that women live longer than men in every country in the world. What then becomes of the widows? Perhaps it is too soon to conjecture about the changes in demographics and their impact on the family. We do know, however, that families will be impacted by these changing forces.

Technology

Technology is rapidly changing the way we live our lives, and it will continue to impact family life in the future. It was only 1978 when the first in vitro fertilization took place. By 1994, 9,000 babies were conceived this way in the United States alone (Martin, 1997, 309). New reproductive technologies will change family structures, as has happened with surrogate mothering and women well into their sixties birthing children.

These technologies, like donor insemination, will have an impact on how the family evolves and what the definition of family becomes. They will also impact adoption, which is a non-technological and traditional activity. What will happen to children who are available for adoption but are not adopted if this new technology continues in a haphazard fashion, as it has so far? And another issue yet to be addressed is the role that human cloning will play in family life in the future.

Finally, we need to consider the information and communication technologies that are proliferating globally. With the expansion of the World Wide Web and the growth of the computer industry, we have seen dramatic changes in how we communicate with each other. Some countries, like China, have tried to control communication between the Chinese and other parts of the world. This is of course quite difficult, as individuals find creative ways to connect with people elsewhere. The Web has changed our lives and how knowledge is transmitted and conveyed. Families are staying more closely connected through e-mail and cellular communications. These technological innovations are sure to continue, with new tools becoming available regularly. How will they change the family? How will this technology impact individuals and societies? The answers to these questions will certainly change the shape of all of our lives in the twenty-first century.

Postscript

As this book comes to its end, I find it imperative to leave you with a few words of observation and conclusion. Throughout the book I have cited many theories in an attempt to explain the complexity of family life and to provide readers with a way to understand what is occurring globally. The two dominant theories that have emerged are feminist theory and post-colonial theory. This world we live in no longer looks the way it did when your parents were your age. In a post–9/11 world, the forces of the West are being challenged. Post-colonial theory suggests that we must shift our lens, to look at a world in which the West is not at the center; that we must de-center the dominant paradigms, to look at countries, ideas, and people who were not in power, and to seek their views as we move further into the third millennium.

Post-colonialism is frightening to those who were once the powerful. It threatens that which has become familiar and comfortable; that is why Americans were so appalled by what occurred on September 11, 2001. Our sense of security and safety was challenged. The people on what was considered the fringe—developing countries, countries in Africa, Asia, and Latin America—are becoming central to the discussion. Their views are aggressively being voiced, and we are forced to listen. We may try to assert our power as a country, but ultimately it is the voices of the unheard that will predominate. It is important that, as students of globalism, we understand that and listen to what is being said. You have been given a lens through which to view what is going on out there, to see that there is a post-colonial message that is being shouted at those of us in the West who will listen. I hope that you will listen.

Feminist theory is also dominant in my understanding of global social change. As I have said, the most significant changes in the twentieth century came about in the situation for women, with progress being made in all spheres of women's lives, and not just in the West. Certainly there is much more to be accomplished, but much has been done. Global feminism is a profound force in bringing about transformation of family life. It is for this reason that I focused on a gendered view of social change and globalization.

Throughout this book, I have shared with you my travels into the world. I attempted to take you on a journey into the world, looking at the family as the lens of analysis. When I was in college, I had traveled no further than New York City (I grew up in Boston). During the past forty years, I have experienced countless countries in all parts of the world. I have learned from my travels just how wondrous the world and its people are. It does not matter whether you are in a village in India, a villa in Italy, a city in Latin America, or on a river raft in the Mekong Delta of Vietnam—people are all the same; people want the same things, to love and to live in peace, to raise their children, to work and to die among their loved ones. It does not matter if one is rich or poor, black, white, African, European, American, Asian, or Latin, we all want the joys of life, and we all suffer the same pains and miseries. While some people's lives are harder than others, they are really no different from you or me. They might look different, they may eat foods that seem weird to us, or have cultural practices that are hard for us to comprehend, but they are trying to make sense of the same inexplicable things that confront us all.

I have written this book as a labor of love. As I said earlier, my father was a Holocaust refugee, and I am of the post-Holocaust generation. The Holocaust occurred because of racism and an exaggerated idea about the evils of difference. I believe that it is imperative that we, as citizens of the world, understand others so that there will not be another Holocaust. As I write this, there are mini-Holocausts going on daily in the world, in places like Rwanda, Bosnia, the Congo. One needs to know about them, and not bury one's head in the sand. That's what happened during World War II, and 8 million people died.

Now for a bit of advice: Go out and experience difference. You do not have to travel far or wide to do so. Look around you, talk to people who are unlike yourself. Find someone who looks different from you or comes from a background far from yours. Smile at that person, introduce yourself, and find out something about him or her. Have a real conversation, not just platitudes; engage in a discussion about who they are and who you are. It will amaze you, it will provoke you, and it will make you a deeper and richer person. Part of the problem with only interacting with folks like ourselves is that we learn so little from them. It is comfortable, but it does not stretch us. I ask you, no, I entreat you: Reach outside of your comfort zone, think outside of the box.

Writing this book has been a joy. I find it a privilege to share my learning with so many people. My students and I have reveled in what we've learned as we have experienced the world. We have observed the changing face of family life and the impact of globalization. Now I challenge you to do the same.

References

Abbott, D., Ming, Z. F., & Meredith, W. (1992). The evolving redefinition of the fatherhood role in the People's Republic of China. *International Journal of Sociology.* 22 (Spring):45–54.

Abrahams, N. (1996). Negotiating power, identity, family, and community participation. *Gender and Society.* 10, 6:768–796.

Aginsky, B. W. (1940). An Indian's soliloquy. *American Journal of Sociology.* Vol. XLVI, No. 1 (July):53–54.

Ahrons, C. (1994). *The Good Divorce: Keeping Your Family Together When Your Marriage Comes Apart.* New York: Harper Perennial.

Allman, J. (1980). Sexual unions in rural Haiti. *International Journal of Sociology of the Family.* 10 (Jan–June):15–39.

Almeida, R. (1996). Hindu, Christian and Muslim families. In McGoldrick, M., Giordano, J., & Pearce, J. K. (eds.), *Ethnicity and Family Therapy.* New York: Guilford Press. pp. 395–421.

Amato, P. (1998). Impact of divorce on men and women in U.S. and India. In Ferguson, S. (editor), *Shifting the Center: Understanding Contemporary Families.* Mountain View, CA: Mayfield Publishing. pp. 412–426.

Arendell, T. (1997). A social constructionist approach to parenting. *Understanding Families.* V. 9. Thousand Oaks, CA.: Sage Publications. pp. 1–44.

Arguelles, L. (1993). Plenary Address: "Intellectual Foundations of Women's Studies: Beyond Political Correctness." National Women's Studies Association, Washington, DC. June. As quoted in Lengermann, P., Niebrugge-Brantley, J., in Ritzer, G. (2000). *Sociological Theory* (5th ed.). New York: McGraw-Hill. p. 470.

Aries, P. (1962). *Centuries of Childhood.* New York: Vintage.

Arroyo, J., Simpson, T., & Aragon, A. (1997). Childhood sexual abuse among Hispanic and non-Hispanic white college women. *Hispanic Journal of Behavior Sciences.* Sage 19, 1:57–68.

Asante, M. K. (1996). The Afrocentric metatheory and disciplinary implications. In Daley, M. (ed.), *Multicultural Experiences, Multicultural Theories.* New York: McGraw-Hill.

Ashcroft, B., Griffiths, G., & Tiffin, H. (eds.) (1995). *The Post-Colonial Studies Reader.* New York: Routledge.

Asmal, K., Asmal, L., & Roberts, R. S. (1996). *Reconciliation Through Truth: A Recognition of Apartheid's Criminal Governance.* Capetown, South Africa: David Phillip Publishers in Asia with Mayibuye Books, University of Western Cape.

Avary, J. (1996). Steering between Scylla and Charyibdis: Shifting gender roles in twentieth century Iran. *NWSA Journal.* 8, 1:28–49.

Baca-Zinn, M. (1998). Feminist rethinking from racial-ethnic families. In Ferguson, S. (compiler), *Shifting the Center: Understanding Contemporary Families.* Mountain View, CA: Mayfield Publishing. pp. 12–20.

Baca-Zinn, M., & Eitzen, D. S. (1993, 1999). *Diversity in American Families.* New York: Longman.

Bad Bargain in Afghanistan. Editorial. (1998 July 13). *New York Times*, p. A16.

Bankston, C. & Zhou, M. (1998). *Growing Up in America: How Vietnamese Children Adapt to Life in the United States*. New York: Russell Sage Foundation.

Barker, J. (1991). Private communication.

Barry, K. (1996). Industrialization and economic development: The costs to women. In Barry, K. (ed.), *Vietnam Women in Transition*. New York: St. Martin's Press.

Barry, K., & Leidholdt, R. (1990). The coalition against trafficking in women. *Woman of Power*. 18:46–49.

Bascom, W. (1968). The urban African and his world. In Fava, S. F. (ed.), *Urbanism in World Perspective: A Reader*. New York: Thomas V. Cromwell. pp. 81–93. As quoted in Hutter, M. (1988). *The Changing Family* (2nd ed.). New York: Macmillan. p. 84.

Baxter, J., & Kane, E. (1995). Dependence and independence: A cross-national analysis of gender inequality and attitudes. *Gender and Society*. 9, 2:193–215.

Bell, A., & Weinberg, M. (1978). *Homosexualities: A Study in Human Diversity*. New York: Simon & Schuster.

Bem, S. (1974). Measurement of psychological androgyny. *Journal of Consulting and Clinical Evaluation*. 42:155–162.

Benedict, R. (1983). Continuities and discontinuities in cultural conditioning. In Silver, H. (ed.). *Socialization of Youth: Evolution of Revolution*. New York: McMillan. pp. 100–108.

Beneria, L. (1997, March). *Women, Work, and the Global Economy* (presentation). Elmira, NY: Elmira College.

Berreman, G. D. (1999). Race, caste and other individual distinctions in social stratification. In Yetman, N. (ed.), *Majority and Minority: The Dynamics of Race and Ethnicity in American Life* (6th ed.). Boston: Allyn and Bacon. pp. 39–56.

Billingsley, A. (1992). *Climbing Jacob's Ladder: The Enduring Legacy of African-American Families*. New York: Touchstone.

Blakeslee, S., & Wallerstein, J. (1995). *The Good Marriage: How and Why Love Lasts*. Boston: Houghton Mifflin.

Boserup, E. (1971). *Woman's Role in Economic Development*. London: George Allen & Unwin Ltd.

Bott, E. (1968). *Family and Social Network*. London: Tavistock.

Breiner, W., & Gordon, L. (1999). The new scholarship on family violence. *Signs*. (Spring) 8:490–531. In Baca-Zinn, M., & Eitzen, D. S. (eds.)., *Diversity in Families*. New York: Longman.

Bumiller, E. (1990). *May You Be the Mother of a Hundred Sons: A Journey Among the Women of India*. New York: Random House.

Burns, J. (1998 May 11). Though illegal, child marriage is popular in parts of India. *New York Times*. Reprinted in Norton, J. (ed.). (1999). *Global Studies: India and South Asia* (4th ed.). Guilford, CT: Dushkin.

Butler, J. (1999). *Gender Trouble: Feminism and the Subversion of Identity*. New York: Routledge.

Caldwell, J. C. (1982). *Theory of Fertility Decline*. New York: Academic Press.

Caldwell, J. C. (1997). The global fertility transition: The need for a unifying theory. *Population and Development Review*. 23, 4 (December):803–810.

Canian, F., Goodman, L., & Smith, P. (1978–79). Capitalism, industrialization, and kinship in Latin America: Major issues. *Journal of Family History*. 3–4:319–336.

Cazenave, N., & Straus, M. (1979). Race, class, network embeddedness and family violence: A search for potent support systems. *Journal of Comparative Family Studies*. 10:281–299.

Centers for Disease Control. (1995). Highlights of a new report from the National Center for Health Statistics. Available on www.cdc.gov.

Chang, J. S. (1996).Negotiating sexual permissiveness in a contemporary Chinese setting: Young people in Taipei. *International Journal of Sociology of the Family*. 26, 1:13–35.

Chapa, J., Hayes-Bautista, D., & Schink, W. (1988). *The Burden of Support: Young Latinos in an Aging Society*. Stanford, CA.: Stanford University Press.

Cherlin, A. (1981). *Marriage, Divorce, Remarriage*. Cambridge, MA: Harvard University Press.

Cherlin, A. (1996). *Public and Private Families*. New York: McGraw-Hill.

Chitauro, M. (1995). *The Role and Status of Shona Women as Revealed in the Language of a Shona Cultural Event.* University of Florida, master's thesis.

Chodorow, N. (1978). *The Reproduction of Mothering.* Berkeley: University of California Press.

Cicirelli, V. (1995). *Sibling Relationships Across the Life Span.* New York: Plenum.

Cockburn, A. (2003). Twenty-first century slaves. *National Geographic.* (September):2–25.

Collins, P. H. (1990). *Black Feminist Thought: Knowledge, Consciousness, and the Politics of Empowerment.* Boston: Unwin & Hyman.

Collins, P. H. (1994). Shifting the Center: Race, class and feminist theorizing about motherhood. In Chang, G., Glenn E., Rennie Forcey, L. (eds.), *Mothering, Ideology, Experience, Agency.* New York: Routledge. pp. 45–65.

Collins, P. H. (1998). Intersections of race, class, gender and nation: Some implications for Black family studies. Special Issue: Comparative Perspectives on Black family life V. 1. *Journal of Comparative Family Studies.* 29, 1 (Spring):27–37.

Collinwood, D. (ed.). (1997). *Global Studies: Japan and the Pacific Rim* (4th ed.). Guilford, CT: Duskin/McGraw-Hill.

Condon, J. (1985). *A Half Step Behind: Japanese Women of the 1980s.* New York: Dodd, Mead. Cited in Hutter, M. (1998). *The Changing Family* (3rd ed.). New York: Allyn & Bacon.

Coontz, S. (1997). *The Way We Really Are: Coming to Terms with America's Changing Families.* New York: Basic Books.

Cornell, C. P., & Gelles, R. (1983). *International Perspectives on Family Violence.* Lexington, MA: Lexington Books.

Corporal punishment of children. (1998). *University of Michigan Journal of Law Reform.* 31, 2:362–367.

Crossette, B. (1998a September 13). Worldwide most are consuming more and the rich much more. *New York Times.* pp. 1–3.

Crossette, B. (1998b July 15). A Uganda tribe fights genital cutting. *New York Times.*

Crossette, B. (1998c June 14). An old scourge of war becomes its latest crime. *New York Times.* Sec. 4, pp. 01, 4.

Crosson-Tower, C. (1999). *Understanding Child Abuse and Neglect.* Boston, MA: Allyn & Bacon.

Cuber, J. & Haroff, P. (1963). The more total view: Relationships among men and women of the upper middle class. *Marriage and Family Living.* 25:140–145.

Culville, R. (1997). Afghanistan's women: A confused future. In *Refugees: Afghanistan and the Unending Crisis.* UN High Commissioner on Refugees. Geneva, Switzerland. VII. pp. 28–29.

Daley, S. (1998a July 9). Workers free wine ends, but South Africans still pay. *New York Times,* p. A1.

Daley, S. (1998b July 23). A postapartheid agony: AIDS on the march. *New York Times,* pp. A1, A10.

Darwin, C. (1859). *On the Origin of the Species.* New York: Modern Library.

Datalounge. (1997 October 29). Netherlands to approve gay adoptions and marriage. Available on the World Wide Web at http://www.datalounge.com.

Datalounge. (1997 November 3). Filipino gays targeted again in the Mideast. Available on the World Wide Web at http://www.datalounge.com.

Datalounge. (1997 December 17a). New Zealand court upholds gay marriage ban. Available on the World Wide Web at http://www.datalounge.com.

Datalounge. (1997 December 17b). Ecuador court repeals anti-gay marriage ban. Available on the World Wide Web at http://www.datalounge.com.

Datalounge. (1998 February 18). Gay Cubans enjoy new freedoms. Available on the World Wide Web at http://www.datalounge.com.

Datalounge. (1998 February 20). Caribbean countries resist gay reform. Available on the World Wide Web at http://www.datalounge.com.

Davis, K., & Moore, W. (1945) Some principles of stratification. *American Sociological Review.* 10:242–249.

Demos, T. (1970). *The Little Commonwealth.* New York: Oxford University Press.

Dickerscheid, J. (1990). Profiles of rural Egyptian women: Rules, status, and needs. *International Journal of the Sociology of the Family.* 20 (Spring):21–20.

Dietrich, K. T. (1977). The myth of the black matriarchy. In Glazer, N., & Waehrer, H. Y. (eds.), *Woman in a Man-Made World: A Socio-Economic Handbook* (2nd edition). Chicago: Rand McNally. pp. 277–285.

Domhoff, G. W. (1998). *Who Rules America: Power and Politics in the Year 2000.* New York: Mayfield Publishing Company.

Domingo, L., & Asis, M. M. B. (1995). Living arrangements and the flow of support between generations in the Philippines. *Journal of History—Cultural Gerontology.* 10:21–51.

Doro, M. (1999 August 4). Available on the World Wide Web at End Violence@edc-cit.org.

Duiker, W. (1999). Private communication.

Duiker, W. T., & Spielvogel, J. (1994). *World History VII Since 1500.* St. Paul, MN: West Publishers.

Durkheim, E. (1893). *Division of Labor in Society.* Rpt. 1964. New York: Free Press.

Durkheim, E. (1897). *Suicide.* Rpt. 1964. New York: Free Press.

Durrant, J., & Olsen, G. (1997). Parenting and public policy: Contextualizing the Swedish corporal punishment ban. *Journal of Social Welfare and Family Law.* 19, 4:443–461.

Efoghe, G. B. (1990). Nature and type of marriage as predictors of aggressiveness among married men in Ekpoma, Bendel State of Nigeria. *International Journal of Sociology of the Family.* 20 (Spring):67–78.

Eisenstein, Z. (1979) *Capitalist Patriarchy and the Case for Socialist Feminism.* New York: Monthly Review Press.

Elder, J. (1996 Fall). Enduring stereotypes about Asia: India's caste system. In *Annual Editions: India and South Asia,* 4th ed. Guilford, CT: Duskin/McGraw-Hill. pp. 140–142.

Eller, C. (2000). *The Myth of Matriarchal Prehistory: Why an Invented Past Won't Give Women a Future.* Boston: Beacon Press.

Elliot, S. (1999). Private communication.

The Embassy of the Czech Republic. (1999). Available on the World Wide Web at http://www.czechcz/Washington/general/general.htm.

End-Violence listserv. (1998 November). Available on the World Wide Web at edc-cit.org.

Engels, F. (1884). *Origin of the Family, Private Property, and the State.* Rpt. 1972. New York: Pathfinder Press.

Esfandiari, H. (1997). *Reconstructed Lives: Women and Islam's Revolution.* Washington, DC: The Woodrow Wilson Center Press, and Baltimore: Johns Hopkins Press.

Espiritu, Y. L. (1997). *Asian American Women and Men.* Thousand Oaks, CA: Sage Publications.

Fausto-Sterling, A. (1993). How many sexes are there? *Gay Liberation News.* May. p. 10.

Feagin, J. R. (1991 November 27). Blacks still face the malevolent reality of white racism. *Chronicle of Higher Education.* p. A44.

Feagin, J. R., & Feagin, C. B. (1993). Adaptation and conflict: Racial and ethnic relations in theoretical perspective. *Race and Ethnic Relations* (4th ed.). New York: Prentice Hall. pp. 21–46.

Feldman, S. (1992). Current themes and issues. In Beneria, L., & Feldman, S. (eds.), *Unequal Burden: Economic Crisis, Persistent Poverty, and Women's Work.* Boulder, CO: Westview. pp. 1–25.

Feinberg, L. (1996). *Transgender Warriors: Making History from Joan of Arc to RuPaul.* Boston: Beacon.

Fessler, R. (1999). Private communication.

Flax, J. (1996). Women do theory. In Rogers, M. (ed.), *Multicultural Theories: Multicultural Experiences.* New York: McGraw-Hill. pp. 17–20.

Fonseca, C. (1991). Spouses, siblings and sex-linked relationships: A look at kinship organization in a Brazilian slum. In Jelen, G. (ed.), *Family Household and Gender Relations in Latin America.* New York: Kegan Paul International.

Furstenberg, F., Jr., & Cherlin, A. (1991). *Divided Families: What Happens When Parents Part.* Cambridge, MA: Harvard University Press.

Gallagher, C. (1999). *Rethinking the Color Line: Readings on Race and Ethnicity*. Mountain View, CA: Mayfield Publishing Company.

Garber, M. (1992). *Vested Interests: Cross Dressing and Cultural Anxiety*. New York: Harper Perennial.

Garcia-Preto, N. (1996a). Latino families: An overview. In McGoldrick, M., Giordano, J., & Pearce, J. K. (eds.), *Ethnicity and Family Therapy*. New York: The Guilford Press. pp. 141–154.

Gelles, R., & Straus, M. (1986). Societal change and change in family violence from 1975–1985 as revealed in two national surveys. *Journal of Marriage and the Family*. 48, 3:465–480.

Gelles, R., & Straus, M. (1988). *Intimate Violence: The Causes and Consequences of Abuse in the American Family*. New York: Simon and Schuster.

Giddens, A.(1982). *Sociology: A Brief but Critical Introduction*. New York: Harcourt Brace Jovanovich.

Gimbutas, M. (1999). *The Living Goddesses*. Berkeley: University of California Press.

Glenn, E. N. (1992). From servitude to service work: Historical continuities in racial division of paid reproductive labor. *Signs: Journal of Women in Culture and Society*. 18, 11:1–43.

Glenn, E. N. (1994). Social constructions of mothering: A thematic overview. In Glenn, E., Chang, G., and Forcey, L. (eds.), *Mothering: Ideology, Experience and Agency*. New York: Routledge. pp. 2–12.

Goode, W. (1963). *World Revolution and Family Patterns*. New York: The Free Press.

Goode, W. (1982). *The Family*. 2nd ed. Englewood Cliffs, NJ: Prentice Hall.

Goodstein, L. (1996). Sexual assessment in the U.S. and Vietnam: Some thoughts and questions. In Barry, K. (ed.), *Vietnam Women in Transition*. New York: St. Martin's Press. pp. 275–286.

Goodwin, P. (ed.). (1998). *Global Studies—Latin America*. New York: Duskin/McGraw-Hill.

Gordon, M. (1980). The ideal husband as depicted in a 19th-century marriage manual. In Pleck, E., & Pleck, J. (eds.), *The American Man*. Englewood Cliffs, NJ: Prentice Hall. pp. 145–155.

Gottschalk, P., McLanahan, S., & Sandefur, G. (1994). The dynamics of intergenerational transmission of poverty and welfare participation. In Danziger, M., Sheldon, H., Sandefur, G., & Weinberg, D. (eds.), *Confronting Poverty: Prescriptions for Change*. New York: Russell Sage.

Gramsci, A. (1932). *Letters from Prison*. New York: Harper.

Gregor, T. (1985). *Anxious Pleasure: The Sexual Lives of an Amazonian People*. Chicago: University of Chicago Press.

Gulati, L. (1995). Women and family life in India: Continuity and change. *Indian Journal of Social Work*. 56, 2:133–154.

Haeri, S. (2000). Obedience versus autonomy: Women and fundamentalism in Iran and Pakistan. In Lechner, F., & Boli, J. (eds.), *The Globalization Reader*. Malden, MA.: Blackwell Publishers. pp. 350–358.

Hagestad, G. O. (1981). Problems and promises in the social psychological of intergenerational relations. In Fogel, R. (ed.), *Aging, Stability and Change in the Family*. New York: Academic Press. pp. 11–46.

Hampton, R. (1987). Race, class and child maltreatment. *Journal of Comparative Family Studies*. 18 (Spring):113–126.

Hampton, R., Gelles, R., & Harrop, J. (1989). Is violence in black families increasing? A comparison of 1975–1985 national survey rates. *Journal of Marriage and the Family*. 51 (November):969–980.

Hare-Mustin, R., & Hare, S. (1986). Family change and the concept of motherhood in China. *Journal of Family Issues*. 7, 1 (March):67–82.

Hareven, T. (1976). Modernization and family history: Perspectives on social change. *Signs: Journal of Women in Culture and Society*. 2, 1:190–206.

Hareven, T. (2000). *Families, History and Social Change*. Boulder, CO: Westview Press.

Harris, A. (1994). Ethnicity as a determinant of sex role identity: A replication study of item selection for the Bem sex role inventory. *Sex Roles: A Journal of Research*. 31, 3/4:233–241.

Hassan, R. (1989). Equal before Allah. *Women's World*. 21–22:11–3.

Haughton, J., & Haughton, D. (1995). Son preference in Vietnam. *Studies in Family Planning*. 26, 6 (Nov/Dec):325–338.

Hawke, A. (1995). Lifting the veil on female mutilation. *UNICEF Information Sheet*.

Health Central News. (1999 January 25). U.S. pregnancy rates leads developed world. Available on the World Wide Web at http://www.healthcentral.com.

Heaton, T. (1990). Marital stability throughout the child-rearing years. *Demography*. 27 (February):55–63.

Heise, L. (1989). The global war against women. *UTNE Reader*. pp. 40–45.

Heller, P. (2000). Private communication.

Hernandez, M. (1996). Central American families. In McGoldrick, M., Giordano, J., & Pearce, J. K. (eds.), *Ethnicity and Family Therapy*. New York: Guilford Press. pp. 214–224.

Hines, P. M., & Boyd-Franklin, N. (1996). African American families. In McGoldrick, M., Giordano, J., & Pearce, J. (eds.), *Ethnicity and Family Therapy*. New York: Guilford Press. pp. 66–84.

Hirtz, F. (1992). The state, family, and social welfare: Notes on the Philippine experience. *Social Development Issues*. 14, 1:71–82.

Ho, C. (1990). An analysis of domestic violence in Asian-American communities: A multi-cultural approach to counseling. In Brown, L., & Root, M. (eds.), *Diversity and Complexity in Feminist Therapy*. New York: Harrington Park. pp. 129–149.

Hochschild, A. with Anne Machung. (1989). *The Second Shift: Working Parents, and the Revolution at Home*. New York: Viking.

Hoffnung, M. (1998). Motherhood: Contemporary conflict for women. In Ferguson, S. (compiler), *Shifting the Center: Understanding Contemporary Families*. Mountain View, CA: Mayfield Publishing. pp. 277–291.

Hooyman, N., & Kiyak, H.A. (2002). *Social Gerontology: A Multidisciplinary Perspective*. 6th ed. Boston: Allyn & Bacon.

Horowitz, A., White, H., & Howell-White, S. (1996). Becoming married and mental health. *Journal of Marriage and the Family*. 58 (November):895–907.

Hosken, F. (1982). *The Hosken Report*. Lexington, MA: Women's International Network News.

Hutter, M. (1998). *The Changing Family: Comparative Perspectives* (3rd ed.). New York: Macmillan.

Iatridis, D. (1990). Cuba's health care policy: Prevention and active community participation. *Social Work: The Journal of the National Association of Social Workers*. 1 (January 31): 29–35.

Ignatiev, N. (1995). *How the Irish Became White*. New York: Routledge.

Ingraham, C. (1999). *White Weddings: Romancing Heterosexuality in Popular Culture*. New York: Routledge.

Interactive Population Center. (2000 November). Available on the World Wide Web at http://www.unfpa.org.

International Food Policy Research Institute. (1995 October). Available on the World Wide Web at http://www.worldbank.

Ishwaran, K. (1992). *Family and Marriage: Cross Cultural Perspectives*. Toronto: Thompson Publishing.

Jackson, J. J. (1974). Ordinary black husbands: The truly hidden men. *Journal of Social and Behavioral Science*. 20:19–27. Cited in McAdoo, J., & McAdoo, J. (1998). The African-American father's roles within the family. In Ferguson, S. (editor), *Shifting the Center: Understanding Contemporary Families*. Mountain View, CA: Mayfield Publishing. pp. 371–384.

Jacobson, S. (1999). Private communication.

Jaret, C. (1995). *Contemporary Race and Ethnic Relations*. New York: Harper Collins College Publishing.

John, D., Shelton, B., & Luschen, K. (1995). Race, ethnicity, gender, and perceptions of fairness. *Journal of Family Issues*. 16, 3:357–379.

Johnson, M. (1996). Violence against women in the family: The U.S. and Vietnam. In Barry, K. (ed.), *Vietnam Women in Transition.* New York: St. Martin's Press.

Jones, G. (1998 February 9). How much truth can we take? *Christianity Today.* pp. 19–24. As reported in *Annual Editions: Race & Ethnic Relations,* 90–100. Guilford, CT: Dushkin/McGraw-Hill. pp. 204–207.

Jung, A. (1990). *Unveiling India.* Calcutta: Penguin.

Kagan, J. (1977). Child in the family. *Daedalus.* 106 (Spring).

Kandel, D., & Lesser, G. (1972). The internal structure of families in the U.S. and Denmark. In Sussman, J., & Cogswell, B. (eds.), *Cross-National Family Research.* London: E. J. Brill. pp. 70–85.

Kaplan, E. B. (1997). *Not Our Kind of Girl: Unraveling the Myths of Black Teenage Motherhood.* Berkeley, CA.: University of California Press.

Kassim, M. S., Shafie, H. M., & Cheah, I. (1994). Social factors in relation to physical abuse in Kuala Lumpur, Malaysia. *Child Abuse and Neglect.* 18, 5:401–407.

Katz, J. (1983). *Gay/Lesbian Almanac: The New Documentary.* New York: Colophon Books.

Kendig, H., Hashimoto, A., & Coppard, L. (1992). Family support for the elderly: An international experience. Oxford Medical Press: *Aging International.* 19, 2 (June):32–38.

Kemp, A. (1998). *Abuse in the Family: An Introduction.* Pacific Grove, CA: Brooks Cole Publishing Co.

Khan, N. (1995). Patterns of child sexual abuse in Zimbabwe: An overview. *Zimbabwe Journal of Educational Research.* 7, 2 (July):181–208.

Kim, B. L. (1996). Korean families. In McGoldrick, M., Giordano, J., & Pearce, J. K. (eds.), *Ethnicity and Family Therapy.* New York: Guilford Press., pp. 281–294.

Kincaid, J. (1988). *A Small Place,* excerpted in Ashcroft, B., Griffiths, G., & Tiffin, H. (eds.). (1998). *The Post-Colonial Studies Reader.* New York: Routledge. pp. 92–94.

Kling, Z. (1995). The Malay family: Beliefs and realities. *Journal of Contemporary Families.* 26 (Spring):43.

Krulfeld, R. (1999). Private communication.

Kuznesof, E., & Oppenheimer, R. (1985). The family and society in nineteenth-century Latin America: A histographical introduction. *Journal of Family History.* 10, 3:215–234.

Laclau, E., & Mouffe, C. (1985). *Hegemony and Socialist Strategy Towards a Radical Democratic Politics.* London: Verso.

Lasch, C. (1977). *Haven in a Heartless World.* New York: Basic Books.

Laskowitz, J. (1998). Private communication.

Laslett, P., & Wall, R. (eds.). (1972). *Household and Family in Past Time.* Cambridge, England: Cambridge University Press.

Laumann, E., Gagnon, J., Michaels, R., & Michaels, S. (1994). *The Social Organization of Sexuality: Sexual Practices in the United States.* Chicago: University of Chicago Press.

Lechner, J., & Boli, J. (eds.). (2000). *The Globalization Reader.* Malden, MA: Blackwell Publishers.

Lee, E. (1996). Chinese families. In McGoldrick, M., Giordano, J., & Pearce, J. K. (eds.), *Ethnicity and Family Therapy.* New York: Guilford Press. pp. 247–267.

Leeder, E. (1994). *Treating Abuse in Families: A Feminist and Community Approach.* New York: Springer.

Lengermann, P. M., & Niebrugge-Brantley, J. (2000). Contemporary feminist theory. In Ritzer, G. *Sociological Theory* (5th ed.). New York: McGraw-Hill. pp. 443–489.

Lens, V. (2002). TANF: What went wrong and what to do next. *Social Work.* July. V. 47, 3:279–291.

Leonard, L. (1996). Female circumcision in southern Chad: Origins of meaning and current practice. *Social Science and Medicine.* 43, 2:255–263.

Lepowsky, M. (1994). *Fruit of the Motherland: Gender Egalitarian Society.* New York: Columbia University Press.

LeRoux, J. (1996). Street children in South Africa: Findings from interviews of street children in Pretoria, South Africa. *Adolescence.* 31, 122 (Summer):423–429.

Leslie, G., & Korman, S. (1985). *The Family in Social Context* (6th ed.). New York: Oxford.

Levinson, D. (1989). *Family Violence in Cross-Cultural Perspective*. Newbury Park, CA: Sage.

Leviton, R. (1993). *Weddings By Design*. San Francisco: Harper.

Lewin, E. (1994). Negotiating lesbian motherhood: The dialectics of resistance and accomodation. In Glenn, E., Chang, G., & Forcey, R. (eds.), *Mothering: Ideology, Experience and Agency*. New York: Routledge. pp. 334–353.

Lewin, L. (1995 December 7). Parents poll shows child abuse to be more common. *New York Times*.

Lie, L. (1996). Class, gender, and ethnicity. *Current Sociology*. 44, 1:35–46.

Linton, R. (1936). *The Study of Man: An Introduction*. New York: Appleton.

Litwak, E. (1960). Geographical mobility and extended family cohesion. *American Sociological Review*. 25:385–394.

Lockhart, J., & Schwartz, S. (1983). *Early Latin America: A History of Colonial Spanish America and Brazil*. Cambridge, England: Cambridge University Press.

Lorber, J. (1998). *Gender Inequality: Feminist Theories and Politics*. Los Angeles: Roxbury Publications.

MacKinnon, K. (1982). Feminism, Marxism, method and the state: An agenda for theory. In Keohane, N. O. et al. (eds.), *Feminist Theory: A Critique of Ideology*. Chicago: University of Chicago Press. Cited in Lengermann, P., & Niebrugge-Brantley, J. (2000). Contemporary feminist theory. In Ritzer, G., *Sociological Theory*. New York: McGraw-Hill. p. 462.

Malinowski, B. (1922). *Argonates of the Western Pacific*. New York: Dutton. Cited in Wolf, R. (1996). *Marriage and Family in Diverse Society*. New York: HarperCollins Publishers. pp. 272.

Maniquis, E. (1985). Kisaeng Tourism in South Korea. *Response to the Victimization of Women and Children*. Journal of the Center for Women Policy Studies. New York: Guilford. 8, 2 (Spring):23.

Mantsiso, G. (1996). Rewards and opportunities: The politics and economics of class in the U.S. In Rosenblum, K., & Travis, T. (eds.), *The Meaning of Difference: American Constructions of Race, Sex and Gender, Social Class and Sexual Orientation*. New York: McGraw-Hill. pp. 97–103.

Mapondera, E. (1997). The family—Shona. Private communication.

Mapondera, E. (1995). Private communication.

Markowitz, L. (1999). Sibling connections: That most vital but overlooked of relationships. *Annual Editions: Marriage and Family*. 1999/2000. Guilford, CT: Dushkin/McGraw-Hill. pp. 121–127.

Martin, G.T. Jr. (1997). The agenda for family policy in the United States. In Arendell, T. (ed.), *Contemporary Parenting: Challenges and Issues*. Thousand Oaks, CA: Sage. pp. 289–323.

Marx, K., & Engels, F. (1848/1948). *The Manifesto of the Communist Party*. New York: International Publishers.

Massey, D., & Denton, N. (1999) American apartheid: The perpetuation of the underclass. In Gallagher, C. (ed.), *Rethinking the Color Line: Readings on Race and Ethnicity*. Mountain View, CA: Mayfield Publishers. pp. 316–336.

Matetakufa, S. N. (1997 July 20). A women's shelter comes to Zimbabwe. *Panos Features: A Third World Oriented News Agency*. London.

Mathabane, M. (1986). *Kaffir Boy: The True Story of a Black Youth's Coming of Age in Apartheid South Africa*. New York: Macmillan Publishing.

Matsui, W. (1996). Japanese families. In McGoldrick, M., Giordano, J., and Pearce, J. K. (eds.), *Ethnicity and Family Therapy*. New York: Guilford Press. pp. 268–280.

Mazur, R. (1991). Impact of repression and guerrilla war: Zimbabwe. *Journal of Developing Areas*. 25:529–540.

Mazur, R., & Mhloy, M. (1988). Underdevelopment: Women's work and fertility in Zimbabwe. (Working paper, No. 164, ISSN 088-5354). Office of International Development, Michigan State University.

McAdoo, H. P. (ed.). (1997) *Black Families* (3rd ed.). Thousand Oaks, CA: Sage.

McAdoo, J., & McAdoo, J. (1998). The African-American father's roles within the family. In Ferguson, S. (compiler), *Shifting the Center: Understanding Contemporary Families.* Mountain View, CA: Mayfield Publishing. pp. 371–384.

McGoldrick, M., Giordano, J., and Pearce, J. K. (eds.). (1996). *Ethnicity and Family Therapy* (2nd ed.). New York: Guilford Press.

McMullen, M. (1999). Private communication.

Meekers, D. (1994). Ethnographic and survey methods: A study of the nuptiality patterns of the Shona of Zimbabwe. *Journal of Comparative Studies.* 25, 3:313–328.

Mennan, F. (1994). Sexual abuse in Latina girls: Their functioning and a comparison with White and African-American girls. *Hispanic Journal of Behavioral Sciences.* 16, 4:475–486.

Menzel, P. (1994). *Material World: A Global Family Portrait.* San Francisco: Sierra Club.

Mere, Q. (1976). Contemporary changes in Igbo family systems. *International Journal of Sociology of the Family.* 6:155–161.

Merton, R. K. (1949/1968). *Social Theory and Social Structure.* New York: Free Press.

Mies, M. (1986). *Patriarchy and Accumulation on a World Scale: Women in the International Division of Labor.* London: Zed Books.

Mies, M. (1999 November). Globalization as Genocide Draft. Presentation: Cornell University, Ithaca, NY.

Miller, B. (1987). Female infanticide and child neglect in rural North India. In Scheper-Hughes, N. (ed.), *Child Survival.* Dordrecht: D. Reidel Publishing Co. pp. 95–112.

Miller, J., & Lewis, P. (1999 August 8). Fighting to save children from battle. *New York Times.* p. 14.

Minority troopers describe a culture of discrimination. Metropolitan Desk. (1999 July 9). *New York Times.* p. B2.

Miralao, V. (1992). Female-headed households in the Philippines. *Philippine Sociological Review.* 40, 1–4 (Jan–Dec):46–56.

Mollica, R., Donelan, K., Tor, S., Lavelle, J., Elias, C., Frankel, M., & Blendon, R. (1993). The effect of trauma and confinement on functional health and mental health status of Cambodians living in Thailand-Cambodian border camps. *Journal of American Medical Association.* 270, 5 (August 4):581–587.

Moodie, T., Ndatshe, V., & Sibuyi, B. (1989). Migrancy and male sexuality in the South African mines. In Duberman, M., Vicinius, M., & Chauncey, G. (eds.), *Hidden from History: Reclaiming the Gay and Lesbian Past.* New York: Penguin. pp. 411–425

Murdock, G. (1949). *Social Structure.* New York: Macmillan.

Murstein, B. (1974). *Love, Sex and Marriage Through the Ages.* New York: Springer.

Newman, D. (1999). *Sociology of Families.* Thousand Oaks, CA: Pine Forge Press.

Ng, V. (1989). Homosexuality and the state in late imperial China. In Duberman, M., Vicinus, M., & Chauncey, G. (eds.), *Hidden from History: Reclaiming the Gay and Lesbian Past.* New York: New American Library. pp. 76–89.

Nobles, W. (1985). *Africanicity and the Black Family: The Development of a Theoretical Model.* Oakland, CA: Black Family Institute Publishers. As quoted in McGoldrick, M., Giordano, J., and Pearce, J. K. (eds.). (1996). *Ethnicity and Family Therapy* (2nd ed.). New York: Guilford Press. p. 68.

Nock, S. (1987). *Sociology of the Family.* Englewood Cliffs, NJ: Prentice-Hall, Inc.

———. (1998). *Marriage in Men's Lives.* New York: Oxford University Press.

Norton, J. (ed.). (1997). *Global Studies: India and South Asia* (3rd ed.). Guilford, CT: Dushkin/McGraw-Hill.

Nwadiora, E. (1996). Nigerian families. In McGoldrick, M., Giordano, J., and Pearce, J. K. (eds.), *Ethnicity and Family Therapy* (2nd ed.). New York: Guilford Press. pp. 129–138.

Ochoa, F., Rojas, P., & Lopez, C. (1997). Economy, politics and health status in Cuba. *International Journal of Health Services.* 27, 4:791–805.

Offe, C. (1977). *Industry and Inequality.* New York: St. Martin's Press.

Offoha, M. (1996). *Ethnic and Cultural Diversity in Nigeria.* Trenton, NJ: Africa World Press.

Ogden, S. (1997). *China* (7th ed.). *Global Studies Annual Editions.* Guilford, CT: Dushkin/McGraw-Hill.

O'Kelly, C., & Carney, L. (1986). *Women and Men in Society: Cross Cultural Perspectives on Gender Stratification.* Belmont, CA: Wadsworth.

Oliver, M. L., & Shapiro, T. M. (1990). Wealth of a nation: A reassessment of asset unequality in American shows that at least one third of households are asset poor. *American Journal of Economics and Sociology,* 49:129–150.

Omari, C. K. (1991). The family of Tanzania. *International Journal of Sociology of the Family.* 21 (Autumn):55–71.

Omi, M., & Winant, H. (1999). Racial formations. In Gallagher, C. (ed.), *Rethinking the Color Line: Readings on Race and Ethnicity.* Mountain View, CA: Mayfield Publishing Co. pp. 9–16.

Osmond, M. W. (1987). Radical-critical theories. In Sussman, M., & Steinmetz, S. (eds.), *The Handbook of Marriage and the Family.* New York: Plenum Press. pp. 103–124.

Otite, O. (1991). Marriage and family systems in Nigeria. *International Journal of Sociology.* 21:15–54.

Peck, M. (Fall, 2002). Syllabus available on the World Wide Web at http://sjsu.edu/depts/social work/swarc/.

Perpinan, M. S. (1985). Strategies in sexual trafficking. *Response to the victimization of women and children.* Journal of the Center for Women Policy Studies. New York: Guilford Press. 8, 2 (Spring):23.

Pillemer, K. (1998). Private communication.

Pino, J. C. (1997). *Family and Favela: the Reproduction of Poverty in Rio de Janeiro.* Westport, CT: Greenwood Press.

Pomerleau, A., Bolduc, D., Malcuit, G., & Cossett, L. (1990). Pink and blue: Environmental stereotypes in the first two years. *Sex Roles.* 22:354–367.

Pong, S. (1994). Sex preference and fertility in Peninsular Malaysia. *Studies in Family Planning.* May/June 25,3.

Popenoe, D. (1988). *Disturbing the Nest: Family Change and Decline in Modern Societies.* New York: A. deGruyter.

Population Crisis Committee. (1988). *Poor, Powerless, and Pregnant: Country Rankings on the Status of Women* (Population Briefing Paper, No. 20). Washington, DC: Government Printing Office.

Price, S., & McKenry, P. (1988). *Divorce.* Beverly Hills, CA: Sage.

Quisumbing, A. (1994). Intergenerational transfers in Philippine rice fields: Gender differences in traditional inheritance customs. *Journal of Development Economics.* 43 (April):167–195.

Quy, L. (1996). Domestic violence in Vietnam. In Barry, K. (ed.), *Vietnam Women in Transition.* New York: St. Martin's Press. pp. 263–274.

Radford, J., & Russell, D. E. H. (eds.). (1992). *Femicide: The Politics of Woman Killing.* New York: Twayne Publishers.

Raffaelli, M. (1997 January). The family situation of street youths in Latin America: A cross-national survey. *International Social Work.* 40, 1:89–100.

Ramsay, F. J. (ed.). (1997). *Global Studies: Africa* (7th ed.). Guilford, CT: Dushkin/McGraw-Hill.

Ramsay, F. J. (ed.). (1999). *Global Studies: Africa* (8th ed.). Guilford, CT: Dushkin/McGraw-Hill.

Rao, V. (1997). Wife beating in rural south India: A qualitative and econometric analysis. *Social Science and Medicine.* 44, 8:1169–1180.

Rerrich, M. (1996). Modernizing the patriarchal family in West Germany: Some findings on the redistribution of family work between women. *European Journal of Women's Studies.* Sage (3):27–37.

Rhee, S. (1997 March). Domestic violence in the Korean immigrant family. *Journal of Sociology and Social Welfare.* 24, 1:63–77.

Rhode, D. (1997). *Speaking of Sex: The Denial of Gender Inequality.* Cambridge, MA: Harvard University Press.

Riphenburg, C. (1997). Women's status and cultural expression: Changing gender relations and structural adjustment in Zimbabwe. *Africa Today.* 44, 1:33–50.

Ritzer, G. (2000 [1996,1997]). *Sociological Theory.* New York: McGraw-Hill.

Rothenberg, J. (1997). Private communication.

Rubin, J., Provenzano, F., & Luria, Z. (1974). The eye of the beholder: Parents' views on sex of newborns. *American Journal of Orthopsychiatry.* 4:512–519.

Rubin, L. (1994). *Families on the Fault Line.* New York: Harper Collins.

Sadker, M., & Sadker, D. (1994). *Failing at Fairness: How American Schools Cheat Girls.* New York: Scribners.

Said, E. (1978). *Orientalism.* Excerpted in Ashcroft, B., Griffiths, G., & Tiffin, H. (eds.). (1995). *The Post-Colonial Studies Reader.* New York: Routledge. pp. 87–91.

Saitoti, T. O. (1995). The initiation of a Maasai warrior. In Hirschberg, S. (ed.), *One World, Many Cultures* (2nd ed.). New York: Allyn & Bacon. pp. 109–119.

St. Jean, Y., & Feagin, J. (1998). The family cost of white racism: The case for African Americans. *Journal of Comparative Family Studies.* 29, 2 (Summer):297.

Salayakionond, W.(1985). Prostitution in Thailand. *Response to the Victimization of Women and Children.* Journal of the Center for Women's Policy Studies. 8, 2:23.

Salazar Parrenas, R. (2002) The care crisis in the Philippines: Children and transnational families in the new global economy. In Ehrenreich, B., & Hochschild, A.R., *Global Woman: Nannies, Maids and Sex Workers in the New Economy.* New York: Henry Holt and Company. pp. 39–54.

Sales, V., & Tuirán, R. (1997). The family in Latin America: A gender approach. *Current Sociology.* 45, 1:141–152.

Sanday, P. R. (2002). *Women at the Center: Life in a Modern Matriarchy.* Ithaca, NY: Cornell University Press.

Sandmaier, M. (1995). *Original Kin: The Search for Connection Among Adult Sisters and Brothers.* New York: Plume/Penguin.

Santa Rita, E. (1996). Pilipino families. In McGoldrick, M., Giordano, J., & Pearce, J. K. (eds.), *Ethnicity and Family Therapy.* New York: Guilford Press. pp. 324–330.

Scheper-Hughes, N. (1992a). *Death Without Weeping: The Violence of Everyday Life in Brazil.* Berkeley: University of California Press.

Scott, E., Ph.D. (1999). Private communication.

Segal, U. (1995). Child abuse by the middle class: A study of professionals in India. *Child Abuse and Neglect.* 19, 2:217–231.

Segura, D. (1986). Familism and employment among Chicanas and Mexican immigrant women. In Melville, M. (ed.). (1988). *Mexicans at Work in the United States.* Houston, Texas: University of Houston Press.

———. (1994). Working at motherhood: Chicana and Mexican immigrant mothers and employment. In Glenn, E., Chang, G., & Forcey, L. *Mothering, Ideology, Experience and Agency.* New York: Routledge. pp. 211–229.

Seligmann, J. (1990). Variations on a theme. *Newsweek.* Special Edition. Winter/Spring: 38–46.

Shapiro, J. (1991). Transsexualism: Reflections on the persistence of gender and the mutability of sex. In Epstein, J., & Straub, K. (eds.), *Body Guards: The Cultural Politics of Gender Ambiguity.* New York: Routledge. pp. 248–279.

Sidel, R. (1974). *Families of Fensheng: Urban Life in China.* London: Penguin.

Sklair, L. (2000). Sociology of the global system. In Lechner, J., & Boli, J. (eds.), *The Globalization Reader.* Malden, MA: Blackwell Publishers.

Smith, P., Dugan, S., & Trompenaars, F. (1997). Locus of control and affectivity by gender and occupational status: A fourteen nation study. *Sex Roles.* 36, 5:51–77.

Smith, R. (1978). The family and the modern world system: Some observations from the Caribbean. *Journal of Family History.* 3, 4:337–360.

Smith-Rosenberg, C. (1989). Discourses of sexuality: the new woman. In Duberman, M., Vicinus, M., & Chauncey, G. (eds.), *Hidden from History: Reclaiming the Gay and Lesbian Past.* New York: New American Library. pp. 1870–1936.

So-kum Tang, C. (1994). Prevalence of spouse aggression in Hong Kong. *Journal of Family Violence.* 9, 4:347–356.

So-kum Tang, C. (1996). Adolescent abuse in Hong Kong Chinese families. *Child Abuse and Neglect.* 20, 9:873–878.

Sorrentino, C. (1990). The changing family in international perspective. *Monthly Labor Review.* 113, 3:4.

Sperling, S. (1991). Baboons with briefcases: Feminism, functionalism and sociology in evolution of the primate gender. *Signs: Journal of Women in Culture and Society.* 17, 11:1–27.

Stacey, J. (1998). Gay and lesbian families are here to stay. In Ferguson, S. (compiler), *Shifting the Center: Understanding Contemporary Families.* Mountain View, CA: Mayfield Publishing. pp. 161–172.

Stack, C. (1974). *All Our Kin.* New York: Harper and Row.

Steyn, A., & Viljoen, S. (1996). The state of family theory and research in South Africa. *Marriage and Family Review,* 22:333–373.

Straus, M. (1994). *Beating the Devil Out of Them: Corporal Punishment in American Families.* Ontario, Canada: Lexington Books.

Strom, R., Strom, S., & Xie, Q. (1996). Parent expectations in China. *International Journal of Sociology of the Family.* 26, 1 (Spring):37–49.

Sutton, C. T. & Broken Nose, M. A. (1996). American Indian families: An overview. In McGoldrick, M., Giordano, J. & Pearce, J. K. (eds.), *Ethnicity and Family Therapy* (2nd ed.). New York: Guilford Press. pp. 31–44.

Swerdlow, J. (1999). Global culture. *National Geographic.* 196, 2:45.

Tafoya, N., & Del Vecchio, A. (1996). Back to the future: An examination of the Native American Holocaust experience. In McGoldrick, M., Giordano, J., & Pearce, J. K. (eds.), *Ethnicity and Family Therapy.* 2nd ed.. New York: Guilford Press. 45–54.

Taylor, R. (1991). Black youth in crisis. In Staples, R. (ed.), *The Black Family: Essays and Studies.* Belmont, CA: Wadsworth Publishing Co.

———. (1997). Who's parenting? Trends and patterns. In Arendell, T. (ed.), *Contemporary Parenting: Challenging Issues.* V. 9. Thousand Oaks, CA.: Sage Publications. pp. 68–91.

Tepperman, L., & Wilson, S. (1993). *Next of Kin: An International Reader on Changing Families.* Englewood Cliffs, NJ: Prentice Hall.

Tilly, L., & Scott, J. (1987). *Women, Work, and Family.* New York: Methuen.

Toffler, A. (1999 August). *National Geographic.* 196, 2.

Tolnay, S. (1999). *The Bottom Rung: African American Family Life on Southern Farms.* Urbana: University of Illinois Press.

Tung, C. (2000). The cost of caring: The social reproductive labor of Filipina live-in home health caregivers. *Frontiers: A Journal of Women's Studies.* Vol. XXI, No. 1/2:61–80.

United Nations Department of Public Information. (1996). *Convention on the Elimination of All Forms of Discrimination Against Women* (pamphlet). Washington, DC: U.S. Government Printing Office.

United Nations Development Fund for Women. (1998). *A Commitment to the World's Women* (UNIFEM brochure). Washington, DC: U.S. Government Printing Office.

United States Bureau of Census. (1995). *Marital Status and Living Arrangements—1994.* Washington, DC: U.S. Government Printing Office.

United States Bureau of Census. (1997). *Statistical Abstracts of the United States.* Washington, DC: U.S. Government Printing Office.

United States Bureau of Census. (2000a). *Median U.S. Income by State.* Available on the World Wide Web at http://www.census.gov.

United States Bureau of Census. (2000b). *Poverty: 1999 Highlights.* Available on the World Wide Web at http://www.census.gov.

Varadarajan, J. (1999, July 4). A Patel motel cartel? *New York Times.* pp. 36–39.

Vatikiotis, M. (1996 August 1). Family matters: Modern-day tensions strain southeast Asia's social fabric. *Far Eastern Economic Review:* 38–40.

Vietnam News Agency. (1996). *Vietnam: Image of the Community of Fifty-Four Ethnic Groups.* Hanoi: Ethnic Cultures Publishing House.

Wallerstein, I. (1974). *The Modern World-System: Capitalist Agriculture and the Origins of the European World Economy in the Sixteenth Century.* New York: Academic Press.

Wallerstein, I. (1989). *The Modern World-System: The Second Era of Great Expansion of the Capitalist World-Economy, 1730–1840.* New York: Academic Press.

Wallerstein, I. (1992). America and the world: Today, yesterday and tomorrow. *Theory and Society* 21:1–28.

Weitzman, L. (1985). *The Divorce Revolution.* New York: The Free Press.

Welter, B. (1973). The cult of true womanhood: 1820–1860. In Gordon, M. (ed.), *The American Family in Social Historical Perspective.* New York: St. Martin's Press. pp. 313–333.

Werner, E. (1995). Resilience in development: Current directions in psychological science. *American Psychological Society.* Cambridge, MA: Cambridge University Press.

White, L., & Riedmann, A. (1992). Ties among adult siblings. *Social Forces.* 71, 1 (Sept):85–102.

White, M. (1987). The virtue of Japanese mothers: Cultural definitions of women's lives. *Deadalus: Proceedings of the American Academy of Arts and Sciences.* 116 (Summer): 149–163.

Widmer, E., Treas, J., & Newcomb, R. (1998). Attitudes toward non-marital sex in 24 countries. *Journal of Sex Research.* 35, 4 (November):349–358.

Wilford, J. N. (1996 March 29). Sexes equal on South Sea Isle. *New York Times.*

Williams, H. (1993). Families in refugee camps. In Tepperman, L., & Wilson, S. (eds.), *Next of Kin: An International Reader of Changing Families.* Englewood Cliffs, NJ: Prentice Hall. pp. 250–255.

Wolf, M. (2000). Why this hatred of the market. In Lechner, J., & Boli, J. (eds.), *The Globalization Reader.* Malden, MA: Blackwell Publishers.

Wolf, R. (1996). *Marriages and Families in a Diverse Society.* New York: Harper Collins.

Wolfgang, M., & Riedel, M. (1973). Race, judicial discretion and the death penalty. *Annals of American Academy of Political and Social Science,* 407:119–133.

Xiaohe, X., & White, W. T. (1998). Love, matches, and arranged marriages: A Chinese replication. In Ferguson, S. (compiler), *Shifting the Center: Understanding Contemporary Families.* Mountain View, CA: Mayfield Publishing. pp. 115–133.

Yoshihama, M., & Sorenson, S. (1994). Physical, sexual and emotional abuse by male intimates: Experiences of women in Japan. *Violence and Victims.* 9, 1:63–77.

Yui-huen Kwan, A. (1995). Elder abuse in Hong Kong: A new family problem for the Old East. *Journal of Elder Abuse and Neglect.* 6, 3/4:65–80.

Zaretsky, E. (1976). *Capitalism, the Family and Personal Life.* New York: Harper & Row.

Zayas, L. (1992). Child rearing, social stress, and child abuse: Clinical considerations with Hispanic families. *Journal of Social Distress and the Homeless.* 1, 3/4:291–309.

Zinn, H. (1999). Drawing the color line: People's history of the U.S. In Gallagher, C. (ed.), *Rethinking the Color Line: Readings on Race and Ethnicity.* Mountain View, CA: Mayfield Publishing Company. pp. 34–45.

Zinsmeister, K. (1990). Raising Kiroko: The child-centered culture of Japan. *American Enterprise.* 1, 2 (March–April):53–59.

Zwingle, E. (1999). Goods move, people move, ideas move, and cultures change. *National Geographic.* 196, 2:12 & 33.

Additional Readings

Anima, N. (1975). *Courtship and Marriage Practices Among Philippine Tribes.* Quezon City, Philippines: Omar Publications.

Barry, K. (1984). *Female Sexual Slavery.* New York: New York University Press.

Bourdillon, M. (1993). *Where Are the Ancestors: Changing Culture in Zimbabwe.* Harare: University of Zimbabwe Publications.

Brenner, S. (1996). Reconstructing self and society: Japanese Muslim women and the veil. *American Ethnologist.* 23, 4:637–697.

Brody, E. (1990). *Women in the Middle: Their Parent Care Years.* New York: Springer. Cited in Hutter, M. (1998). *The Changing Family* (3rd ed.). New York: Allyn & Bacon.

Brown, S. (1977). Household composition and variation in a rural Dominican village. *Journal of Comparative Family Studies.* 8, 2:257–267.

Bunch, C. (1995). Transforming human rights from a feminist perspective. In Peters, J., & Wolper, A. (eds.), *Women's Rights-Human Rights: International Feminist Perspectives.* New York: Routledge. pp. 41–48.

Collins, P. H. (2000). Toward a new vision: Race, class and gender as categories of analysis and connection. In Rosenblum, K., & Travis, T. M. (eds.), *The Meaning of Difference: American Constructions of Race, Sex and Gender, Social Class and Sexual Orientation.* New York: McGraw-Hill. pp. 213–223.

Ehrenreich, B., & Hochschild, A. (2002). *Global Woman: Nannies, Maids and Sex Workers in the New Economy.* New York: Metropolitan Books.

Flanzer, J. (1993). Alcohol and other drugs are key causal agents of violence. In Gelles, R., & Loseke, D. (eds.), *Current Controversies on Family Violence.* Newbury Park, CA: Sage. pp. 171–181.

Garcia-Preto, N. (1996b). Puerto Rican families. In McGoldrick, M., Giordano, J., & Pearce, J. K. (eds.), *Ethnicity and Family Therapy.* New York: The Guilford Press. pp. 183–199.

Gelles, R. (1993). Alcohol and other drugs are associated with violence—they are not the cause. In Gelles, R., & Loseke, D. (eds.), *Current Controversies on Family Violence.* Newbury Park, CA: Sage.

Gelles, R., & Loseke, D. (eds.). (1993). *Current Controversies on Family Violence.* Newbury Park, CA: Sage.

Gordon, M. (1964). *Assimilation in American Life.* New York: Oxford University Press. Cited in Feagin, J. R., & Feagin, C. B. (1993). Adaptation and Conflict: Racial and Ethnic Relations in Theoretical Perspective. *Race & Ethnic Relations* (4th ed.). New York: Prentice Hall. pp. 21–46.

Hart, D. (1977). *Compadrinazgo: Ritual Kinship in the Philippines.* De Kalb, IL: Northern Illinois University Press.

Herdt, G. (1982). *Rituals of manhood: Male initiation of Papua New Guinea.* Berkeley: University of California Press.

Herman, J. (1981). *Father-Daughter Incest.* Cambridge, MA: Harvard University Press.

Kridge, E. J. (1975). Women-marriage, with special reference to the Lovedú—its significance for the definition of marriage. *Africa.* 44:11–37.

Lamanna, M., & Riedmann, A. (1997). *Marriages and Families: Making Choices in a Diverse Society* (6th ed.). Belmont, CA: Wadsworth.

McAdoo, H. P. (1997). Transgenerational patterns of upward mobility in African-American families. In McAdoo, H. P. (ed.), *Black Families* (3rd ed.). Thousand Oaks CA: Sage.

Morgan, R. (1984). *Sisterhood Is Global.* Garden City: Anchor Books.

NiCarthy, G. (1989). From the sounds of silence to the roar of a global movement: Notes on movements versus violence versus women. *Response to the Victimization of Women and Children.* Journal for the Center for Women Policy Studies. New York: Guilford Press. 12, 2:3–10.

Oboler, R. S. (1980). Is the female husband a man? Woman/woman marriage among the Nandi of Kenya. *Ethnology.* 19, 1:69–88.

O'Toole, T. (1996). *Understanding Humankind: A Global Introduction to Social Science.* Aurora, CO: Davies Group.

Park, R. (1993). Adaptation and conflict: Racial and ethnic relations in theoretical perspective. In Feagin, J. R., & Feagin, C. B. (eds.), *Race and Ethnic Relations* (4th ed.). New York: Prentice Hall. pp. 21–46.

Parsons, T., & Bales, R. (1955, 1966). *Family, socialization and the interactive process.* New York: Free Press.

Renzetti, C., & Curran, D. (1995). *Women, Men and Society: The Sociology of Gender* (3rd ed.). Boston: Allyn & Bacon.

Sapir, E. (1958). *Selected Writings of Edward Sapir in Language, Culture and Personality.* Berkeley: University of California Press.

Scanzoni, J. (1983). *Shaping Tomorrow's Family: Theory and Policy for the 21st Century.* Beverly Hills, CA: Sage Publications.

Scheper-Hughes, N. (ed.). (1992b). *Child Survival.* Dordrecht: D. Reidel Publishing Co. pp. 95–112.

Schmidt, E. (1992). *Peasants, Traders and Wives: Shona Women in the History of Zimbabwe, 1870–1939.* Portsmouth, NH: Heinemann.

Staples, R. (ed.). (1991). *The Black Family: Essays and Studies.* Belmont, CA: Wadsworth Publishing Co.

Strom, R., Strom, S., Shen, Y., Li, S., & Sun, H. L. (1996). Grandparents in Taiwan: A three-generational study. *International Aging and Human Development.* 42, 1:1–19.

Thorne, B. (1982). Feminist thinking on the family: An overview. In Thorne, B., & Yalom, M. (eds.), *Rethinking the Family: Some Feminist Questions.* New York: Longman. pp. 1–24.

Wallerstein, I., & Smith, J. (1991). Households as an institution of the world economy. In Blumberg, B. L. (ed.), *Gender, Family, and Economy: The Triple Overlap.* Newbury Park, CA: Sage. pp. 225–241.

Westfield, A. (1997) The emergence of the democratic Brazilian middle-class family: A mosaic of contrasts with the American family. *Journal of Comparative Family Studies.* 28, 1 (Spring):25–54.

White, L. (1992). Ties among adult siblings. *Social Forces.* 71, 1 (September):85–102.

Whorf, B. (1966). *Language, Thought and Reality.* Cambridge, MA: MIT Press.

Wikan, U. (1982). The Xanith: A third gender role? In Wikan, U. (ed.), *Behind the Veil in Arabia: Women in Oman.* Baltimore, MD: Johns Hopkins Press. pp. 168–186.

Wilson, W. J. (1984). The urban underclass. In Dunbar, L. W. (ed.), *The Minority Report.* New York: Pantheon.

Wilson, W. J. (1996). *When Work Disappears: The World of the Urban Poor.* New York: Knopf.

World Health Organization. (1992). Female circumcision. *European Journal of Obstetric Gynecological Reproductive Biology.* 45:153.

Author Index

Subject Index

Abortion, 119, 133, 247
Achieved status, 42
Adolescents
    among the Maasai, 223–224
    in Denmark, 209
    in Malaysia, 207
    pregnancy in, 39
    sexuality among, 39, 222–223
    as a social construction, 221–223
Affectional and emotional needs
    fulfilled by families, 41–42
Afghanistan, 132
    gender construction in, 145–147
Africa. *See also* individual countries
    affectional and emotional ties between
        family members in, 42
    AIDS in, 133–134
    apartheid in, 152, 153–157
    childhood in, 219
    colonization of, 69
    domestic violence in, 253–255
    family life in, 102–109
    female circumcision in, 46,
        134–135, 254
    genocide in, 164–165
    homosexuality in, 102–103
    as a peripheral area, 13, 131
    polygamy in, 32
    sibling relationships in, 228–229
    and the slave trade, 101–102
    as third world, 19
    women's roles in, 105–106, 107–108
African American families
    fathers of, 215–216
    gendered racism and, 173
    grandparenting in, 231–232
    health of, 161
    matriarchy among, 30, 84, 1616
    mothers of, 211

    point-of-entry theory and, 82–83,
        157–159
    racism against, 157–163, 171–173
    sibling relationships in, 225, 226
    social mobility among, 45, 160–161
    violence among, 240–242
African Americans, change in families of,
    83–84, 270
African National Congress, 155
Agriculture, gender inequality and,
    131–132
AIDS, 133–134, 157
Albania, 164, 267
Alcoholics Anonymous, 46
Alcoholism, 46, 157, 204, 244–245, 252
Angola, 158
Anguilla, 190
Antigua, 16
Apartheid, 152, 153–157
Arranged marriages, 34–35, 119, 178,
    182–183, 185–186
Aryan Nation, 159
Ascribed status, 42
Asia. *See also* individual countries
    collectivist societies of, 205
    colonization of, 69
    dependency theory and, 14
    emigrants to the United States form,
        88–93
    families of, 109–119
    homosexuality in, 111
    and the media, 127
    as a peripheral area, 13, 131
    third world countries of, 19
Asian Americans, 88–93, 270
    motherhood and, 211
    racism against, 172
    violence among, 241–242
Australia, 69

About the Author

Elaine Leeder is Professor of Sociology and Dean of the School of Social Sciences at Sonoma State University. She holds an M.S.W. from the Wurzweiler School of Social Work of Yeshiva University, a Masters of Public Health from the University of California at Berkeley, and a Ph.D. in Sociology from Cornell University. She was a practicing psychotherapist from 1967 to 1992. From 1977 to 2001, she taught in the Sociology Department at Ithaca College and coordinated the social work minor at that institution. She currently teaches Introduction to Sociology and has taught courses on social change, family violence, and the treatment and prevention of family violence and social policy. She is the author of *The Gentle General: Rose Pesotta, Anarchist and Labor Organizer* (1993) and *Treating Abuse in Families: A Feminist and Community Approach* (1994), as well as articles on women's history, treatment of child abuse perpetrators, domestic violence, and spirituality. She has taught courses on the Holocaust to undergraduates at Sonoma State University and Ithaca College as well as to college professors at the United States Holocaust Memorial Museum in Washington, D.C. Leeder has traveled around the world twice on Semester at Sea, and has visited many programs and universities throughout the globe in an effort to understand the diversity and complexity of family life.